CW01510575

My films consist of a series of idealisms reflected in the idea of beauty. Now beauty can be a terrible thing, beauty can be twisted and abused.

Kenneth Anger
A Demonic Visionary

Alice L. Hutchison

Black Dog Publishing

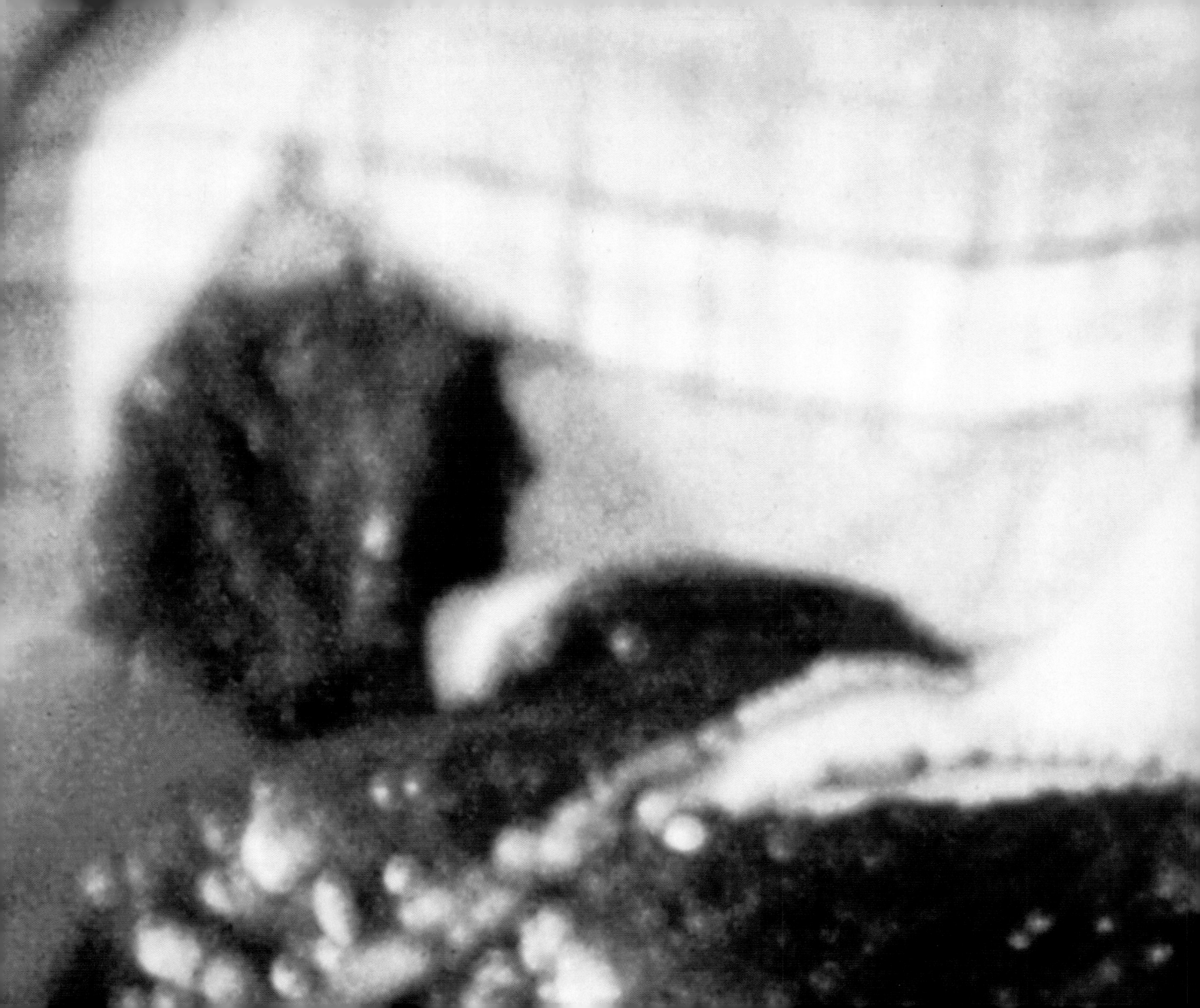

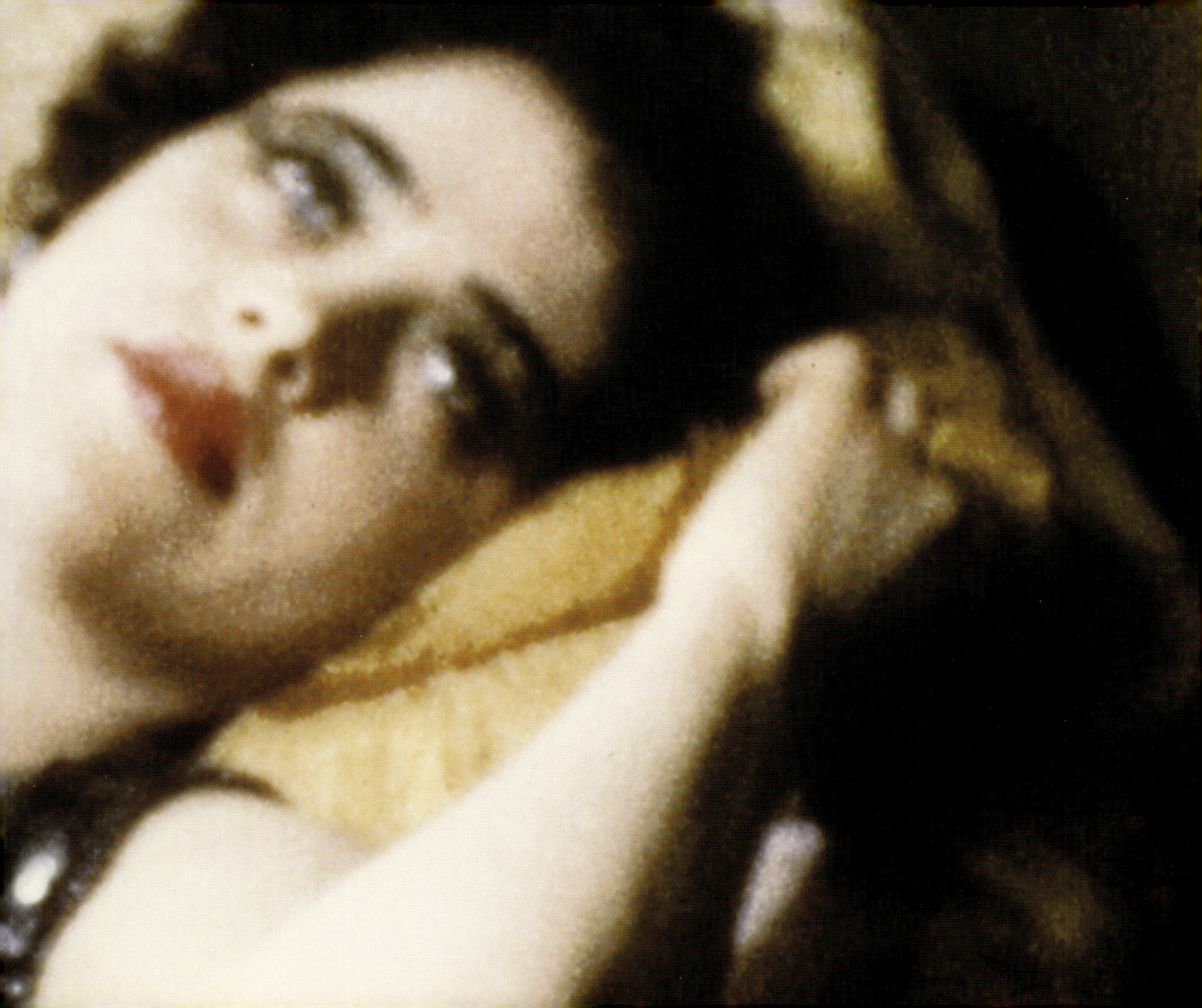

By the most heart-wrenching efforts one
gains the phosphorescent layer of myth, which
is at the foundation of all of our existences.

Contents

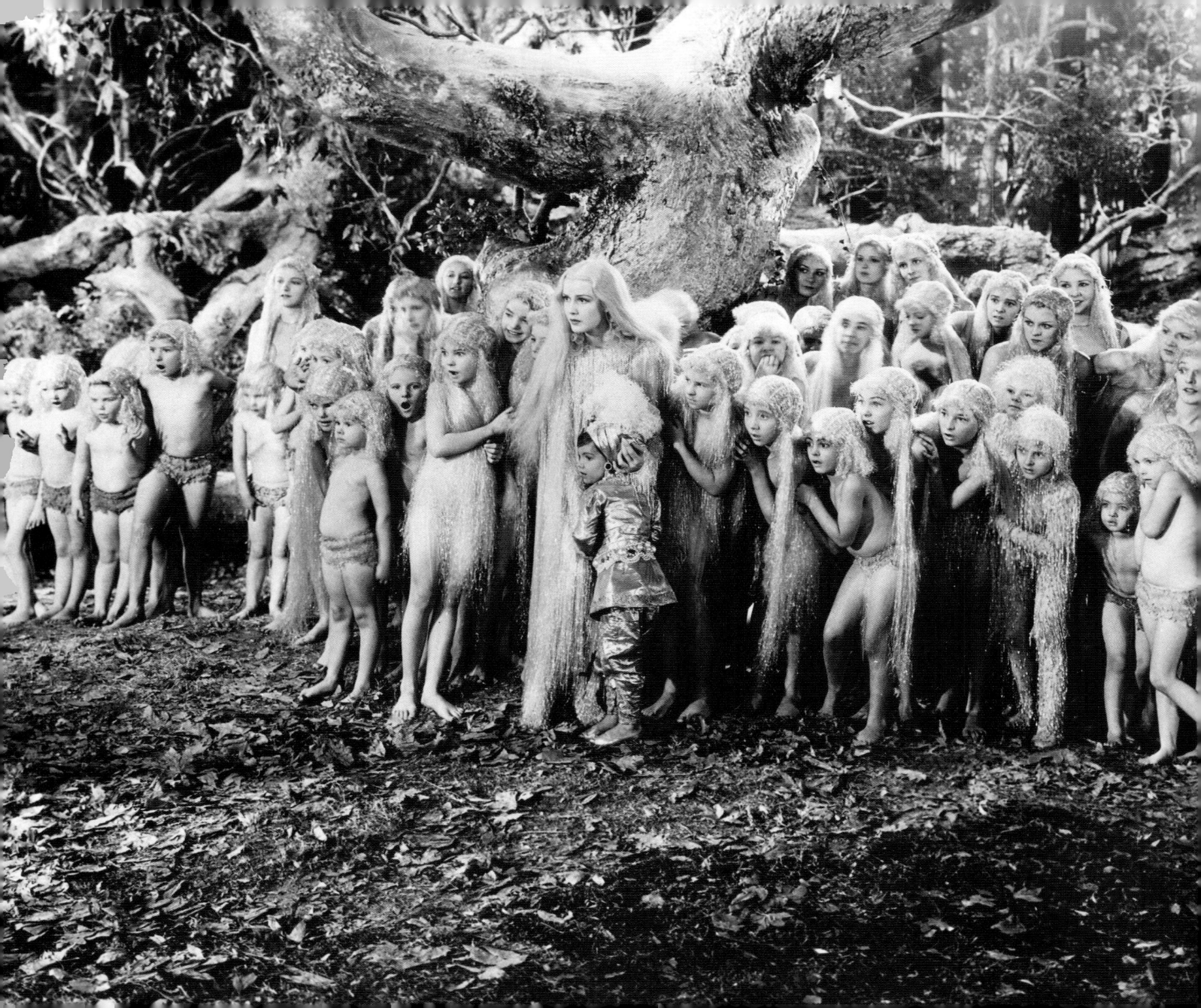

Preface

A study of Kenneth Anger's full body of work is long overdue, however this is by no means an exhaustive attempt to discuss his complex oeuvre. For the first time, Anger has agreed to the production of new stills and frame enlargements from his films for reproduction. A visual publication of still images and written commentary cannot encapsulate, or attempt to stand in for the experience of viewing his films. With reels and reels of 16mm film, I viewed each of the thousands of tiny film frames with a magnifying glass to find quintessential images, a demanding curatorial or editorial project in itself. What emerged was a miraculous microcosm of individually beautiful photographic images, viewing what is usually perceived as fleeting moments in motion. Many of only one or two frames, these images only appear subliminally when watching the film, secrets previously privy only to the filmmaker. To hold them still for a moment gives us the opportunity to explore Anger's vast pan-cultural references, hermetic systems, allegory and symbolism, mythology, folk-law and purported autobiography, to gain a more profound understanding of his work.

The book necessitates a discussion of film that encompasses art, literature, theater, music, psychology, psychoanalysis, film history and theory. Covering 60 years of counterculture aesthetics as could only be found in Anger's singular oeuvre, this publication consolidates English and French texts for the first time – archives and correspondence collected internationally, interviews with Anger, commentaries by Stan Brakhage, Anaïs Nin, Samson De Brier, Carolee Schneemann, Jonas Mekas, Robert Haller and their contemporaries – as well as recent projects that have not been discussed in film anthologies or journals, with Jonas Mekas and Robert Haller at Anthology Film Archives in New York permitting extensive reproduction of seminal texts from *Film Culture*.

This book seeks to cast Anger's work as an artist-filmmaker into a wider historic context, which does not attempt to exhaustively analyze, verbalize, decode or demystify the abundant symbols and visual language that his films present. Rather, it is a dedication to one of the twentieth (and twenty-first) century's most influential and under-recognized artists.

A Midsummer Night's Dream, 1935, dir. Max Reinhardt and William Dieterle, featuring Kenneth Anger

Time Must Have A Stop

Kenneth Anger

Hotspur, *dying*:

But thought's the slave of
life, and life's Time's fool

And Time, that takes
survey of all the world,

Must have a stop

Shakespeare, *Henry IV, Part I*

Think about it: for 100 years, the film-watching public has
been fooled. Whether watching a crowd of workers
leaving the Lumière factory in 1895, or waves crashing
onto rocks, or a train arriving in a station, the audience
has been taken in by the illusion of life, when all it is
seeing is a series of projected still photographs, with an
interval of darkness between each one. The willingness
to believe – and the persistence of vision – have given us
the Cinema.

As a filmmaker, cutting my own films, I was always aware
and captivated by the seduction of the miniature images,
the frames, flowing like a cascade as the lighting, the
color and the action changed. In the viewer on my cutting
table I could stop time, and isolate one picture as the
essence of the moving event.

Thus was born the idea of Kenneth Anger's ICONS.
[These] individual frames [were selected] from several of
my films that I thought could stand on their own as an
arresting and compelling image[s]. In some cases, I have
enlarged the filmstrip to show several frames, to capture
the blur and flow of actual movement. In other cases,
such as the close-up of Anaïs Nin or of Samson De Brier
from INAUGURATION OF THE PLEASURE DOME, I have
stopped the frame on a fleeting smile, or the sardonic
glint of the eye. Ah, to capture, to slow, to arrest time –
the World's Illusion. Of course it will escape again – as
escape it must. The March of Time is inexorable.

IT'S ALWAYS THERE
TAUNTING YOU
FASTER, FASTER.

YOU HATE IT. CURSE IT.
RESPECT IT. WORSHIP IT.
IT'S TIME.

AND THE ONLY WAY
TO BE A MASTER MAGICIAN
IS TO BEAT IT

TIME MUST HAVE A STOP

What *is* the Present? It is nothing more than a point upon the line of Time, where the infinite Future is separated from the infinite Past.

Metaphorically: A FRAME OF FILM.

Going still further, it is the invisible instant, the theoretical atom of Time, trillions of times more than 24-frames-per-second, where the non-existent Future meets the non-existent Past. Can such a point – the super-super-super-super film frame – be said to exist?

For the Present to exist it must have some sort of duration, however short. It must exist for some measurable moment of Time, this META-FRAME, however small. For if it doesn't exist for a single moment, a molecular shutter-flash, it cannot be said to exist. Furthermore, this moment, this Cosmic Frame, must have some duration of its own, however small.

But if a moment has duration, it must have a Past and a Future, like a piece of film, a beginning and an end. In our Cosmic Cutting Room, we must sub-divide this moment, then, and eliminate its Past and its Future in order to isolate its Present – the ultimate freeze-frame – if it has any Present at all. In our Cosmic Cutting Room we must cut it up into instants, and *must keep on cutting it up* until we get an instant so small that it has no fractional part of a Past or Future remaining in it.

When we have accomplished this, we will have come to the true atom of Time – the ULTIMATE FRAME – but we will have eliminated *duration*.

A true atom of Time must have no duration whatever. It must have no Past or Future in it or it will not be a pure NOW; it will be contaminated with Then-ness and Yet-ness. A true atom of Time – one cell of the body of God Chronos – must have no Time-dimension at all. Therefore it cannot exist at all, in Time, for without duration existence is impossible.

Now what has become of the Present? Our isolated, single film frame? It cannot exist for more than one indivisible instant, one atom of Time, and this atom of Time cannot exist at all. Consequently the Present cannot exist at all, even as a theoretical point where the non-existent Past meets the non-existent Future. The Present is the most obviously unreal and unprovable tense of all three; it surely *did not* exist in the Past, it surely *will not* exist in the Future; and it cannot be allowed any duration, for a fraction of an instant, NOW.

So it is clear that the Present does not exist!

If, as has been "proved", on the unspooling reel of Time, neither the Past, the Present nor the Future exist NOW; and if it is impossible to prove that any one of them *did* exist or *will* exist, then it cannot be proved that Time itself has *any existence whatsoever*.

STOP THE PROJECTOR.
CUT THE CURRENT.
EXTINGUISH THE PROJECTION LAMP.
THE MAGUS PROCLAIMS:

TIME MUST HAVE A STOP.

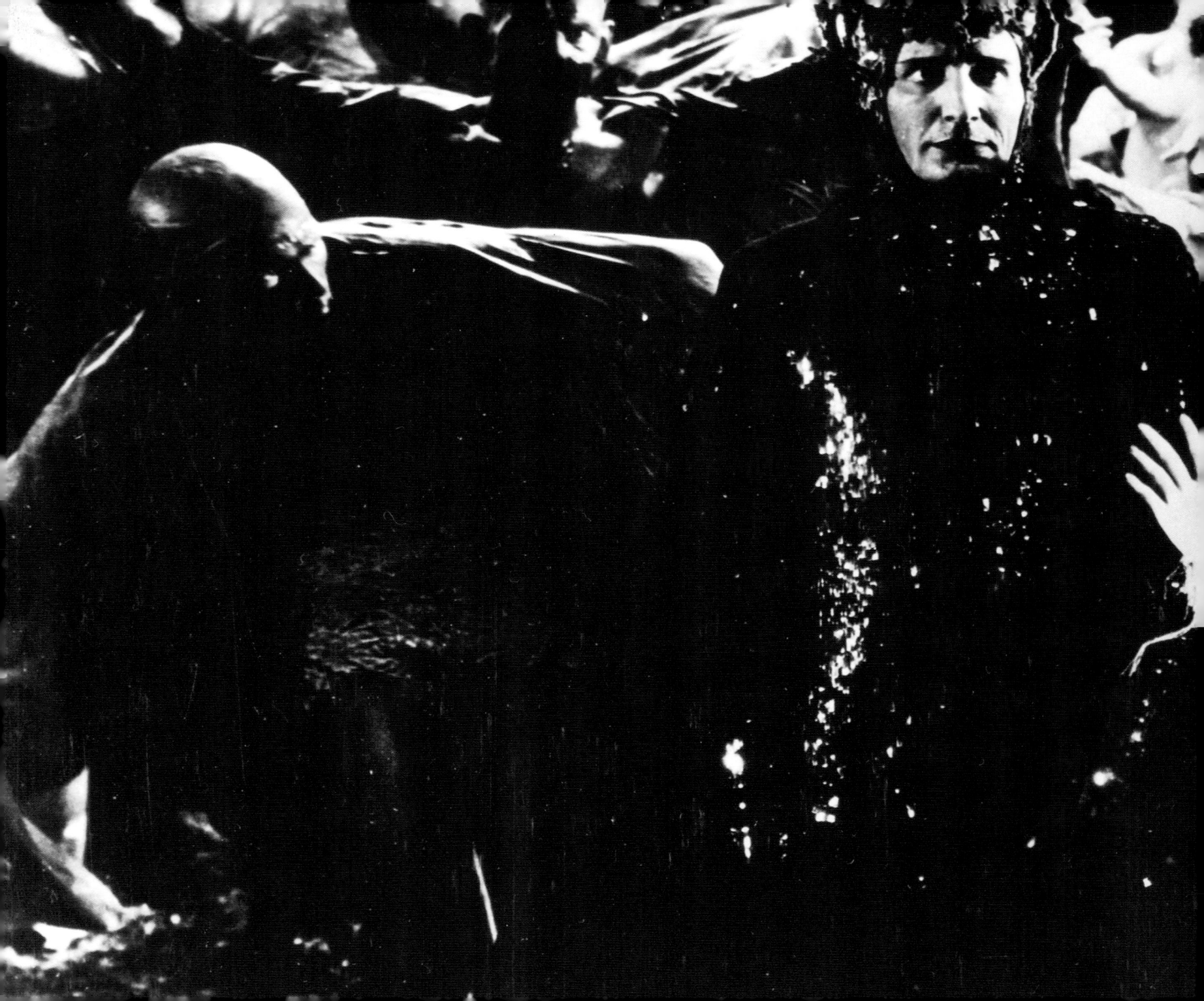

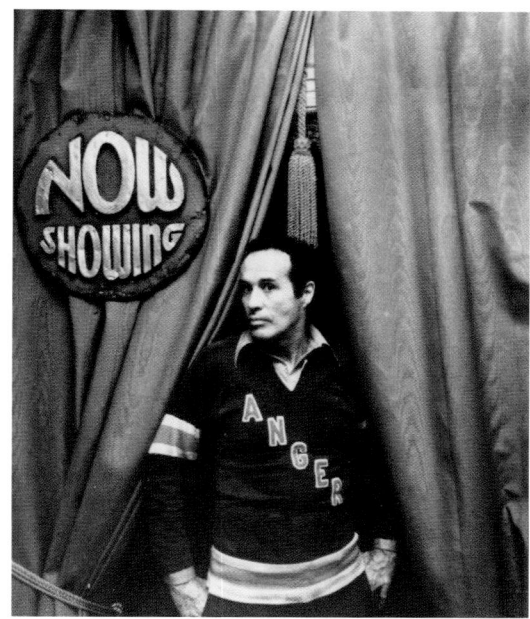

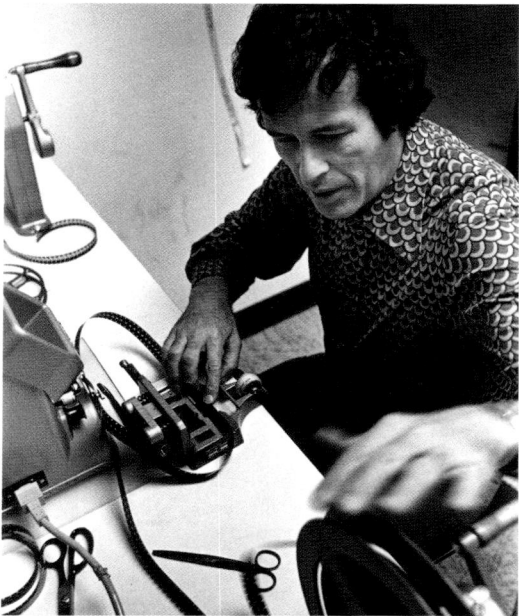

"rational" processes of modernity. As in *The Arcades Project*, "an experiment in the technique of awakening," Benjamin expressed awakening as an historical and generational process as well as an individual one. Anger has said that he would prefer to project images directly into his viewers' minds; his films still continue to stimulate or awaken the perceptions and tap into the primal sensory faculty of viewers. As Anger has often cited, in Shakespeare the conscious life is revealed as a type of trance. "Drama is born in the renunciation of magic," critic Northrop Frye has stated (recalling Prospero breaking his staff and relinquishing his powers in *The Tempest*); as Anger would have it, magic is the renunciation of drama. Neither the initiates of ancient lore nor modern occultists considered the macrocosm in terms of space and time, but rather in spheres of transcendent consciousness. Animist and fantastic beliefs of our past culture(s) are reawakened, exposing audiences to the archaic power of magical thought, a filmic mimesis, a reversal of the suppression of ancient pagan beliefs, removing the separation between old fictions and new realities.

This page: portraits of Kenneth Anger by Robert Haller
Next pages: production stills from *A Midsummer Night's Dream*, 1935

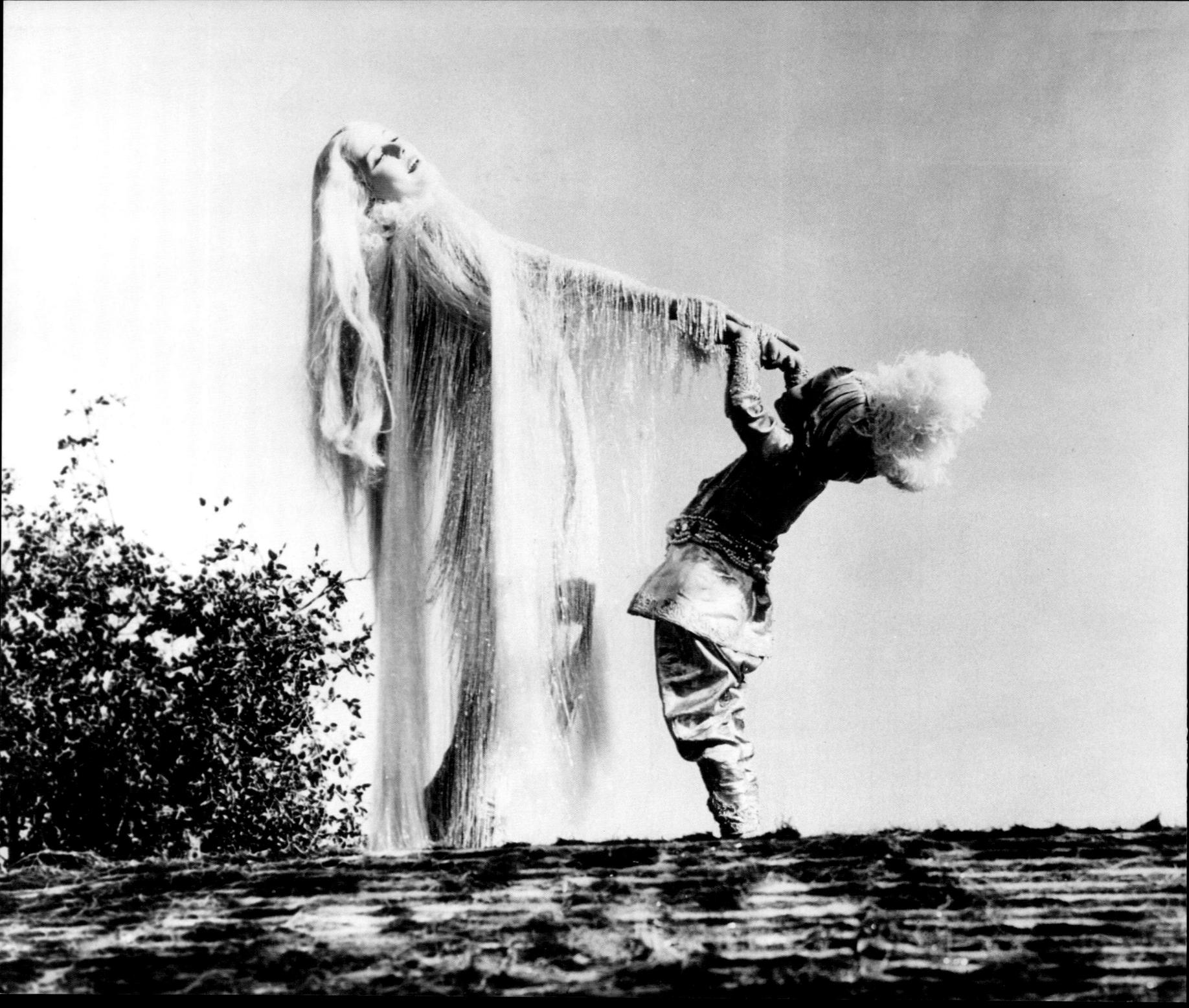

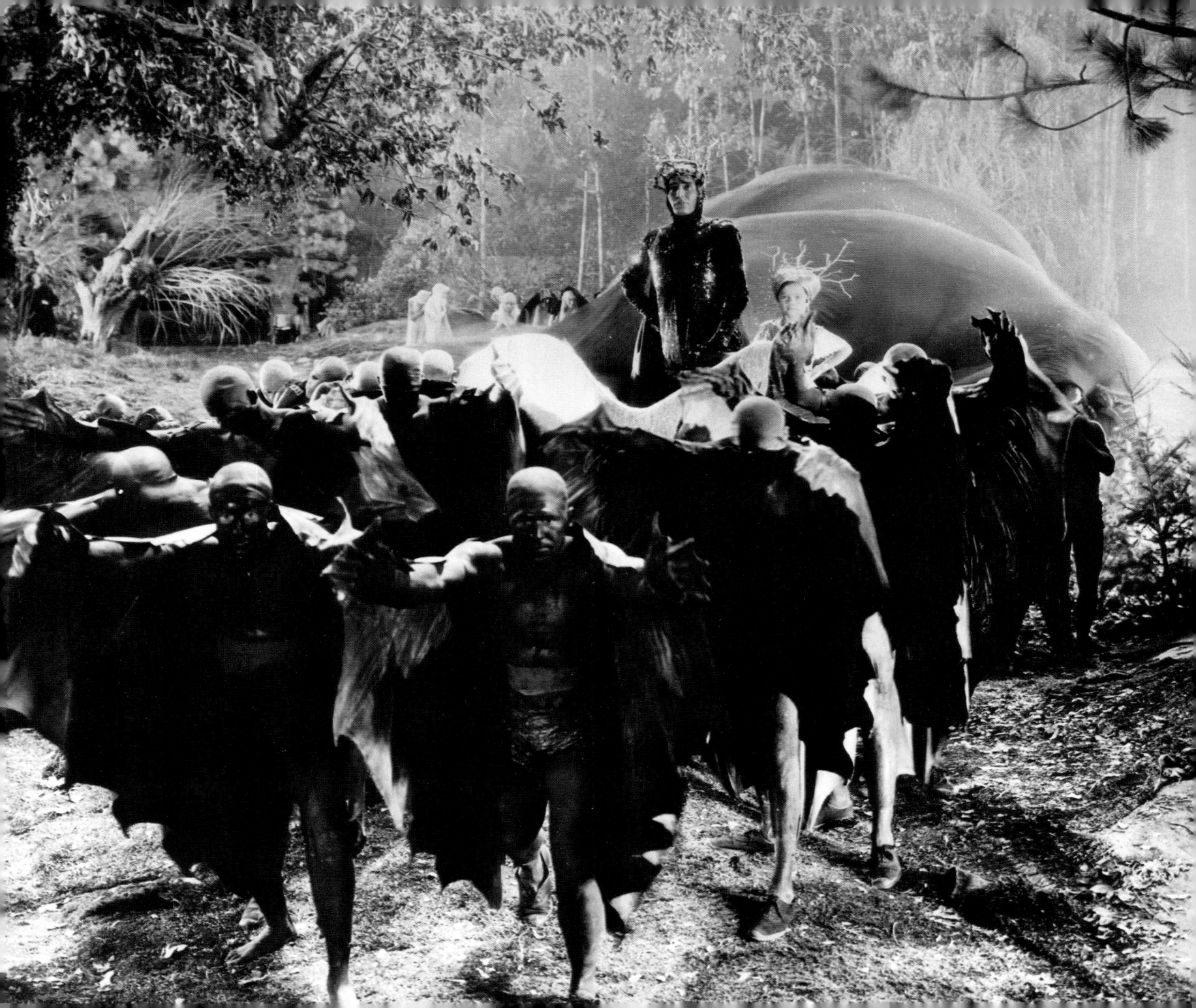

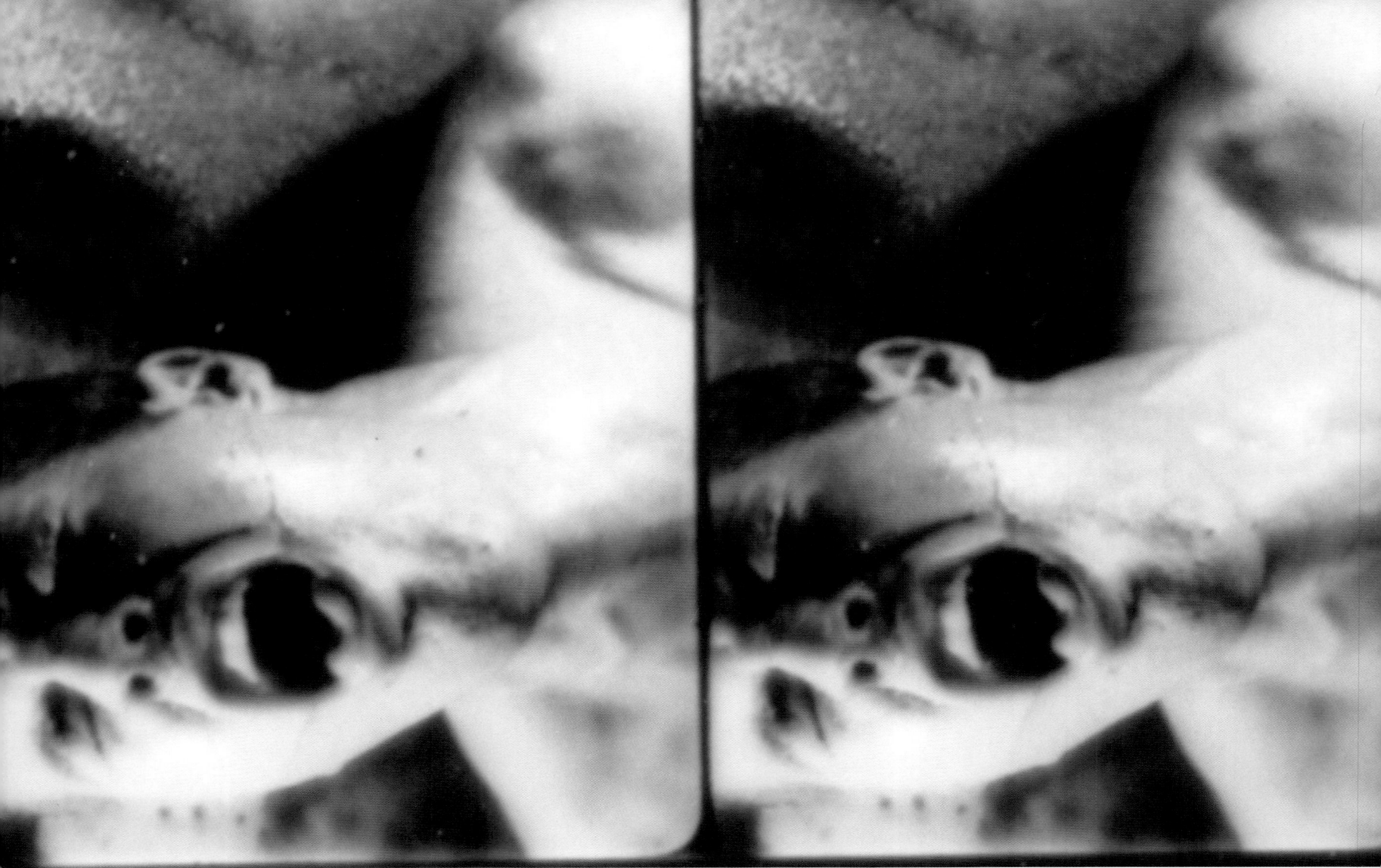

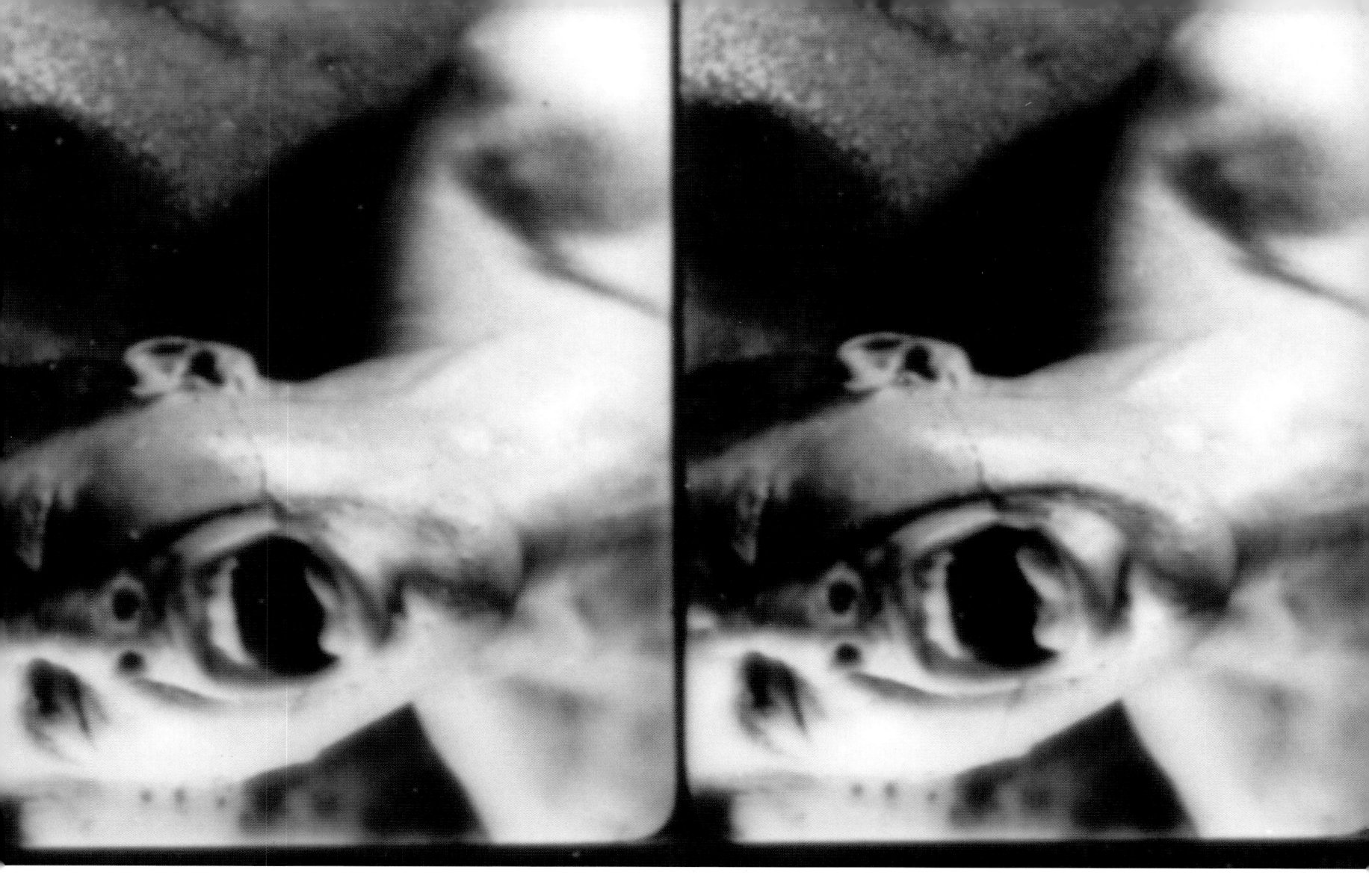

1. Los Angeles in the 1940s

Self-taught, Kenneth Anger began making and screening films with his family's 16mm Kodak home movie camera from the age of seven. Growing up in Los Angeles, film became an inescapable frame of reference and medium of expression from an early age. As a child Anger attended dance cotillions (Shirley Temple was one of his partners), participated in *Baby Burlesques* and appeared in Max Reinhardt and William Dieterle's 1935 film adaptation of *A Midsummer Night's Dream*.[1]

Although these films may all be lost, he completed seven short films prior to 1947, conceiving, directing, photographing, creating his own props and costumes, and editing the films himself. As we can only surmise from the existing descriptions, specific images from these early films were to recur in Anger's subsequent work.[2] His first film, *Ferdinand the Bull*, was made in 1937, and in 1941 he created *Who Has Been Rocking My Dream Boat?*; described by Anger as an atmospheric montage of children enacting war games in the summer before Pearl Harbor. A similarly titled song by the Ink Spots provided Anger's first use of popular music as an ironic counterpoint to the visuals. While early avant-garde filmmakers such as Bruce Conner syncopated and synchronized rhythmic editing of images with a soundtrack, Kenneth Anger can be credited for introducing pop music as a film soundtrack.

Who Has Been Rocking My Dreamboat?, was filmed in Santa Monica with a cast of neighborhood children. Using rapid cross-cutting, the play-world of children was shown overshadowed by war. A "newsreel holocaust," (an onslaught of documentary images mimicking the assault on Pearl Harbor), was flash-cut across their reverie, with the children then falling to the ground in mock death while smoke billowed over their still bodies. The following year, Anger utilized the family Christmas tree in a ritual burning, in *Tinsel Tree*, 1942, in which he painstakingly hand-colored the individual film frames with scarlet and gold over-tint. Branches of the tree decked with baubles and tinsel were then stripped and burnt in close-up. That year, he also directed the science fiction inspired *Prisoner of Mars*, filmed with elaborate miniatures and costumes created himself. Anger was the "boy elect from earth" in his first formal use of a serial-chapter aesthetic (structured sequences creating "chapter breaks"). As a sci-fi rendition of the Minotaur myth, Anger as the chosen boy of the future rocketed to Mars, and landed in a labyrinth littered with the bones of previous travelers.

While at Beverly Hills High School, Anger first began researching Jean Cocteau and Jean Genet as well as French Symbolist literature. He made his first variant on Cocteau's *Les Enfants Terrible*, called *The Nest*, in 1942. Following which, he conceived and filmed the half-hour *Escape Episode* in Los Angeles in 1944, which he described as an experimental study showing a conflict of moral values. Set in a decaying stucco-gothic seaside church, it was a free adaptation of the Andromeda myth. Following the psychology of the protagonist, a sensitive adolescent girl (Marilyn Granas, the stand-in for Shirley Temple), the film became increasingly subjective. Stifled by the hand of religious fanaticism, the girl encountered a "nature boy," Perseus, on the beach and the pair conspired to break parental bonds. The film premiered at the Coronet Theater in Hollywood in 1947. The last of these seven lost films, *Drastic Demise*, 1945, was filmed with a hand-held camera plunged into the hysteria of the anonymous delirious crowds of V. J. Day on Hollywood Boulevard. Constructing a dialectical *frisson* between negative and positive images in the frenzy of the euphoric crowd *vis-à-vis* the end of the war and the birth of the atomic age, this film marked the ambivalence of V. J. Day with a mushroom cloud end. It had an accompanying original score for percussion. *Escape Episode*, *Drastic Demise*, and *Fireworks* were featured at the San Francisco Museum of Modern Art, and offered as a package for screenings in 1947. From these descriptions, it is apparent that later motifs and themes were contained in these works. For instance, the ritualized burning of the Christmas tree returns in *Fireworks*, whilst the act of self-preparation (ablutions and mirrors) in *The Nest* was to mark *Puce Moment*, *Scorpio Rising* and *Kustom Kar Kommandos*. The mirror-signals of "the perfect pair" in *The Nest* reappear as Isis and Osiris signaling across the desert in *Lucifer Rising*. *Who Has Been Rocking My Dreamboat?* and *Invocation of My Demon Brother* show private worlds threatened by war, perpetual violence and chaos.[3]

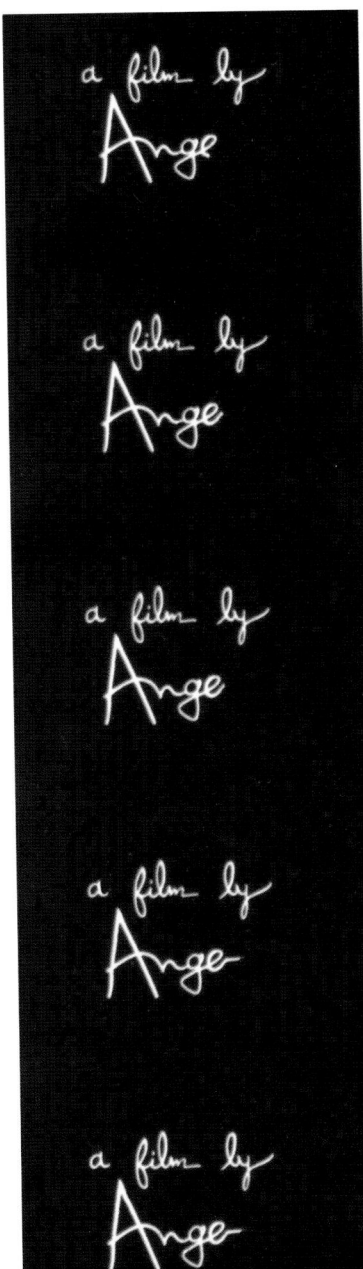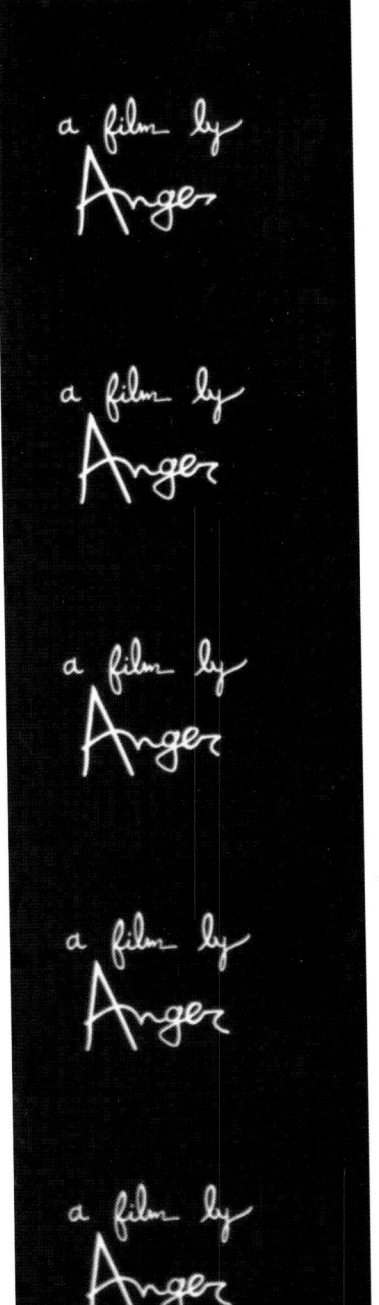

Film strips from the title sequence of *Fireworks*, 1947

It was this same year that Anger first encountered Nin in San Francisco. Harry Smith had organized a screening of *Fireworks* at the San Francisco Museum of Art (SFMOMA), which ran a successful Art in Cinema program through the 1940s, at which time Harrington and Anger met San Francisco-based independent filmmakers James Broughton and Sidney Peterson. The SFMOMA Art In Cinema's program signaled an unparalleled occasion for collaboration within the burgeoning West Coast avant-garde American community in the 1940s between filmmakers, poets and writers, and artists. At this time, Anger and Curtis Harrington had set up their own distribution company in Los Angeles, Creative Film Associates, renting primarily European avant-garde films from the Museum of Modern Art in New York and screening them for the first time in Los Angeles, alongside their own work and those of their contemporaries. Following Deren's seminal Provincetown Playhouse screenings which she called "Three Abandoned Films" (after Valéry's, "a work of art is never finished merely abandoned") Amos Vogel established New York's Cinema 16 in 1947, the first organization to specialize in the distribution of avant-garde film and the longest-lived and most successful film society in American history (at its height it had 7,000 members, and inspired a nationwide network of smaller film societies).[27] Symposiums were also held, most notably that with Maya Deren, Dylan Thomas and Arthur Miller debating the poetic possibilities of film:

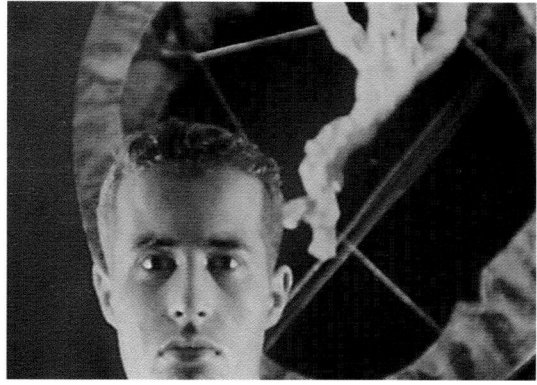

> You get a montage of images, that is, a poetic construct, after which what follows is a dramatic construct that is essentially "horizontal" in its development [i.e. a narrative progression]. The same thing would apply to dream sequences. They occur at a moment when the intensification is carried out not by action but by the illumination of that moment. Now the short films, to my mind (and they are short because it is difficult to maintain such intensity for a long period of time) are comparable to lyric poems, and they are completely "vertical," or what I would call a poetic construct, and they are complete as such.[28]

> What you would say in words should be said instead in images.[29]

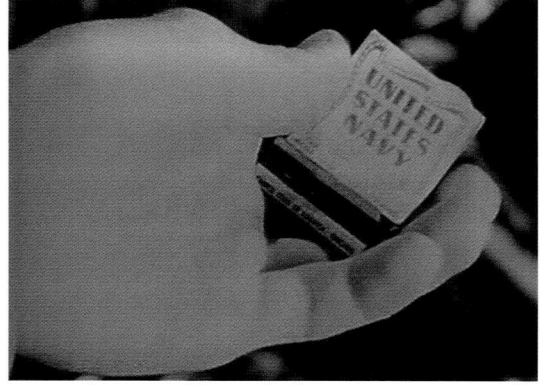

Anger discussed the violent Zoot Suit riots that began in downtown Los Angeles in 1943 prior to making *Fireworks*, which sparked his fascination with the image of the sailor.[30] The marauding, bullying, clean-cut young sailors remained archetypal figures for Anger, in a highly personalized eroticization of the sadistic events four years earlier. Although it is uncertain whether Anger had access to this book at the time, Cocteau's *Le Livre Blanc* had referred to the port town of Toulon and its obliging sailors.[31] Los Angeles in 1943 was a major training and transit point for military personnel, and saw itself on the front lines of the war in the Pacific. Sailors, soldiers, and marines stationed in the area were in direct competition for the attention of the ladies with the local "zoot suiters," with the situation soon turning

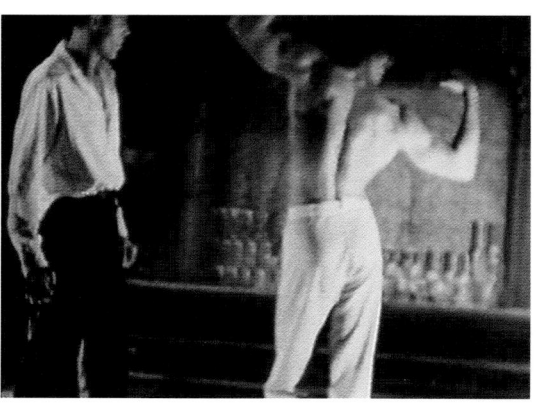

Top: "Anger's clay sculpture of the "Risen Furious Christ", which casts a shadow in the mirror image in the film"
Middle: "Smoking was actively encouraged in the U.S. military during World War II and the post war 40s"
Bottom: "15 year old Junior Body Building champion"

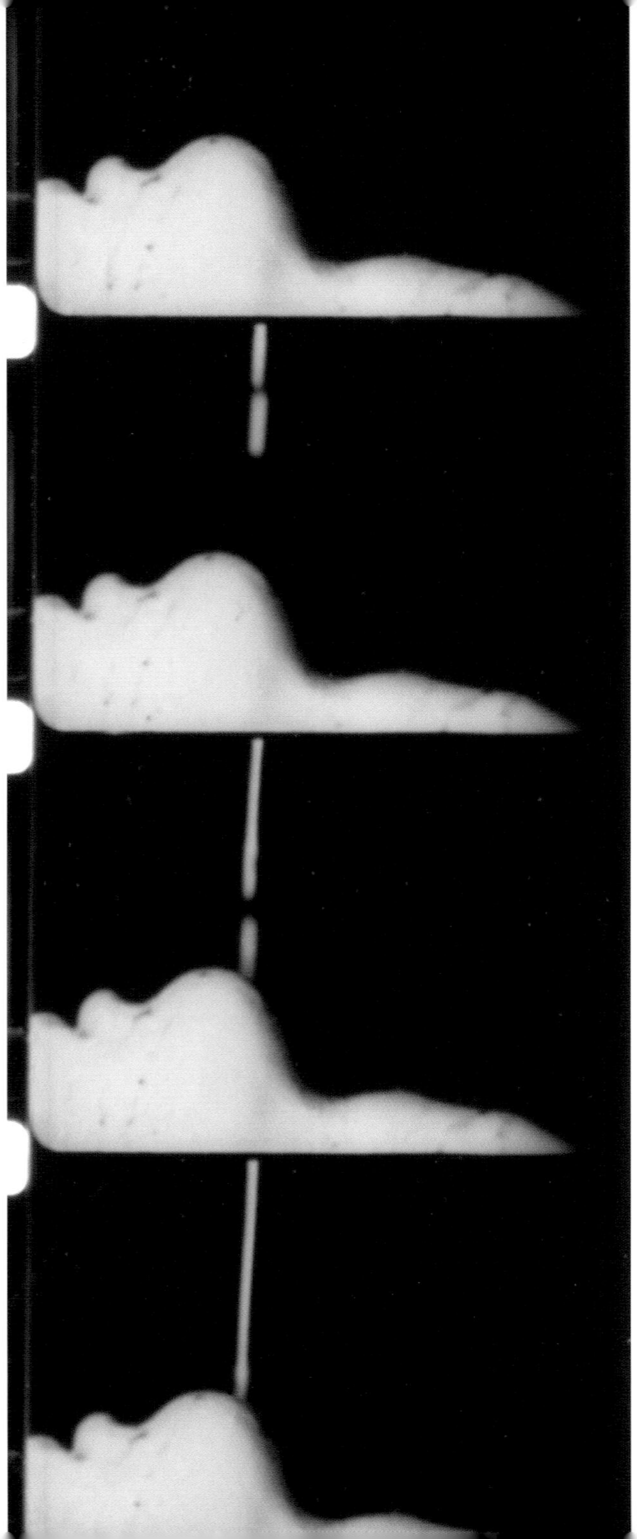

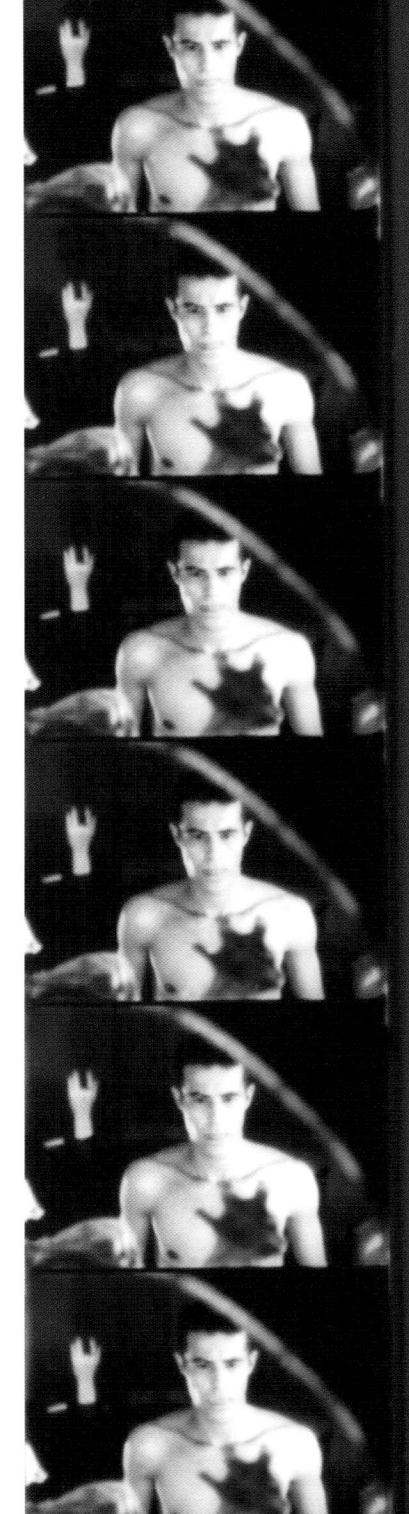

into a "war" against Mexican "pachucos" (young punks), who were demonized by a conservative media. A growing youth counterculture mixed with a rebellion against cherished social norms, led to the criminalization of what was assumed to be a youth gang.

The dream of aggression has as its target not only Anger himself, but the external society which acts as omnipotent repressive force. Thus in its iconography of matches, Christmas trees and Roman candles, it satirizes social institutions in the manner of Buñuel's *L'Age d'Or*. As Anger himself has ironically put it: "This flick is all I have to say about being 17, the United States Navy, American Christmas and the Fourth of July."[32]

The repressive American society from which *Fireworks* emerged was not about to uphold Anger's artistic aspirations, and so the support he received from France encouraged him to leave for Paris, particularly when there was hardly an established audience for such work: neither fitting into the established modern art realm nor that of commercial film. A private screening of *Fireworks* and Harrington's *Fragment of Seeking* was held in Los Angeles around 1948 at the Schindler House for modern art's denizens of the day, amongst whom were John Cage and Merce Cunningham. The audience would not look nor speak to them after the screening, then Cage approached them saying, "well of course young gentlemen, you must realize these have *nothing* to do with art." Seeing everyone in complete shock and utter silence Mrs. Schindler announced: "We have discussed the films amongst us, and we have decided that you are two very sick boys."[33] The response in France however was ecstatic; Cocteau was adamant that Anger was one of the most important new filmmakers, one able to convey the interior world of desire, at once forbidden, invisible and dangerous, not only depicting homosexuality but also of personal fantasy. An ability to transcribe sensations, a transition to immaterial ideas was a new concept in film, one that Cocteau and Genet were grappling to manifest, and here it was, finely wrought by an American teenager.

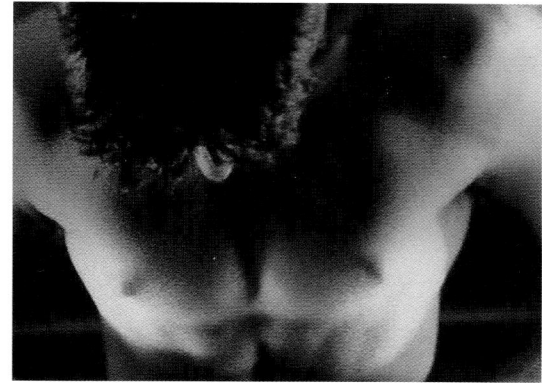

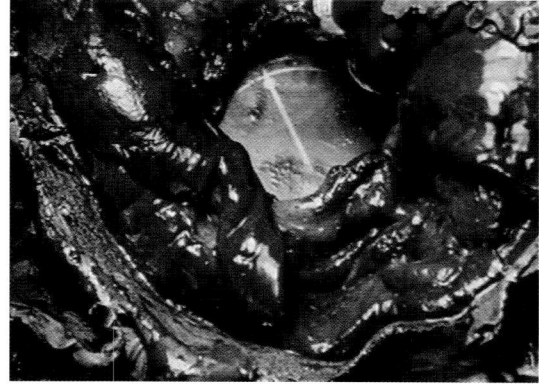

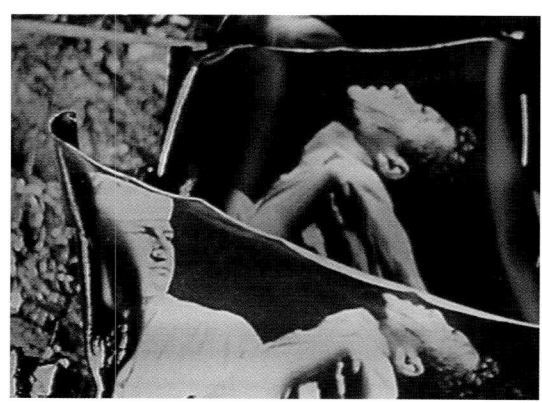

Next page, from left: "smashing beer bottle; stabbing with broken bottle; Anger's hands covered in blood; the oh-so-strong Gordon Gray, U.S.C. football hero, carries the 138-pound Anger easily; crotch, match and Roman candle; transformation into Christmas Tree – note the bandage covering "missing" heart; hand-painted Solar Lover: Head as Light"

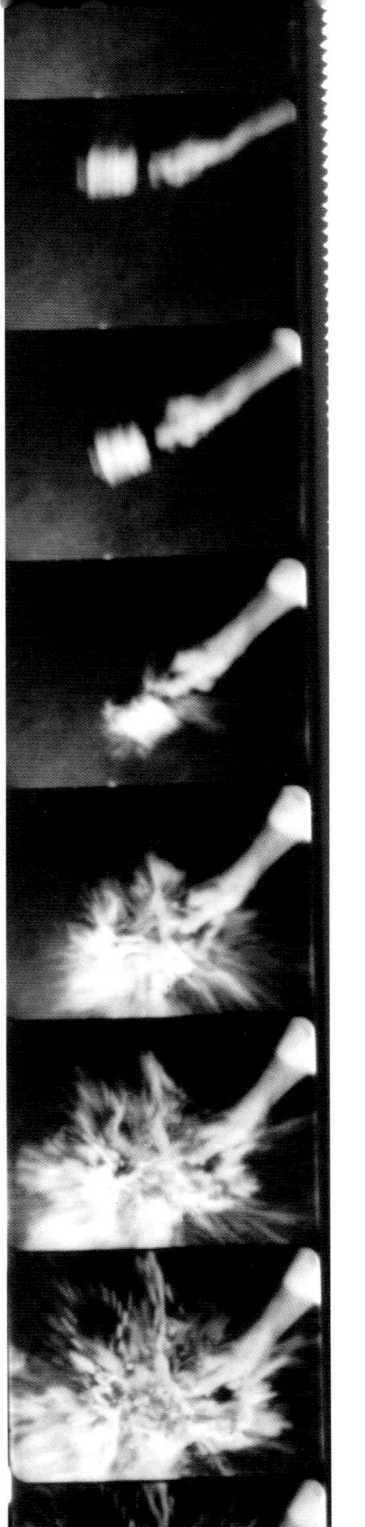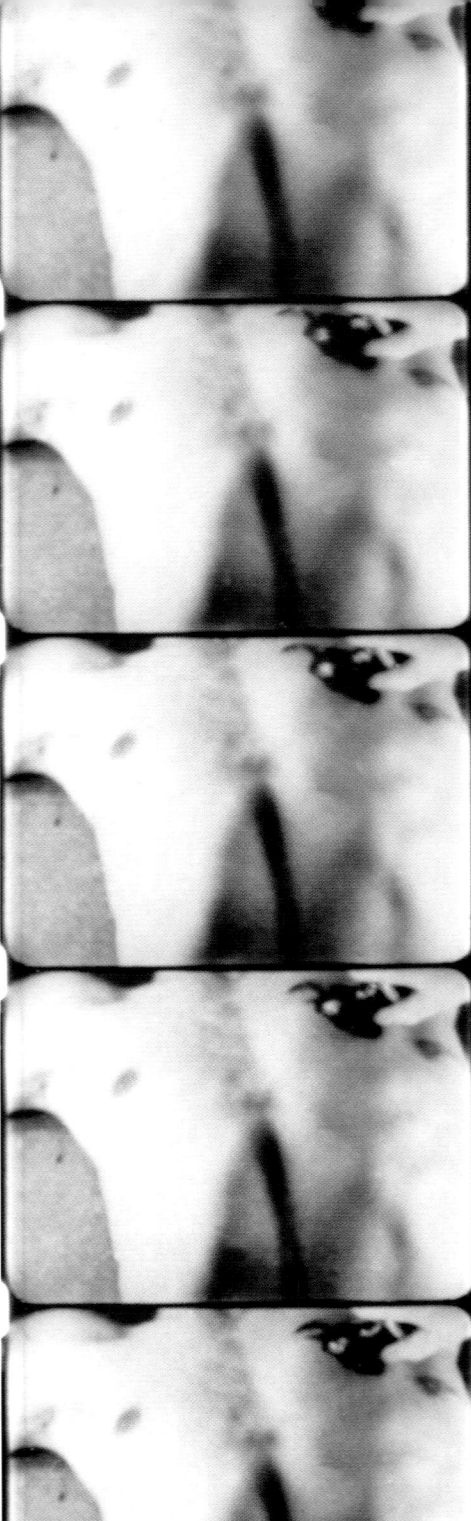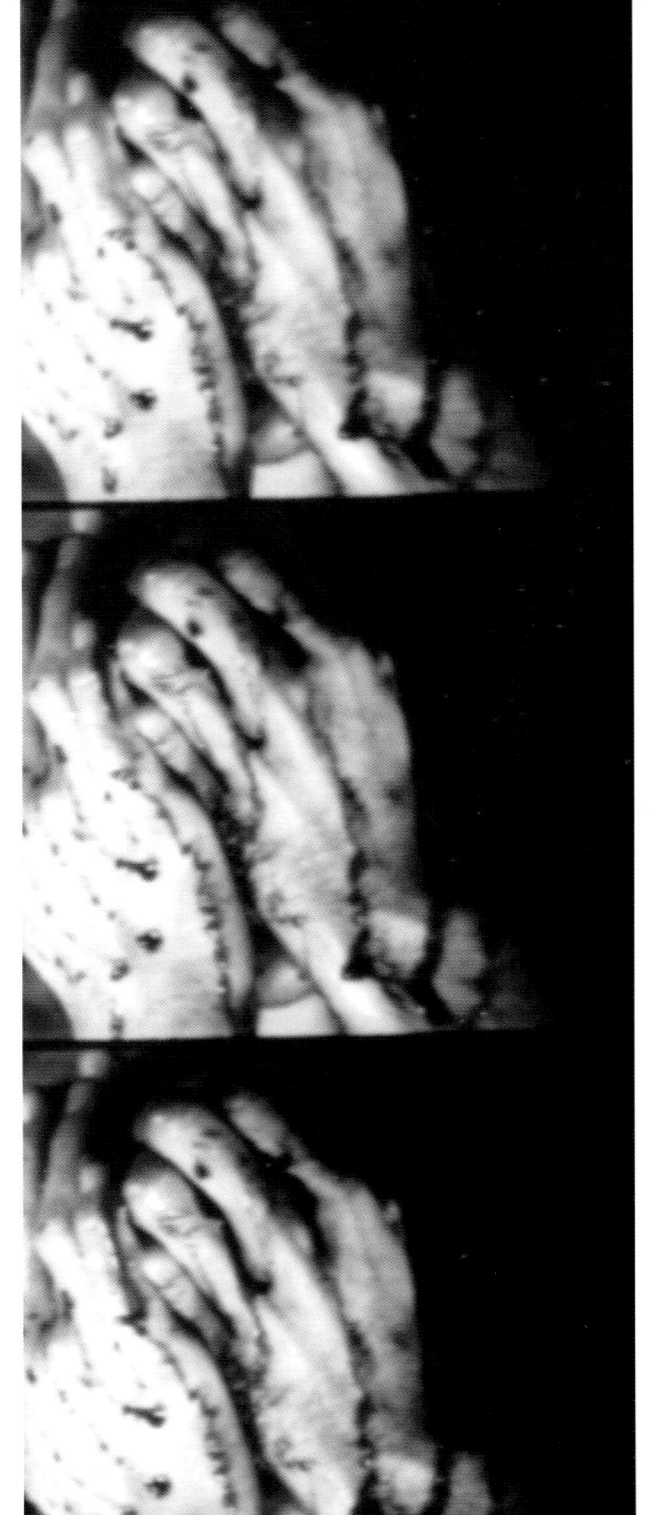

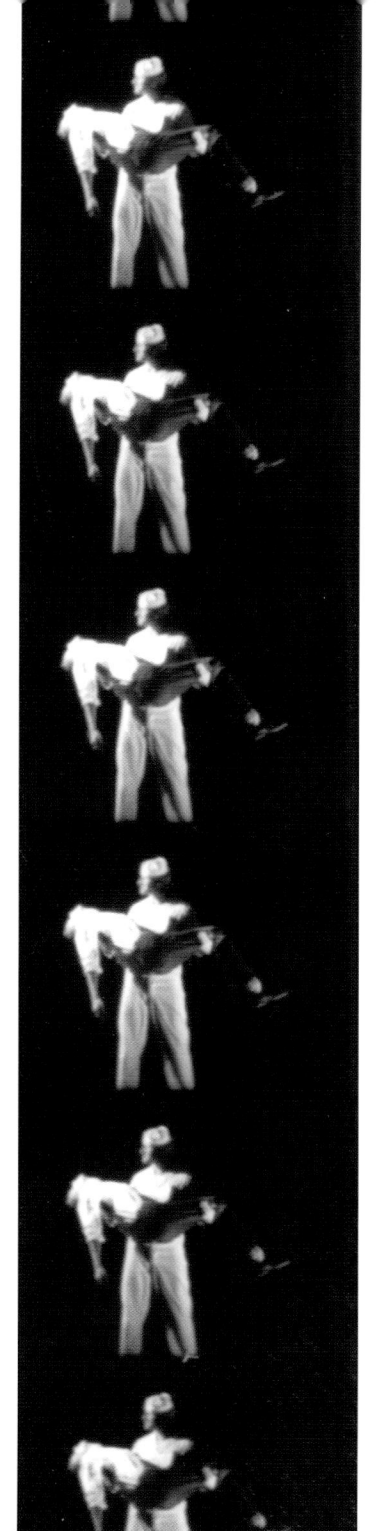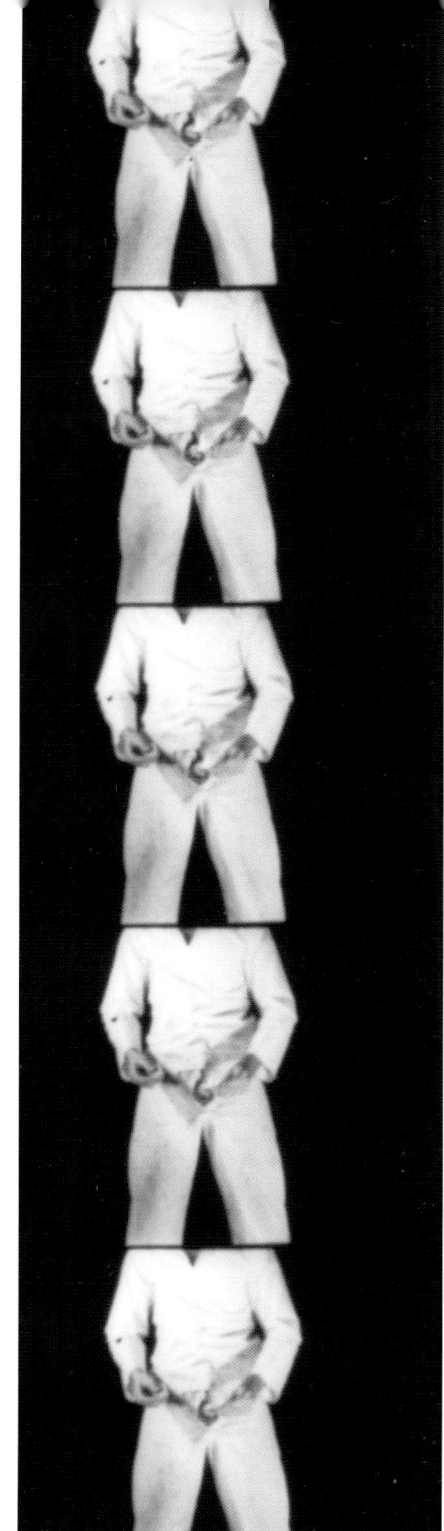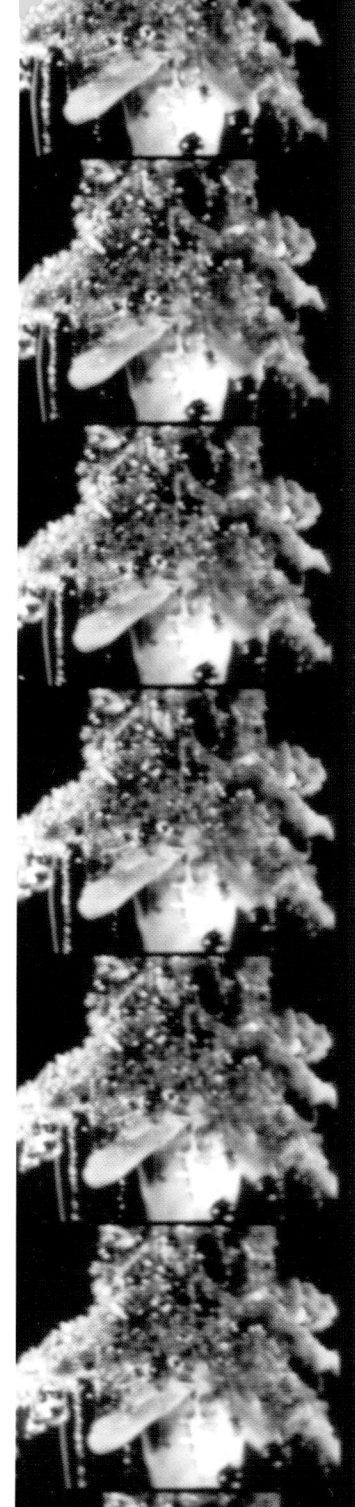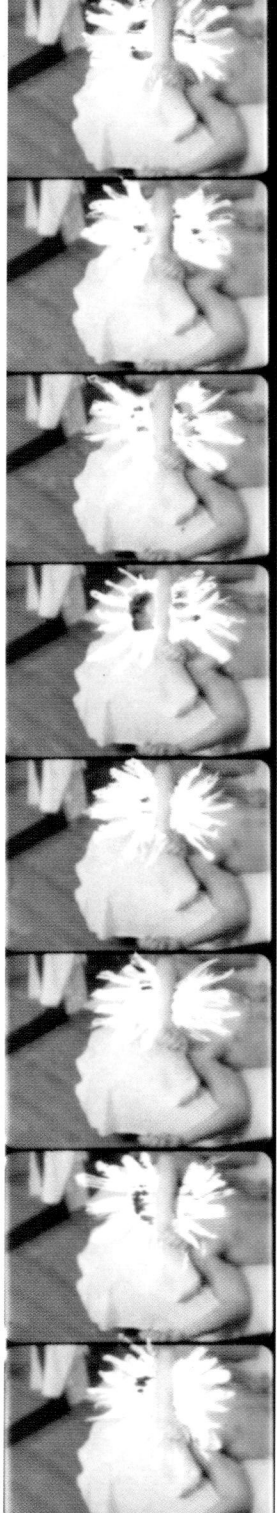

Application d'Artifice

Kenneth Anger [34]

Fireworks was screened in Paris in 1949 following the Biarritz festival and Anger found his first avid advocate in the press, Jean Boullet, who also encouraged Anger to write about his film. Boullet discussed *Fireworks* in the context of the classics of avant-garde film, *L'Age d'Or*, *Un Chien Andalou*, *L'Ile du Docteur Moreau*:

> ... this extraordinary confession, this flaunted declaration, turns upside down and disrupts all that we know about film and eroticism up until this point. The contribution of *Fireworks* is similar in the cinematographic domain to that of Jean Genet in contemporary literature.... Without a taste for gratuitous scandal and violence.... The beauty of certain images (the steps of the sailors advancing towards the victim), the daring innovation of its realization, the extraordinary nerve that he had in daring to make the film; it deserves to come out of the shadows where it is being held. *Fireworks* deserves to leave the world of discreet projections, its quasi-clandestine situation distorts judgment and fools the eye.... It is the first confession in provocative images of the cinema. [35]

A year later Boullet dedicated an issue of *St. Cinema des Près* to *Fireworks* and the young director, and encouraged Anger to submit his own statement on the film. Anger's first published writing (originally in French) is included here for the first time in English.

Kenneth Anger's *Fireworks* ranks among... the true honors of the cinema. We are delighted to be the first to have broken the silence of the press in regard to *Fireworks*. Silence that strangely facilitated the work of those repressed, cowardly and envious.

Without doubt certain people soon discovered Anger and his film (in measure which served their own personal publicity). Their concerns are pointless. *Fireworks* is no longer to be "discovered." We are responsible to take care of this work. Today *St. Cinema des Près* is publishing the first article by Kenneth Anger on his film.

Kenneth Anger is twenty years old. – J.B. [36]

The inventions of the unknown
demand new forms.

Arthur Rimbaud

I chose cinema as the mode of personal expression for its potential and capacity for disruption: it is the surest means to incite change. As an art form, it exceeds the "aesthetic" and becomes experience. My cinema "is alive" when the spectator forgets that they're seeing a work of art[ifice]. You see my films or you don't see them – there's no veil of appreciation. *Fireworks* emphasizes a vital drama: the sexual arena of adolescence. It does not seem to me that social organisms have taken a position in regard to the question; similarly, it is unthinkable that the screen must be restricted to a special category of images: I place myself quite beyond that position!

By the most heart-wrenching efforts one gains the phosphorescent layer of myth, which is at the foundation of all of our existences. I will not lie: the landscape of *Fireworks* reaches toward terrifying tunnels of anguish, toward nights of hallucination and burning tears – near steep walls of pain – toward deserts and forests of terrible and obsessed desire.

The buds of eroticism planted upon the bare flesh and deeply rooted in the mind have flourished nevertheless, in tranquillity, solemnity and in the ideal realm of the dream universe. In the dream, the experience is transformed – the chains torn apart and the measures without the counterweight of emotion are put in balance. The vision of the dream was uniquely submissive to the instrument that was waiting for it. A small expenditure of practical sorcery gathers the material and personnel necessary for the production: in an application of total energy, *Fireworks* was filmed in the continuous space of 72 hours. Objectively presented in the language of a dream, *Fireworks* is to coax out the sparks of the psyche of each dreamer. And it is to them I address my work. The synthesis accomplished in the dream is the richest treasure that floats until we drift to sleep; it supplies the ticket to raise our flight toward the troubled waters of experience, and also as a compass to locate our fates. With my researches in cinema, I am trying to restore the dream to its primal state of reverence. *Fireworks* remains for me a key to existence: it re-presents research toward experiencing integrality.

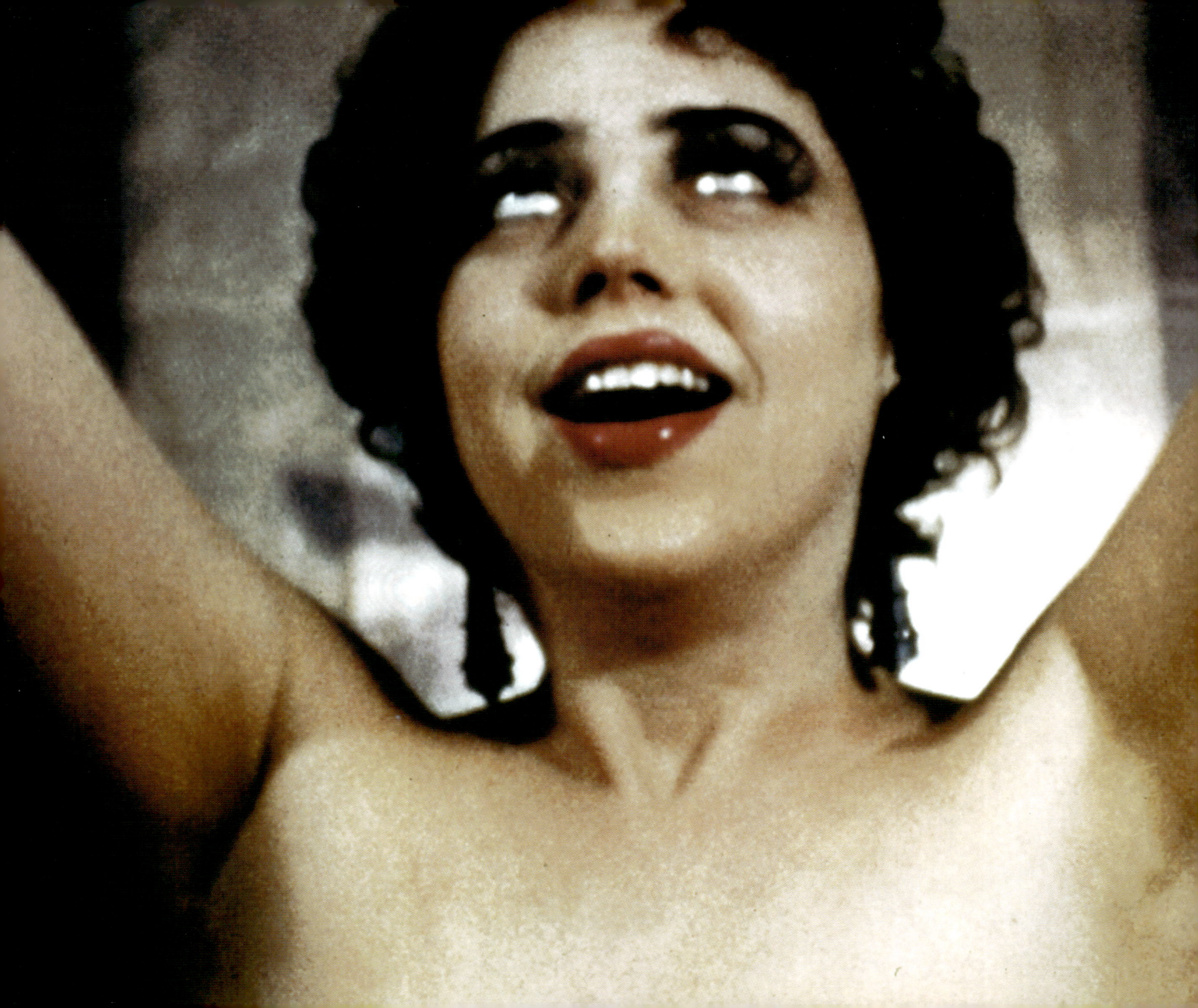

Puce Moment

1949/1970

6 minutes

35mm, color

Music by Jonathan Halper

Puce Women, 1949, was originally conceived as a feature length film on the women of Hollywood in the 1920s, and Anger's first use of color. It was to be a study of their lifestyles, their clothes, their cars, their houses, their social patterns, with an all women cast (including their elegant wolfhounds). Anger stated, "*Puce Women* was my love affair with mythological Hollywood. A straight, heterosexual love affair... with all the great goddesses of the silent screen... filming ghosts. The project was doomed, because a freeway to the San Fernando Valley was put through all those lovely 1920s houses. That was a sad day for Hollywood, the beginning of the end."[37] This project reflected Anger's concerns with the myths and decline of Hollywood. "For him more than for any other avant-garde filmmaker Hollywood has been both his matrix and the adversary."[38]

The opening sequence captures rows of shimmering sequined and beaded 1920s flapper-style gowns pushed – lunging and shimmying – toward the camera as if to don the spectator and share in the act of "dress up" in a ritual of assuming identity. Each frame celebrates the beauty of surface texture and color. Intimate close-ups on soft powdered cheeks, fluttering black false eyelashes and glossy red lips are intercut with images of fabrics and beads, fur, glistening perfume bottles and shots of the dresser as she steps into turquoise satin pumps; the camera studies each, relishing the individual surfaces and textures in fetishizing close-ups.

Puce is the color of her sequined gown. It was the name of a purple-green iridescent color that was very popular in the 1920s – puce and tango were jazz colors.[40]

Puce is the changeable color of the lowly flea, the iridescent color of her 1920s gown.[39]

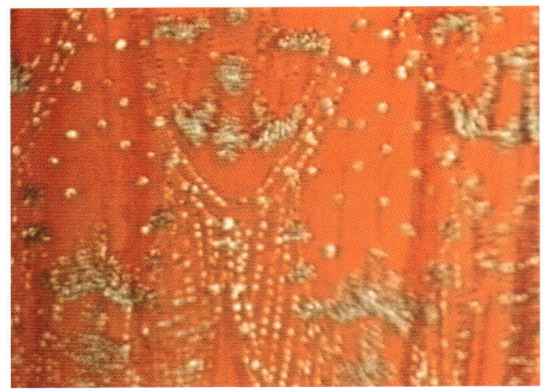

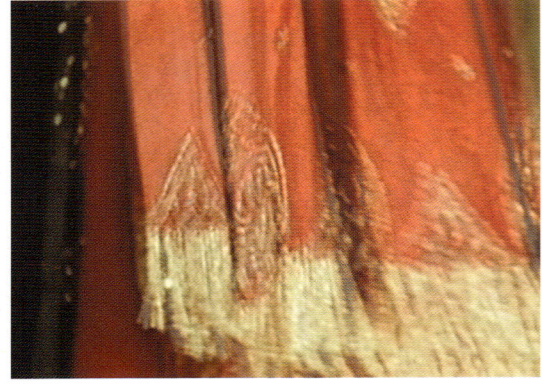

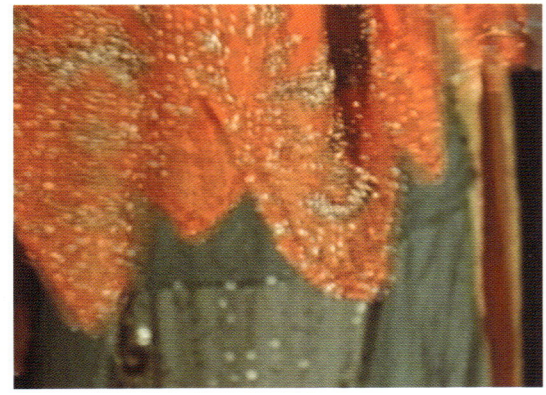

The fragment of *Puce Women* as it exists and was re-edited as *Puce Moment* is a "sketch" in which one of these "goddesses" selects her frock, deliriously attends to her toilette, lounges around on a chaise longue (which appears to "float" outside to a glistening view of the Hollywood Hills), and steps out armored in jewels and wolfhounds. Yvonne Marquis, Anger's star, disappeared after the filming in Mexico, where she ultimately captivated President Cardenas, who made her his mistress. After re-editing the existing footage from 1949 in London with a contemporary soundtrack by Jonathan Halper ("Leaving My Old Life Behind," and "I'm a Hermit"), ironic *frisson* was created between the images and the lyrics. Combined with the visuals of shimmering 1920s dresses and a languishing Hollywood star, the suggestion here is an ironic renunciation of drag dressing, an escape from the fetishization of costume and a possible climb "out of the closet."[41] *Puce Women*, as Anger states "ended up by being a moment, but it was supposed to be a feature film and it used a series of stunning women denoting various times of day. There was Miss dawn, Miss morning, Lady noon, Dame afternoon, and Dowager evening, and so the fragment was one little bit of it, which I called *Puce Moment*."[42] A fantasy on the mansions built for stars of the silent movies (sunlight falling through bubbles held by hermaphroditic, stained-glass figures and reflecting in the waters of Pola Negri's swimming pool), *Puce Moment* was made a long time before a general revival of interest in the period. Neither "story," nor "acting," nor the deployment of splendors of the past: all allusions are condensed into a moment, a poetic evocation, that crystallizes the sensuality of memory, accessories as objects chosen to evoke Hollywood, a flash of fabric or the fugitive steps of a woman with dogs on a leash.[43] It is an evocation of the 1920s and, more specifically, to use its maker's word, an homage to the American painter Florine Stettheimer, whose cosmetic éclat of color and spindleshank figures are a reflection and memento of that period.[44] A film from the 1920s that Anger was particularly fond of was the proto-psychedelic, Beardsley-inspired *Salomé*, 1923, Oscar Wilde's historic fantasy, starring and produced by Alla Nazimova, in which she appears in a number of fantastical costumes.[45] In Wilde's eroticized version of the biblical tale, Salomé is an irascible rebel princess, maximized by the *mise-en-scène* filmic fantasy.

Puce Moment is Anger's Symbolist world of sensually perceived phenomena, luxurious and glamorous, capturing Baudelaire's "phosphorescence of decay." The Rococco clutter of *Puce Moment*'s style of decadence, an introspective microcosm reflected in the soundtrack, is not "simply a refusal to communicate with the world, but also a self-preoccupied attempt to create another world through the cult of sensationalism."[46]

Of his surviving film "sketches," Anger had said:

> My approach to art is the Egyptian one.... You might as well make it in steel or carve it in the hardest granite. If it's a statue of the god or goddess you adore and it takes you 20 years to make, the chances are that an eye, a smile, a wrist, something of that figure is going to survive, maybe even when mankind is just a question mark in future archeology.[47]

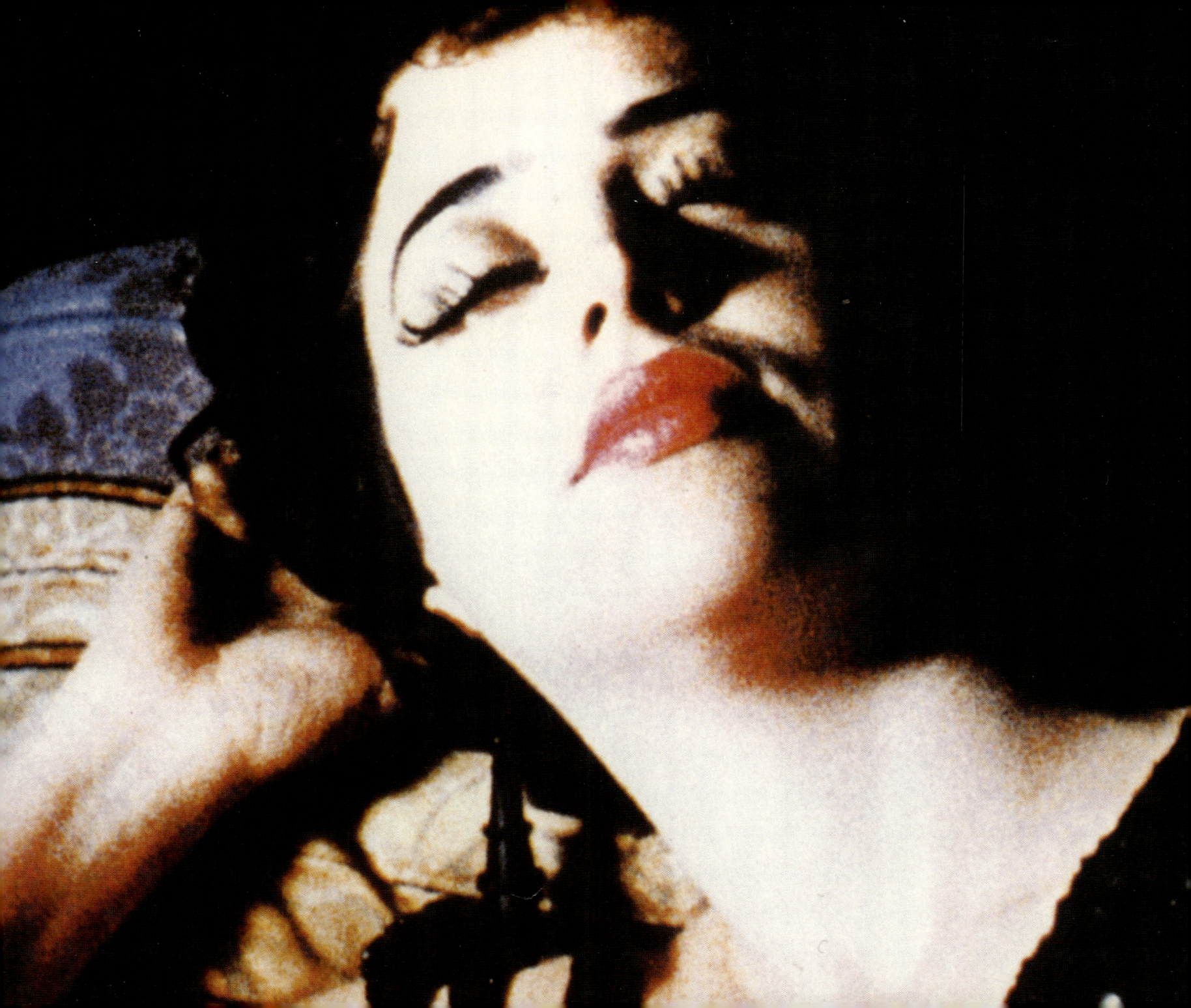

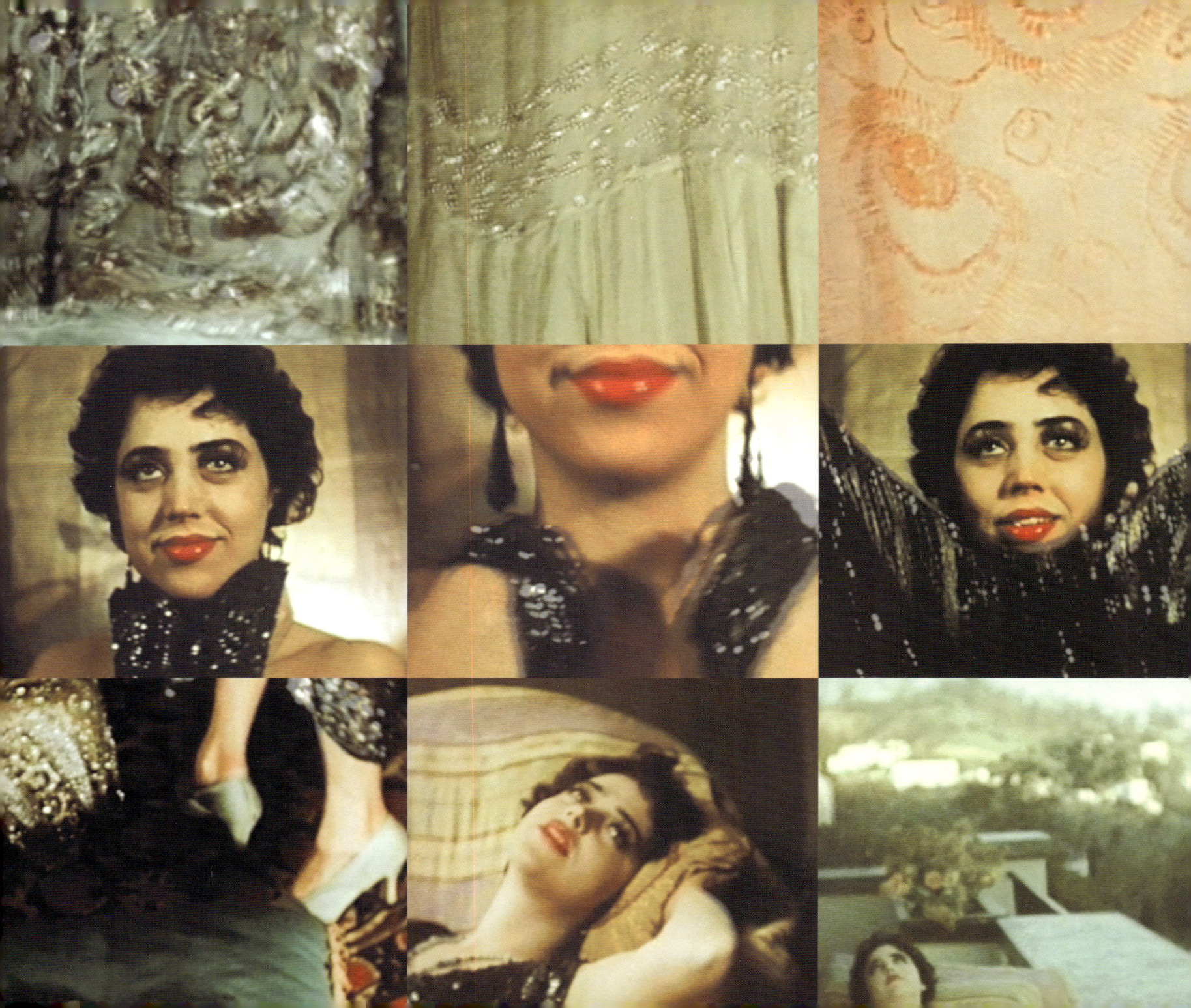

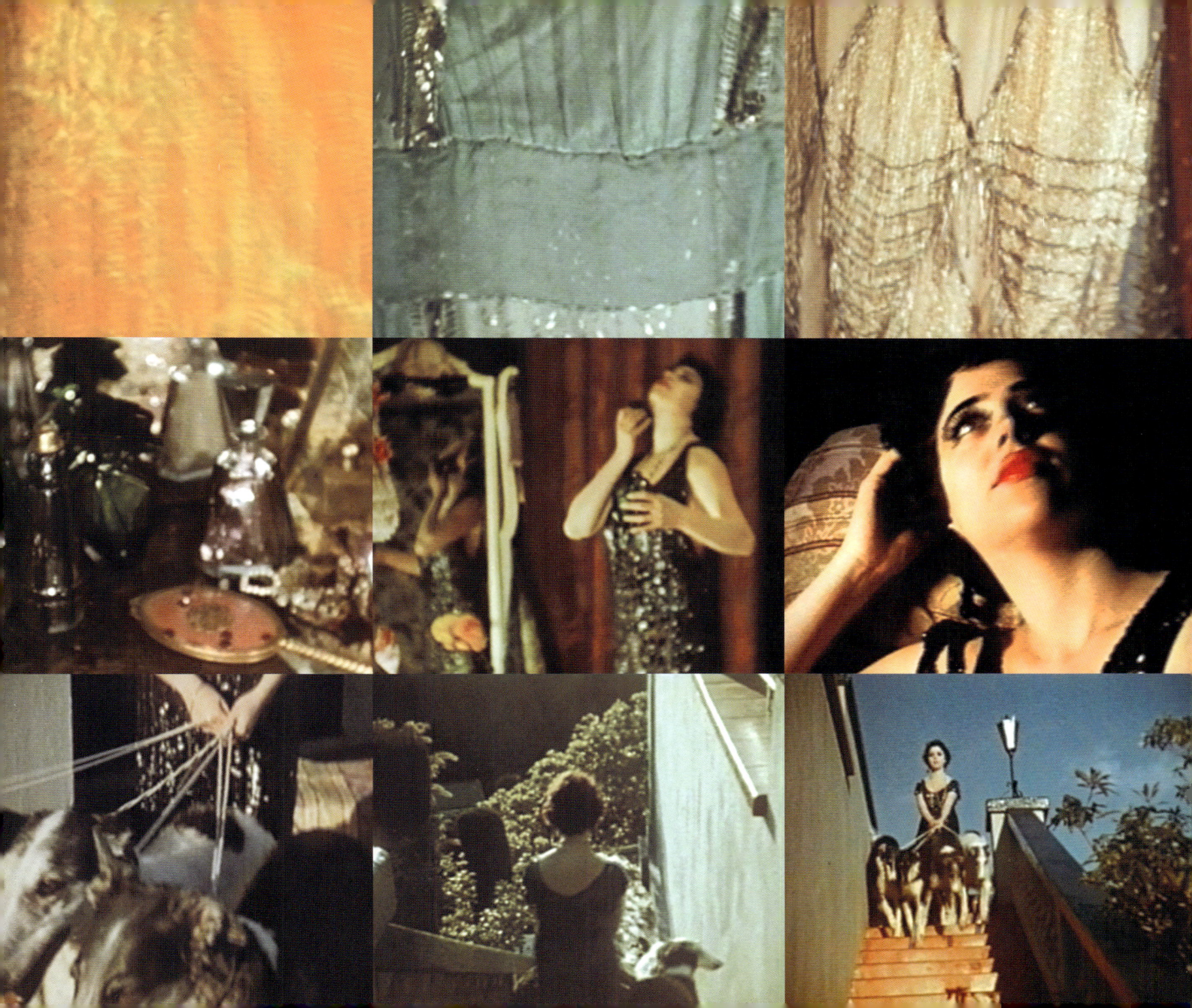

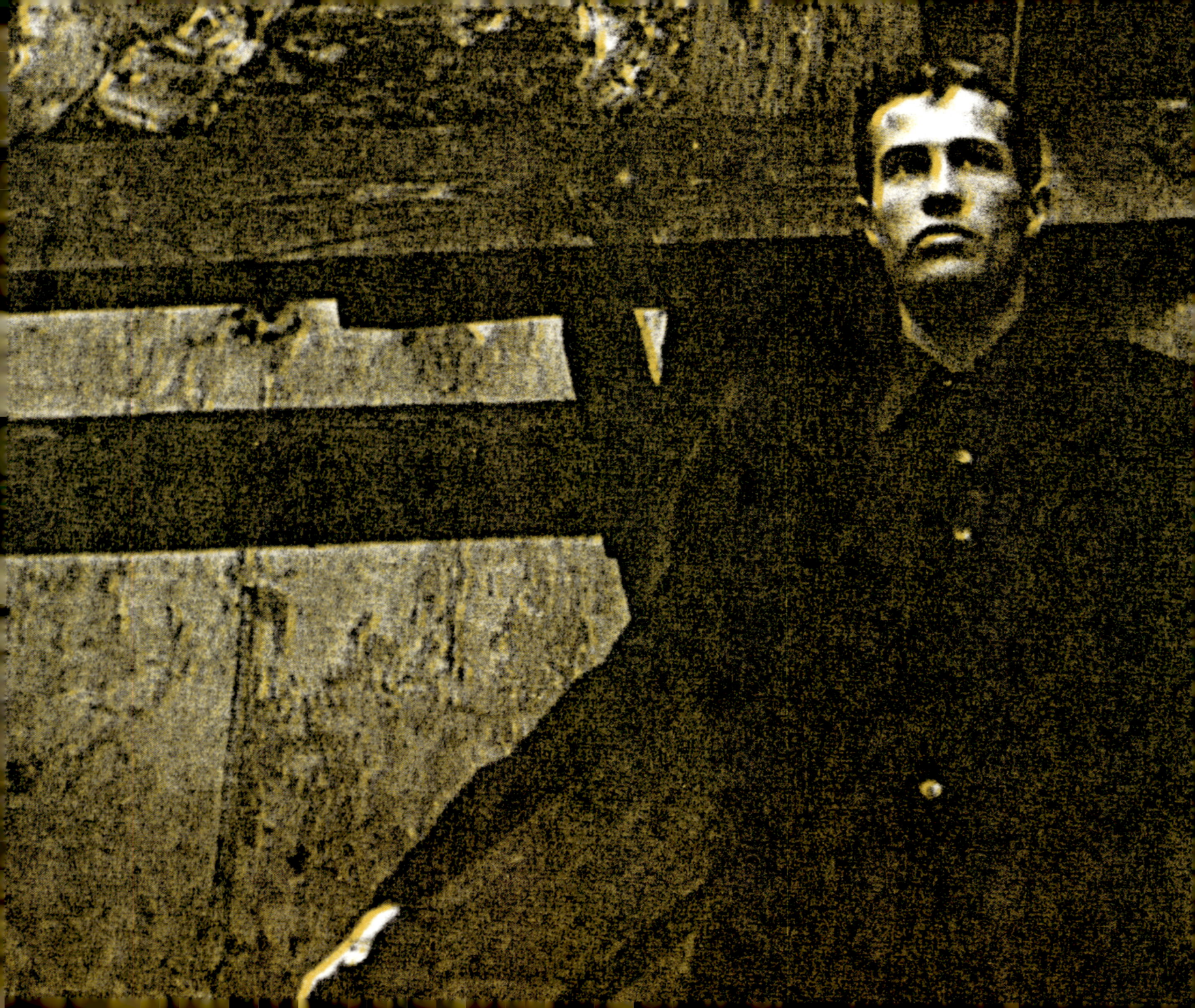

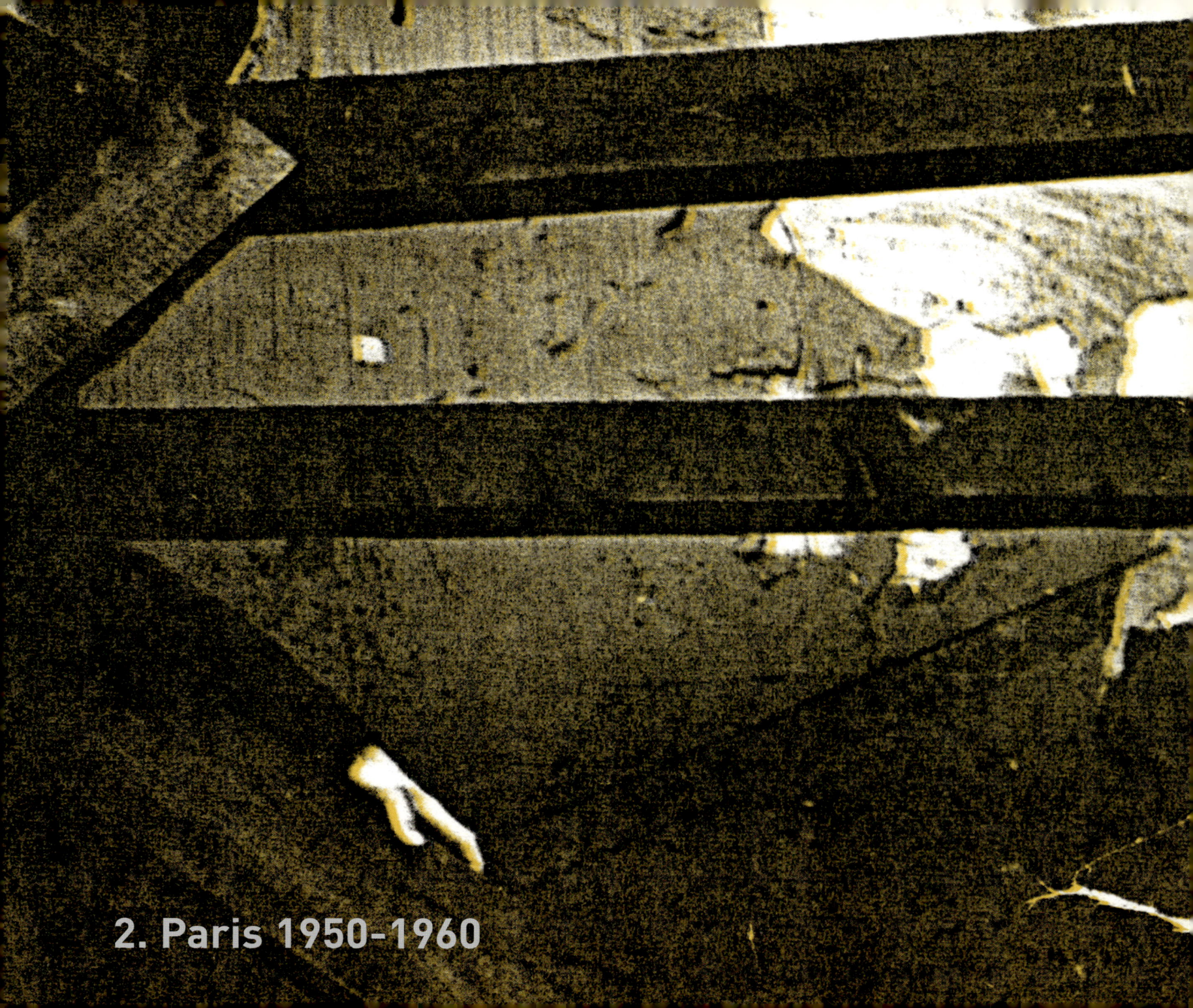

2. Paris 1950–1960

At the beginning of 1950, Anger arrived in Paris, finding lodging in an artist's studio behind Notre-Dame, beside the Seine. With Cocteau's letter in hand, Anger had anticipated attracting a "sympathetic producer," and his first mission was to seek out Cocteau. Fortunately at that same time, a ballet work of Cocteau's, *Le Jeune Homme et la Mort*, was playing at the Theater of the Champs d'Elysées.[1]

At the end of one performance Anger succeeded in meeting Cocteau, announcing his enthusiasm concerning the spectacle and proposed to derive a film that he would shoot himself. Cocteau gave his full endorsement followed by a letter expressing his confidence, in order for Anger to find a producer. In spite of his celebrity, none of Cocteau's films had been profitable at that time, and despite the recommendation, Anger's plans to film a 35mm Technicolor 20 minute short began to fall through. However, he succeeded in shooting a test of the ballet in 16mm black and white. Due to lack of funding, he had to shoot it outside (primarily for light) in Jean Babilée's garden in freezing midwinter. Due to the icy cold, steam appeared to issue from the dancers' mouths.[2]

Simultaneously modern and archaic, an innovator of forms concerned with archetypal symbolism, in Cocteau, Anger found not only a role model, but also a supporter. He had always regarded Paris as a locus of inspiration through literature, poetry and early avant-garde film and his decade based in France enabled him to explore his francophile fascinations and conceive projects such as the ambitious visualization of *Les Chants de Maldoror* and later *Histoire d'O*.

His involvement with the Cinémathèque Française, and its founder Henri Langlois, became the other major relationship for Anger in Paris. It put him in direct contact with the work of his aesthetic mentors, predecessors and sources: Méliès, the Lumière brothers, René Clair, Abel Gance and Sergei Eisenstein, as well as countless lost classics of the cinema from the unparalleled, if chaotic archive at the Cinémathèque. After filming *Rabbit's Moon* in 1950, Anger discovered the original reels of Eisenstein's *Que Viva Mexico!* and for Langlois, he was the ideal candidate to reconstruct the film according to Eisenstein's notebooks, providing the occasion to directly confront the question of montage.

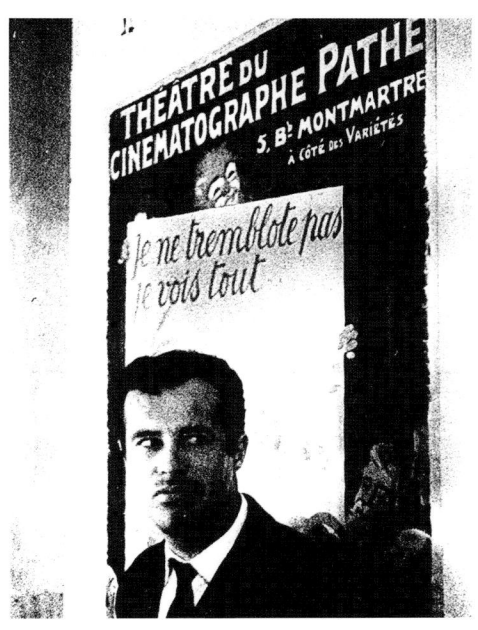

The Turkish-born Langlois founded the Cinémathèque with filmmaker Georges Franju in 1936, and since then, had been accumulating a vast film archive, at a time when films were infrequently revived, even routinely destroyed, and film history was an arduous chore. While Hollywood was churning out new films every day without consideration for the survival of early work and hundreds of silent classics were destroyed and irretrievable – from von Stroheim to Murnau – the Cinémathèque was adamant that these films should be preserved for posterity and screened. The Cinémathèque mounted daily screenings, providing a basis for the dialogue which evolved with *Cahiers du Cinéma*, whose young critics were soon to be *Nouvelle Vague* directors, such as François Truffaut and Jean-Luc Godard. Remunerated in the finest French *haute cuisine* meals, Anger shared with Langlois a love for silent films – an essence of cinema that could be expressed visually, through surface appearances (as Anger conceived *Puce Moment*) – which Langlois recognized and encouraged.

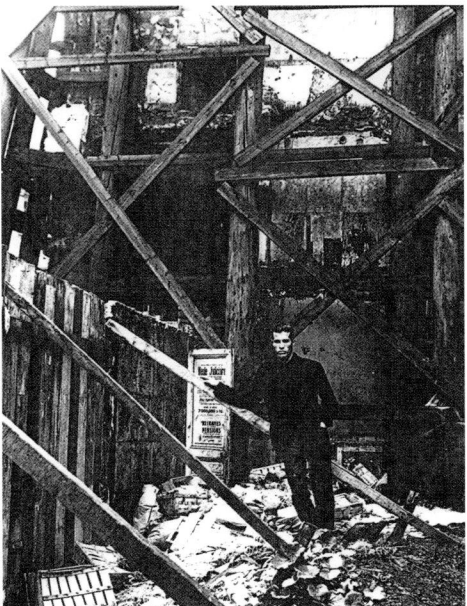

This page and previous: portraits of Anger, Paris, 1950 (photographer unknown)

Previous page and bottom left: "photographs taken on site of collapsing eighteenth century building on the Left Bank of Paris: location chosen for *Maldoror* in 1950"

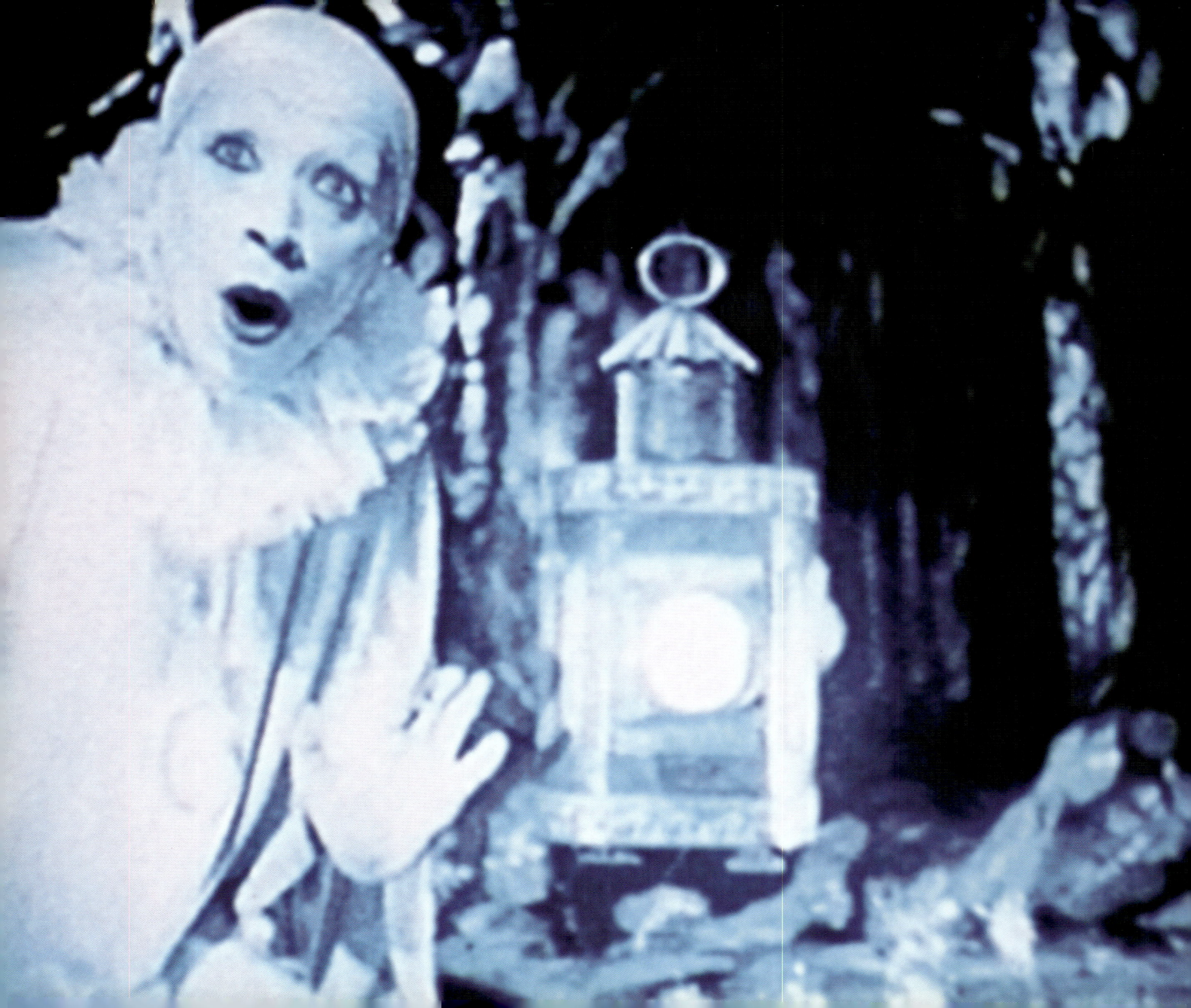

Rabbit's Moon

1950/1971/1979

15 minutes

Music by The Temptations[3]

Short version

7 minutes

16mm, skip frame printing, tinted black and white

Music by Andy Arthur

After the tests for *Le Jeune Homme et la Mort*, Anger then began filming *La Lune des Lapins* in a studio behind the Pantheon, loaned by producer Pierre Braunberger one midsummer August weekend in 1950. Using 35mm black and white film that had been given to him, he began another choreographed project using dancers but soon lost the use of his sound stage complete with the ornate set of a tinseled forest (which he had painstakingly created single-handedly). For 20 years the film was stored in the Cinémathèque Française until Anger rediscovered it and prepared to work on it again while he was in London in 1970, where he had it reduced to 16mm, re-shot a few of the graphic images, and had the entire film printed through a blue filter. First he edited it with a soundtrack by The Temptations ("I Only Have Eyes For You" and "You Took My Life and Threw It Away"), and then, in the current version, 1979, with the ironic tragi-comic "Things that go bump in the night" Andy Arthur sound-track, which Anger referred to as the "kiddie version." It was released in 1971 as *Rabbit's Moon*. Anger originally described it as "... a lunar dream utilizing the classic pantomime figure of Pierrot in an encounter with a prankish enchanted Magic Lantern."[4]

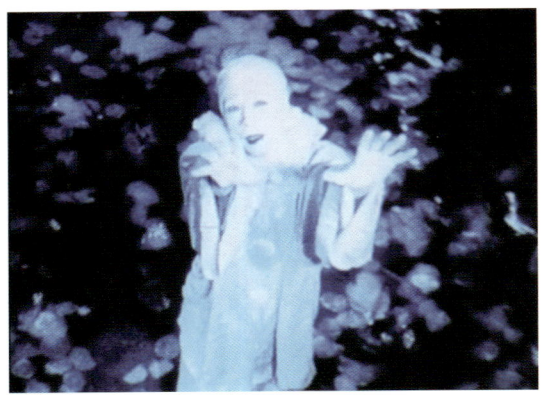

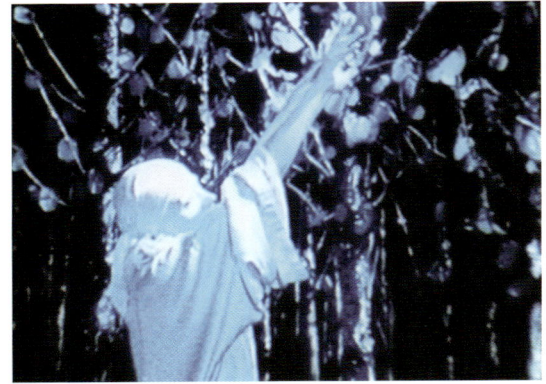

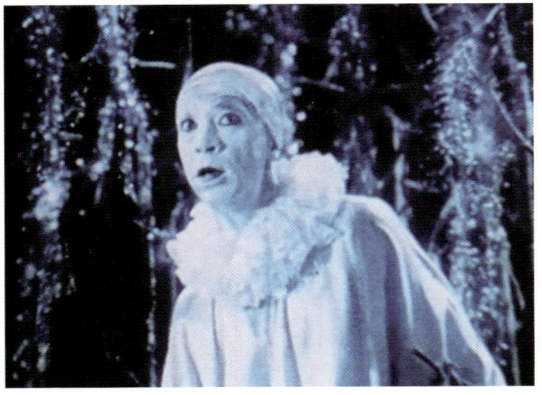

The Commedia dell'Arte tradition had Pierrot, among other things, as a common fool, a thief, an affable street urchin grown up; Columbine, a pretty, bawdy, working-class girl; and Harlequin, an Italian version of the clever court-jester, often associated with magic and death. The characters were presented again and again by various playwrights, most notably in France by Regnard and Dufresny, in many situations and with many twists of characterization, to create an archetypal mode around which many variations could be played out. In Anger's portrayal, Pierrot is in a clearing in an enchanted forest. He gazes at, reaches for, and jumps toward the moon. He is desolate and consoled by two small boys, offering up a mirror and a mandolin (his habitual attribute instrument in Commedia dell'Arte), offering two options, reflection or expression, for the demoralized Pierrot. Harlequin appears; does a few tricks, which fascinate and frighten him. He shows a magic lantern, reveals the sun, and conjures a small stage upon which Columbine is prancing. Pierrot yearns for her love, attempts to impress her by offering her the astral rays of the moon, but is rejected. Harlequin is amused and he snatches her into his arms. Exaggerated and mannered, Pierrot (Anger's earthly presence), again hopelessly tries to touch the moon. Like Charlie Chaplin's Tramp, he rebounds when thrust down. In the artificiality of the stock-characters and synthetic set, one senses an attempt at distancing that the artist-filmmaker wanted to attain to make a self-referential work. The pop soundtrack spins the tragedy into an ironic, sardonic romp. Cinema as an instrument of magick was employed self-reflexively in *Rabbit's Moon*.[5] Here the Magick Lantern creates an image of Pierrot's affection, but Columbine is stolen by Harlequin, and the hapless Pierrot is left alone under the pitiless gaze of the moon. In 1953, discussing why production of the film was halted, Anger had said: "The film was to have been a fable of the Unattainable (the moon, always out of frame) combining elements of Commedia dell'Arte with Japanese myth...."[6] Marjorie Keller suggests:

> If one takes the title of *Invocation of My Demon Brother* literally, then *Rabbit's Moon* can be seen as the other side of the story, the exorcism of Anger's old film demons, by conjuring them within the magic circle, passing outside the perimeter and establishing ritual death as the final sloughing off of the limitation of the past. All this is done through an "auto-filmographical" type of narrative – calling on the spirit of Hollywood, the phoniness of its naturalism and Reinhardt's creation of Anger's archetype of himself. The Changeling; Magic and Ritual, in their lowest form as tricks and, higher, visions, astrology, sun and moon worship, and their overriding unity in the force of light projection; and high and low culture, theater and rock'n'roll.[7]

Rabbit's Moon was also the most personal of all of Anger's films to date, characterized by the sublimation of unrequited love. Anger has only cryptically referred to this period, a time when he was debilitated by deep depression and left Paris for an extended journey through Europe and Egypt. Retrieving the film was, for him, like finding a love letter two decades later; and he turned it into an emblematic quip on his survival from heartbreak and juvenile hardship, with the exaggerated, mannered and contrived actions of the Commedia dell'Arte characters play acting roles in a faux and ultimately cruel game of love and courtship. In a letter to Stan Brakhage about the recovery of the footage of *La Lune des Lapins*, he refers to the theme of perpetual death and resurrection:

> Hence the disturbance when even in written form – and even from someone I dearly love – I am confronted with some "evidence" of what I "was." I've got thru (got thru so far) "travelin' light" and I will deny – even the existence of shadow-baggage of "my" past. It "may" have occurred – someone else may have "seen" it happen – were their eyes shut? Perhaps I blinked while my eyes sped past. I cannot confirm anything – it may have happened to "him" – one of the I's, one of the many I's I've escaped from (that was a close call!) sometimes (not very often) leaving my shed skin in the form of a film by the side of the road where I fled for others to ponder on (if they noticed it at all). For my films have exor-cised me usually of weight of sight so that I may see anew.[8]

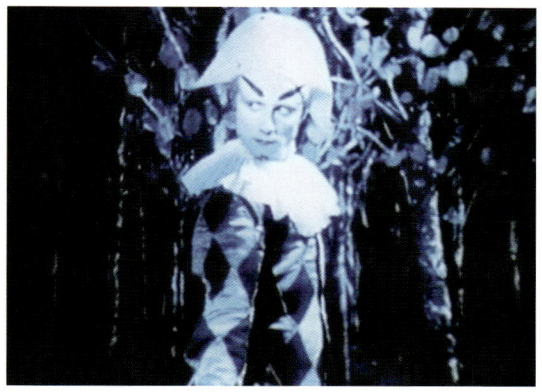

The closest reference in Anger's filmography is the dreamer in *Fireworks*, that part of himself that is subject to earthly desire and torment. In *Rabbit's Moon* Anger tends to mock the seriousness, authenticity and dubiousness of the role of poet, as Cocteau so earnestly applied to his oeuvre, and *Rabbit's Moon*, could be seen as an intentionally sardonic counterpart to *Death of a Poet*:

> Pierrot is the poet searching for the unattainable. The moon is... illusion ill met by moonlight. Harlequin is the cruel jester, the trickster with his slapstick. Other people's tragedies make us laugh. The huckster of invisible wares and the magic lantern.... Columbine is full of grace and teasing malice and prettily mocks the poet and his moon. The rabbit is my soul. Thus before the concluding shot of Pierrot's fall from the sky, the entire film preceding is a flashback – dying's memory of the adolescent's life experience – what I know of life up to that time. And cutting the film is what I have learned since.[9]

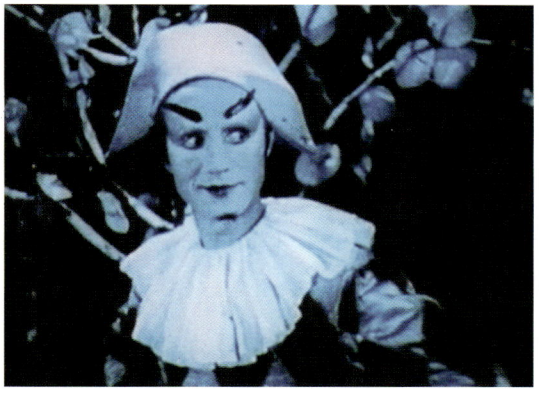

Keller summarized:

> More than others within the avant-garde tradition, Anger manifests explicitly the love-hate of Hollywood. He instills the complexities of high tragedy in a seemingly simple narrative, by stretching the limitations of what are painfully private meditations on his own past. They are transformed into a more universal meditation that illustrates the similar processes of life and death of ideas – a philosophical possibility when both are essentially questions of will. The coincidence of those two disillusionments – the breaking of conventional cinema's tricks which distort and hide reality and vision, and the very personal re-evaluation that he makes of his life works, myths, and essential concerns – is Anger's art in *Rabbit's Moon*.[10]

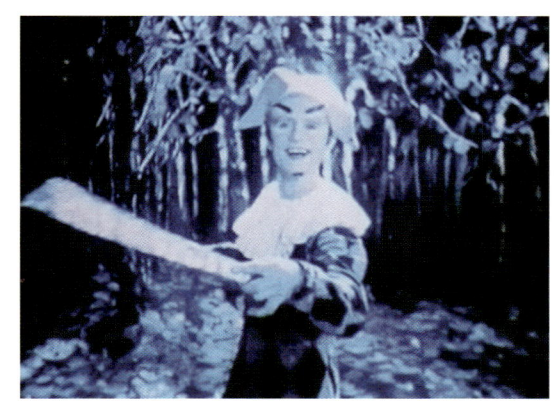

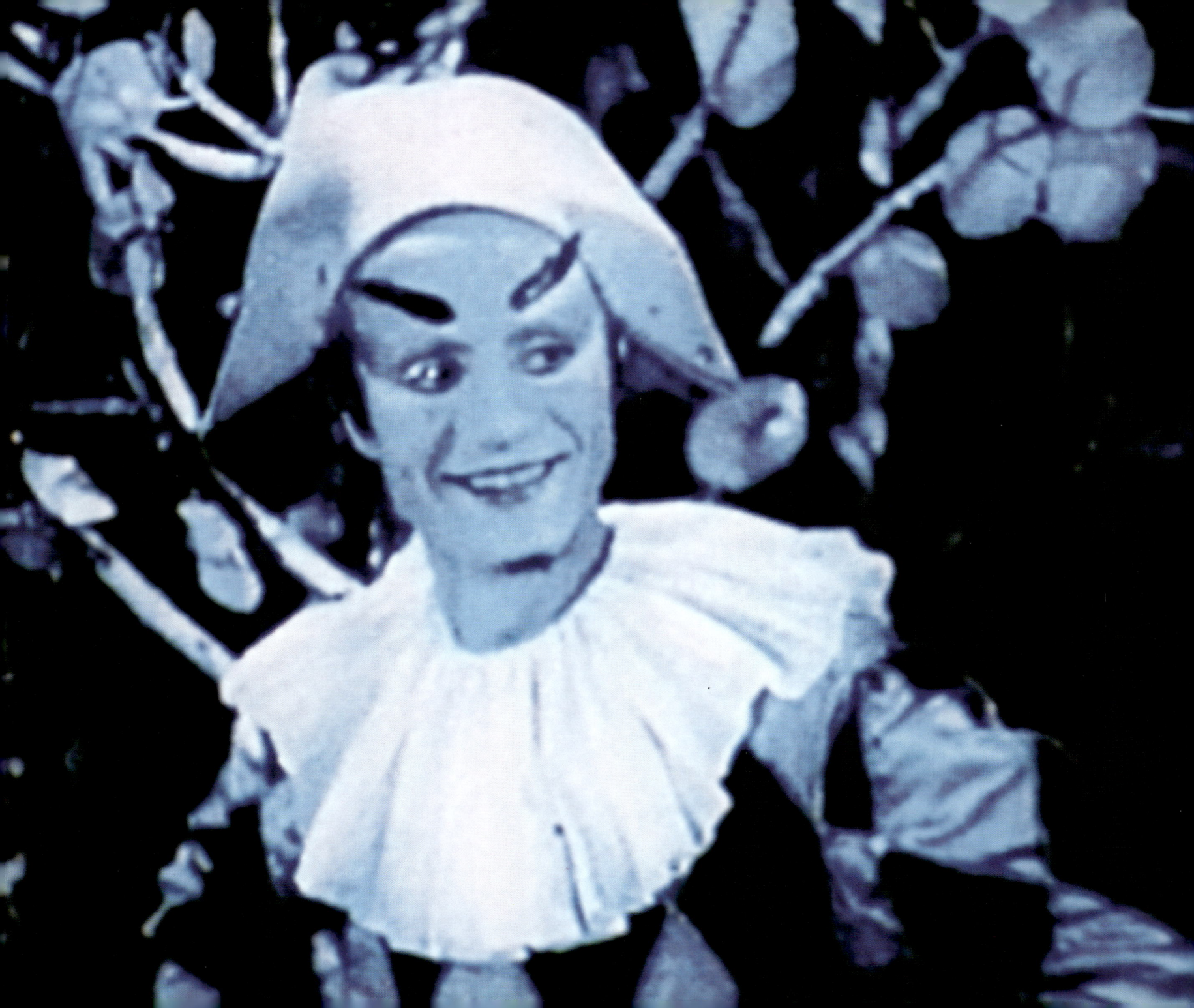

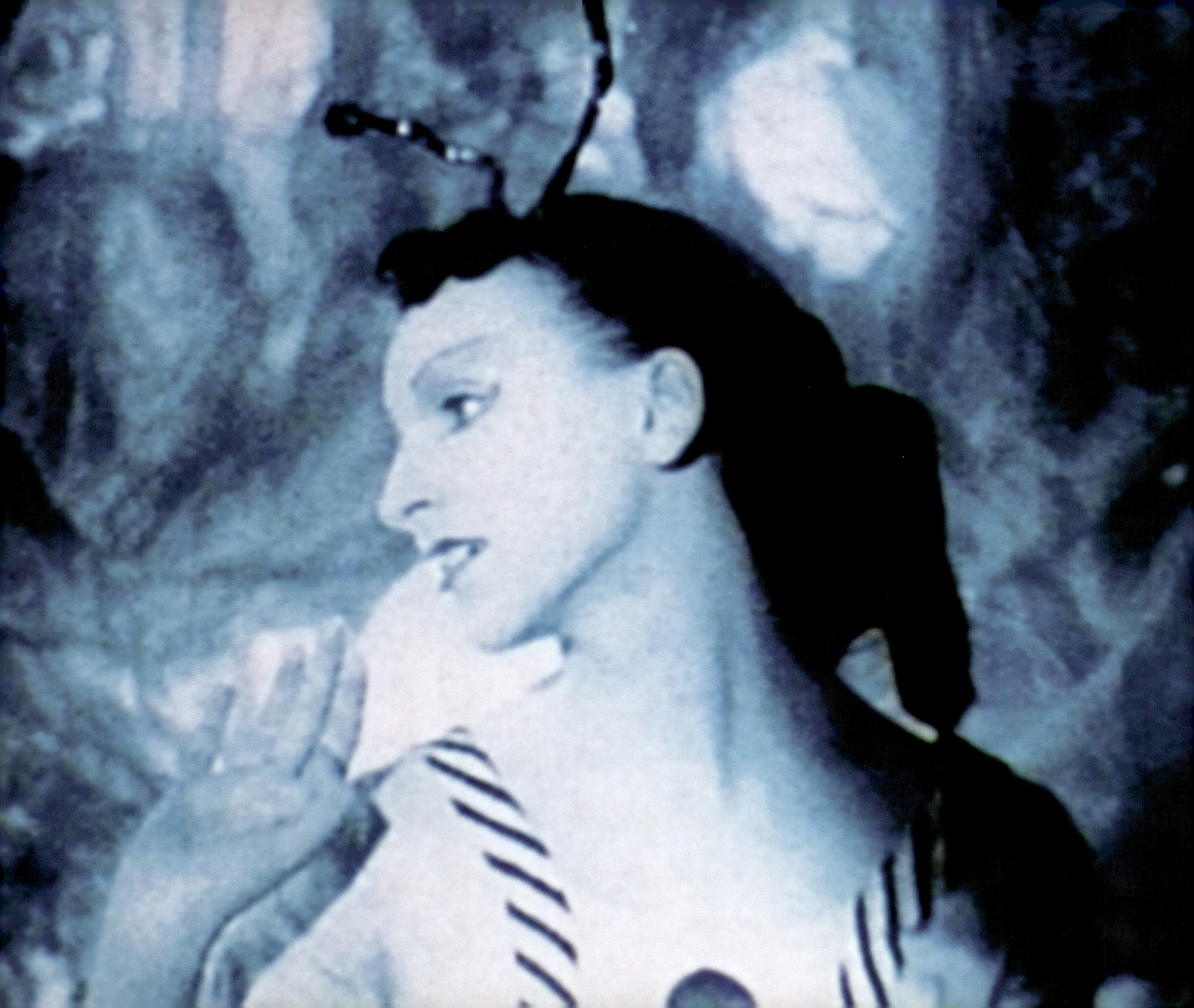

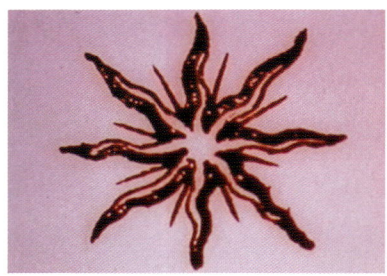

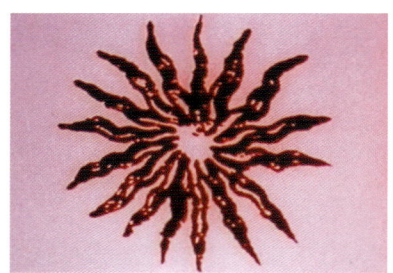

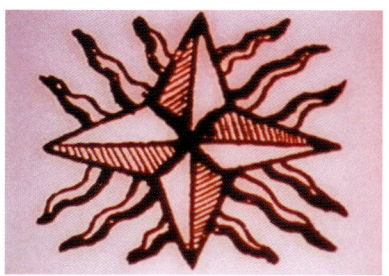

The magic moon is an homage to George Méliès, an illusionist par excellence conjuring apparitions, particularly *Voyage dans la lune* (*Voyage to the Moon*), 1902. Méliès serendipitously discovered stop-motion photography, and went on to discover fading, dissolving, masking, superimposition, slow motion, fast motion and reverse motion: an arsenal of tricks. In short, he learnt how to use film to manipulate reality (between 1896 and 1913 he made hundreds of films, wrote the scripts, designed and painted the sets, ran the camera, directed the action and often played the lead role in his stage-inspired spectacles).

With *Rabbit's Moon*'s full and intricate montage style, it is fruitless to go into lengthy descriptions of the sequences of events (something which could be applied to most of Anger's films). The film can be seen many times before the narrative acquires the internal logic necessary for a coherent understanding. Description is inadequate, as a combination of asynchronous and synchronous sound and image montage is used, and cannot be translated with its inherent cinematic force into a language event. "The subtleties, the ironies, the ecstasies are lost, that rely so heavily on the particular, discriminating sensibilities of the eye to the image, not the word, and the ear to the tune."[11] Again, the music soundtrack has intrinsic appeal as a structural element, with Anger offering insight into the function and mechanism of such songs within teen culture in the United States, attributing their popularity to their ability to make manifest the "desire to escape into the romanticism of the death wish."[12] Anger describes *Scorpio Rising* as the story of "death and resurrection," a description fitting enough of *Rabbit's Moon*, making evident the parallel between their endings – a wiped out biker and whimsically suicidal Pierrot. The fascination with light and its source, a primal and broad human concern, and a struggle to bring light out of the realm of myth, to show the process of internalization and process of a working relationship with the elemental, are the self-reflexive themes of *Rabbit's Moon*. Had Anger been able to complete the film, as planned, Pierrot would have become lost in the wood, discovered a metro station there, and found within it an infinite series of images of the moon ("Eclipse" shoe polish posters) extending away into the darkness.[13]

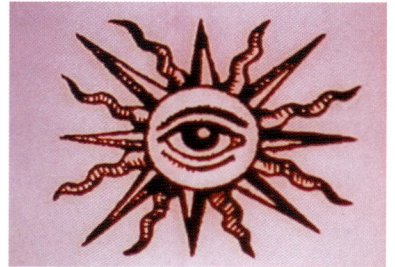

Page 50: "Pierrot with antique eighteenth century "lanterne magique" lent from the collection of the Cinémathèque Française (returned intact!)"

Previous page left: "Harlequin: first appearance of Lucifer – the prankster in Anger's work"

Previous page right: "the tease – Columbine – a name now forever associated by the first school shooting massacre in the U.S. years later. The actress was gallant in her agreement to shoot through the night despite killer fatigue"

Opposite: "all costumes and makeup by Kenneth Anger. "Magic Forest" set entirely hand-fashioned by Anger in the Films du Panthéon studio"

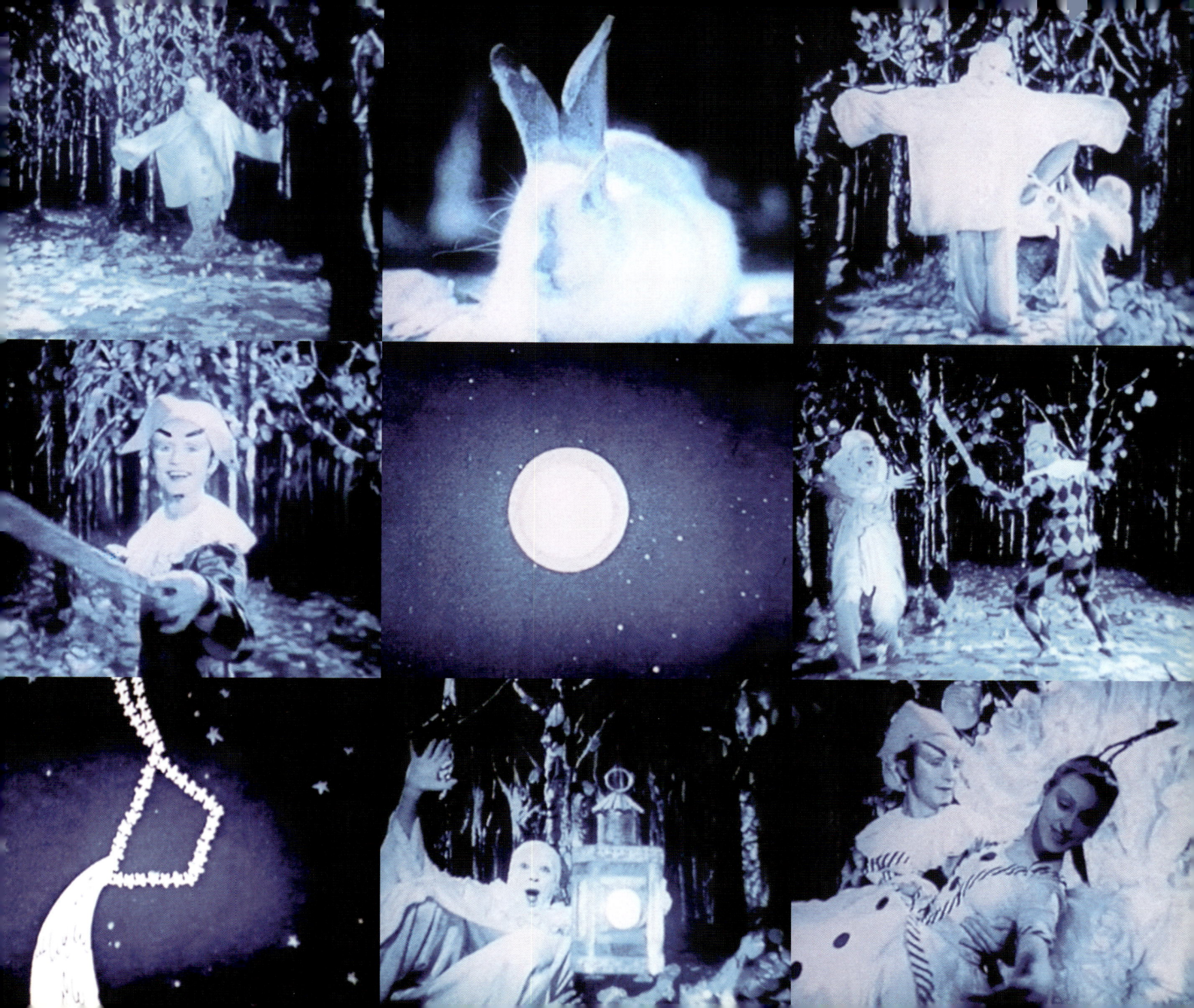

Que Viva Mexico!

1931

16mm, black and white (reduced from original 35mm nitrate negative)

Silent

Conceived and directed by Sergei Eisenstein, photographed by Eduard Tisse (never cut by Eisenstein)

Edited by Kenneth Anger, 1950, at the behest of the Cinémathèque Française for presentation at the Antibes Film Festival

In 1950 Kenneth Anger met Henri Langlois and Mary Meerson at the Cinémathèque Française. He worked as their assistant periodically over many years to follow, leading to a lifelong friendship. Anger had occupied himself by organizing exhibitions and screenings, putting the archives in order, cataloguing the silent American films, and succeeding to recover the original titles of certain films. He also worked on inter-titles and sub-titles. During his time at the Cinémathèque he had discovered the unfinished Sergei Eisenstein reels in the archives, a film Eisenstein was never to see completed in his lifetime. Langlois had authorized Anger to realize a montage of these reels according to the original scenario of the film, and he was responsible for the first full assembly, editing the extant footage according to Eisenstein's original film treatment published in the leftist journal *Experimental Film*.[14]

Diego Rivera, David Siqueiros and Jose Orozco were "guides and teachers" to Eisenstein, cameraman Eduard Tisse and G. V. Alexandrov upon their arrival in Mexico, traveling north, south, east and west, covering thousands of miles. "A feature of this land struck us as amazing. A hundred miles meant the difference between epochs; separating the pre-Columbian Mexico from that of the time of the Spanish conquest, the Mexico of feudal rule, from modern Mexico."[15] All Eisenstein had to guide him was a brief outline that resembled a prose poem. As a visual artist, Eisenstein's maxim was "Go the way the material calls you."

His brief for the film consisted of:

> Four novels framed by prologue and epilogue, unified in conception and spirit, creating
> its entity.... Different in landscape, people, custom. Opposite in rhythm and form, they
> create a vast and multi-colored Film-Symphony about Mexico. Six Mexican folk-songs
> accompany these novels, which themselves are but songs, legends, tales from different
> parts of Mexico brought together in one unified cinematic work.[16]

Without a detailed script to work from, they shot incessantly (a prodigious amount of about
170,000 feet, which did not bode well with the producers). That the film was never returned
to the director to complete and was confiscated by the producers, became an international
outrage. Eisenstein had also broken his agreement with the Soviet government by remaining
too long in Mexico, and it had been rumored in Moscow that he had had contact with the
exiled Trotsky. His filmmaking liberties were subsequently severely curtailed.

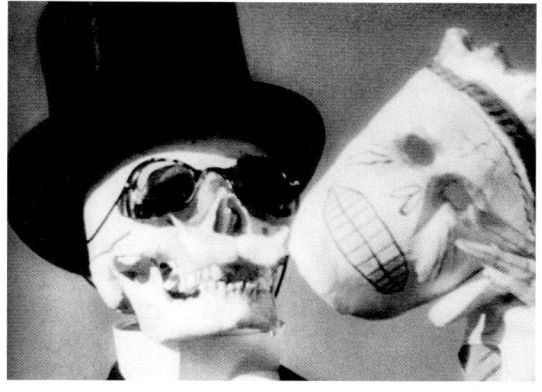

Various shorts and features have been compiled out of the vast quantity of material shot by
Eisenstein in Mexico over a period of 17 months from 1930 to 1931. The best known are
Thunder Over Mexico (supervised by Sol Lesser, 1933), *Time in the Sun*, (supervised by Marie
Seton, 1940) and *Study for a Mexican Film by Eisenstein* (compiled by Jay Leyda, 1957), this
last being a four-hour assemblage of rushes which comes closest to Jean-Luc Godard's
ideal of putting the pieces "end to end." Anger viewed Sol Lesser's version when he was a
young child, which he remembers as both profoundly disturbing and riveting. Although the
rushes were edited by the producer's commercial Hollywood studio, disregarding
Eisenstein's original conception and editing, the photography bore an aesthetic that focused
on ritual, eroticism and mortality. In seeing this film, Anger was exposed to two aesthetic
approaches that would become hallmarks of his own cinematic practice: Eisenstein's editing
montage which utilized cross-cutting of diverse scenes to bring out the 'interior meaning' of
events and personalities; and an unconcealed focus on sado-masochistic eroticism, which
reached its zenith in death.

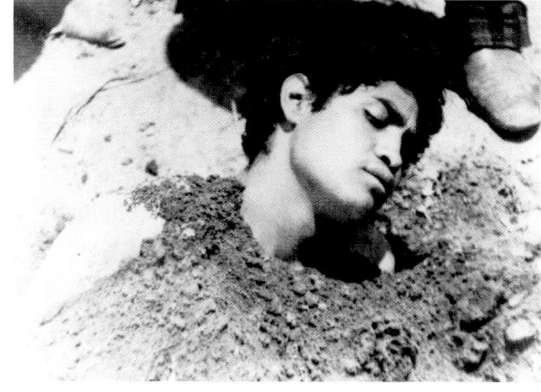

Anger modestly discussed the film in an interview with Robert Haller and John Burchfield in
1978, underplaying his own editorial virtuosity:

> I don't think it's any great revelation. It was just that nobody before me had put the film in
> the right order – to Eisenstein's written scenario. There's a wonderful buildup to dawn in
> Deathday. It starts with guttering, flickering candles in the dark, and then gradually the
> dawn comes, the scene gets lighter and lighter, until finally you see the people sitting
> around the graves in the morning light, and then it bursts into a carnival. These shots
> were gathered from four different shorts.... That sort of thing was interesting for me to
> work on, but the prints I was given to work with were dupes in 16mm, so it was like a
> study or reference film.[17]

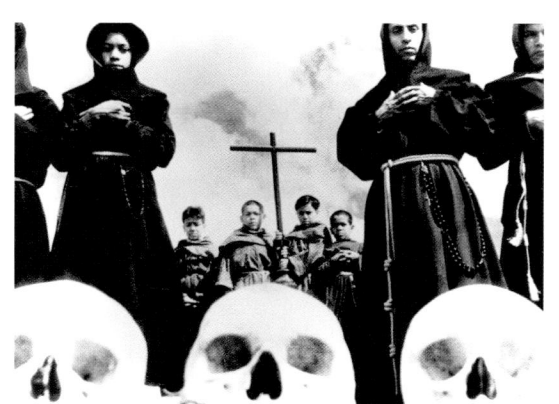

Top: "Death and Candy"
Middle: "earth and martyred Mexican rebel"
Bottom: "the Church and Death"

Modesty and the Art of Film

by Kenneth Anger[18]

In 1951 Anger wrote an article for *Cahiers du Cinéma*, "Modesty and The Art of Film," an eloquently voiced complaint about Hollywood and mainstream film's obsession with "the grandiose, the epic, the big" – that is, the blockbuster, commercially-driven cinema, rather than the modest scaled and more lyrical, poetic and personal. Anger argued that the large-scale productions necessitated a rigid commercial control that sacrifices freedom and spontaneity for the sake of an overly refined style and formulaic narrative and plot. Anger described the neglected art of this kind of more abstract, non-realist cinema with a call to "personal lyricism," to "restore faith in a pure cinema of sensual revelation," and to "re-establish the primacy of the image."

"Capturing the immediate moment" is unquestionably the principal condition of artistic creation. The poet who can seize the first spark of his inspiration at the very second it strikes and preserve it on the back of an envelope with the stub of a pencil; the native who because he is happily in love takes a bit of clay from the river bank and a few minutes later leaves an insouciant divinity to dry in the sun... how we envy them, those of us who work with film.

The problem, for every artist, is to hold this reflection of the divine fire of inspiration in the direction and the essence of his work, since he well knows how this transient fire, this flash of light which appears out of the night and has to be given expression – and yet which sometimes has the incandescent force of a newly born volcano – is a fragile thing: a witch's light, St. Elmo's fire.

What Eisenstein called "the first vision."

What a strange paradox, then, is the film medium, that magnificent and terrible instrument born out of our time to tempt and torture our creative imagination. Without in any way lessening our enthusiasm for it as an art form, I don't think we – the children of this era – are wrong to call it an imperfect medium... imperfect and terrifying.

Let us look quite honestly for a moment at some of these imperfections, at once trivial and monumental, while never forgetting the specificity of an art in which the smallest speck of dust can quickly assume the menacing proportions of the Rock of Gibraltar.

Every artistic discipline needs its tools in the finest condition. Taken separately, those of the cinema have a capricious fragility: they have to be adjusted and handled with extreme care; they are not at all suited to untidy minds. Considerable scientific knowledge is recommended before going near these machines... which are also depressingly heavy, large and inflexible and need great strength to handle. They are all so interconnected that the slightest mistake in the procedure from the movement of the camera which unwinds the virgin film stock to the setting of the projectionist's arc lamp – can ruin the whole enterprise.

To master the complications which these machines present, the filmmaker inevitably has to accept the collaboration of assistants, advisers, technicians... something that is more difficult to handle than the machines themselves: individual personalities. The actual material – film – has to be handled with care, because it can quickly be destroyed or irreparably damaged by a change in temperature, a chemical defect, or simply by oil, dirt or dust. Finally, this means of expression is the costliest ever. The artist cannot avoid taking into account that anti-poetic object – finance and that incomprehensible being the financier, who is forever invariably and unforgivably asking the same question: why?

Of course, we force ourselves to overcome these imperfections and to accept them as the challenge thrown down by this age of technology, since above all else we love cinema. These difficulties can in no way lessen the attraction of this promise of immortality, this certainty that there finally exists a mirror held up to the fleeting face of nature, a means of holding on to "the inexhaustible flow of visions of beauty" which endlessly die and are reborn and which make of the contemplation of beauty a feeling imbued by the sadness of its disappearance, a way of holding on to the moment, a weapon with which to challenge the implacable unfolding of time – there is the miracle, the true miracle of film.

Breaking through the barrier of these mechanical shortcomings can only be achieved by a conscious return to simplicity, to the direct relationship between the camera and the artist.

The widespread idea that films necessarily involve the complex farce of the commercial cinema has its antithesis in a field of Japanese rice, where Okamoto wades in with a 16mm camera in his hand and achieves a totally different creative result. This Japanese film poet cut himself off from the script department, the studio, projectors, film crews and even the camera tripod, and went off by himself into the countryside in pursuit of his celluloid poems. His wonderful visual "silent songs" – intimate and totally free – elicit my unbounded admiration. There is even an additional poetry in these slightly flickering images that are freed from all contingencies. Heir to a culture traditionally enamored of the small and the refined, this poet does not scorn the 16mm camera, considering its lightness and its small size to be every bit to his advantage. He started out with an 8mm camera, and had it existed he would have used a 4mm camera. The dream of a personal, free, pure cinema can be fulfilled as long as you are modest.

Using the simplest of means of an art with lyrical associations is the very basis of the Japanese aesthetic and my own most precious memory of that culture. I shall never forget how the lesson was taught me, when I was a child, by my Japanese drawing teacher.

I had done a sketch of a seascape, a holiday memory, on which I'd worked laboriously and I took it to my master for criticism. He looked calmly at my grimy "Western" page, on which in my enthusiasm I'd tried to put everything I had seen, and then with a slight smile he took a sheet of rice paper, dipped his brush in the ink, and in a flash there before me was the essence of the scene: three brush strokes, the outline of Mount Fuji, the island and its pine trees, the sweep of the bay.

This Japanese love for economy of expression is found in tanka, poems in five lines, and in haiku, which have a mere three lines.

Mastery of these forms of expression is regarded as the highest literary aspiration. The story is often told of the pupil who had composed the following haiku:

Clipping the wings
Of a flying dragon
Is pepper dust.[19]

To which his master replied:

Pepper dust
Give it wings
It's a flying dragon.

A magical evocation born out of the rigors of choice. In their extreme limitation some forms have the suggestive force of an echo resonating endlessly in the imagination. Witness this brilliant example by the classical master Bashu:

What a piercing cold I feel.
The comb of my deceased wife on the floor of the room
Under my heel.

Western poets could profit from such an exercise of discipline, just as we filmmakers might bear in mind the lesson of Okamoto's films, which evoke in two or three images of high lyricism the poignant drama of an orphan, an aquatic flower, devotion to a doll or to a "perfect friendship."

Let's give our Western poets the opportunity to reflect on the possibilities offered by three lines, by three brush strokes, and – or our film poets – by three images. The result may well be surprising.

In contrast to this art of lyrical evocation, the Western tradition – from Michelangelo to Griffith via Beethoven – most often aspires to the grandiose, the epic, to the "big." Though of the works of these artists it is not the "smaller scale," more poetic, more personal ones that we cherish most: we don't prefer Michelangelo's sonnets to the Sistine Chapel, Beethoven's quartets to his symphonies, *Broken Blossoms* to *Intolerance*.

We admire the epic, but we are moved by the lyrical. This is even more evidently the case with comedy. What better example than the crystallization of the meaning of improvisation in Keaton or Chaplin – a meaning which, in the field of cinema, already belongs to a "lost art." It is the improvised moments that remain the most precious.

In the art of film, the divine spark of intuition very quickly arouses the desire for total control. The studied composition of the epic leads us to the "frozen realms" of Eisenstein and late-period Dreyer, Sternberg and Bresson. We admire the formal beauty of these works but their coldness fails to move us. The spectator must "appreciate" the quality of these works before "feeling" them, competently analyze the ingenuity of the camera movements and the merits of the lighting before being involved in the action. The veil of judgment is drawn between the spectator and the drama.

Since it is now an imperative of the film industry that a film must be carefully prepared, designed and rehearsed in advance to avoid financial disaster, it is not surprising that the "greats" of cinema have tried to overcome these complications through a rigid intellectual control. But these proceedings increasingly take the form of rites, and in sacrificing freedom and spontaneity in this way the "icy masters" have at the same time stifled audience "response." Their works are increasingly becoming "ends in themselves," exercises in highly refined style, but they lack the irreplaceable qualities of improvisation.

Looking at the work of these film intellectuals, we find ourselves watching something where concern for perfection of detail and nuance has led to the filmmaker betraying the motivations and the object of the drama. The dynamic elements of the drama of the dramatic structure have been ousted, the flow of emotions dissipated, and with every gesture and every shadow becoming more perfect the rhythm gets progressively slower until the film is no more than a carefully studied series of vignettes. The initial value as drama, the power of catharsis, is lost.

Note also the growing tendency in today's commercial films to break the action up into "frames" or flashbacks, often accompanied by the inopportune presence of a commentary whose superimposition on the visual action constantly means us having to switch from the realm of the immediate to that of nostalgia for the past. To put it another way, the filmmaker is saying "This happened" or "This happened to me" rather than the vital "This is happening" or "I am."

This widespread neutralizing of the essential point of cinema – its power to simulate real experience – enshrines its more off-putting tendency. So we are now in the cul-de-sac of stylization. From the mouths of the half-dead people who pronounce the oracles of the contemporary screen should come a freedom charter: the restoration of the persuasive poetics of the lyrical image. A freedom that is only possible through the artist's intimate view through the lens of his camera, in a word through "personal cinema."

It was precisely this "cinematic" potential for expressing spontaneity that attracted me as a form of personal art.

I saw its disruptive strength: a way of bringing about a change. This means of expression can transcend the aesthetic to become experience. My ideal was a "living" cinema that explored the dynamism of the visual communication of beauty, fear and joy. I wanted my personal cinema to transmute the dance of my interior being into a poetry of moving images that would create a new climate of spiritual revelation where the spectator, forgetting that he or she was looking at a work of art, could only become one with the drama. I knew that an art like this needed only the simplest of means: Okamoto and the lesson of Japanese aesthetics had shown me the way.

With a hand-held 16mm camera I shot my first series of short haiku. This was my apprenticeship in the marvels that surround us, waiting to be discovered, awake to knowledge and life and whose magical essence is revealed by selection. At 17, I composed my first long poem, a 15 minute suite of images, my black tanka: *Fireworks*.

I had seen this drama entirely on the screen of my dreams. This vision was uniquely amenable to the instrument that awaited it. With three lights, a black cloth as décor, the greatest economy of means and enormous inner concentration, *Fireworks* was made in three days.

An example of the direct transfer of a spontaneous inspiration, this film reveals the possibilities of automatic writing on the screen, of a new language that reveals thought; it allows the triumph of the dream.

The wholly intellectual belief of the "icy masters" of cinema in the supremacy of technique recalls, on the literary level, the analytical essays of a Poe or the methods of a Valéry, who said: "I only write to order. Poetry is an assignment."

At the opposite pole to these creative systems there is the divine inspiration of a Rimbaud or a Lautréamont, prophets of thought. The cinema has explored the northern regions of impersonal stylization; it should now discover the southern regions of personal lyricism; it should have its prophets.

These prophets will restore faith in a "pure cinema" of sensual revelation. They will re-establish the primacy of the image. They will teach us the principles of their faith: that we participate before evaluating. We will give back to the dream its first state of veneration. We will recall primitive mysteries. The future of film is in the hands of the poet and his camera. Hidden away are the followers of a faith in "pure cinema," even in this unlikely age. They make their modest "fireworks" in secret, showing them from time to time, they pass unnoticed in the glare of the "silver rain" of the commercial cinema. Maybe one of these sparks will liberate the cinema....

Angels exist. Nature provides "the inexhaustible flow of visions of beauty." It is for the poet, with his personal vision, to "capture" them.

Up to now, poetry has followed a wrong course: rising to the heavens or crawling along the ground, it has ignored the principles of its existence and, not without reason, has constantly been rebuffed by decent people. It has not been modest... the finest quality that ought to exist in an imperfect being.

Lautréamont, *Les Chants de Maldoror*

Les Chants de Maldoror

1951-1952

16mm, black and white

In a moment of aberration I might seize your arms and twist them as one wrings water from washing, or snap them with a crack like two branches, forcing you afterward to eat them. Taking your head between my hands in a soft, fond manner, I might sink my greedy fingers into the lobes of your innocent brain, thence to extract (with a smile on my lips) a blubber effective for bathing my eyes – sore from the eternal insomnia of life.... Doubtless the body has stayed caked across the wall like an overripe pear and has not dropped to the ground. But dogs know how to perform high leaps, if one isn't careful.[20]

Le Comte de Lautréamont's genre-defying poem-novel of demon-maddened youth, *Les Chants de Maldoror*, is unique in the history of literature in its exalted lyrical prose, containing passages of gruesome sadistic horror, vivid phantasmagoric abjection, and blasphemy verging on the uproarious.[21] The innovative use of language combines novel, poem, epic, canto and song – a veritable alchemy of the word. Anger had wanted to undertake the shooting of a two-hour long color film inspired by this work, which he had greatly admired. It was one of his greatest ambitions for many years to create a visual translation of *Maldoror*. Like Lautréamont, Anger is a macabre humorist in whom it is difficult to distinguish where sincerity ends and mystification begins.

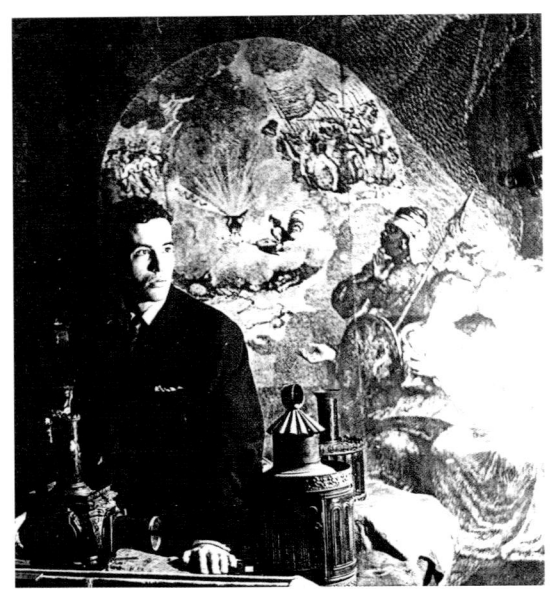

"If our culture is too rooted in language, and that culture is unsatisfactory or the time has come to reshape it, we must first attack language and remake it."[22] The destructive nature of sexuality was a Symbolist theme adopted by the Surrealists and inherent in *Maldoror*. Held by the Surrealists as an ideal of the *poète maudit* in their desire to shock the bourgeois, Buñuel stated: "To produce in the spectator a state which could permit the free association of ideas, it was necessary to produce a near traumatic shock...."[23] This was most stunningly rendered in the famous sequence of *Un Chien Andalou*, 1928, with a tight close-up of a woman's face seemingly having her eyeball slashed open with a knife – literally a visual assault on the viewer. André Breton considered *Maldoror*, in all of its Symbolist Decadence the "dead sea scrolls" of Surrealism. Breton and the Surrealists particularly adored *Maldoror*, and the phrase "as beautiful as the chance encounter of a sewing machine and an umbrella on a dissecting table" became a key textual avatar and Surrealist mantra. They hailed Lautréamont as a forefather who, with Baudelaire and Rimbaud, was part of an unholy trinity of genius. This revolutionary classic had remained truly an underground work, little discussed and less read. Unnoticed on first publication in 1868, by the end of the century it had become a *cause célèbre*; "an epic-poetic testament reveals a shrouded twilight world, half-ecstasy, half-nightmare of angels, grave diggers, madmen and perverted children."[24] The author of *Maldoror*, Isidore Ducasse, was born in Montevideo in 1846. Little is known of his life but *Maldoror* was prodigiously written in his early twenties, as he apparently died at the age of 24. Under the *nom-de-plume* of Le Comte de Lautréamont he published *Les Chants de Maldoror*, and his only other published writing, under Ducasse, was *Poesies*, 1869. Alexis Lykiard, in an introduction to his translation of *Maldoror*, described how he was "... faced with strange puns and punctuation; with curious syntactical constructions which weave unexpected opposites into daring new patterns; with grim continually dissolving ecstatic lyrical flights in a cloud of ambiguities and teasing commas...."[25]

Anger meticulously prepared pre-production sketches and requested permission to shoot in certain quarters of Paris conserved for their nineteenth century appearance. The Surrealist "fringe" of Ado Kyro considered it sacrilege for a young American to attempt to create a film version of *Maldoror*, and lambasted Anger.[26] Anger succeeded in shooting a section, "Hymn to the Ocean," on the beach at Deauville. Despite incorporating professional dancers from the Marquis de Cuevas' Ballet dancing on the surface of the water (in fact upon tables placed just below the surface), the project revealed itself to be too ambitious. Anger shot the sequence of the war between the flies and pins by placing a quantity of pins in a revolving drum, as well as a dozen flies, shaking it up and filming it in slow motion. Anger described it: "My scenario follows the "exalted" style of Lautréamont's text finding visual equivalents."[27] Threatened with reprisals from Kyro if he continued shooting, Anger was not intimidated, but again lack of funds obliged him to abandon the project.[28] The sections of the film that were completed is stored in the Cinémathèque Française, but its exact whereabouts in the archive is unknown, with no images from the film being currently available for reproduction.

Portrait of Kenneth Anger in his spiritual "home," the Magick Lantern Room in the Cinémathèque Française c. 1950 (photographer unknown)

Julia Kristeva based a great part of her seminal text *Revolution in Poetic Language* (*La Révolution du langage poétique*), analyzing Lautréamont's *Maldoror*, within her discussion of the rupturing social possibilities of Symbolist poetic language.[29] Kristeva's thesis developed the notion that nineteenth century post-Symbolist avant-garde literature, specifically *Maldoror*, performs a revolution in language that transforms the structure of literary representation – a revolution in poetic language analogous to a political revolution, a form of anarchic expression. Anger had first articulated a similar view in his text "Modesty and the Art of Film," seeing "its disruptive strength: a way of bringing about a change." The writings of Lautréamont and Mallarmé are examples of the revolution in language staged by disruption, that poetic language can reactivate the semiotic force in language through its sounds and rhythms, denoting an essentially mobile and extremely provisional articulation of the discourse of representation "as rupture and articulations (rhythm), precedes evidence, verisimilitude, spatiality, and temporality."[30]

Anger's often anarchic visualization of poetic language was at once abject and lyrical, humorous and sublime: a sensibility steeped in Lautréamont. Kristeva further elaborated the revolutionary aspect of poetic language, especially the relationship between poetic language and the speaking subject (or self-played role as protagonist, as Anger's film *Fireworks* could be applied here). Poetic language puts the speaking subject in crisis. Here she proposed that the rhythms of poetic language not only violate the grammar of language but also render syntax indeterminate. In a similar way, mainstream narrative cinema relates to Anger's "poetic" dialectical logic in film. Instead of dialogue and plot structure, the rhythm of images and soundtrack create a non-narrative progression. Poetic language operates between sense and nonsense, making it clear that signification is a process that is not completely controlled by a unified subject. The two registers, semiotic and symbolic, of poetic language suggest a split subject, the split subject of psychoanalysis who operates between unconscious and conscious realms. Lautréamont's "split" and duality, and Baudelaire's attraction of opposites, mirror Eisenstein's "montage of attractions." Again, this idea is characteristic of Anger's evolving film practice, and the creation of his own realm between the conscious and unconscious:

> The representation of the "character" that becomes the place of this process is one the normative consciousness finds intolerable. For this "character's" polymorphism is one that knows every perversion and adheres to none, one that moves through every vice without taking up any of them.... His is the wisdom of artifice, which has no interiority and is constant rejection. He is familiar with the social organism and its paranoid reality but makes light of it and, for them, he is an unbearable monstrosity.[31]

The Revolution of Poetic Language further applies to Anger in the process of marginalization of his own work in the light of the dominant production of commercial cinema:

Under what conditions does it become indispensable, censored, repressed, or marginal?... in the history of signifying systems and notably that of the arts, religion, and rites, there emerge, in retrospect, fragmentary phenomena that have been kept in the background or rapidly integrated into more communal signifying systems but point to the very process of significance. Magic, shamanism, esoterism, the carnival, and "incomprehensible" poetry all underscore the limits of socially useful discourse and attest to what it represses.[32]

An analogy to be drawn here is Anger's relationship to Hollywood, and mainstream media ideology: "Under what conditions does this "esoterism," in displacing the boundaries of socially established signifying practices, correspond to socioeconomic change, and ultimately, even to revolution? And under what conditions does it remain a blind alley, a harmless bonus offered by a social order that uses this "esoterism" to expand, become flexible, and thrive?" – a prediction of our current media culture, where "subcultures" are grist for the mill.[33] But Anger was in tune with a 1950s and 60s counterculture "revolution" or at least a new generation defining itself against the old guard of extreme repression, as expressed in *Scorpio Rising*. However, the film's subject matter was quickly cannibalized by mainstream Hollywood, and so too his antiestablishment renegade style, just as the Beatles' song "Revolution" has been emptied of its original meaning and used as a retro soundtrack for a Nike shoes commercial. Kristeva summarized that Lautréamont implied social rejection and negation through abjection and rupture of language. The Surrealists upheld this morpho-syntactic destruction in their quest to rupture societal repression or morés, which was further taken up by Anger as a spontaneous alignment to a burgeoning counterculture. Abjection was key to refusal.

Anger was influenced by Rimbaud's "alchemy of the word," conscious of poetry's incantations likened to witchcraft – incantations to hypnotize with visual symbol and rhythm, reactivating the senses through sensual correspondences:

> I invented the colors of the vowels! – "A" black, "E" white, "I" red, "O" blue, "U" green. I regulated the form and movement of every consonant and with instinctive rhythms, I prided myself on inventing a poetic language accessible to all the senses sooner or later. I reserved translation rights.[34]

The complexity of Anger's visualizations brings to mind Antonin Artaud's thoughts on the boundaries of language: "... so capable of multiplying, splitting apart, turning inside out with its glistening little cracks, its dimensions, its narcotic highs, its penetrating and toxic injections, and all this then will be found to be all right, and I will have no further need to speak."[35] Anger's filmmaking stems from the boundaries and inadequacy of language: "To me, it's not a matter of finding an equivalent of words. But to find images, which are like hieroglyphs and so, are the visual equivalent of those words. It was letting the power of images as dreams reach the unconscious."[36]

Histoire d'O

1959-1961

20 minutes

16mm, black and white

Silent fragment

Filmed in Paris, from the novel *Histoire d'O* by Pauline Réage (Dominique Aury), 1954

Histoire d'O was first published by Jean-Jacques Pauvert in Paris in 1954, the same publisher of Kenneth Anger's original French edition of *Hollywood Babylone*. The author, Dominique Aury, only revealed her real identity in 1995 and *The Story of O* has become a polemical and contentious issue for both conservative censorship and feminist ire.[37] Following the publication of the Marquis de Sade in 1951 (also published by Pauvert), Aury thought it would be more interesting and original to see through Justine's eyes, the Marquis' object. The result has been described as a highly crafted literary pastiche of de Sade and quickly became one of the most translated French books of all time, although it has suffered from mistranslations of the lyrical French original, with parts of the text being completely removed in some instances. Based on the author's discrete love letters, the book narrates, in an insolently elegant style, the experiences of a young woman who confesses her desire to be enslaved by her lover, traversing the delicate line between horror and pleasure, through the practices of a secret society. Upon his return to Paris from extensive travels through Europe and North Africa (as discussed in the following chapters), Anger conceived his own interpretation of *Histoire d'O*.

Anger described his discreet and oneiric version of this sado-masochistic fairytale as containing no explicit sex scenes or violent sado-masochism, relying on imagination to fill the gaps. He states "*Histoire d'O* follows the narrative of Pauline Réage's book, rendered as a silent film with sound effects and music."[38] The sado-masochistic scenes lit by torches and supposed to take place at the Roissy Chateau were filmed in old vaulted cellars that Anger had discovered in Paris. The project was abandoned after Anger found that money given to him by the boyfriend of the girl playing "O" was part of the ransom paid out to kidnappers of Eric Peugeot, heir to the French automobile empire. It also transpired that the girl was the daughter of the Minister of Finance in the de Gaulle administration, who accepted the role in a spirit of rebellion, and when her parents heard about the film they immediately forbade her further participation.[39] Only 20 minutes of the planned feature-length 90 minutes was shot.

> At the time when I approached the *Story of O* it was years before anything like that had been done and I saw it as an act of defiance. I shot 20 minutes of the script. I conceived of the film as a "fairytale for adults," and it was done in a very discreet style, very cool. No violence was ever shown, that was the big thing. Except for a little bruise or mark, all of the violence was implied. Since then we've had a so-called liberalizing of censorship codes, but I haven't seen any great works of art emerge as a result. We're still waiting for the Fragonard or the Jean Renoir, who can deal with sexuality in a way that is art.[40]

The project to film *Histoire d'O* is discussed by Olivier Assayas in his book on Anger, which he describes as "one of the missing works in the history of cinema" and although he was not the only filmmaker capable of rendering the subject, he was, Assayas ventures, the only one worthy of making it, fully aware of confronting all its complexities and implications, without exploiting or cheapening its subject matter for commercial interest.[41] It was Anger's only fiction-adaptation project (*Maldoror* was far more abstract). Themes of ritual, of preparation, attention to the accoutrements and fetishistic accessories, of masters and slaves (or, rather adepts), of characters role-playing roles which were aspects of their own personalities (as in *Inauguration of the Pleasure Dome*) intersected with Anger's interests, which he was able to convey with elusive subtlety.[42]

> ... a poetic film, rather than pornographic. My idea was to realize a film with a very limited circulation, as George Bataille and others had done when they had written very meticulous erotic literature... my model was Bresson's *The Women of the Bois de Boulogne*... where the beauty of the images removes a part of the severity of the subject. I did not wish to show explicit things – not even the whipping... finally, I shot 20 minutes without sound, on the Left Bank in Paris, in the old cellars, on beautiful medieval staircases worn by the centuries – I had used several to give the impression that the staircases descended endlessly.[43]

The sado-romanticism of *Histoire d'O* is an underlying theme throughout Anger's films, most apparent in *Fireworks*.[44] Anger's next film *Scorpio Rising*, made upon his return to the U.S. from France, and discussed in Chapter Six, was to explore the iconography of brutality of another secret society – a motorcycle gang. Themes of domination and submission, where equally fetishistic accessories act as talismans within ritualistic preparations, define the embattled rebels as willing masochists satisfied in their own abuse in the climax of a death wish.

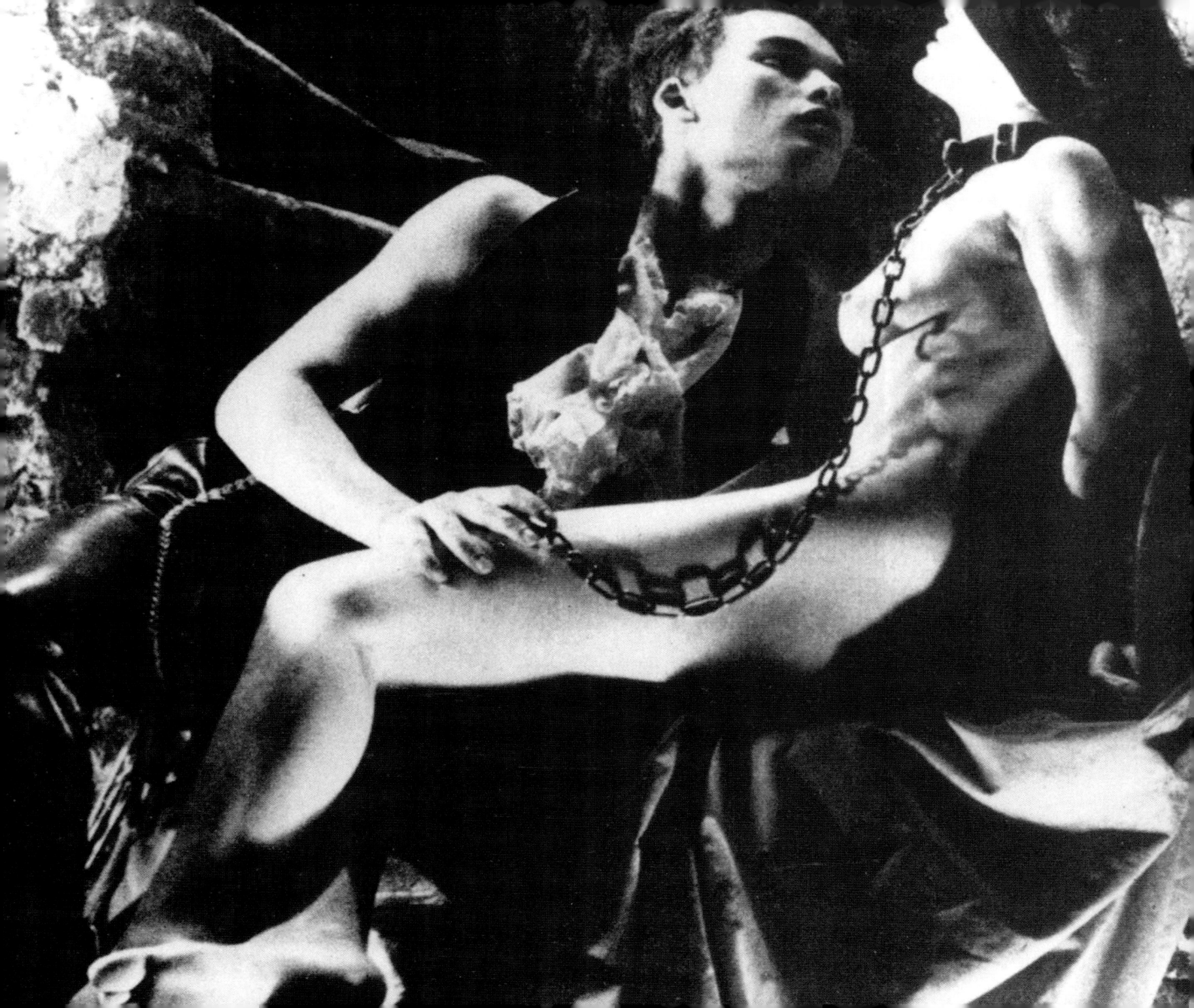

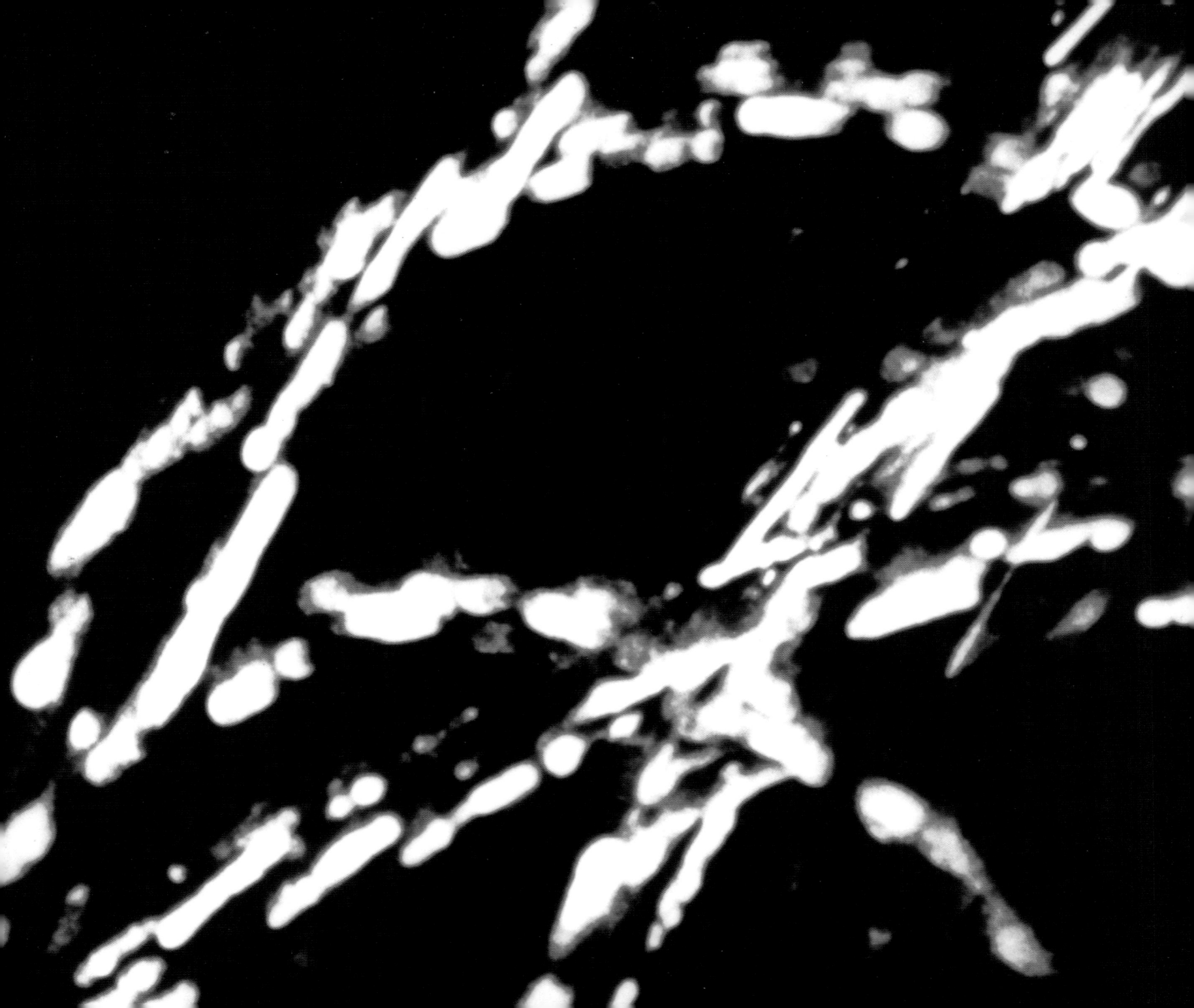

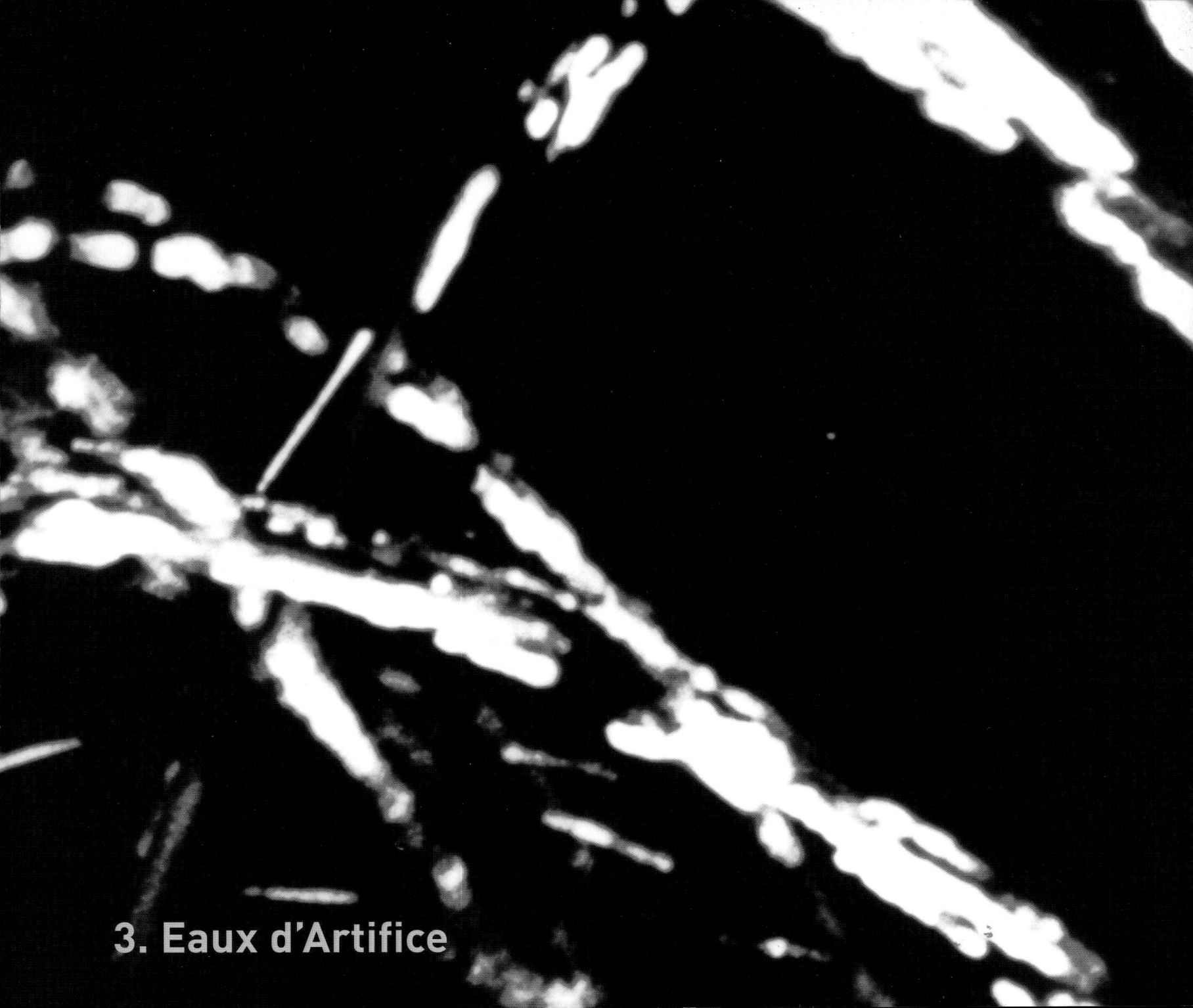

3. Eaux d'Artifice

Early 1950s Egypt and Rome

Before Anger's return to Paris at the end of the 1950s, he traveled to Egypt in 1951 and then, in 1952, to Rome. Throughout his travels, he wrote regular letters to Mary Meerson, the co-director of the Cinémathèque Française, a selection of which are reproduced here. Fascinated by Egyptian civilization, he planned to film in the land of the pyramids *Hymn to the Sun*, a feature film for which he wrote a detailed synopsis and obtained permits to begin filming. He went to Luxor in December 1951 and to Cairo in January 1952 but found himself in the midst of dire political turmoil and rioting known as Black Saturday, the day Cairo burned: destroying the Shepheard's Hotel, and many other "Europeanized" landmarks. What began as an anti-British riot against the British taking over the Suez Canal soon turned xenophobic, with the burning and destruction of many foreign-owned and occupied companies including picture theaters.

The film synopsis exists as a written sketch conveying the vibrant, chaotic co-existence of modern and ancient worlds, but was never realized due to Anger having to leave Egypt sooner than anticipated. *Hymn to the Sun* was Anger's most detailed outline of a film in progress and provided a vivid account of the environment through which he was traveling (including specific locales that Aleister Crowley had inhabited), and the sudden ensuing riots in which he witnessed the deaths of acquaintances. The full transcript is archived in the Bibliothèque du Film in Paris, with the first two pages reproduced overleaf. From details such as the protagonist's pet monkey Thot Moise (a wink to Fritz Lang's constant companion) who is suddenly stricken down by a snake charmer's cobra in the desert, to the scrabbling third class train carriages crossing Egyptian terrain, to the fire-ravaged city in chaos in the final scene, it is again, a poetic evocation of turmoil. Unable to continue with this project, Anger decided to leave Egypt for Rome.

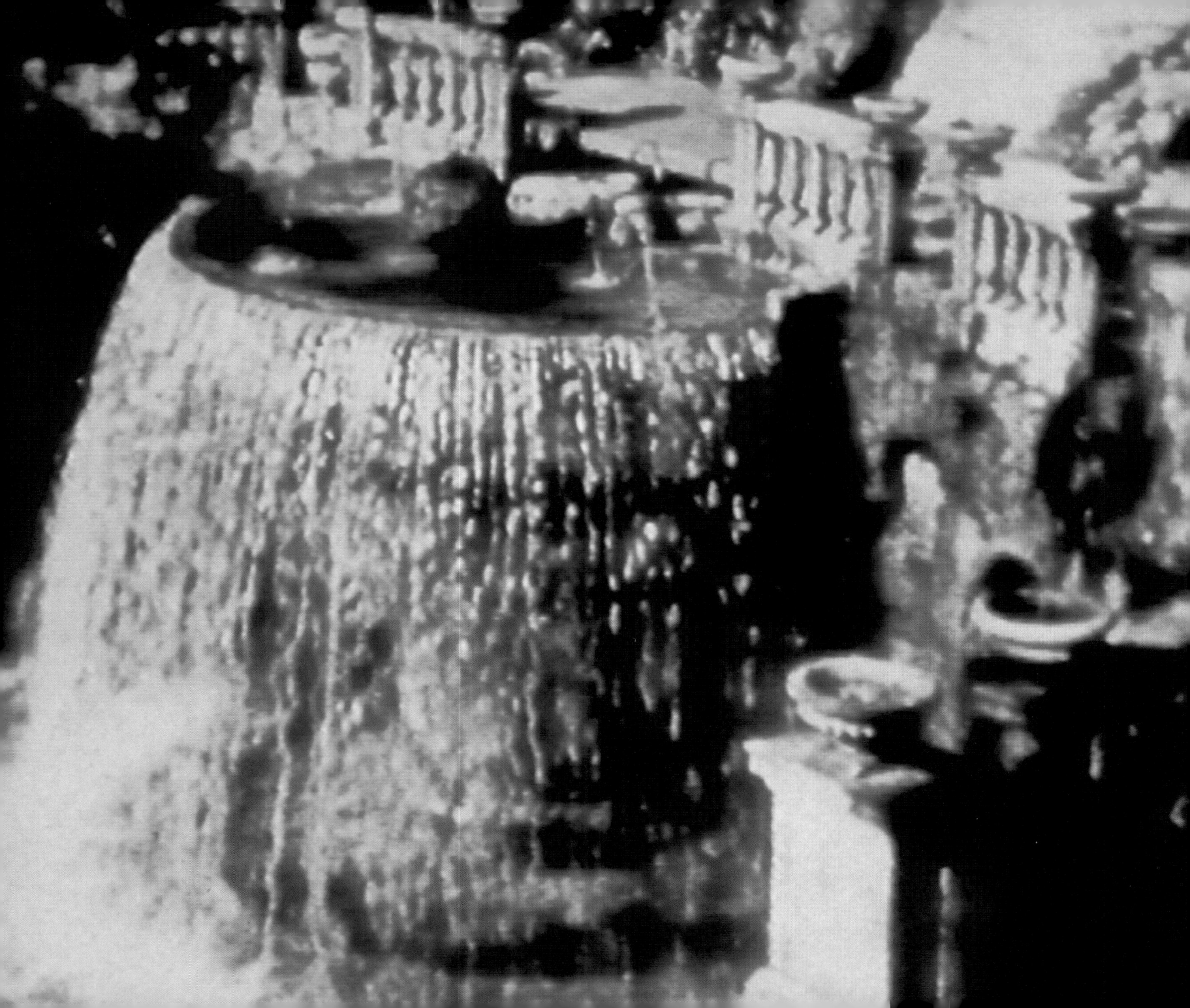

OUTLINE

1.   Hallway. R. walks down hallway to mirrored door. Rings bell.
Reflection of self in glass. Sensation of uneasiness, as before.
The nature of the door. Is admitted into apartment.

2.   Apartment. Oriental servant admits R, passes on into salon.
Description of salon, same as R. remembers it. Precious objects and
strange odors. L. enters, with pets. Conversation with R, mentioning
planned trip to Egypt. L offers R port. Mentions theories of Baron.
R fascinated. L suggests that R come along on trip, goes out to tell
J of R's arrival. L returns with J. J expresses interest that R might
accompany them on trip. J and L introduce Thot-Moise. Conversation
mentioning plans for trip, monkey, etc. 3.

R's room, later that night. R revues history of acquaintance with L
and J. Puzzling points. Excited over idea of trip. Dream.

4.   Hotel lobby, later that week. R waiting for L to stop by for him
in car. C C stops by to bid him farewell. Conversation with C C
mentioning L and R. Long wait, C C says she must go. R phones L who
says they are trying to catch Thot Moise. Asks R to wait. Finally
L stops by in car, but alone. Says J is still trying to catch Thot
Moise. They leave for apartment.

5.   Apartment. General chaos of departure, they succed in capturing
Thot-Moise.

6.   The Car Ride. Driving at Night. Arrival at hotel, early morning.
Sleep all day. Room terrible chaos, monkey has broken things. Hotel
owner makes them pay. Again driving at night. J talking and talking.
Avoid flooded area outside of Lyon. Second hotel. Again monkey damage
Sneak out before it can be found out.

7.   The villa. Arrival at the villa of J's mother, who died two years
before. Received by caretaker, who was disciple of J's mother. J&L
bring two boxes out of the vaults, while R talks to caretaker and muses
upon death of J's mother. They are served vegetarian meal, and depart.

8.   The boat. Before the departure. R finds his cabin in intermedi-
iare, J retires to his room in 1st and L goes off on an errand. L
arrives at last minute. The departure. L introduces R to M, who is
going back to Egypt after six months in Europe. They discover they
are both in intermediare.

9.   The Voyage. L & J are mostly invisible. R knocks on door of
their cabin but no answer. Conversations with M and his friends.
Finally meet L and J one late twilight in lounge. Conversations.
Other days -- knock on door of cabin, finally answered by L. Cabin in
great disorder. Monkey in bathroom. J in bed, looking at talismans.
Tell of plans to show them to King who collects things. R wonderingly
examines talismans. J asks to borrow nail scissors from R. Descriptions
of sea and nights. Passing Stromboli in early morning. Straits of
Messine. The Greek islands. Endless feeling of Voyage. Again visit
to cabin of J & L. Packing talismans into socks to evade customs.
Thot Moise eats talisman -- is finally recovered after much consternatio
10. Lebanon. Arrival in Beyrut harbor in early morning, R looks out
porthole. Says goodbye to Tunisian boy who is going to study in Lebanon
They have decided to take car together to see either Baalbek or Pere
Charbel Pere Charbel wins due to J's insistence. Hungarian woman
cannot go because of her passport, is furious. They go off in taxi.
Through Beyrut, and into country side following coastline. Stop at
Byblos. Inspect ruins, find miniature stage. Antics upon stage, J's
posturing. Crusaders castle. Leave and wind their way up into mountain
At the shrine of Pere Charbel. Very prosperous, being modernized.
Priests with long beards. Gaudy shrine. Running wall. L buys bottle
of eau Pere Charbel, booklet listing miracles, and photograph of Santa
Claus vision. They get into car and go off. Stop for lunch at house
of friend of M's. Above Adonis river, tremendous mountains. After
lunch, go on to temple of Astarte. Dusk falling. Helped down muddy sli
pery trails by Turkish boys. Dramatic spot. Tremendous cliffs.
Waterfall and river cominf from huge cavern in rock. Go up to mouth,
like entrance to Inferno. L & J standing on precipice like Dante &
Virgil. Turkish boy takes R in tunnel under ancient tumbled rocks,
Byzantine picture of Virgin in glass frame. Boy kisses virgin. R
kisses boy. They go out, near full moon is out. Struggle back to road.
R. asks for money and gives boy tip. In the dusk they drive back down
through the barren mountains, filling up with clouds. Darkness.
Around and around and down. Through little settlement blazing with
crude light. No time to go to haschish parlour. Back at dock.
Argument with cab driver, J makes big scene and refuses to give him
another penny. Back on boat, R tired and ill seeming.
11. Haifa. R awakes ill. In Haifa harbor. Some sort of trouble.

This page: the first two pages of unrealized scenario *Hymn to the Sun*
Next pages: letters to Mary Meerson

19th Dec. 1951
Luxor

Dearest Mary,

I'm sending off this note so you'll know that so far this trip has
worked out wonderfully. I'm too overwhelmed by it all to attempt
much description at the moment, but during the week I've been here
in upper Egypt, I've been shown the temples at Luxor, Karnak, the
tombs in the Valley of the Kings, etc. etc. by the best
Egyptologists of the Symbolist school who have explained their
theories to me on the spot. I want to see as much as possible
first so I can plan the work I want to do here. I'm so thankful
for the film!

I only wish you were here to share with me this beauty. Such a
serenity radiates from this land! And the sun, of course, is
magnificent. I already feel renewed. My first film project here
must necessarily be something very simple — I think first a study
of the light as it changes over the landscape.

Mary, I do hope that your knee is well again. Please drop me a
line telling me how you are, c/o Maison des Arts. With all my love
for ever and ever,

Kenneth

26 Feb. 52
Roma

Dearest Mary,

I do hope you received the card I sent you when I first arrived in Rome. Just a month ago today the disaster occured in Cairo that so changed my plans. Two of my friends were killed and half of my possesions burned up. It's too bad I couldn't have finished my film project "Hymn to the Sun" but as you can see, bad luck dogs me everywhere. Nevertheless I sold some photos I took to "Life" magazine — the Feb. 11 issue — and they at least covered my plane trips.

Spring has arrived here in Rome and as I find it no more expensive than Paris, I believe I'll stay here for a while. However I will have to return to Paris for a few days to put my things in order. I do wish, dear Mary, you'd please drop me a card so I can have some idea how you're getting along. After all, I still love you, don't you ever forget that, and I'm concerned about you. It seems that our dream of Egypt is off for the time being, but maybe there is somewhere else. Please drop me just a line, Mary, I want to hear from you so much. I miss you.

Love, Kenneth

c/o American Embassy Roma

78

November 17 1952
VIA CILICIA 51
ROMA

DEAREST MARY,

I've been meaning to write to you for some time but still was hoping to
receive some word from you. Somehow it is very discouraging to be writing to
someone knowing that it is very unlikely ever to receive an answer, even if
her heart is in the right place. It's rather like mailing the letter in a tree
trunk. I think it's just too neurotic and awful that you can't at least send
me a post card from time to time.' What other sign do I have that you still
think of me from time to time? After all, it's also hellishly hard for ME to
write, yet I do manage to do it because I still LOVE YOU.

I have no way of knowing whether you're still concerned about me or whether
you've forgotten me altogether. I do know my own concern for you and desire to
know how you are and how things are working out for you.

The truth of it is, dear Mary, that again I'm crying out desperately for help.
I'm sorry to report that the ship is again beyond control and is headed for
the rocks. Nothing physical this time, it's a crise d'angoisse irrationelle
which has left me completely smashed. Is anyone surprised? Of course I
couldn't have gone on much longer — building on hopeless hopes — and now I
have ceased going anywhere. So I'm stuck here in the vi[s]cious ring of Mania
and Melancholy which is literally running me into the ground. Who can help me?

I wondered if there's a dim chance of Dr. Fulchignoni knowing of some Doctor
or Psychotherapist here that might agree to see me. Naturally someone who
speaks and understands English. The catch is I have no money to pay for such
an interview. So what am I to do?

It is impossible for me to leave here so I will stay on, hoping to hear from
you or other source. If you yourself can't write can't one of the secretaries
at the Cinémathèque type up a note for you? I had hoped long ago to have
received some names of people here who might have taken an interest in my work
or who to write to at the Cineteka Italiana who might arrange something for me
here. Yet I've had no word. Now unfortunately work is out of the question
until I again learn how to stay alive.

I'm sorry to trouble you about this Mary. Yet if you can think of some course
of action at this time please do try to contact me. Believe me, I wouldn't
have written you if I didn't know that the matter at hand is an urgent one.

WITH ALL MY LOVE AS EVER, KEN

KENNETH
VIA CILICIA 51
ROMA ITALIA

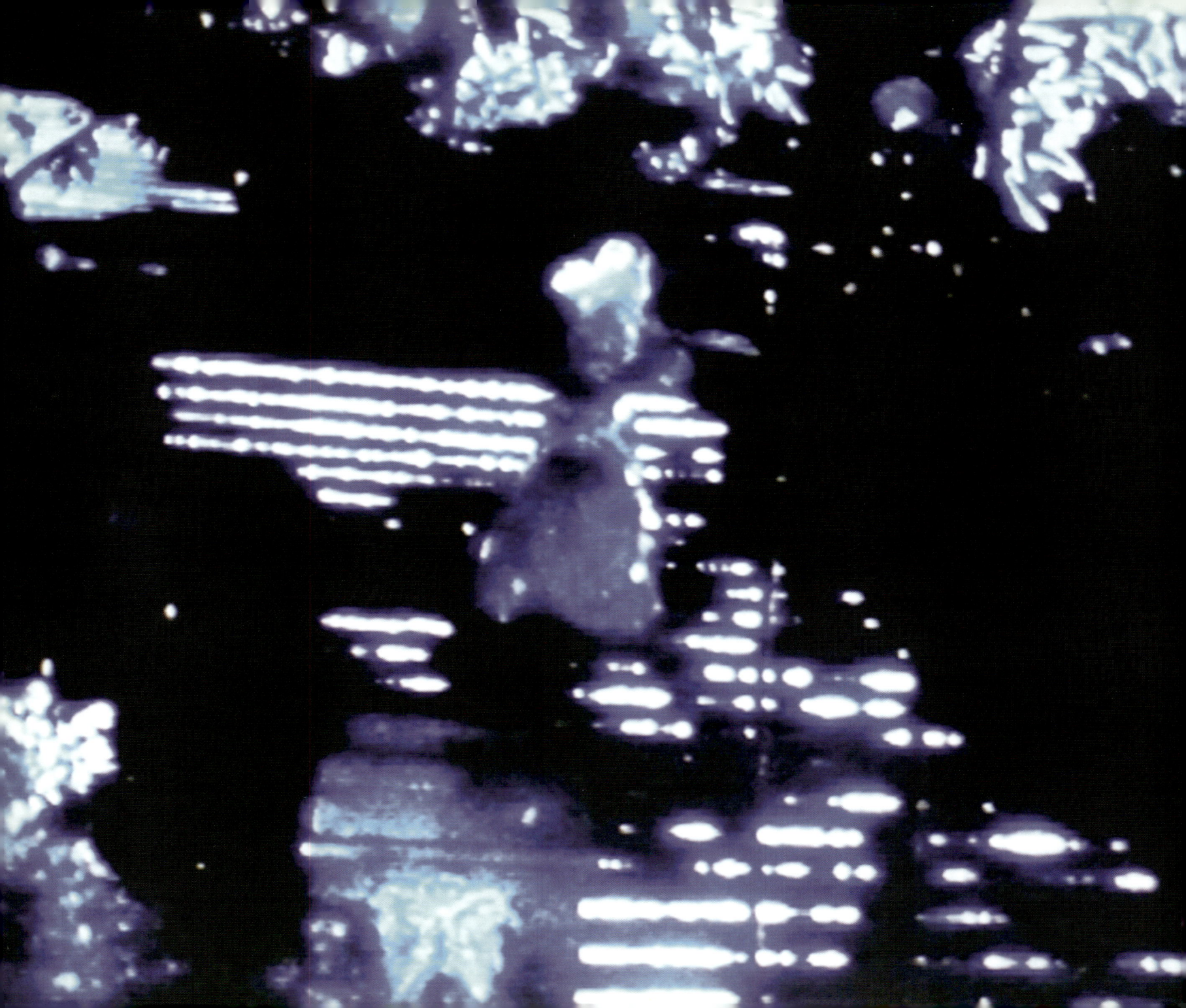

Eaux d'Artifice

1953

13 minutes

16mm, tinted black and white

Music by Vivaldi, "Winter" from "The Four Seasons"

Once Kenneth Anger had settled in Rome, he conceived of a film with a mythological theme on ancient deities. However, this transformed into an attempt to make a film in four parts, synchronizing the Baroque setting of Tivoli with music to create a film-symphony through dynamic montage. The working titles were "acque barocche" and "il mistero dell'acqua."[2] The Villa d'Este at Tivoli on the outskirts of Rome was constructed in 1550 under the direction of architect Piero Ligorio, and is best known for its sumptuous gardens animated by fountains: a Baroque maze of staircases, gargoyles, fountains and balustrades. Conceived as a counterpoint to *Fireworks*, Anger could only complete the first part of the film, set to Vivaldi's "Winter" from "The Four Seasons." The title does not exist as a correct phrase in French, but is Anger's own pun for "water-works" playing on the words "feux d'artifice" – fireworks; a dialectical counterpart to his earlier film. A decadent fugue of water and light, the short film becomes another rite of finding identity. Anger describes it as "Hide and seek in a night-time labyrinth of levels, cascades, balustrades, grottoes, and ever-gushing, leaping fountains, until the Water Witch and the Fountain become One."[3]

Anger mentioned in an unpublished letter to Mary Meerson:

> I now have a camera available, through an American friend who is living here for the time being; the problem of course is lack of film. I have with me the last five rolls of 16mm Reversal which I picked up in Paris, but I would need ten more before beginning on the project I have in mind. I think I explained to you before my idea for the fountains and gardens of the Villa d'Este at Tivoli. It is a perfect subject, all I need is the camera, sun, and film.... Of course my original plan for the film was to do it in color, but I have given up on that idea as it would be too "cher" from every point of view. The most important thing is the montage dynamics, which is just as effective in black and white.[4]

The patron of the Villa d'Este and the fountains of Tivoli, Cardinal d'Este was also a source of fascination for Anger. As a Cardinal from one of Italy's foremost aristocratic families, he was not content leading a life of supreme materialistic decadence and scandalous debauchery, and became more interested in the worship of pagan gods, conducting numerous Dionysian rituals and ceremonies often within the gardens of the Villa. The film is at once documentary and oneiric, and Anger did not neglect elements of the symbolic order. The lunar light controlling the dream and the unconscious evoked in *Fireworks* and *Rabbit's Moon*, also baths the realm of *Eaux d'Artifice*. The moon emanates domination upon the physical, terrestrial worlds, constituting the astral matrix. The omnipresent water evokes symbolism of the source of life, rituals of purification, baptism and the essential element of regeneration.

The "actress" in the film, playing a character bedecked in eighteenth century evening dress with plumed feather headdress, jewels (and black domino mask), was Carmilla Salvatorelli, a circus midget Anger encountered in Italy. She was employed to alter the perception of scale, chosen to make the dimensions of the gardens loom more spaciously. Carmilla has been described as "the evocation of a Fairbank heroine" in "pursuit of the night moth."[5]

> To watch *Eaux d'Artifice* is to become very aware of the artifice of the film (and implicitly, of all films). Anger fashions a drama of flight and observation with his synchronization of the images to Vivaldi's music, and the visual manipulation of gargoyles seeming to leer at the running figure.[6]

The film was shot on black and white through a deep red filter, then printed with a blue filter on color stock giving the scenes shot during the day a nocturnal atmosphere. Certain frames, such as the close-up on the fan were hand-tinted green. The precision of dynamic montage and image-sound synchrony cut to Vivaldi's "Four Seasons" has rarely been matched in the history of film and, as Robert Haller noted, this was a departure for Anger. In later films such as *Scorpio Rising*, Anger freely intercut dissimilar images to work with what Eisenstein called intellectual montage, but in *Eaux d'Artifice* he followed the opposite mode of film editing, the Pudovkin method of linkage, a syntagmatic continuity and chain of sequences, instead of Eisenstein's montage of collisions and conflicts.[7] Unlike *Fireworks*, the film is non-narrative, and primarily rhythmic, with its elements paced to the diminutive heroine, from the speed of the zooms (close-ups on the mask-like faces of the water spirits carved in stone), to the cascading jets of water slowed to emulate sparkling jewels and unfamiliar abstract shapes. The film is driven primarily by the montage around the music which builds to a crescendo when "the water witch" dissolves into the fountain with a flash of her fan.

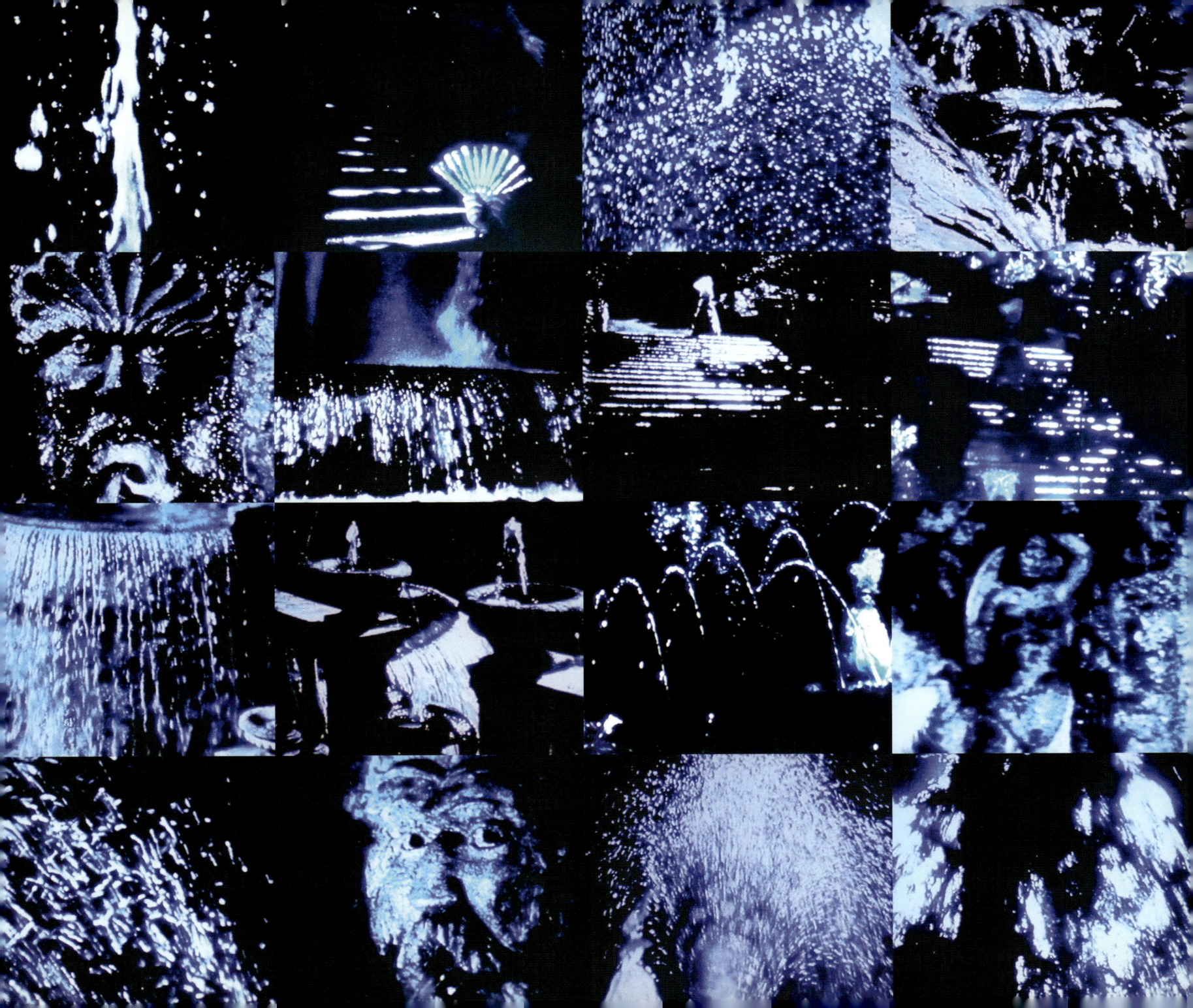

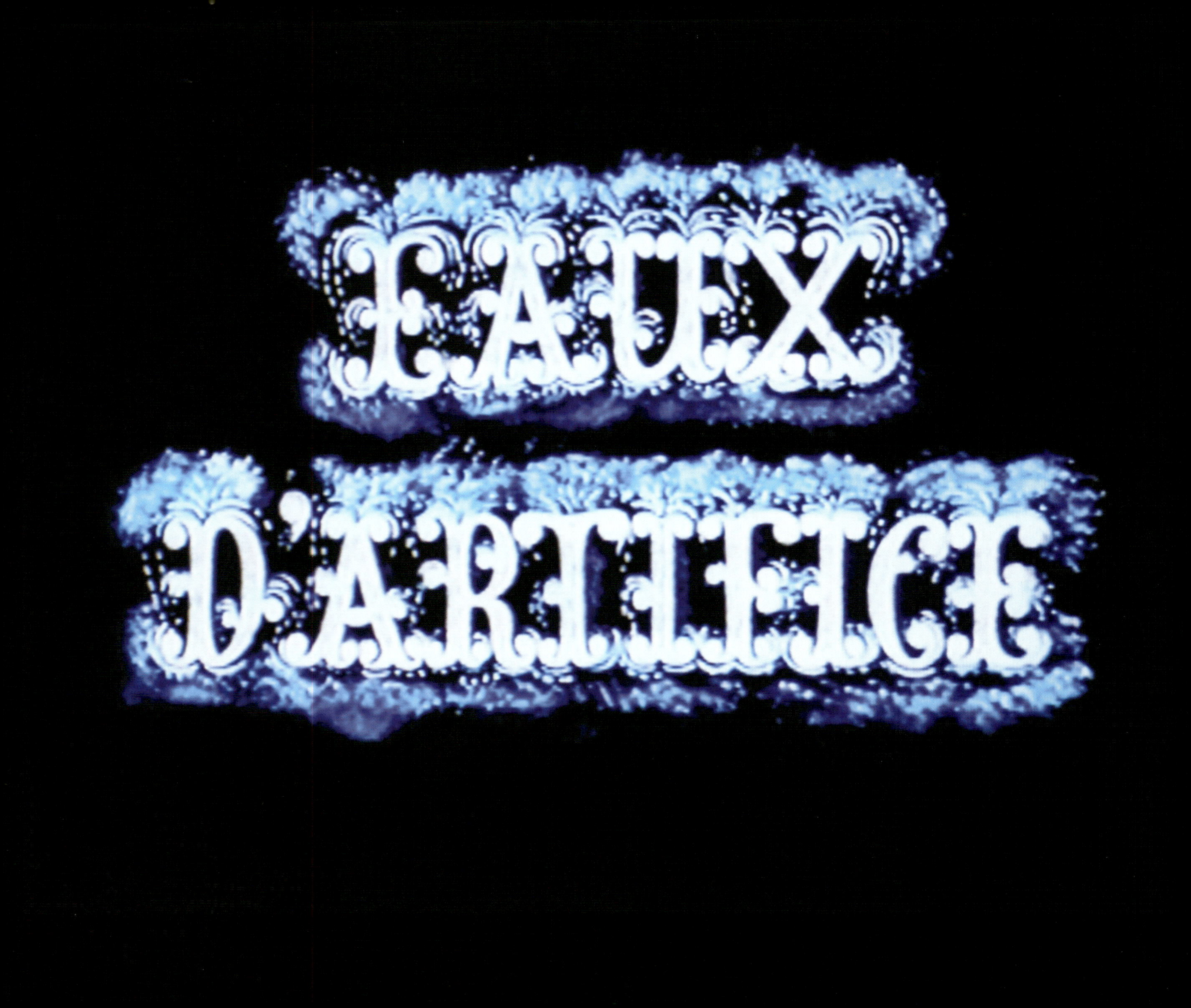
EAUX
D'ARTIFICE

This abstract quality in the film has rarely been discussed. In simply photographing the jets of water in motion (filmed at a variety of speeds, with some sequences extremely slowed), flickering with dancing light, the image could almost be likened to an action painting.[8] Montage is indeed artifice and an abstraction of objective reality. The impression of movement was a conscious concern for Anger, and prior to the action painters such as his contemporary Jackson Pollock (who coincidentally created *Blue Poles* a year earlier), Anger had been interested in the impressionist method and aesthetic, and specifically James McNeill Whistler.[9] Whistler's compositions and harmonies, sketches, and his studies of light on water, favor lyricism over an optical and scientific approach to visualizing impression, light and movement. This is reflected in his preference to call his paintings "nocturne," "caprice," "symphony" and other terms from musical forms. The visual-musical analogy is clearly a key aspect of Anger's pioneering work in film in this respect extending Eisenstein's "Synchronization of the Senses."[10] Whistler proposed that, like music, a painting should not need to depict a particular character or event but that the composition, form and color were the primary elements. Three or four dashed lines or haphazard swirls of color could become a scene. His paintings were also studies of contrasting textures, with the effects of silk, tapestry, gold leaf and printed paper indicated by an economy of brushwork, while the composition is also influenced by Japanese and Eastern design. As discussed in "Modesty and the Art of Film", the economy of the "sketch" – a succinct visual statement distilling an essence – was close to Anger's aesthetic, manifest in *Eaux d'Artifice*, increasing the dynamism of compositions. As Eisenstein stated, the sketch is often more alive than the finished canvas: "Our first and most spontaneous perceptions are often our most valuable ones, because these sharp, fresh, lively impressions invariably derive from the most widely various fields."[11] Aldous Huxley proclaimed the new cinema as a new form of visionary art, and hoped that it would presage the supercession and early demise of non-representational painting.

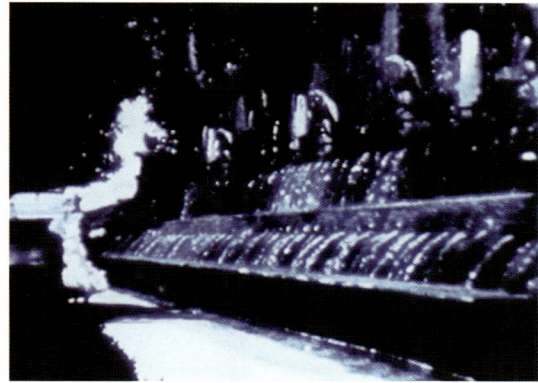

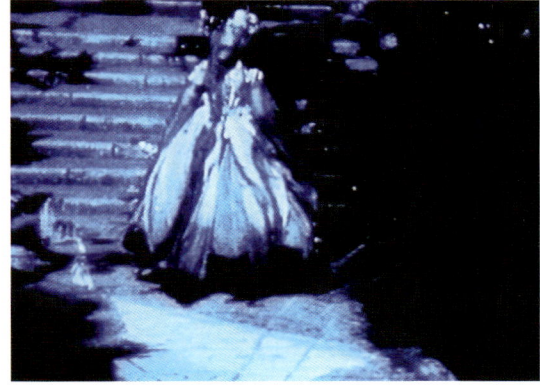

P. Adams Sitney made the point that a synthesis has bound the "visual" and the "dynamic" in a supposed opposition to the "literary" (in regard to Deren and Peterson specifically), which could also apply to *Eaux d'Artifice*. In the dialectic of abstraction, such "dynamic visualists" maintain the position that the filmmaker as artist accomplish all of the multiple tasks required of a larger crew. This position holds that the filmmaker should be his/her own cameraman and editor (which Anger, for the most part has always been, in maintaining his unmitigated vision). The visualist approach implies the synthetic unity of functions which the film industry has kept separate. "A corollary to the same proposition demands that the filmmaker appropriate the whole visual field, leading ultimately to an expressionistic employment of anamorphosis, superimposition, painting on film... the emergence of this aesthetic during the reign of Abstract Expressionism is not a coincidence."[12]

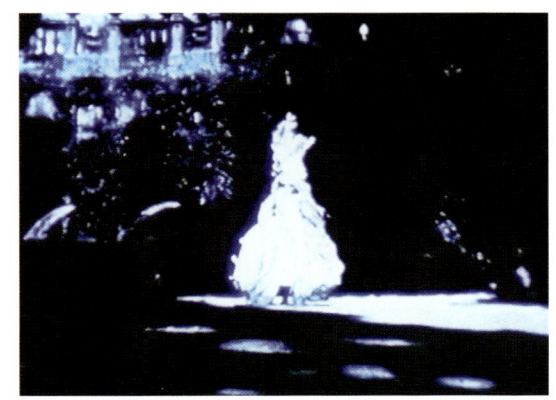

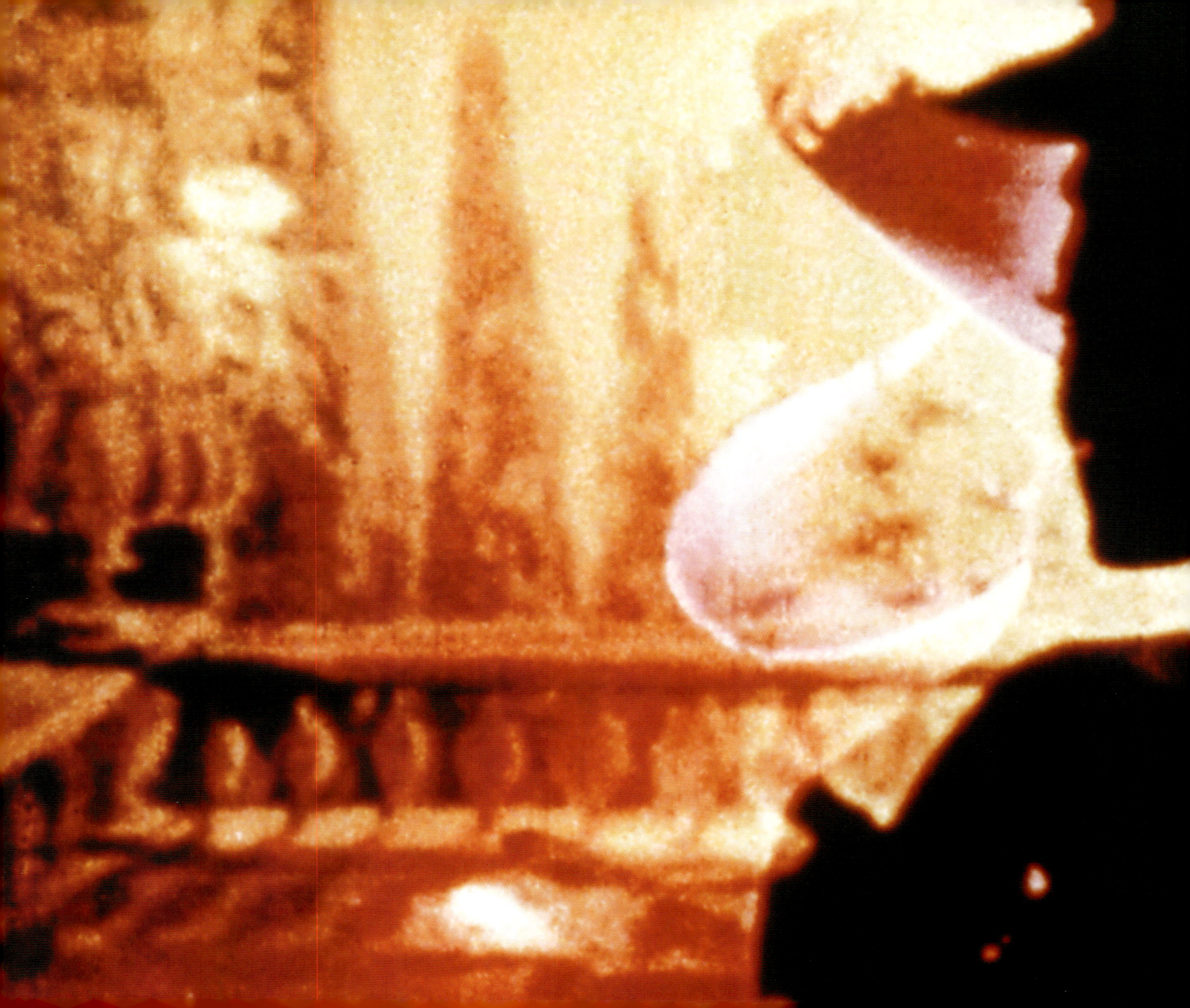

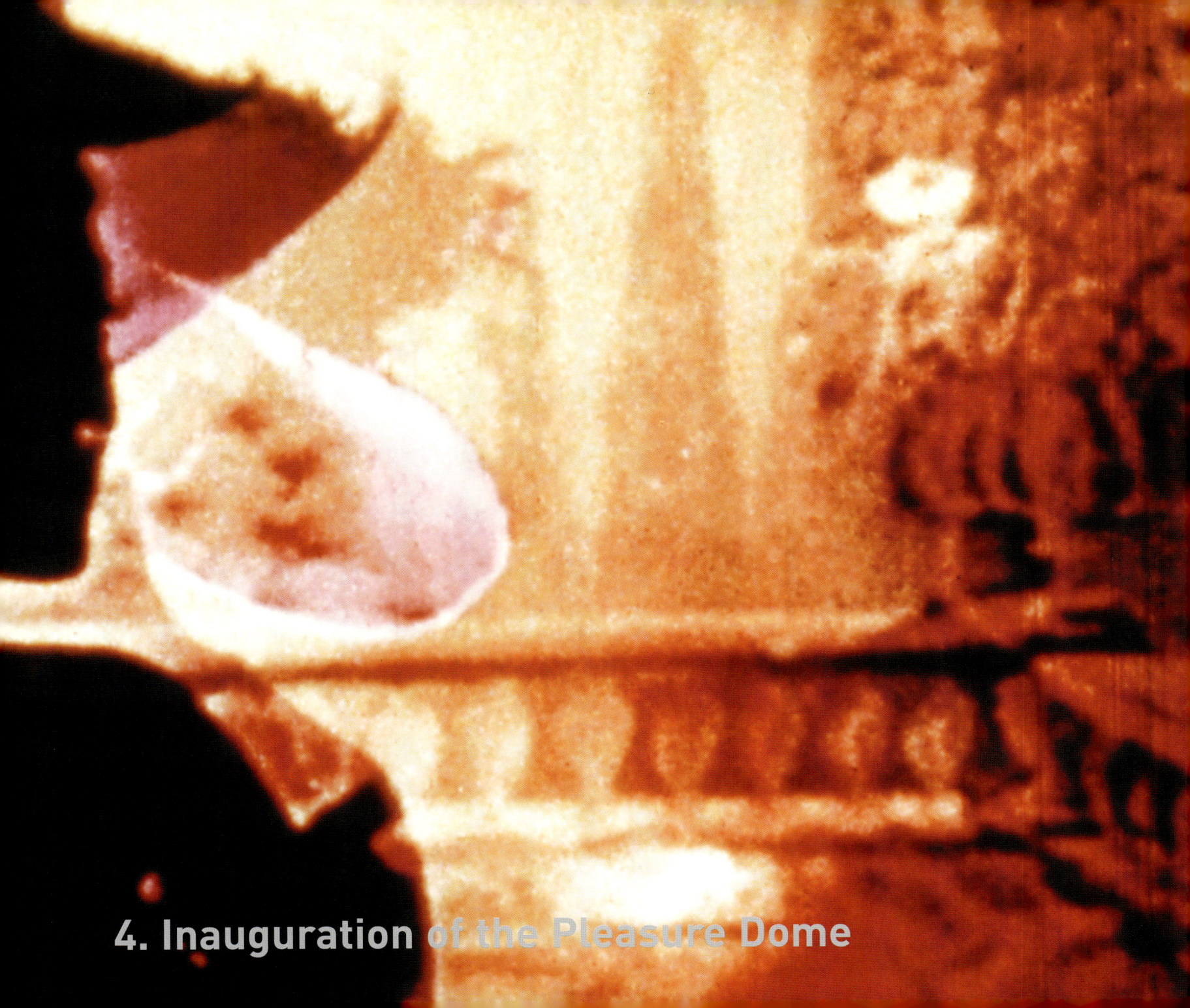

4. Inauguration of the Pleasure Dome

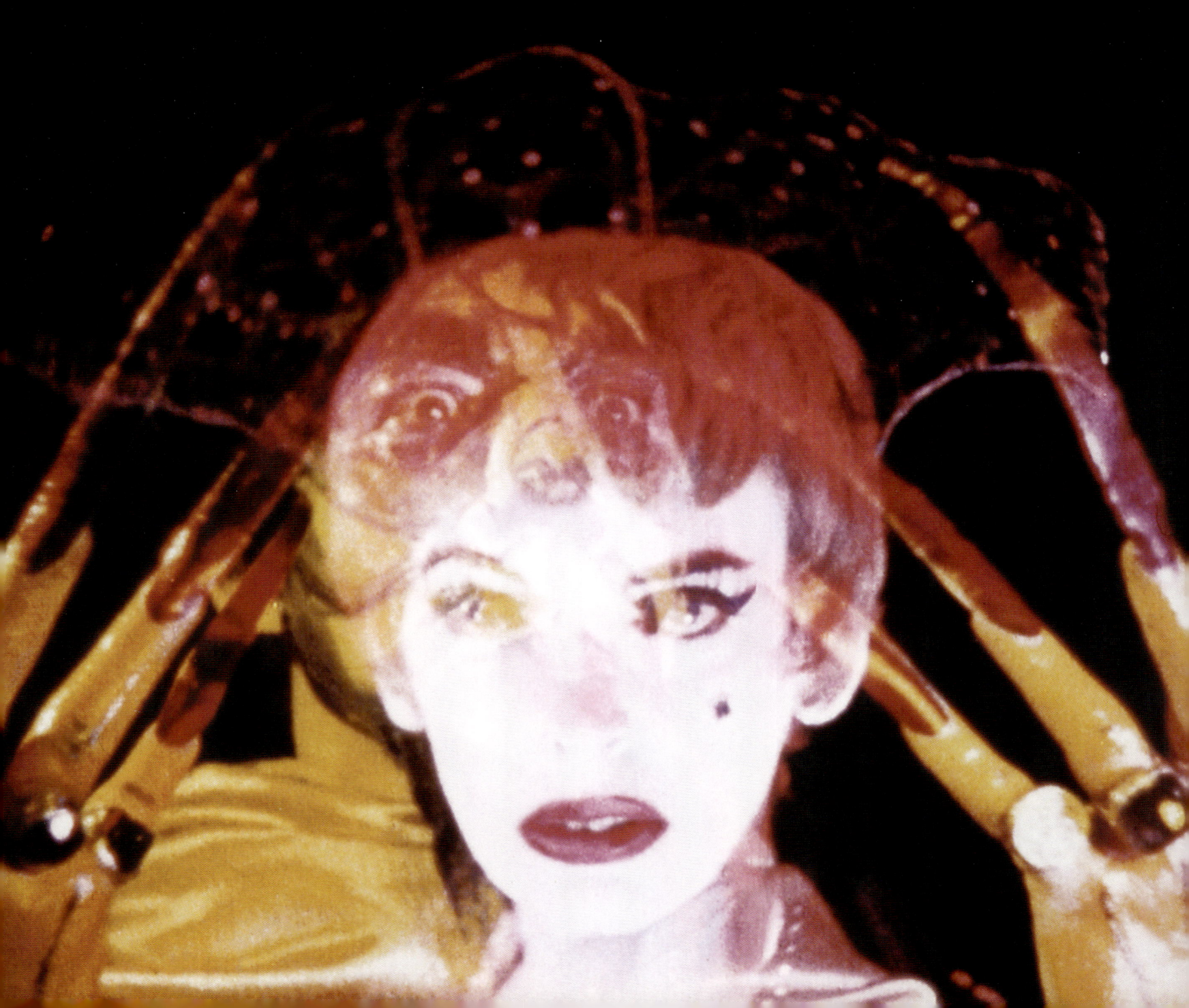

Inauguration of the Pleasure Dome

1954/1966

38 minutes

16mm, color

Music by Leoš Janáček, "Glagolithic Mass"

Following his time in Europe, Anger returned to Los Angeles to settle a family inheritance and began filming *Inauguration of the Pleasure Dome* from the proceeds. When asked why he made *Inauguration of the Pleasure Dome* in America, Anger replied:

> Because America is the Pleasure Dome of the world... the materialistic dream is so strong, that you have to be of the purity of Parsifal to banish Klingsor's castle... there'll always be a penalty to pay for these artificial paradises.[1]

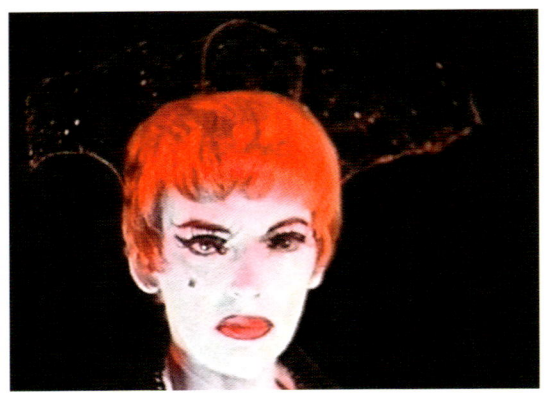

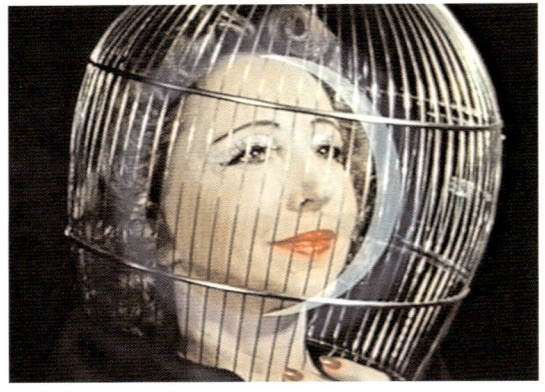

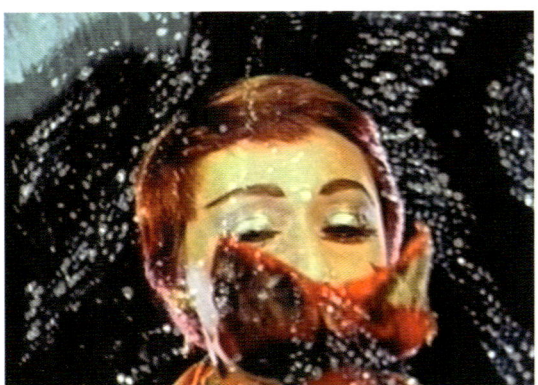

The lavishly costumed magic masquerade party derived from the dramatic neo-pagan rituals of Aleister Crowley, featuring various characters from classical mythology and a pantheon that is distinctively Anger's: the Great Beast and the Scarlet Woman, Shiva, Osiris, Astarte and Pan, and Cesare the Somnambulist, from *The Cabinet of Dr. Caligari*. Anger himself called the event "an improvised happening." As the celebration becomes more orgiastic, the characters become high on an hallucinogenic brew and transform with costume, make-up and personality changes. The film itself enters a hallucinated crescendo of editing and superimposition, amplified with a progressive use of color, with tints multiplying and deepening as the tension mounts to the climax of the destruction of the god Pan by his worshippers. The film experimented with psychometric qualities, pulling a viewer out of the regular space-time continuum into another level of consciousness. With *Inauguration*, Anger's works begin to assume the form of religious rituals, here, centering on the consumption of the Eucharist:

> The legend of Bacchus that's the pivotal thing and it ends with the God being torn to pieces by the Bacchantes... but rather than using a specific ritual, which would entail quite a lot of the spoken word as ritual does, I wanted to create a feeling of being carried into a world of wonder, and the use of color and phantasy is progressive. In other words, it expands, it becomes completely subjective – like when people take communion and one sees through their eyes...[2]

Inauguration has undergone several transformations, with at least four versions completed. The definitive, or at least current version, which is in circulation as part of Anger's *Magick Lantern Cycle*, is the *Sacred Mushroom Edition (Lord Shiva's Dream)*, 1966, with a soundtrack of "Glagolithic Mass" by Leoš Janáček. The original version, 1954-1956, had eccentric music by Harry Partch and was 41 minutes long. An innovative 1958 version was projected on three screens, using three simultaneous projectors, with three acts entitled "The Talisman," "The Banquet Of Poisons," and "The Ceremonies of Consummation." The three-screen synchronous projection for the climactic final two-thirds, debuted at the second experimental film festival during the Brussels World Fair, 1958. Anger was familiar with Abel Gance's split-screen technique pioneered for the epic *Napoléon*, 1927, which he had seen during his period at the Cinémathèque in Paris.

Top: Marjorie Cameron
Middle: Anaïs Nin
Bottom: Renate Druks

In the psychedelic 1966 version, more superimposed stills of Crowley and images of the moon were added to the first part of the original film, at strategic points. Calculated by the filmmaker to be experienced under the effects of LSD, it had quintuple imposition, using footage of the naked souls in Hell from Lachman's 1935 *Dante's Inferno*, a Hollywood spectacle, which were mainly crowd scenes of burning, printed in red. It was in the final third of Anger's film, where once images on two flanking screens had appeared, that major changes were made in the 1966 version. Superimposition, sometimes many layers deep, replaced the earlier linear development and montage. To the multiplication of his characters he also added most of *Puce Moment*. In 1992 funding from his friend J. Paul Getty, allowed him to complete a lavish and luxurious visually reworked version that featured added effects and more superimposition.

Aleister Crowley's concept of occult initiatory rituals provided the governing internal logic of the film, a concept which applies to Anger's films in general but most certainly to *Inauguration*, and the films that were to follow: *Scorpio Rising*, *Invocation of My Demon Brother* and *Lucifer Rising*. In 1956 Anger's synopsis for the films' premiere in New York was as follows:

> The Abbey of Thelema, the evening of the "sunset" of Crowleyanity. Lord Shiva wakes. Madam Satan presents the mandragore, and a glamor is cast. A convocation of enchantresses and theurgists. The idol is fed. Aphrodite presents the apple; Isis presents the serpent. Astarte descends with the witchball, the Fairy Geffe takes wing. The gesture of the Juggler invokes the Tarot Cups. The Elixir of Hecate is served by the Somnambulist. Pan's drink is venomed by Lord Shiva. The enchantment of Pan. Astarte withdraws with the glistening net of Love. The arrival of the Secret Chief. The ceremonies of Consummation are presided over by the Great Beast – Shiva and the Scarlet Woman – Kali.[3]

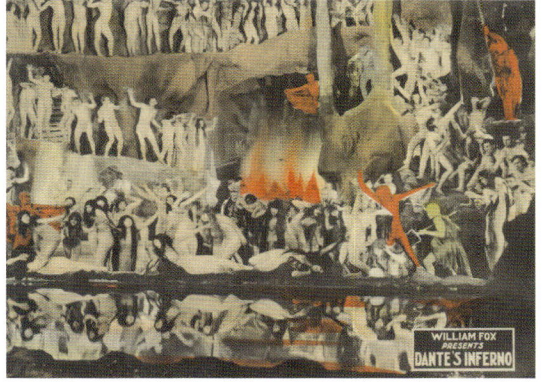

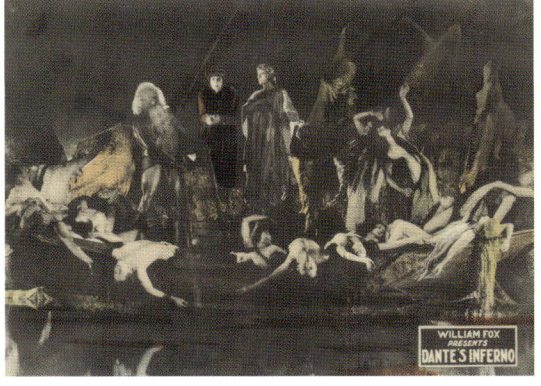

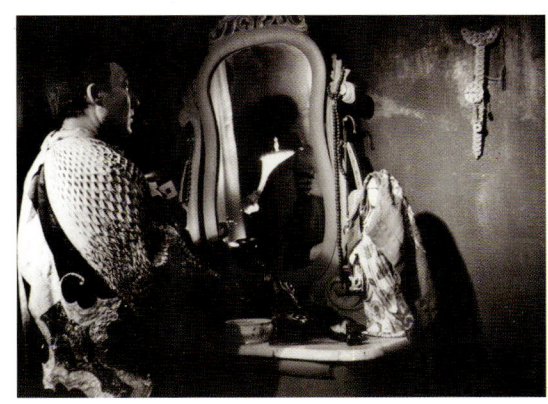

Top and middle: first silent 1920s version of *Dante's Inferno*, hand-painted lobby cards from the collection of Kenneth Anger
Bottom: set photograph from *Inauguration of the Pleasure Dome*

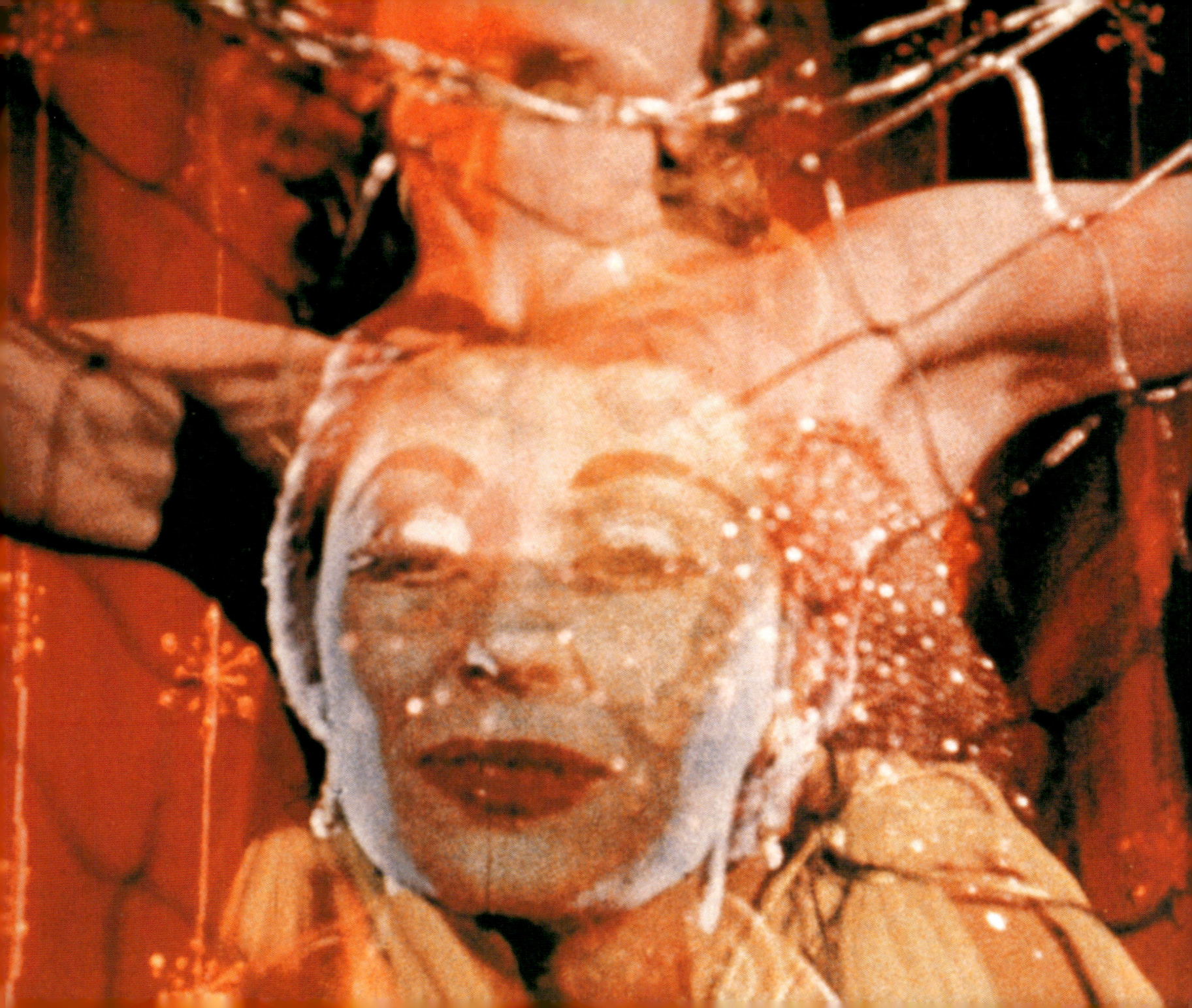

The perpetual transformations and revisions of Anger's own films, and most particularly this one, is quite unique of any filmmaker, defying the expectations of film as mechanical reproduction."[4] On the occasion of his Spring Equinox program at the Film-Makers Cinematheque in New York in 1966, this version began with a reading of the whole of Coleridge's *Kubla Khan* from which Anger derived the original title of the film. His program notes were as follows:

INAUGURATION OF THE PLEASURE DOME

Sacred Mushroom Edition Spring Equinox 1966

Otherwise known as "Lord Shiva's Dream"

"A Eucharist of some sort should most assuredly be consumed daily by every magician, and he should regard it as the main sustenance of his magical life. It is of more importance than any other magical ceremony, because it is a complete circle. The whole of the force expended is completely re-absorbed; yet the virtue is that vast gain represented by the abyss between Man and God. The magician becomes filled with God, fed upon God, intoxicated with God. Little by little his body will become purified by the internal lustration of God; day by day his mortal frame, shedding its earthly elements, will become in very truth the Temple of the Holy Ghost. Day by day matter is replaced by Spirit, the human by the divine; ultimately the change will be complete; God manifest in flesh will be his name."

– The Master Therion (Aleister Crowley), *Magick in Theory and Practice.*

Anger's notes were followed by Aleister Crowley's poem "One Star in Sight."

As much as the film itself has metamorphosed so have Anger's commentaries, which mirror the mutable panoply at this convocation of gods of orgy and disorder. Metamorphosing characters of *Inauguration* include Shiva, the Hindu god/dess of destruction and regeneration, indicating a disintegration of the life-forms associated with a celestial cycle. Samson De Brier transforms from Lord Shiva, to the Egyptian god Osiris, Cagliostro – the great mesmerist, Nero, and the Great Beast 666 of the Apocalypse; while Lady Kali becomes The Scarlet Woman. These improvisational transformations added to a visually extravagant spectacle. In the opening sequence the camera slowly pans up an art nouveau-style title and a sparkling string of jewels, which are ingested by Lord Shiva, a symbolic numinous opening scene, in which he ceremonially bejewels himself before an ornate mirror – a signal to his transformation and entry into another realm. The precious stones are talismans, symbolic of intrinsic visionary value and natural magic, vision inducing and transporting.[5]

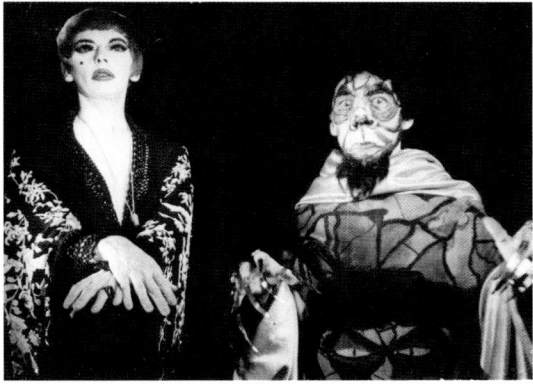

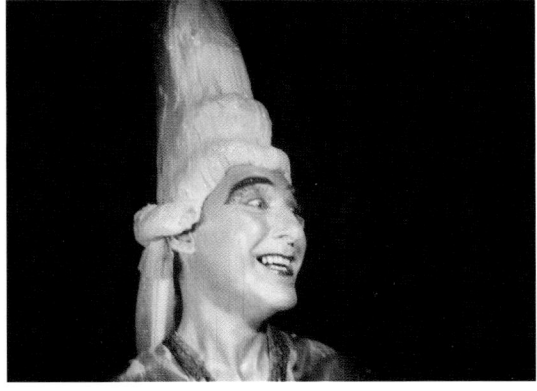

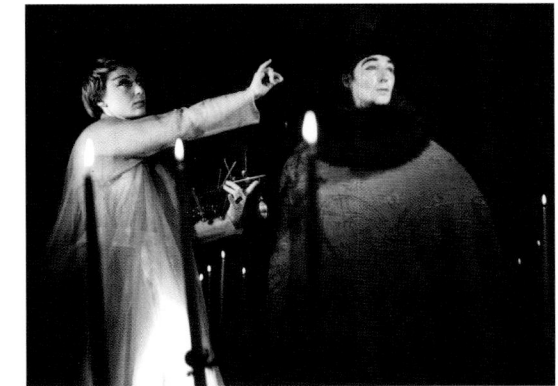

This page: "set photographs showing transformations of Samson De Brier"
Top: "with Cameron as Scarlet Woman"
Middle: "De Brier as Prince Youssopov"
Bottom: "with Renate Druks"

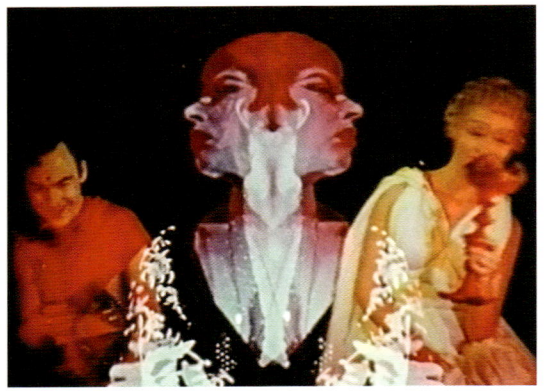

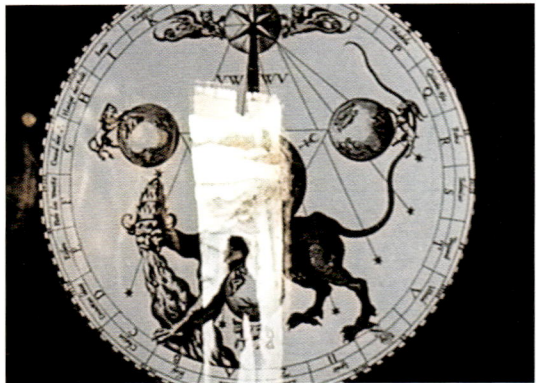

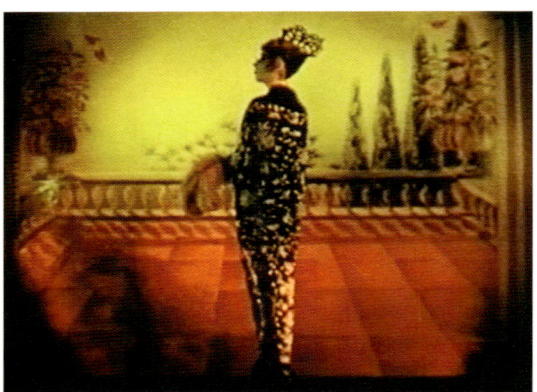

Inauguration of the Pleasure Dome articulates the "hypnotic resonance" of combined images. From the opening credits and title the film explores spatial relationships through the vertical plane (although this quickly gives way to overtonal construction.[6] The slow beginning, rising through the psychedelic hysteria of the second act to the climax of the film (the consumption of Pan, the Eucharist), and the attempt to arouse a near-religious fervor in the spectator in the pacing of the montage, as in Eisenstein's *The Old and The New*, with both films building slowly to culminate in an ecstatic peak which signifies the end of the film. "There was no need for a dominant narrative thread, a transposition of the idea into the realms of fiction in order to make it intelligible. His aim was direct and immediate communication of the theme."[7] Anger also explores "vertical montage" in *Inauguration of the Pleasure Dome*, a technique Eisenstein theorized and which has become one of the prevalent visual forms of our time (being used, for example in music video production and contemporary artist's films alike). Combining heterogeneous but significant elements: animations, pictures within pictures, sound effects and music; a "polyphonic" dynamic is created. While Eisenstein did not put his vertical montage theory into practice, Anger did so in *Inauguration of the Pleasure Dome*, with a complexity that was only rivalled with his own *Invocation of My Demon Brother*. Recognizing vast possibilities and the productive combination in using sound as a counterbalance to the picture (aligning the images with the score), a synchronous arrangement of the various aspects within the frame or shot (in this case, the complex superimpositions) communicates on simultaneous levels.

This page top: "Two-faced woman: Cameron as Scarlet Woman"
Middle: "Alchemy and doorway to another dimension"
Bottom: "Cameron as Scarlet Woman. Costume, belonging to De Brier, is one of Valentino's Spanish shawls"
Opposite: "watchful eyes of green-faced godling Samson De Brier"
Page 96: "Triple Threat: Cameron as Scarlet Woman, Head of Scarlet Woman and Samson De Brier as The Great Beast"
Page 97: "Samson De Brier as Nero with Joan Whitney as Aphrodite"
Pages 104-105: from left to right: "Samson De Brier as Lord Baphomet, the "owl King", stoned suspension of the Orgy: Joan Whitney, Paul Mathison as Pan, Renate Druks"

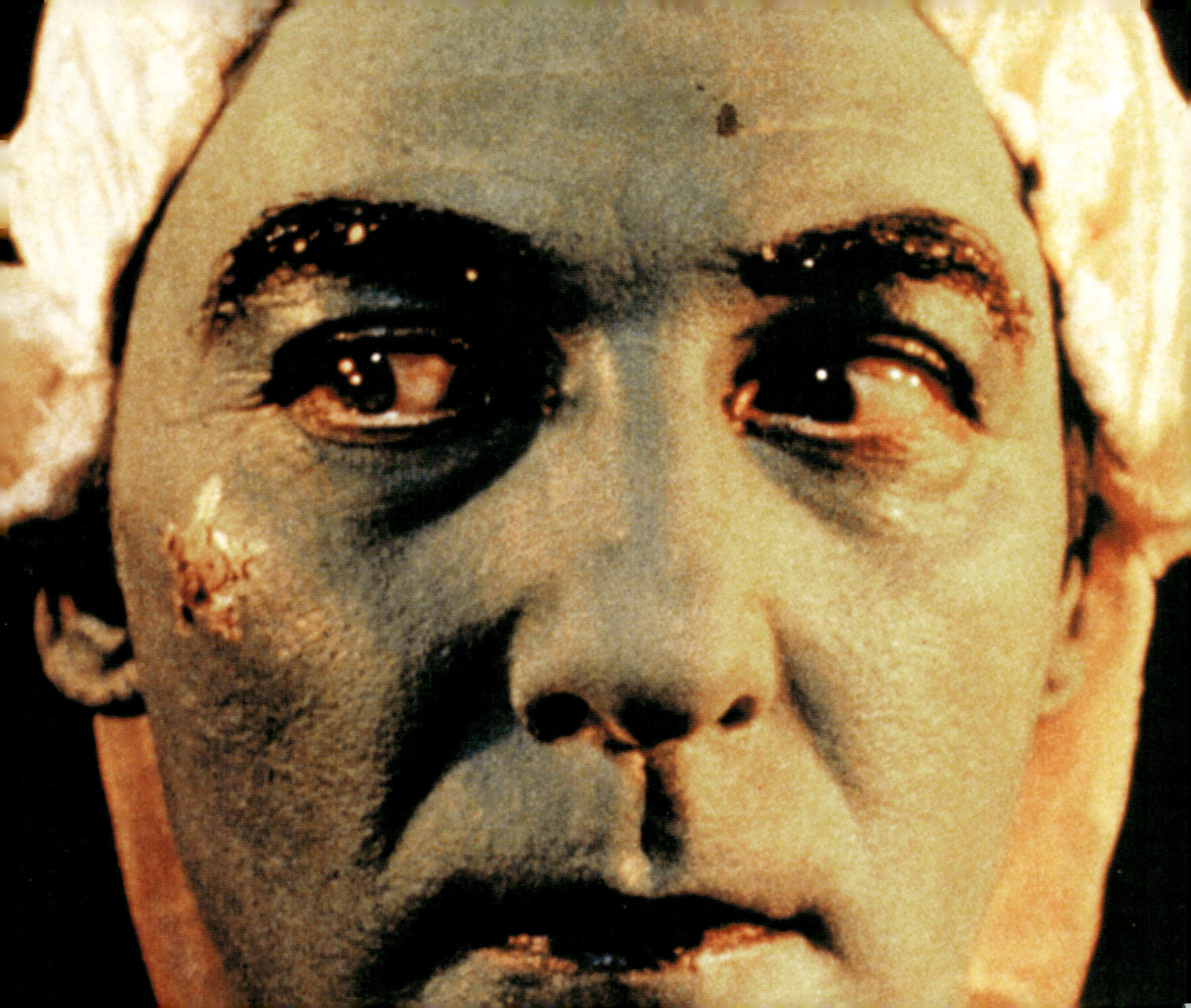

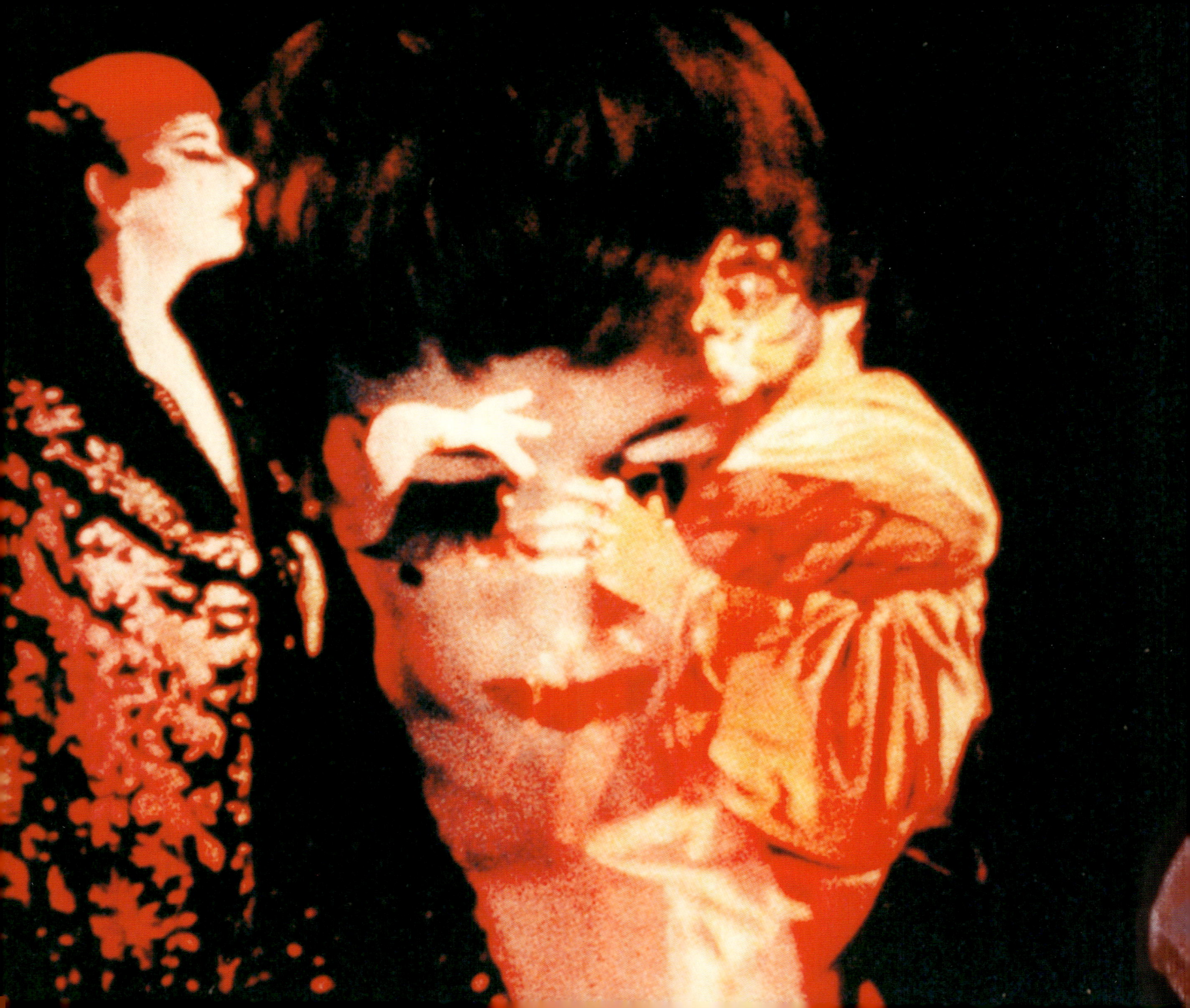

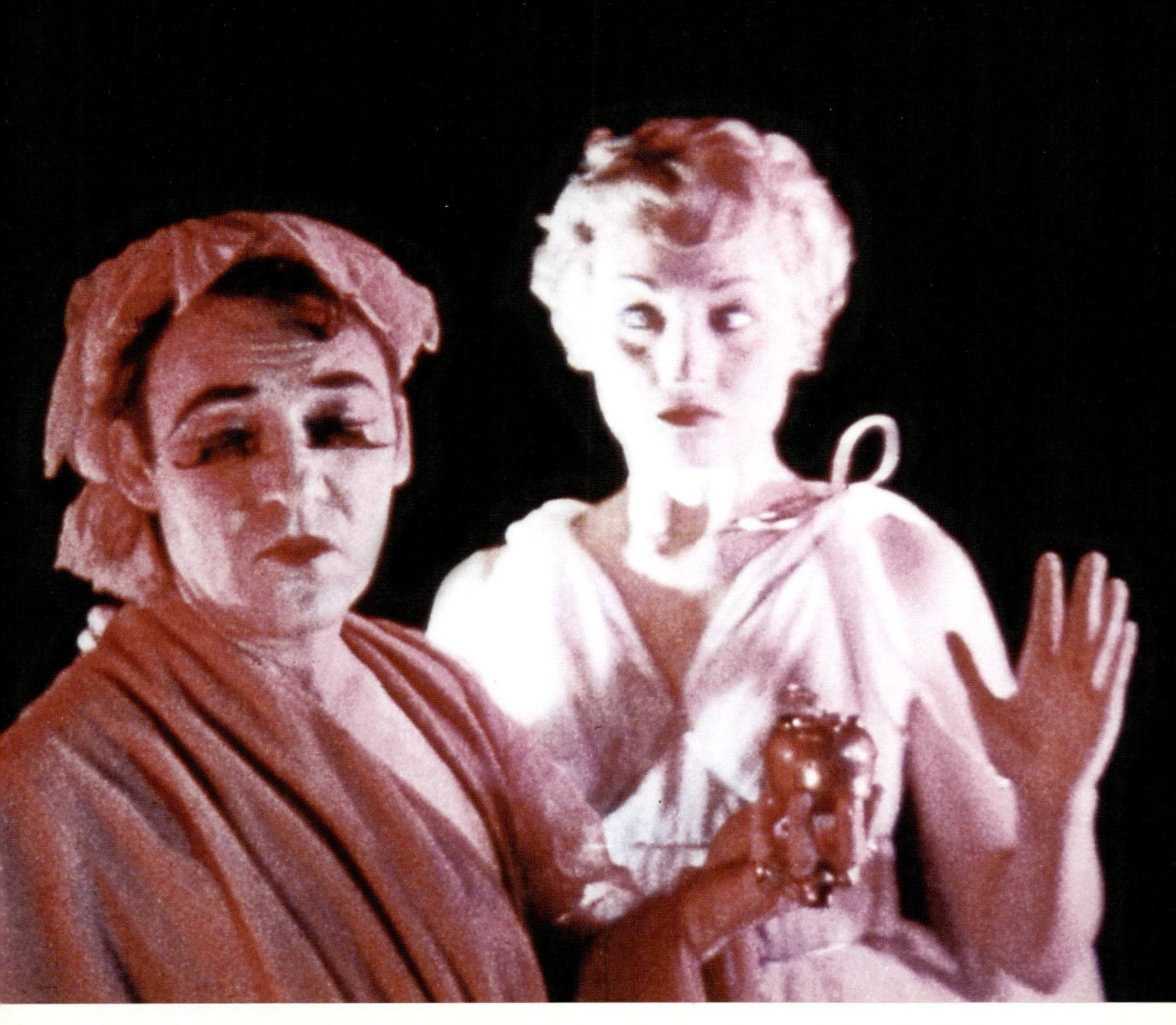

He was dressed as Hecate, goddess of the moon, earth, and infernal regions, sorcery and witchcraft. Only one heavily made-up eye was visible. His long black fingernails were made of black quills. The rest was all a towering figure of lace, veils, beads, and feathers.

Curtis Harrington was the somnambulist from *The Cabinet of Doctor Caligari*. He walked with his hands in front of him as if he had been hypnotized, and slim as he was, looked the part. His madness was to be caught in an archetypal figure.

Samson De Brier's madness was identification with an Eastern potentate. He was absolutely covered with jewels, and his fine dark Oriental eyes suited his fantasy....

... Kenneth Anger felt that the masquerade "Come as Your Madness" resembled a dream he had, which he had painted and which hung in Samson De Brier's studio. He decided to make a film of it [*Inauguration of the Pleasure Dome*]. We were to come in the costumes we wore. He said to me: "I want you as Astarte, the goddess of light. You are a magic person. I want to capture that luminosity which startled everyone at the party. It is an inner light and so difficult to capture."

We filmed in Samson's apartment from seven o'clock to one o'clock in the morning.

Part of the room was painted, gold ceiling, black walls; another room was made to look like a cave, all gold and red, with beaded, iridescent curtains. There was a backdrop painted to represent a Venetian scene. Most of the colors were intensified and created by the use of gels. Under the floodlights, Paul looked like a blond Nordic god.

Samson's apartment was ideal for the film, for he had trunks filled with costumes, textiles, costume jewelry, fans, lace, old photographs, gloves, scarves, veils, feathers.

Kenneth was working in the same way as Maya Deren; he wanted to capture the elusive aspects of our personalities, undirected, spontaneous, accidental. Renate stood in front of the backdrop with her large hat, looking very beautiful, laughing, laughing as only she can, so fully and unrestrainedly, abandoned and total. Peter as a little prince, shy, daydreaming, as if he were walking through a fairy tale. Peter, the gentle, dreaming boy, like a child from another planet. I thought of him as Saint-Exupéry's Little Prince. He has beautiful, liquid-blue eyes, a wistful face, and a manner so remote that he seems to be sleepwalking. Cameron, with a frightening mask of dead-white, chalky face and ink-black eyebrows and eyelashes, looked as if risen from the dead. A large voracious mouth and narrow slanted eyes. She is surrounded by an evil aura, which fascinates Paul, Curtis, and Kenneth.

We worked all through a weekend. We all felt we needed to know the meaning of Kenneth's dream, so that we could act in it. But he did not confide in us. The scenes seemed disconnected, and the characters changed costumes and personalities. There was chaos because the theme was unknown. I stepped into the room through a window. Paul had wrapped me in yards and yards of blue muslin as in a cocoon. My head was in the birdcage I wore at the masquerade. My lace-stockinged foot slowly descended on a fur bench which seemed to bristle at the touch. The contact with the fur was sensual, the fur seemed to raise its hairs to encounter the foot.

Paul said: "In the film Samson is the false man, the man of many faces, that is why he changes costumes and make-up all the time. The various women, Renate as sensuous romantic love, Joan as the virgin beauty, Cameron as the satanic woman, and you as the woman of light, all offer him gifts which he rejects. Curtis brings him the wine of ecstasy from the caves of the unconscious. They all drink and are transformed. You, Anaïs, refuse the drink. You have no need of it. You are Astarte, goddess of the moon. I, the romantic lover, reach in vain for the unreachable moon."

Cameron sat on a thronelike chair and took out a lifeless breast. There was a cave, web-like, labyrinthian, in which I danced, in the light of red gels. Samson ate pearls, Paul drank from a goblet, Kate acted a Cleopatra gone mad.

Beads fell off one of the flapper costumes. We were cutting our bare feet on them. I picked up a broom to sweep them and Kenneth would not let me.

"You are Astarte," he said.

At first Astarte was illuminated in the film, shed her light, but Cameron became a stronger figure as evil, a hypnotic figure, and the mood of decadence and destruction won out. Renate, with her Austrian beauty, very much like Luise Rainer but more voluptuous, represented the joy of sensuality. I, the ecstasies of the dream. Paul struggled out of the grasp of orgiastic women to reach for Astarte.

Renate had made Samson up to look like the Great Beast. His mouth was made invisible by paint and another mouth appeared on his chin. A duplicate mask was designed on his chest. His nails were a foot long, made of lacquered cardboard. He shook them in people's faces and the threatening gesture frightened everyone. He frightened himself too. As a degenerate potentate greedily swallowing all his jewels he was the best actor among us. Curtis Harrington was serving the drink which created ecstasy. Kenneth Anger asked Peter to dip his finger in the goblet, touch his tongue with it, and fall into a deep trance. Renate suddenly felt she did not want to see her child poisoned. She rebelled against this scene. For her it was not a symbolic act but a real danger. Kenneth argued that it was symbolic and that he was merely asleep. Renate was deeply disturbed and no one could convince her that she was confusing symbolism and reality. After a long battle, she surrendered. The scene was filmed. To see Cameron sitting with one breast uncovered and Peter tasting the elixir was to feel a chill of fear that her witch's milk might be the source of the goblet's content. Renate's interpretation of Kenneth's film was that it was an extension of the masquerade. It was a portrayal of people's madness. The reality and the madness mingled and that made chaos and confusion. The links were missing, as in madness. There was a distortion. Love became hatred, ecstasy became a nightmare. Those who began with a sensual attraction ended by devouring each other. The elixir, which Kenneth said came from the unconscious, Renate saw as coming from infernal regions, whipping the madness to dizzying heights from which it would collapse.

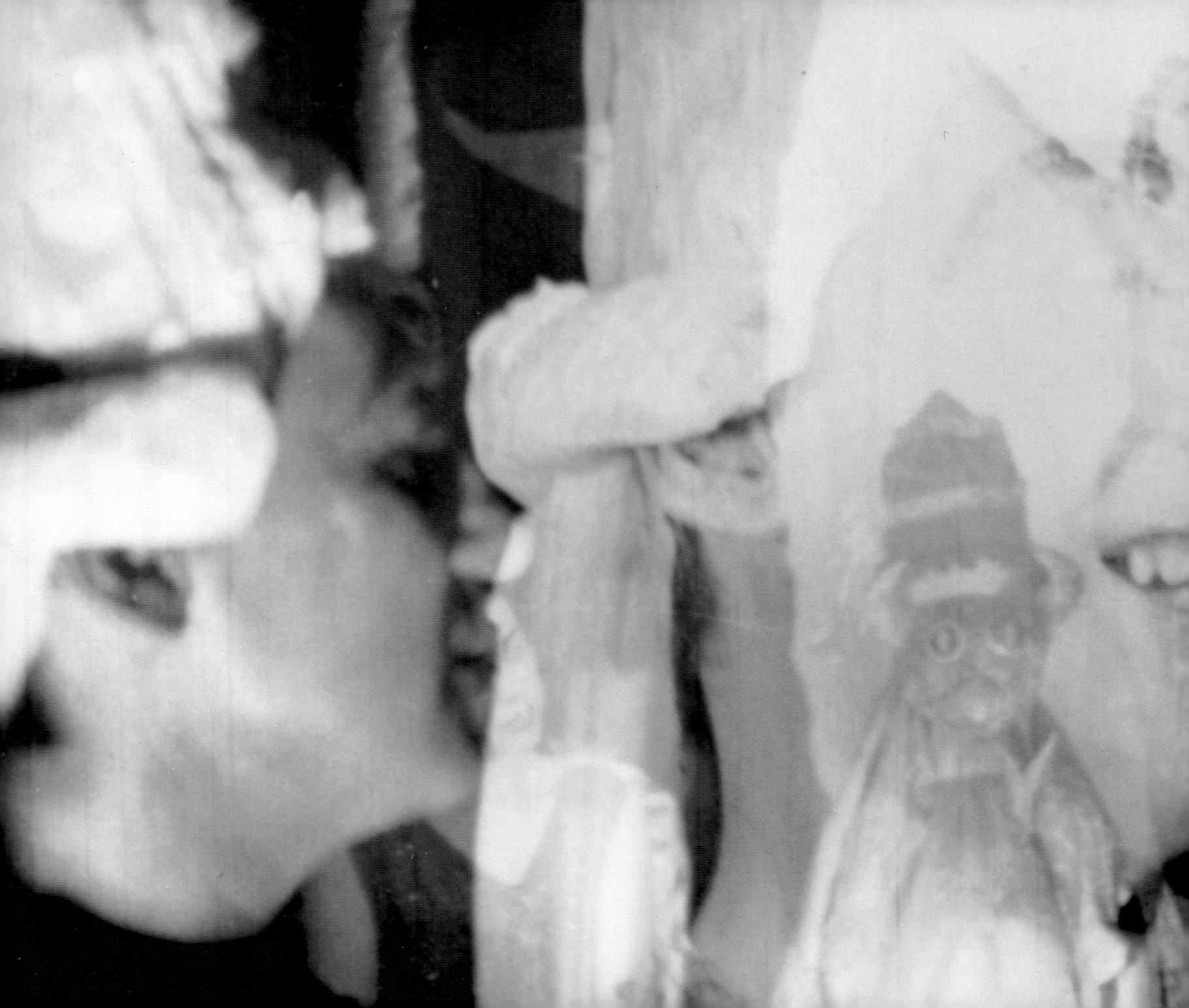

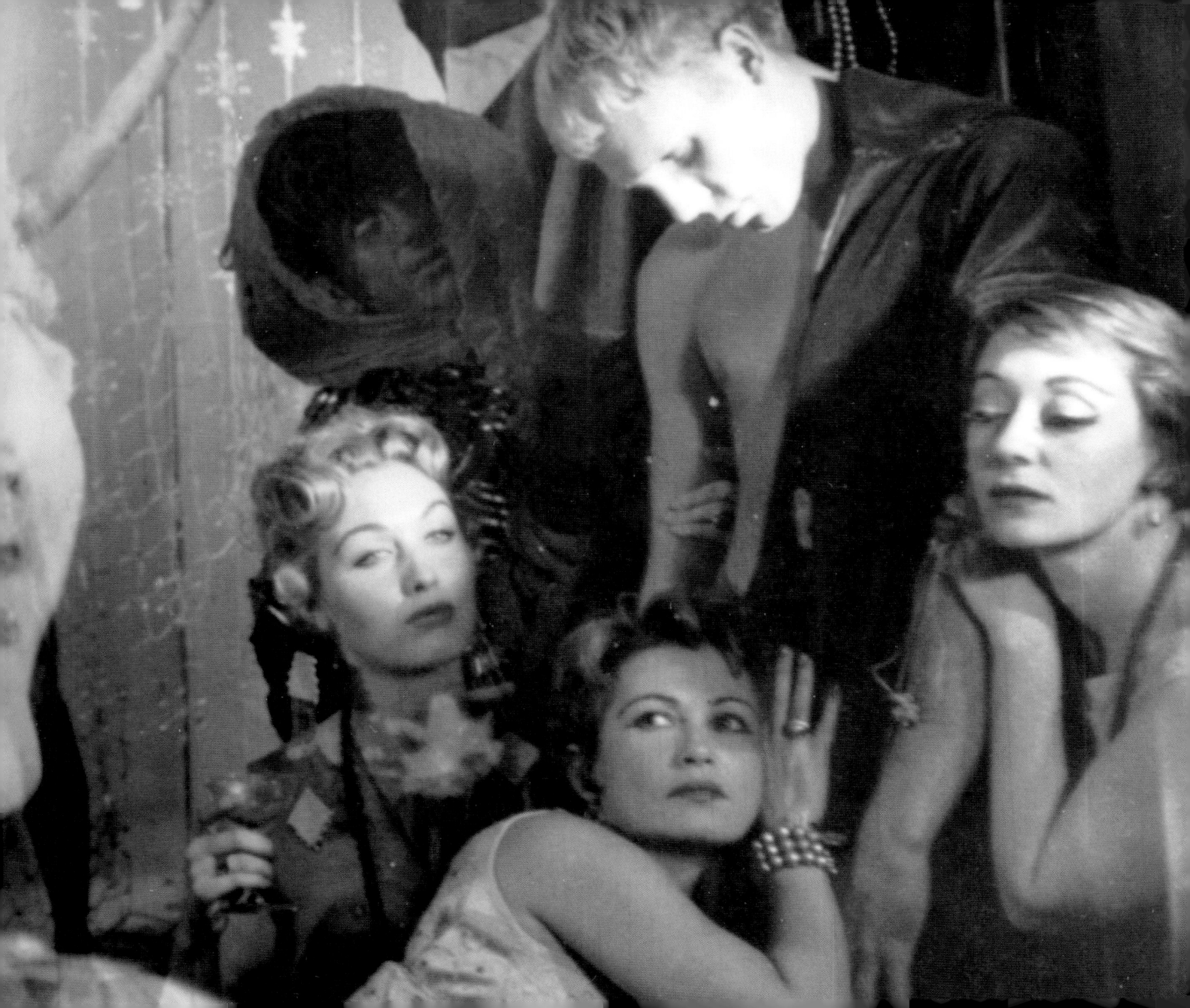

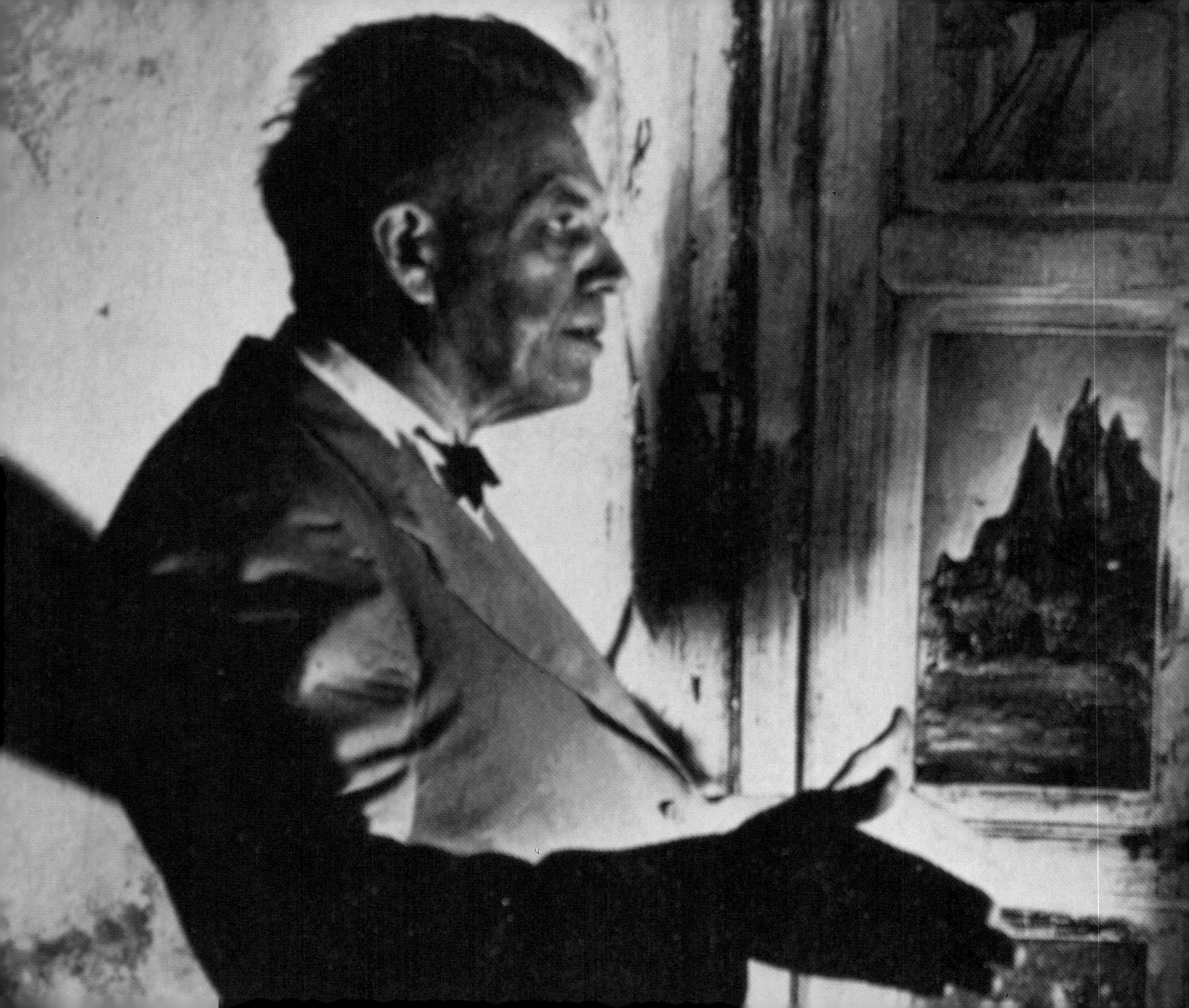

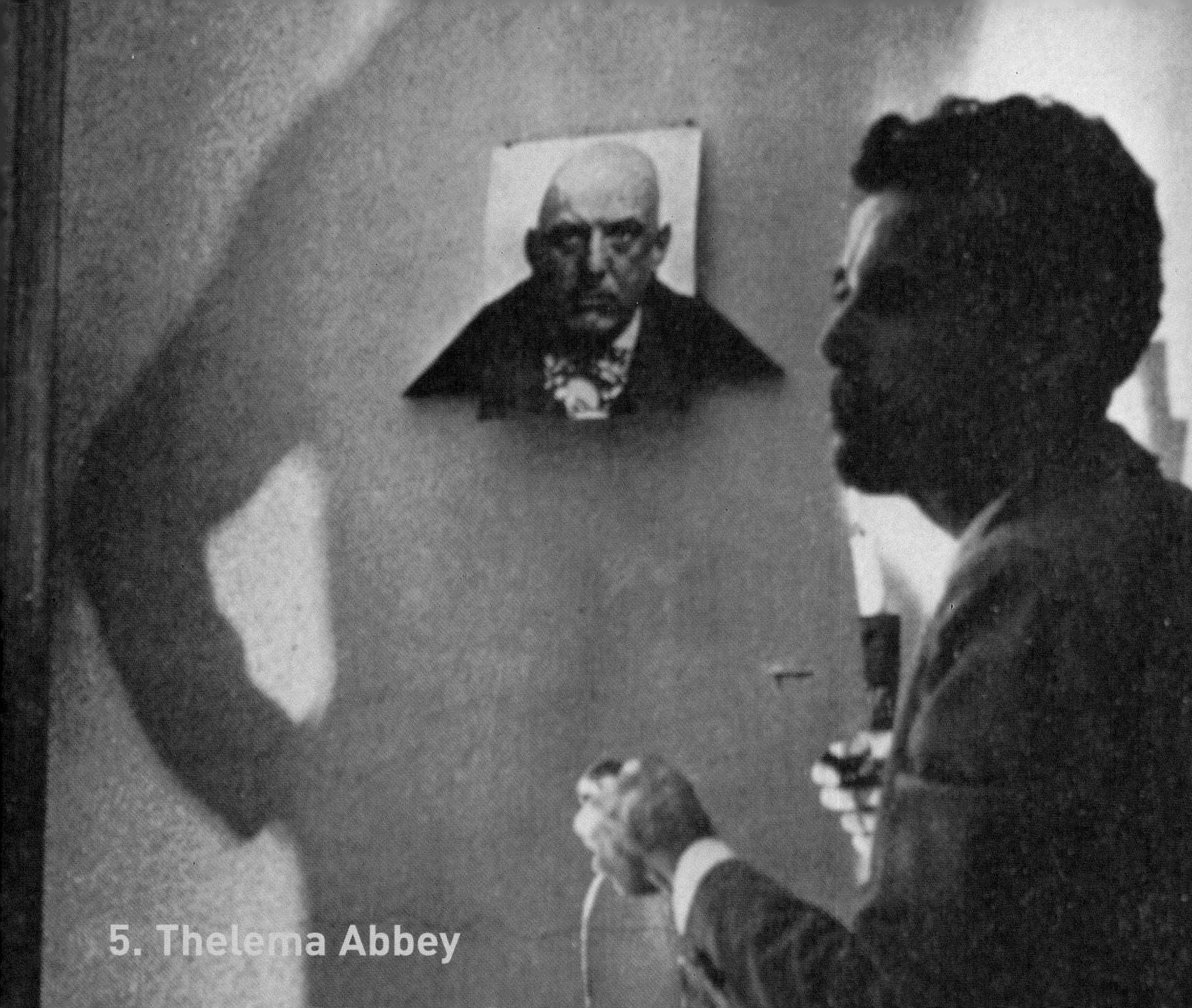

5. Thelema Abbey

Anger
C/o Poste Restante
Cefalù — Sicily

15. Oct. 55

My dear Henri,

I hope that the situation is well at the moment for you at the
Cinematheque.

I've been very ill lately, with rheumatic fever, but now after two weeks
under medication, I feel a bit better.

I came to this little village, hoping to find traces of the English
magician, Aleister Crowley, who lived here in 1920. It was Crowley who had
inspired the Ingram film "The Magician." So I found Crowley's villa,
abandoned for 30 years. Mussolini's police drove Crowley out of Sicily in
1923, and all the symbolic frescoes in the villa were covered with a coat
of whitewash. I gained permission to work in the villa, and I've found all
the frescoes almost intact, under the coat of whitewash. It is a very good
subject for a film shot in color, but firstly I must take photos to sell in
England, where "Crowley, the black sorcerer" is still famous.

I thought of making a "reconstruction" of a "black magic ceremony" in the
photos. To make these photos, it would be very useful for me to have the
costume of the sorcerer used in "Enfants du Paradis" — the blue velvet robe
with the word "ABRA." If you can lend the costume to me for one month only,
I would be very grateful. It would be very easy for me to add red velvet
ribbons and a mask, in a way that the costume doesn't appear the same.
What's more, you can rest assured that I will take utmost care of the
costume. It would be good to send it in a package marked "CLOTHING —
VESTITI" — Joyce could send it I think. My address is: ANGER
C/o POSTE RESTANTE
CEFALÙ — SICILY

Another thing, I could make use of the robes of Maë Murray, Clara Bow and
Barbara La Marr at the Cinematheque.

Best wishes,
Kenneth A.

La 2ème page
~~de la~~
manque

Anger
℅ Poste Restante
Cefalù – Sicilie
15. Oct. 55

Mon cher Henri,

J'espere que la situation est bien en ce moment pour vous et la Cinémathèque.

J'étais très malade ce dernier temps, avec de la fièvre rheumatique, mais maintenant après deux semaines de soins du médecin, je me semble un peu mieux.

J'ai venu dans cette petite village, esperant de trouver des traces du magicien Anglais, Aleister Crowley, qui a habité ici en 1920. C'était Crowley qui a inspiré le film d'Ingram "The Magician". Alors j'ai trouvé le villa de Crowley, abandonné il y a 30 ans. Crowley fut chassé de la Sicilie en 1923 par la police de Mussolini, et tous les fresques symboliques dans le villa était couvert d'une couche de peinture blanche. J'ai gagné permission de travailler dans le villa, et j'ai trouvé tous les fresques presque intact, sous la couche de peinture blanche. C'est un très bon sujet pour un film en couleurs, mais 1rement je dois prend les photos pour vendre en Angleterre, où "Crowley, le sorcier noir" est toujours fameux.

2.

J'ai pensé de faire dans les photos un "reconstruction" d'un "Ceremonie de la Magie Noir". Pour faire ces photos, il serait très utile a moi d'avoir le costume du sorcier utilisé dans "Enfants du Paradis" – le robe blu velours avec le mot "ABRA". Si vous pouvait prêter le costume a moi pour un mois seulement, je serais très reconnaisant. Serait très facile pour moi de ajoute les rubans en velours rouge et un masque, d'un façon que le costume ne paraît le meme. De plus, vous pouvait être tranquille que je prendrai tous les soins avec le costume. Serait bien de l'envoyer dans un paquet marquée "VETEMENTS - VESTITI" – Joyce pouvait l'envoyer je crois. Mon adress est:

ANGER
℅ POSTE RESTANTE
CEFALÙ - SICILYE.

Autre chose, je pouvais faire don de les robes du Maé Murray, Clara Bow + Barbara la Marr à la Cinémathèque, si ça serait interessant pour vous.

Bien à vous
Kenneth
A.

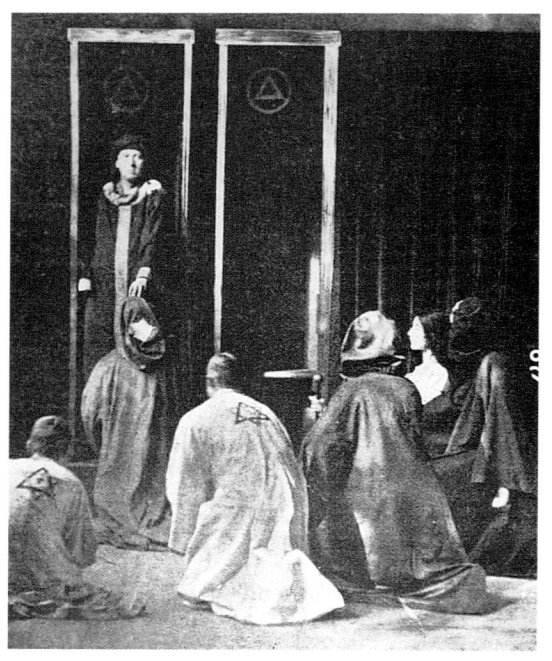

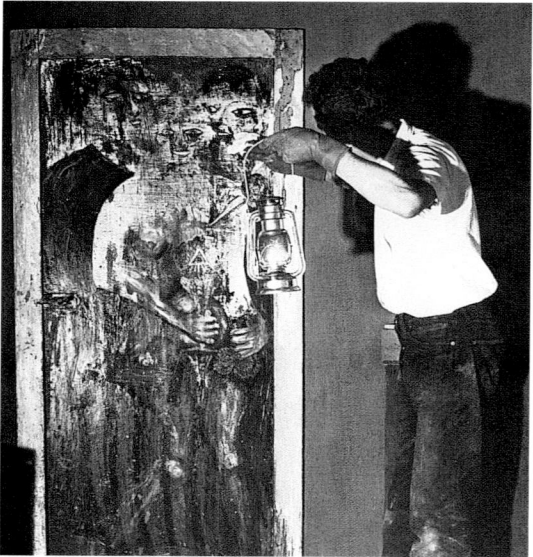

stimulated the re-emergence of magic (primarily amidst the upper classes of Victorian society). The motive for incorporating the ancient Rosicrucian tradition and new rituals into Freemasonry had been to bring renewed vitality into rites which had lost their original meaning and vigor in a maze of lifeless symbolism. As a recent Rosicrucian address states:

> We must remember that Rosicrucianism itself was "no new thing" but only a revival of still earlier forms of Initiation, and was a lineal descendant of the Philosophies of the Chaldean Magi, of the Egyptian priests, of the Neo-Platonists, of the Hermetists of Alexandria, of the Jewish Kabbalists and of Christian Kabbalists such as Raymond Lully and Pico della Mirandola. The nominal Founder of our Society – Christian Rosencreuz, did not invent, at least in our modern sense of the word, the doctrines he promulgated, and which we should now study. It is narrated that he journeyed to Arabia, to Palestine, to Egypt and to Spain, and in the seats of learning in those countries he found and collected the mystic lore, which was made anew by him into a code of doctrine and knowledge.[4]

But later members of this Lodge would create breakaway movements which were out of keeping with the traditions of Freemasonry and Rosicrucianism. Such a breakaway movement was the Golden Dawn. The Hermetic Order of the Golden Dawn was a quasi-masonic organization founded in England, whose members studied comparative religions. It was organized into a Masonic system of degrees and inner circles complete with elaborate rituals with colorful ceremonial robes, incense and dramatic oaths. One theory was that Lucifer was the light-bearing god (as the morphology of the name attests), not the devil of conventional Christianity. The Golden Dawn lacked the sexual bias of Freemasonry by admitting female members, amongst whom was Constance Wilde, Oscar's wife; other prominent members included Aubrey Beardsley, Florence Farr (Director of the Abbey Theater and close friend of Bernard Shaw), Bram Stoker (author of *Dracula*), and Sir Gerald Kelly (Crowley's first wife was his sister Rose), President of the Royal Academy; all of whom studied the Kabbalah.

Crowley joined The Hermetic Order of the Golden Dawn in 1898 while still an undergraduate at Cambridge. His progress through the preliminary grades was sure and swift, but he was bluntly refused entry for the grade of Adept because of his "unsavoury reputation" (promiscuity and bisexuality bothered Yeats, not to mention his experimentation with drugs). His mentor initiated him in the Paris Temple of the Order, which sparked off the fierce eruptions that brought about the speedy dissolution of the Golden Dawn. When Crowley established his own Lodge he quickly shed the amateur techniques of the cult and began in earnest the practice of his own magic in a new and effective form. Crowley stated:

> In my third year at Cambridge, I devoted myself consciously to the Great Work, understanding thereby the Work of becoming a Spiritual Being free from the constraints, accidents, and deceptions of material existence. I found myself at a loss to designate my

Top: Aleister Crowley conducting the *Rite of Saturn* in Thelema Abbey, 1910
Bottom: Kenneth Anger restoring the Babalon door at Thelema Abbey, 1955

work, just as H. P. Blavatsky some years earlier. "Theosophy," "Spiritualism," "Occultism," "Mysticism," all involved undesirable connotations. I chose therefore the name "Magick" as essentially the most sublime, and actually the most discredited, of all the available terms.[5]

In his poetry and theoretical writings, Crowley had filtered the sexual psychology of Freud through the Jungian concept of collective unconscious and symbolism, deriving his occult theories from Judeo-Christian mysticism of the Rosicrucians, the Freemasons, and his interpretations of the Kabbalah. He was also to rediscover the mythological parallels between ancient cultures, and the symbols which transcend religions and cultures: emblems of a Jungian (pan-cultural) collective consciousness. As a wealthy young heir, Crowley traveled the globe from Mexico to China, Africa and the Middle East, accumulating knowledge of diverse cults and religions, publishing, in addition to poetry, comprehensive studies and guides on everything from astrology, numerology and tarot to tantric sex, yoga, I Ching and Sufism.

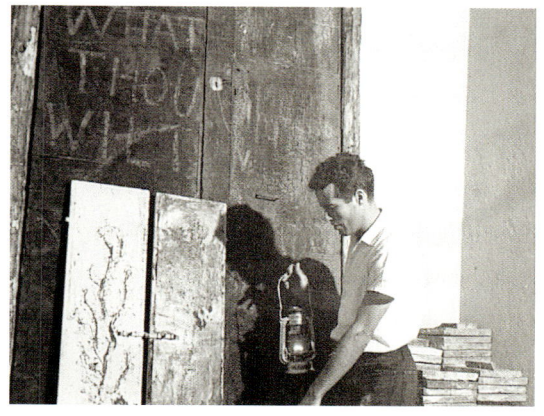

Although he wrote some of the most influential and widely read books on alternative religion of recent times, Crowley's notoriety was based on his use of sexuality as a sacramental ritual. His studies concentrated on all forms of sexual illuminism and by 1912, he had reached the Ninth Grade of a clandestine Lodge in Berlin – Ordo Templi Orientis – concerned specifically with sexual magick. Crowley was sought out by the Ordo Templi Orientis to head its British division, for whom he wrote *Gnostic Mass* in 1913, as well as the *Manifesto of the O.T.O..* Invoking Babalon, the initiate graduated to the highest degrees in which the sexual act took the central place in the ceremony. By the time Crowley had settled into Thelema Abbey, he was treading in the medieval footsteps of Landulf of Capua, the Klingsor of the anti-Grail who dominated all spirits, whether good or evil, from his eyrie in castle Merveille.[6] And it was on a nocturnal visit to the site of Klingsor's castle at Kalot Enbolot that Crowley first invoked the Anti-Christ into manifestation, the Beast of the Revelation.[7] Reference to the Grail is made in *Gnostic Mass*.

Aleister Crowley's own Lodge, the Argentinum Astrum (Silver Star), remains closely affiliated with the O.T.O., both following the Law of Thelema. It was named after the ultimate level of the tripartite structure of the Golden Dawn: The First Order (or Golden Dawn itself), the Second Order (the order of the Rosy Cross) and finally, the Argentinum Astrum, to which no human could aspire. Crowley's extensive use of hermetic symbols (as outlined in *The Book of the Law*, *Magick in Theory and Practice*, *777 – Book of Correspondences*, etc.), were referenced as if a series of tarot cards flashed at the reader, each evoking a specific association. The theology of Thelema postulates all manifested existence arising from the interaction of two cosmic principles: the infinitely extended, all-pervading space-time continuum; and the atomic, individually expressed "principle of life and wisdom." The interplay of these principles gives rise to the principle of consciousness which governs

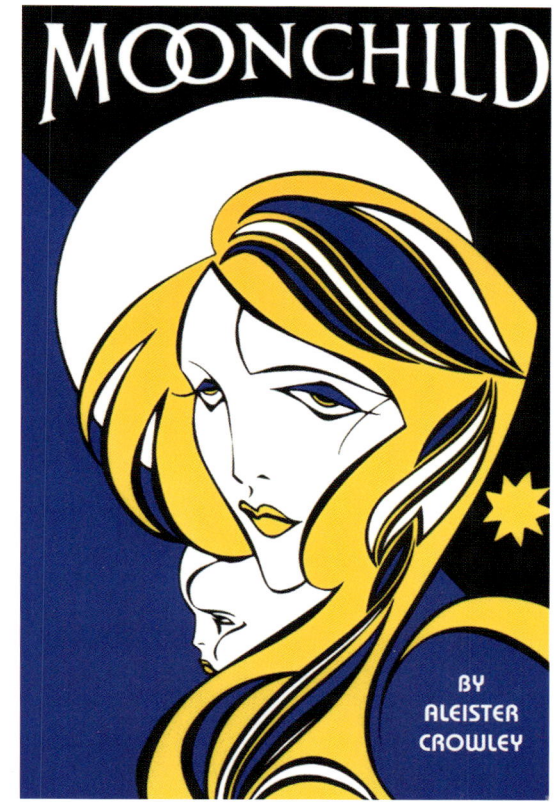

Top: Kenneth Anger uncovering the frescos, 1955
Bottom: cover of Aleister Crowley's book *Moonchild*, 1929

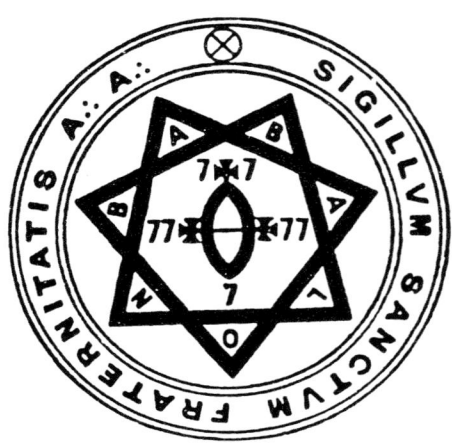

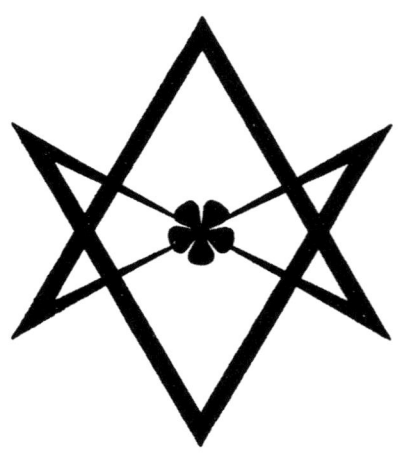

existence. In *The Book of the Law*, the divine principles are personified by a trinity of ancient Egyptian Divinities: Nuit, the Goddess of Infinite Space; Hadit, the Winged Serpent of Light; and Ra-Hoor-Khuit (Horus), the Solar, Hawk-Headed Lord of the Cosmos, who become personages and references in Anger's later work – specifically *Invocation of My Demon Brother* and *Lucifer Rising*. The Thelemic theological system utilizes the divinities of various cultures and religions as personifications of specific divine, archetypal and cosmic forces. Thelemic doctrine holds that all the diverse religions of humanity are grounded in universal truths; and the study of comparative religion is an important discipline for many Thelemites.

Anger had researched Crowley independently from an early age, but he also had a link to the Beast himself through Jack (John) Parsons, a ground-breaking scientist and co-founder of the Jet Propulsion Laboratory in Pasadena, California who was to attain leadership status of the Agape Lodge of the O.T.O. in the mid 1940s. Parsons befriended actress Jane Wolfe who had lived at Thelema Abbey in Cefalù before returning to California after their eviction by Mussolini. Parsons had also become partners with L. Ron Hubbard, the founder of Hollywood's Church of Scientology (Parson's was so taken with Hubbard he forgot his obligation and violated his oath to the Order, revealing to Hubbard the secret grades of the O.T.O.). According to his own writings and all other reports, Parsons apparently conjured his "magickal partner" Cameron (born Marjorie Cameron), The Scarlet Woman whom he was to marry. She literally arrived after an extensive ritual upon his doorstep. Parsons wrote to Crowley: "I have my elemental! She turned up one night at the conclusion of the Operation, and has been with me since, although she goes back to New York next week. She has red hair and slant green eyes as specified. She is an artist, strong-minded and determined, with strong masculine characteristics and a fanatical independence. If she returns she will be dedicated as I am dedicated!"[8] Cameron, Parson's wife, was Anger's Scarlet Woman a year prior to his *Thelema Abbey* documentary in his film *Inauguration of the Pleasure Dome*. With similar serendipity, she arrived on the set having not met Anger previously, brought by mutual friends, and ended up becoming the most potent figure in the film. The flame-haired Cameron, a poet and artist, was to form a close alliance with Anger, and was embodied in Curtis Harrington's film *Wormwood Star*, 1955, and also appeared in *Night Tide*, 1960.[9] In Parson's collected writings, he provides insight into Crowleyan O.T.O. rituals, and Parson's own dilemma pursuing Thelema and conquering the Abyss. He outlines both *The Book Of Babalon* and *The Book Of Antichrist (The Black Pilgrimage)*, detailing specific rituals. The grueling invocation to conjure his "elemental" (Cameron) within the Babalon Working, for instance, lasted several days. Jack Parsons was tragically killed in an explosion with volatile substances in his garage in Pasadena. After the death of her husband, and having become friends, Anger lived with Cameron for a period. For both, magick was integral to their respective life-works. He discussed Magick in relation to his films:

Magick is a word that has been lost and it needs to be found again. For primitive man, magick was so much a part of daily experience that it was simply a fact of life. Later it was displaced – partly by science – but as far as I'm concerned it still exists. As an artist I can believe what I want. I agree with Crowley's definition that magick is the science of causing change, and whatever causes change is therefore an act of magick. But formal knowledge of magick is not necessary to appreciate my work. My films are not an appeal to the intellect. They are an appeal to the level of dream logic and to the emotions.[10]

Having filmed the closely-knit group of Thelemites at Samson De Brier's house in Hollywood, Anger had every reason to travel to the Abbey himself to discover what remained. This project was at once a pilgrimage, a commissioned job (for *Picture Post*) and first hand contact with Crowley's legacy. Recently, Kenneth Anger discussed the current state of Crowley's Abbey:

> Thelema Abbey has been abandoned by its owners, as a large sports stadium has been built directly in front of it by the city of Cefalù, destroying the view and rendering it useless. It is in an advanced state of decay, without protection so that doors and shutters have been stolen; the walls with the Crowley murals I uncovered in 1955 are still there.[11]

An Italian documentary crew is making a film about Kenneth Anger and his travels for Italian television (titled *Anger IO*) for which Anger returned to Sicily in the summer of 2004 to do the commentary.

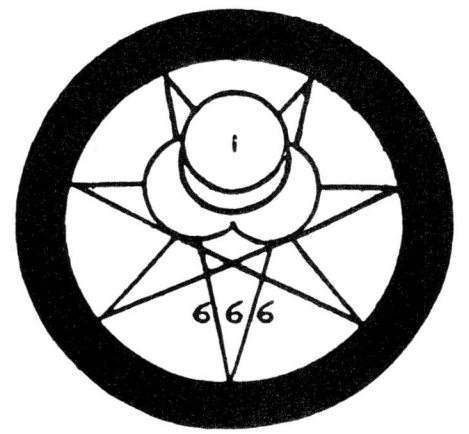

Astrum Argentinum symbols,
designed by Aleister Crowley

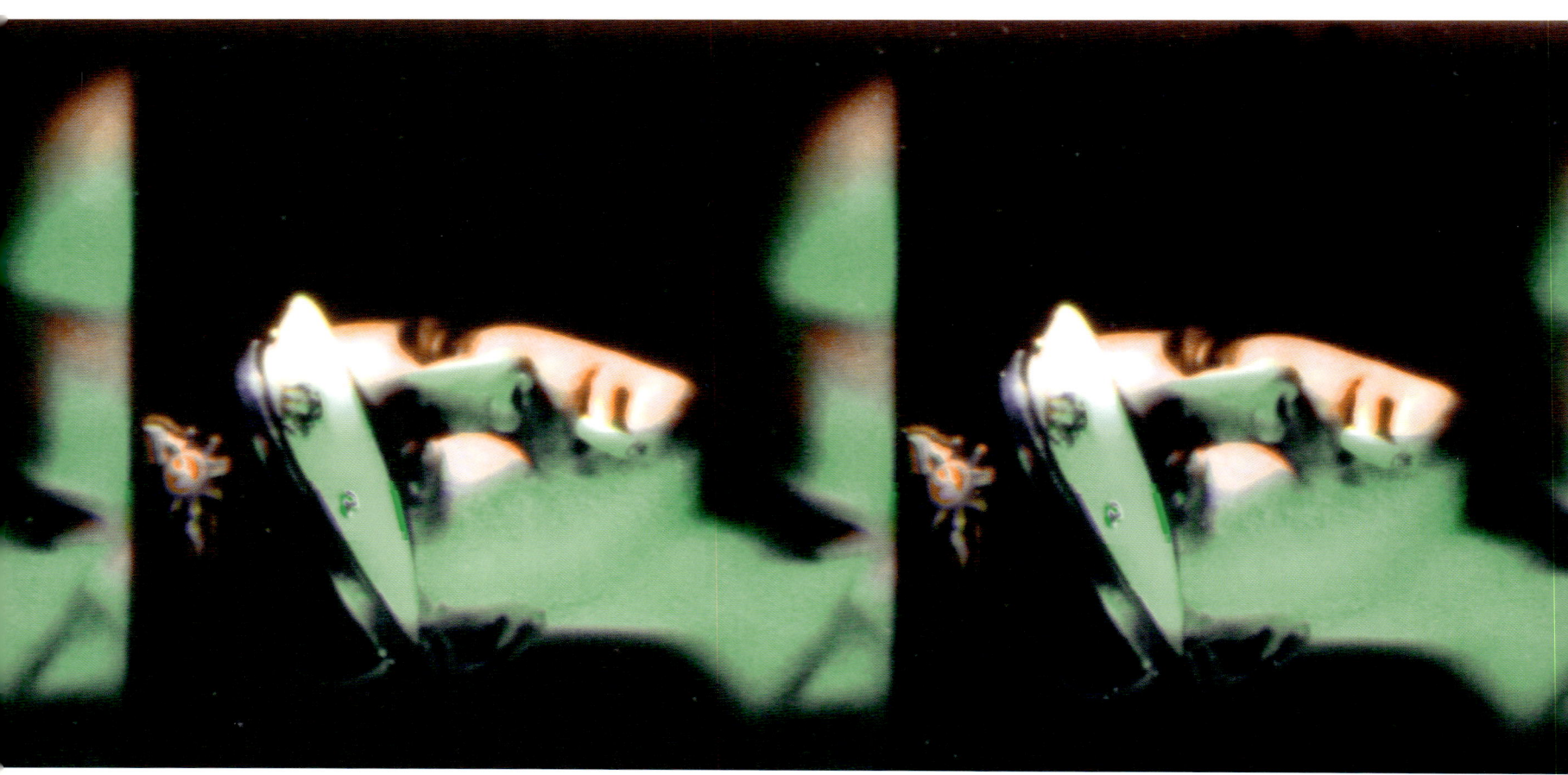

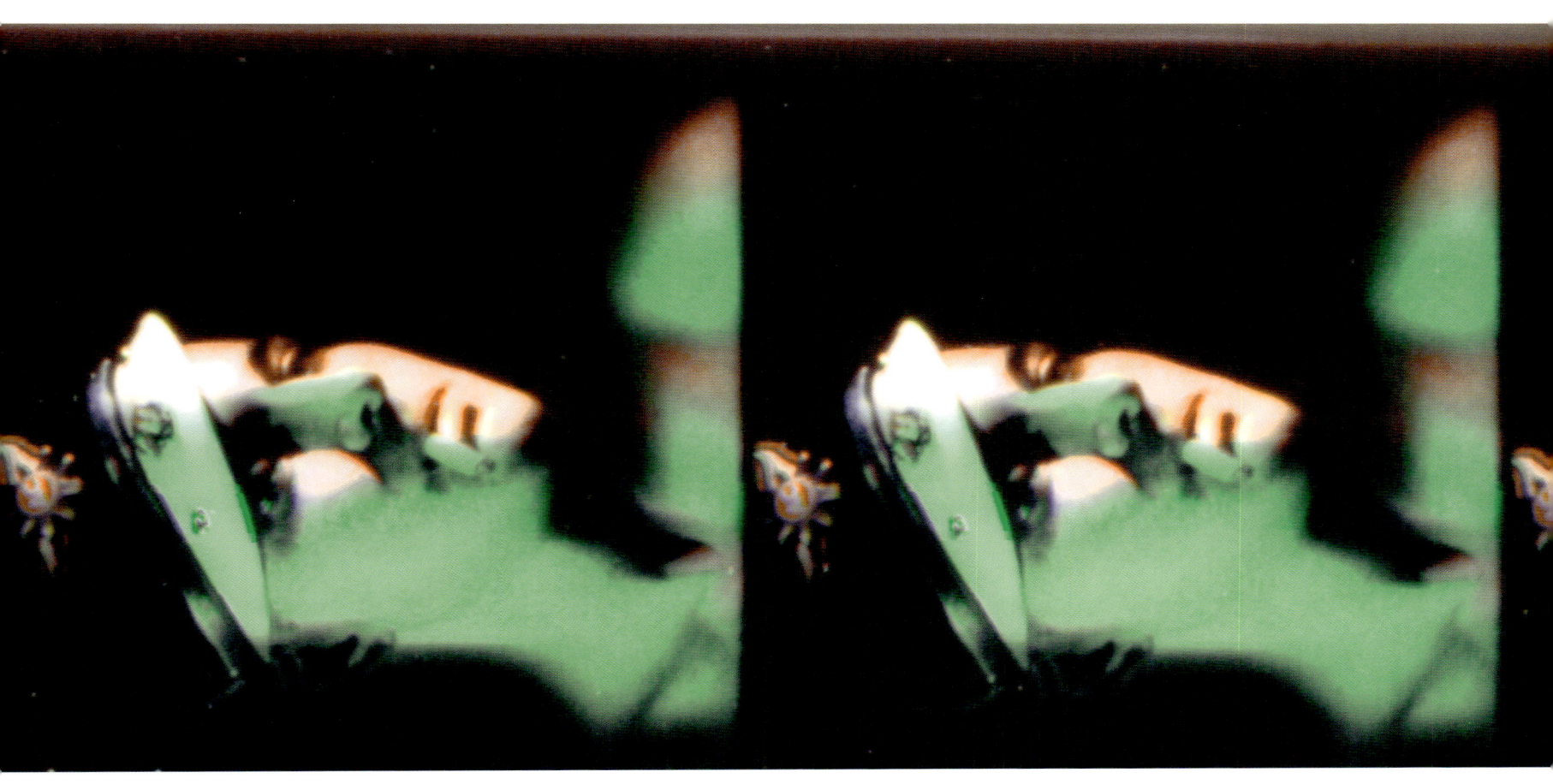

6. Scorpio Rising

At the end of the 1950s, Anger was living in Paris, where, to great success, he had published the French version of *Hollywood Babylon* in 1959. However, he did not succeed in finding producers who would help him realize his major European film projects, specifically *Maldoror*, and so with Stan Brakhage's encouragement, he decided to return to the United States.

In the letters reproduced here, Anger is in correspondence with Henri Langlois and Mary Meerson from the Cinémathèque Française, dicussing Hollywood memorabilia that he had bought for the archive. Anger's double-edged interest in the golden years of Tinseltown, as depicted in *Hollywood Babylon*, also provided the background for his next film, *Scorpio Rising*. One of his best-known projects, *Scorpio* merges Anger's interest in youth culture and popular music, with a subversive use of imagery and innovative editing techniques.

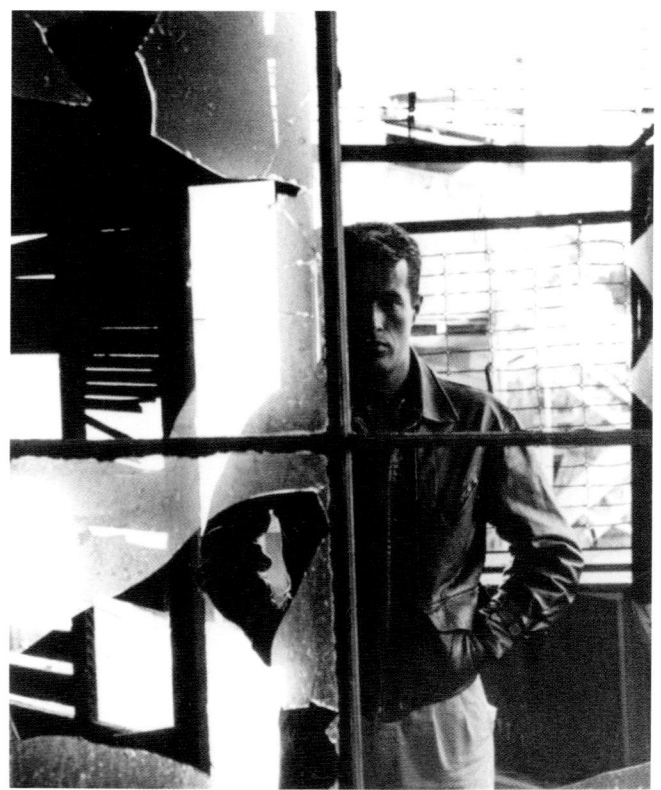

Hollywood 5 April 62

Dear Henri,

Enclosed is a photo of a bust of James Dean that I think may be of
interest to you for your museum. (price and details on the back).
If it does interest you I'll do what's necessary here with my
funds (luckily I have a little at the moment) and the C.F. can
reimburse me later in Paris. (I'll only return when the political
situation calms!!!)

I've already bought for you: a United Artists press book from
1930. That's a gift from me. Also a very rare Fatty Arbuckle
poster. OK? Did you receive the catalog from the Larry Edmunds
Bookshop? They have very interesting things — but expensive. Let me
know if you find things that interest you — as I know the library
director, it is always possible to get a good price from him.

I am in the middle of "negotiating" for the red jacket that Dean
wore in "Rebel" and the blue jeans from "East of Eden" with a
collector — but it's not that easy!

I'll do my best for you here "outside the studio" — with the
private collectors for example — but no doubt, Lotte will do
better than I within the "studios." I hope you liked as much as I
did, the photograph, without makeup, taken in a train station, of
our dear Louise [Brooks]

Best wishes to you and Mary Best wishes always,

Kenneth

5957 Barton Avenue
Hollywood 38 Calif.

April 26 62

Dearest Mary,

I was very happy to have seen Henri here at last in Hollywood,
though I could have been more help in showing him around if he had
allowed a few more days here! As it was, luck was with him and he
managed to see quite a few interesting people — from Evelyn Brent
to Mae West — for such a short visit. He also practically "bought
out" the cinema collection of Larry Edmund's bookshop — though the
amount of money involved is quite a lot, I think it is an
excellent thing as in another year or so everything would have
been snatched up by the Sol Lesser Museum or the University of
California. I was so pleased to have found for the Cinémathèque
the program for "Birth of a Nation" which you should have
received, as well as the other film programs I sent you before,
the United Artists 1930 press-book, etc etc. Also I bought with my
own money a rare press-book for Theda Bara's "Salomé," a Fatty
Arbuckle poster which Henri is carrying back on the plane, and 50
copies of sheet music including the theme song from Murnau's "4
Devils", Griffith's "Woman of the Pavements," and early musicals.
These I have shipped off to you, with another package of film
books.

Enclosed is a Scorpio year book for you dearest Mary, and for
Henri. I have "Scorpio Rising" in my sign, Verseau — which would
explain our affinity! I miss you dear, very much — you must plan a
visit here, too — all my love as always, your own

Kenneth

c/o Menken
62 Montague St.
Brooklyn 1, NY
USA

My dear Henri,

Enclosed is the cutting from the New York Times today of the death
of Tod Browning. I hope that the Cinémathèque could eventually make
him a good "homage." I've been in New York for some time —
Hollywood has finally bored me. That's nothing new. I met Carlos
here.[2] He told me that the hundred dollars that you gave him before
leaving New York was for him, not for me. Curious, isn't it? At
any rate, don't worry, I'm not in great need for the moment.
Anyway it's hard. I've started a film here in color, on the cult
of the motorcyclist. But not at all "The Wild One"!!

Tell Mary that I am finally in the middle of doing a new film, she
will be pleased.

I miss you all,

Warm wishes,

Kenneth

The Dead

Stan Brakhage[1]

In 1958 Stan Brakhage visited Kenneth Anger in Paris where he filmed his silent black and white film *The Dead*, 1960. The main location was the graveyard of Père Lachaise, on the Seine, with the film including images of Anger.

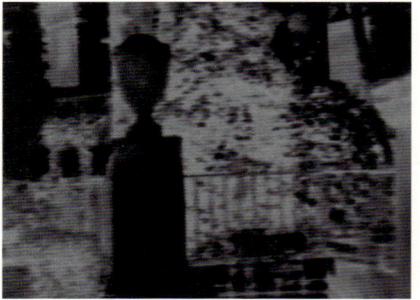

I used material only shot in Paris because that was a total world of something that, if I'd leave it long enough until it impinged on me directly in life, would have a total form of its own.... I had to find, realize re *The Dead* that somehow all images of death or all concepts of it are structured here in life.

... I had no idea at the time of shooting that Kenneth Anger, as an image, would be used in *The Dead*. I was running out the end of a reel, which I wanted to get out of the camera so I could put in the color film for doing the shots of the Seine. So I said, "Well, I have no picture of you, still or otherwise." We were sitting in a café; so I took the image of Kenneth. It was only when I relooked at that footage that I realized that one level of what I meant by *The Dead* was how I saw Kenneth and what he was encased in. I saw him as a concept. Seeing him as one of the dead. I had great concern and care and love for him at that moment. He was years without working, trapped by concepts of the nineteenth century with no way to break out, almost a destroyed man, and yet still living... that was the important thing. All the rest of the people in *The Dead* – are dead. They're the walking dead; but he was a living dead. So he became my double in a sense – my "stand-in," you might say. He was the image that was most immediately available for me to cast out there as [a] statement: "Do you want this?... Do you want to be trapped by all those symbols?... Do you want to be trapped six ways sideways by concepts that are ahead of where you actually are?" And then my answer was: "No!"

Then I could structure *The Dead* by way of the concept of the future as that through which we can't live. When we're living through it it's different from the concept of it. It's comparable to how you can't live through death. So the question becomes one of all that is pitched out of life; how the walking dead come to be that; and how what is sculpted in stone becomes concept of what is sculpted out of stone; and how the living people do relate to that, and how even trees, shaped that way and so ordered and structured, become living dead and like the walking dead, who are people so dead on their feet that you can't even use the word "living" in relationship to them... well, not Kenneth. He was shining with all that beauty and concern with life; and yet he was trapped six ways sideways by forms he had pitched ahead of himself – all that he wanted to do (such as film *Maldoror*) and could not find the means or the money to do. This was intensely painful to me. I would have given anything to have found a way for him to do what he wanted, not only to see *Maldoror* done by Kenneth Anger, or maybe not even foremost for that reason, but to let Kenneth have a way to accomplish it so that he could have gotten through it and could have gone on. He was ultimately defeated. There's new hope for Kenneth now, because he did escape from that trap which *Maldoror* posed for him, and he is back in the United States and has a new film in progress.

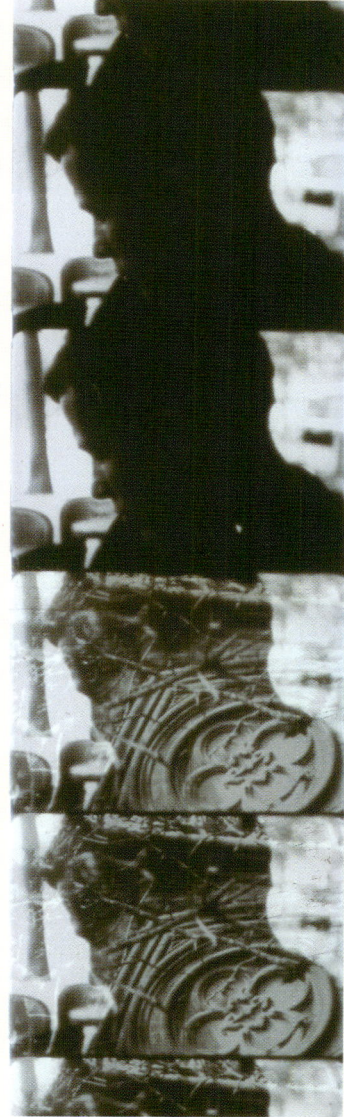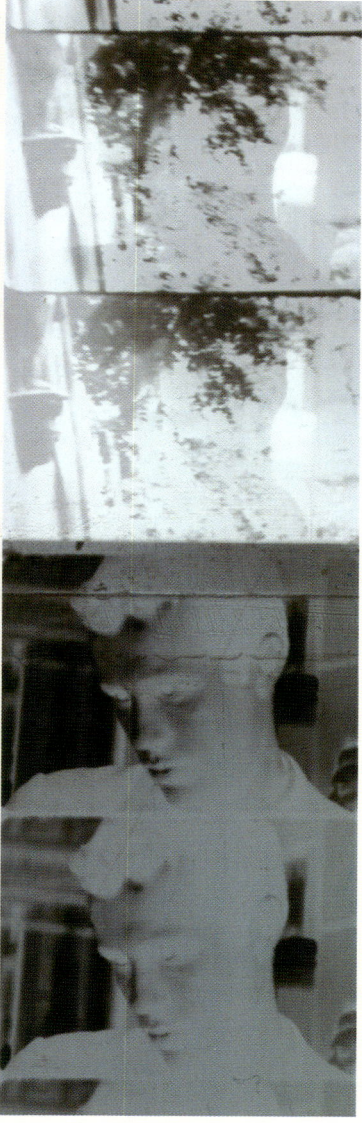

Stan Brakhage, *The Dead*, 1960,
courtesy of the Estate of Stan Brakhage and Fred Camper,
www.fredcamper.com

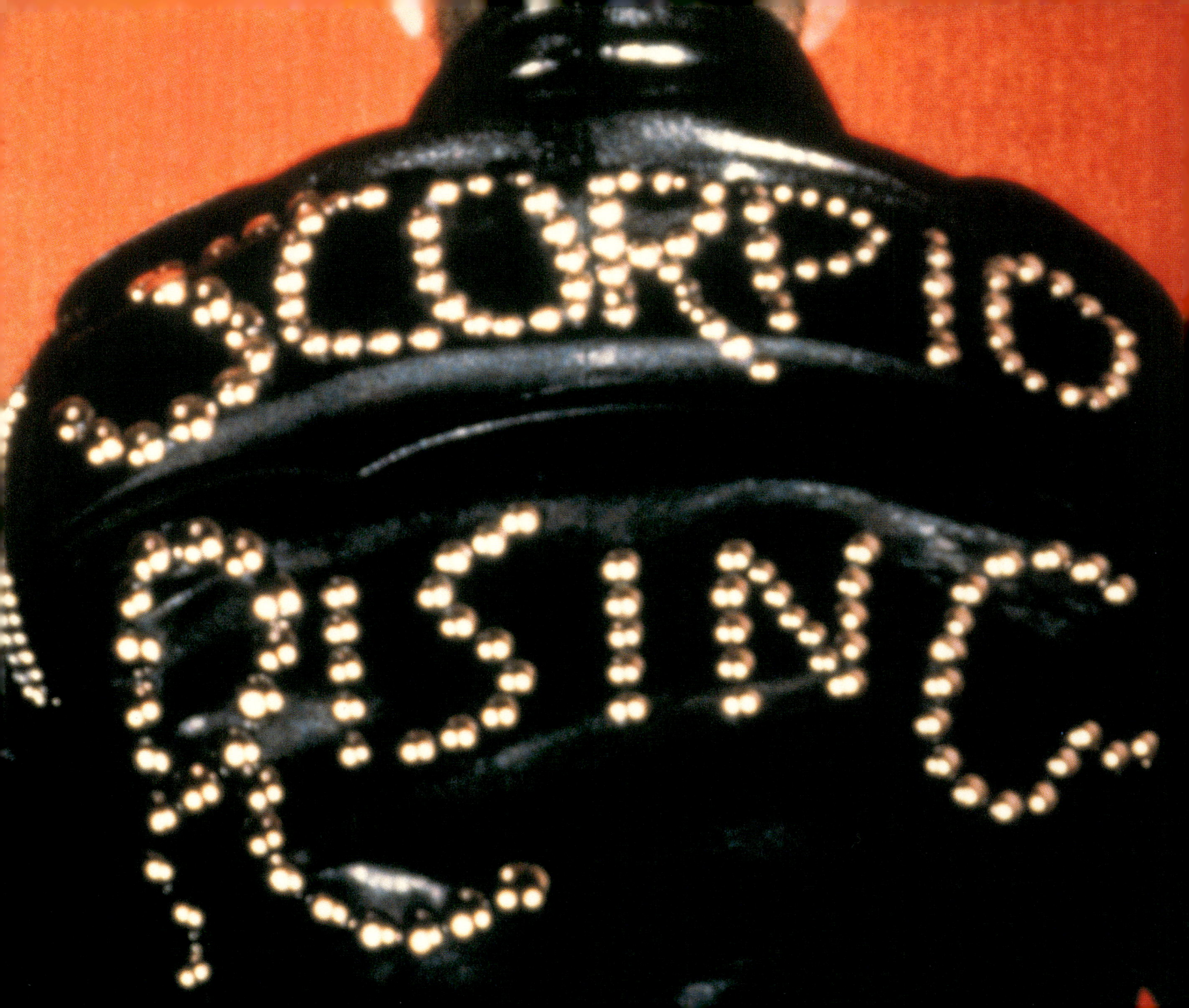

Scorpio Rising

1963

29 minutes

16 mm, color, Ektachrome ER

Music by Ricky Nelson, Little Peggy March, The Angels, Bobby Vinton, Elvis Presley, Ray Charles, The Crystals, The Ran-Dells, Kris Jensen, Claudine Clark, Gene McDaniels, The Surfaris

What *Scorpio* represents is me cluing in to popular American culture after having been away for eight years, because I had been living in France for that long. When I came back, I spent the first part of the summer of 1962 at Coney Island on the beach under the boardwalk. The kids had their little transistors, and had them on. It's one of the things that I call a magical happening, the way it worked out, because every single song that I used in *Scorpio* came out at the time that I made the film. For instance, "Blue Velvet," which I use for the "dressing adagio" in *Scorpio*. I was in the final week, where I had to get the track re-recorded and I wanted something slower for this part. Bang, there it was out just on time. And it was just like it was made for the picture, or the picture was made for it – a perfect marriage, because it has the blue of the blue jeans. The whole three minute sequence was just made for it.[3]

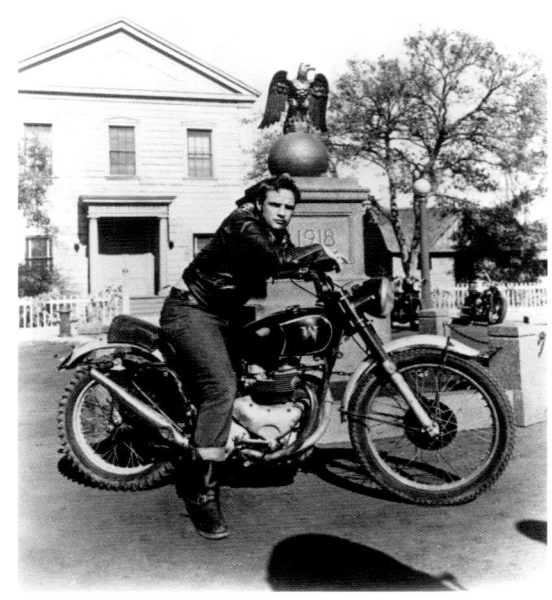

In 1953, the 29 year old Marlon Brando created an unforgettable archetype of the hell-raising motorcyclist in *The Wild One*. Brando originally took on the role as an exploration of a character who stood for a belief in a counterculture revolution, but after the release of the film, he denounced his involvement. His immediate interest was to portray this new type – the hipster – but the production turned it into another moralizing tale of youth gang violence. Brando, of course, became a cult figure, but he was not satisfied with the outcome of the movie: "We started out to do something worthwhile, to explain the psychology of the hipster. But somewhere along the way we went off track... all that we did was show the violence."[4] Due to the film's violent theme it was banned in Britain until 1968. The film in the end takes on the directorial perspective of the law, the police and the authorities, isolating the wild one as a hoodlum gangster.

Despite the film's phenomenal appeal and the mass acceptance of the cyclist as modern anti-hero, the wave of cycle films did not really begin until a full decade later, after Kenneth Anger's *Scorpio Rising*. Little known now, in 1966, Roger Corman and American International Pictures joined forces to create an extravagantly successful exploitation film, *The Wild Angels*. By invitation only, it was the only U.S. entry at the Venice Film Festival that year. With its banal dialogue, mad-cap editing and wild imagery, the film represented the Hell's Angels, which was considered by the Venice jury as a cinematic work of art (unfortunately unaware of its blatant plagiarism and cannibalizing of Anger's *Scorpio Rising*). There was practically no plot, but a band of Hell's Angels-type cyclists, led by Heavenly Blues (Peter Fonda) and "Mike" (Nancy Sinatra), cruising the countryside involving themselves in heavy-drinking, pot smoking, gang fighting and various sorts of criminal activity from violent vandalism to rape. The film was quickly followed up by dozens of lesser imitations. Jack Nicholson riding the highways in *Hell's Angels on Wheels*, Dennis Hopper in *The Glory Stompers*, both 1967. Eventually Fonda, Nicholson and Hopper were united for *Easy Rider*, 1969, a film that would transcend the cycle genre and temporarily redefine the American cinema. All of a sudden the cult of the rebel motorcyclist replaced cowboys as American popular heroes. In a 1966 interview Anger discussed his subjects of *Scorpio Rising*:

Spider: What are the bike riders in *Scorpio* like? Were they a typical motorcycle gang?

Anger: This group was from Brooklyn. There are some superficial similarities to other groups like dress and attitudes, but some go a lot farther. Like, the Hell's Angels go farther than most groups. My group doesn't have a name. They just hang around together. Most of them are married, have a couple of kids already, are in their early twenties. They got married just after high school. Most of them have jobs, either as truck drivers, mechanics, or unloading fish down at Fulton's Fish Market. Most of them have an Italian background. I see the bike boys as the last romantics of this particular culture. They're the last equivalents of the riders of the range, the cowboys. The horse has become a mechanical thing, but it has the appeal that horseback riding has – it's out in

Previous page: leather jacket used in title sequence of *Scorpio Rising*, hand-studded by Kenneth Anger
This page: Marlon Brando in *The Wild One*, 1953, set photograph
Opposite left: "Bruce Byron *walks* to Biker's Halloween Party on Eighth Avenue, New York"

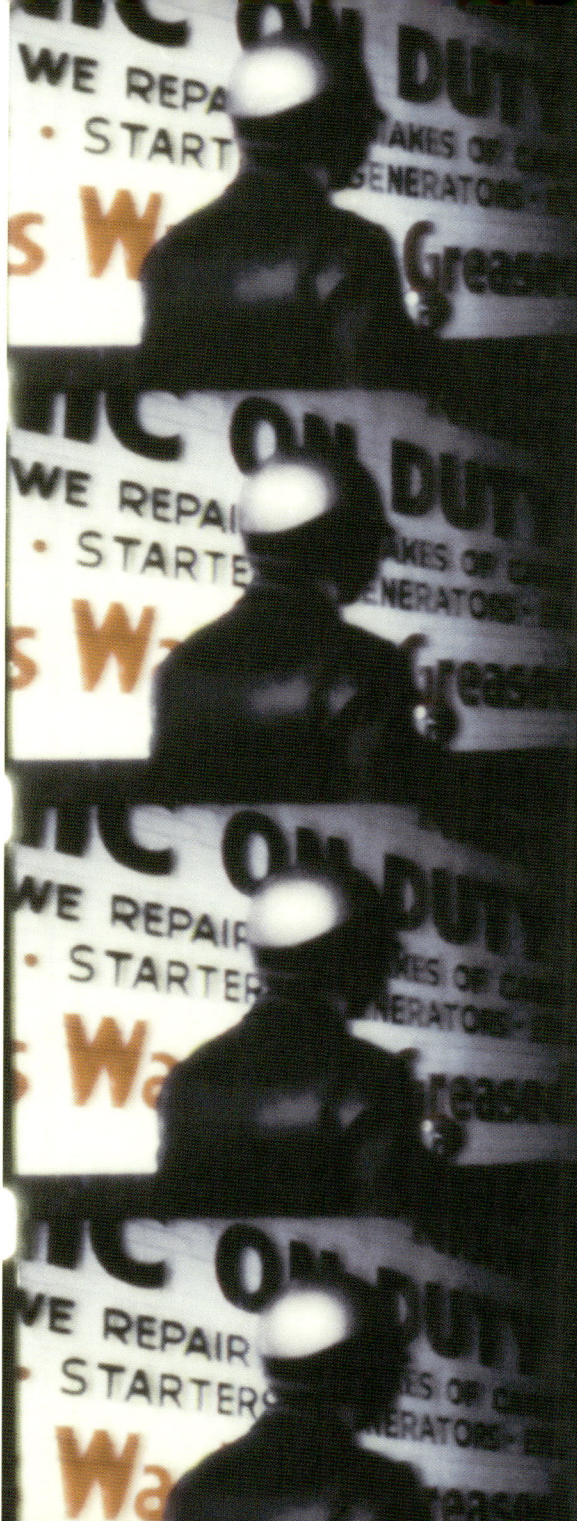
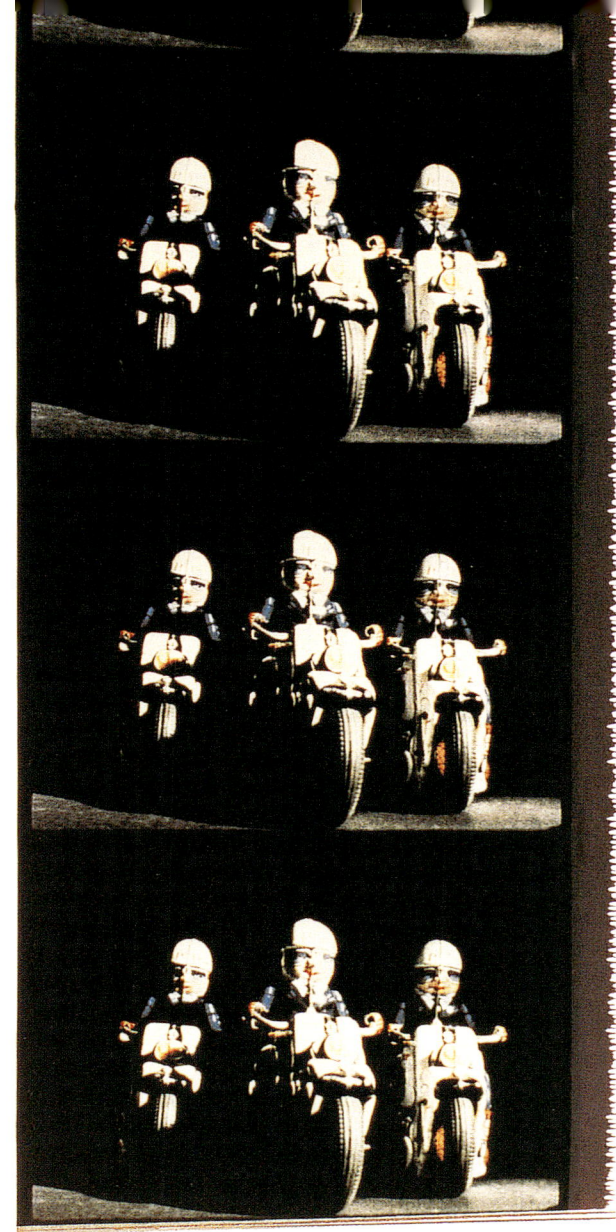

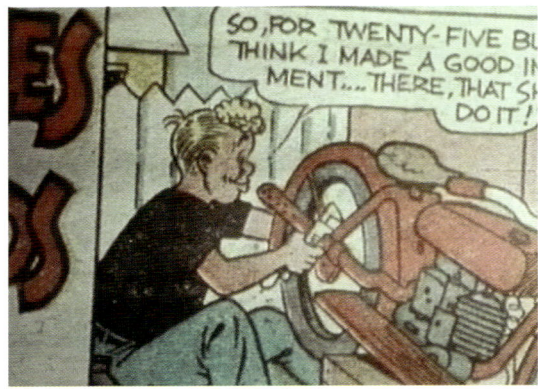

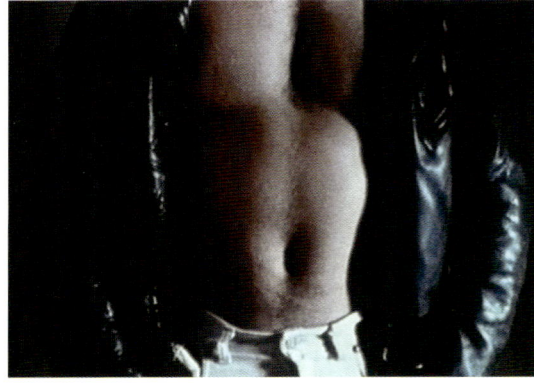

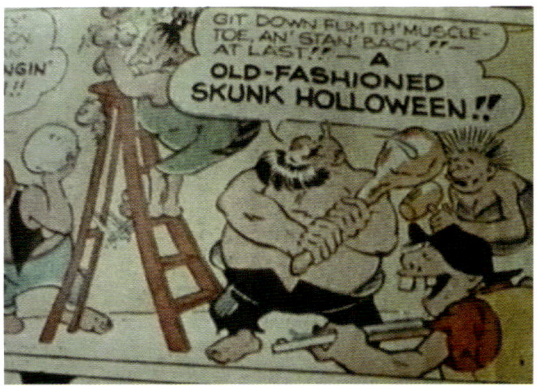

the open air and you're really in contact with the elements and danger. Also, skill is required to ride one and not flip, not go down. There used to be large areas where they could ride without being bugged by cars or bugging cars in return, but now the cars have taken over everything. Groups like the Hell's Angels have so completely got this image going. For instance, I was out with three of them here in North Beach and they didn't even have a bike – they came in a car. But just because they wore their colors, little sleeveless Levi jackets with "Hell's Angels" on them, suddenly we had two patrol wagons with riot dogs surrounding us. Just for three guys! It's like the fuzz were going to put down an insurrection. We managed to split. But now whenever the Angels are recognized they are going to be buffed by the fuzz, and this brings out the worst in them.[5]

Upon his return to America in 1962, Anger had become fascinated with contemporary youth cults. *Scorpio Rising* manifested a certain romantic vision and mythology of the American "barbarian." Filmed in Brooklyn while he was living with colleague filmmakers Marie Menken and Willard Maas, *Scorpio Rising* was edited and completed in San Francisco.[6] To the uninitiated spectator, this film might seem to be merely a warning of a rising tide of anomie and violence.[7] It is certainly an assault upon middle-class American values, including a satire on Hollywood's use of homosexual men as heterosexual icons. However, as well as being a harbinger for a new era (an era of disruption, protest and refusal), the year *Scorpio Rising* was shot, 1962, was, according to astrology, the end of the 2000 year-long Piscean Age and the beginning of the Aquarian Age. For occultists (including Anger) this was interpreted as being the end of a period of Christian domination and the beginning of a period of pagan domination. The film invokes the breaking away from and purging of the old "sin-sickened" age of violence, destruction, and death, leading to resurrection in the new age. Teen culture (pop songs, drug use, motorcycle cultists and adoption of cult icons and symbols) became manifestations of fomenting demonic forces. "A portrait of violence, an exercise in black humor, a document of motorcycle cultists, and one spectacular death wish."[8]

As much as it was an exploration of biker-boy style and the filmic construct, this half hour film encapsulated social rage and a deep distrust of authority. Like Bertolt Brecht before him, or Günther Grass, Anger was one of the first offspring of the post war era to explore cynicism and skepticism of authoritarian values, particularly promulgated by the brain-washing media; and a sense that the populace had to practice a new kind of vigilance, if not open anarchic outrage against those values. Quoting Shakespeare, with the planetary alignments to back him up, Anger put it: "Crabbed age and youth cannot live together: Age is full of grief, youth is full of pleasure."[9] Foreseeing the 1968 student uprisings – a fundamental clash between the generations – Anger commented in 1966:

That's why there is a kind of war going on between the students and the Regents and Administration. That generation has proven that no dialogue is possible. They and the young cool just aren't the same race... the reason the Regents are now so upset is that the only thing the big wheels – the business wheels – want from a college graduate is a replacement part. They want minds that can think about all these electronic problems or run computers, but that's to replace parts, because they always need new ones... I really think there's a subterranean state of war.[10]

Anger was one of the first filmmakers to embody social critique incorporating documentary elements (newsreel footage), and to simulate external violence through a filmic construct. In *Scorpio Rising* the footage of Third Reich rallies, of Hitler, and of the checkers with swastikas, is certainly used for its shock effect, implying the potential fascist postering implicated in hero-worship. Anger took as many taboo emblems and hurled them together; but their juxtaposition with quintessential American icons and the local authorities raised the question of the American government's (and consequentially, Hollywood's and the media's) culpability in the formation of youth cults. These suggestions were made through the montage of images, remaining ambiguous and obliquely suggestive. The objective, almost ethnographic distance to American culture could only have been achieved from having spent the decade of the 1950s in Europe, a timely escape from McCarthy black-listing.

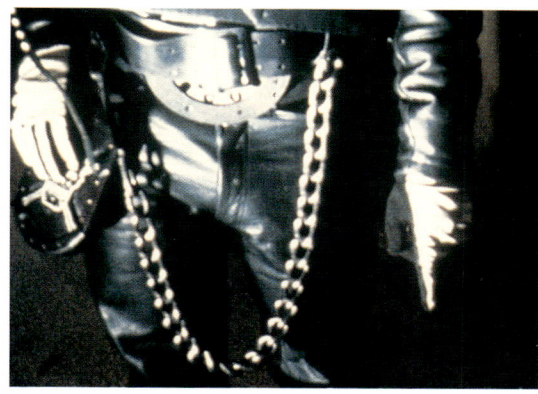

The presence of Third Reich imagery and fascist symbols in *Scorpio Rising* could also perhaps be explained as the film's commentary on mass culture or blind religious following. By juxtaposing images of Hitler and Jesus with popular icons like Marlon Brando, James Dean, Gary Cooper as the sheriff in High Noon, Bela Lugosi as Dracula, and comic book characters with homoerotic subtexts, the film establishes an analogy between media myths and greater historical and religious myths, ironically binding together incongruous rebel leaders. From this perspective, the film relates the adoration of media and religious icons to the violence of fascism, leaders and followers. After readying himself in a room plastered with posters and memorabilia of his cult icons, Scorpio steps out into the night. Shots of his tougher-than-leather black motorcycle boots crossing the Brooklyn sidewalks are inter-cut with footage of the Apostles stepping out to preach the word. The editing of the scene cleverly applies Eisenstein's conflict of directions to evoke a Western-like showdown, and to suggest, tongue in cheek, a union of opposites. The production of off-screen glances and the juxtaposition of images ironically with the lyrics regulates the film's interpretations of popular texts. Through quotation and allusion, the film pulls a host of cultural icons into its own circle of (homosexual) desire. The overall trajectory of this scene depicts the slippage from the witty appropriation of mass cultural identities (Jesus as Leader of the Pack) to the final outbursts of sado-masochistic violence, insinuating the biker's adoption of identities and styles disseminated by the media. Anger treats the degrading rites of initiation administered by such all male groups as fraternities, lodges and the military of his own

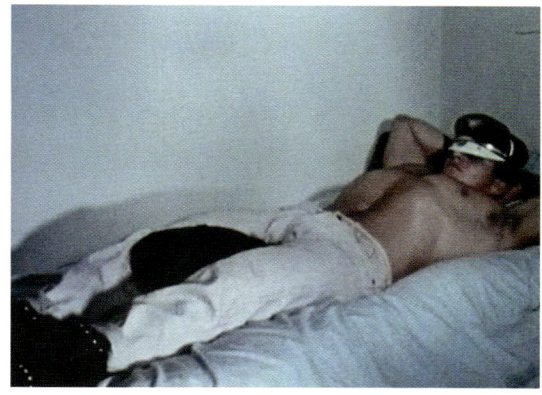

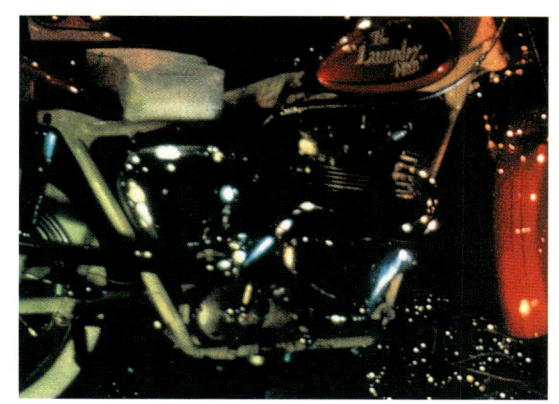

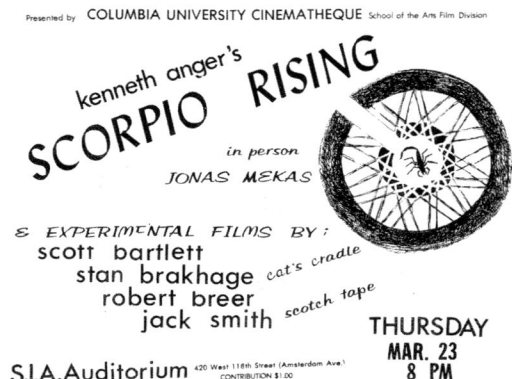

Presented by COLUMBIA UNIVERSITY CINEMATHEQUE School of the Arts Film Division

kenneth anger's
SCORPIO RISING
in person
JONAS MEKAS

& EXPERIMENTAL FILMS BY:
scott bartlett
stan brakhage *cat's cradle*
robert breer
jack smith *scotch tape*

S.I.A. Auditorium 420 West 116th Street (Amsterdam Ave.) CONTRIBUTION $1.00

THURSDAY
MAR. 23
8 PM

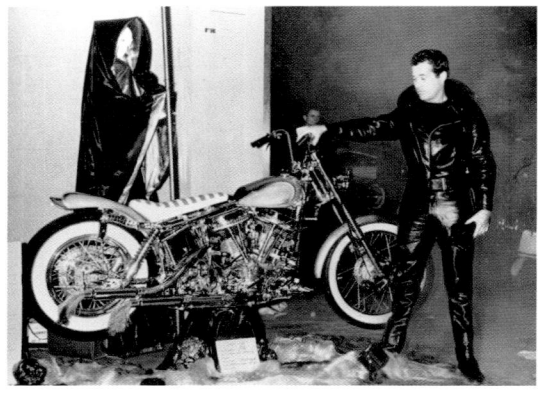

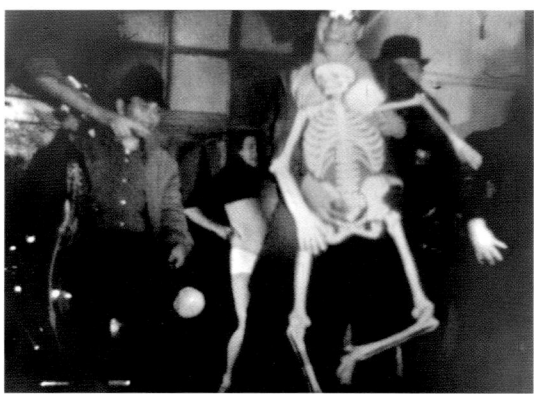

culture, where repressed sexuality expresses itself in ritual acts of brutality and degradation, as if it were an obscure tribal system.

Subversive statements are buried in coded metaphors and double entendres throughout the film. Questions and themes of repressed desire are literally fleshed out and exploded on screen in fast-cut sequences in which subliminal shots of a full frontal, pelvic thrusting, or a boys' orgy, are inter-cut with scenes from a black and white Sunday school religious epic in which Jesus gives sight to a blind man. These visual subversions are mirrored in the use of pop music, as male and female roles are conflated, playing with an audience's pre-conceptions, as the trials and tribulations of romantic love in the lyrics are transposed into a homoerotic context proposing sexual role reversal. The music of the time expressed a frank sexuality at odds with the Christian puritanical mores that the previous generation cherished, including Elvis, who was, according to Anger "the first dirty star."

The pivotal role of pop songs can be seen in the film's structure. There are 13 "chapter breaks" measured by the 13 songs of the soundtrack, with the fact that 13 is the number in any coven, including the Christian one, with Jesus as "leader of the pack." Anger spoke of the film in four parts:

Part I: Boys and Bolts (masculine fascination with the Thing that Goes)

Part II: Image Maker (getting high on heroes: Dean's Rebel and Brando's Johnny: the True View of J. C.)

Part III: Walpurgis Party (J. C. wallflower at cycler's Sabbath)

Part IV: Rebel Rouser (The Gathering of the Dark Legions, with a Message from Our Sponsor)

Rock'n'roll songs such as "Leader of the Pack", "My Boyfriend's Back", "Blue Velvet", Elvis' "Devil in Disguise", and "Wipeout", are incongruously cut to images of motorcycle gangs, comic books, and Hollywood icons Marlon Brando and James Dean. While the avant-garde artists of the day were influenced by, and privileged jazz, taken to be an equivalent, or aural parallel to free-form painterly abstraction, Anger utilized pop music to accentuate a contemporary sensibility.[11] As Carel Rowe pointed out, Anger's *Scorpio Rising* is placed in specific "AM radio time," the time zone in which a song got the most airplay on popular radio, and therefore the time when the film is forever taking place.[12]

In over six decades as a filmmaker, Anger's work has consistently been embedded with a Crowleyean iconography that encouraged the rejection of authority and socially approved role

Top: poster for *Scorpio Rising*
Middle: "Kenneth Anger with "Grim Reaper" bike, which won a prize at a Manhattan motorcycle show"
Bottom: set photograph
Opposite: Victor Childe

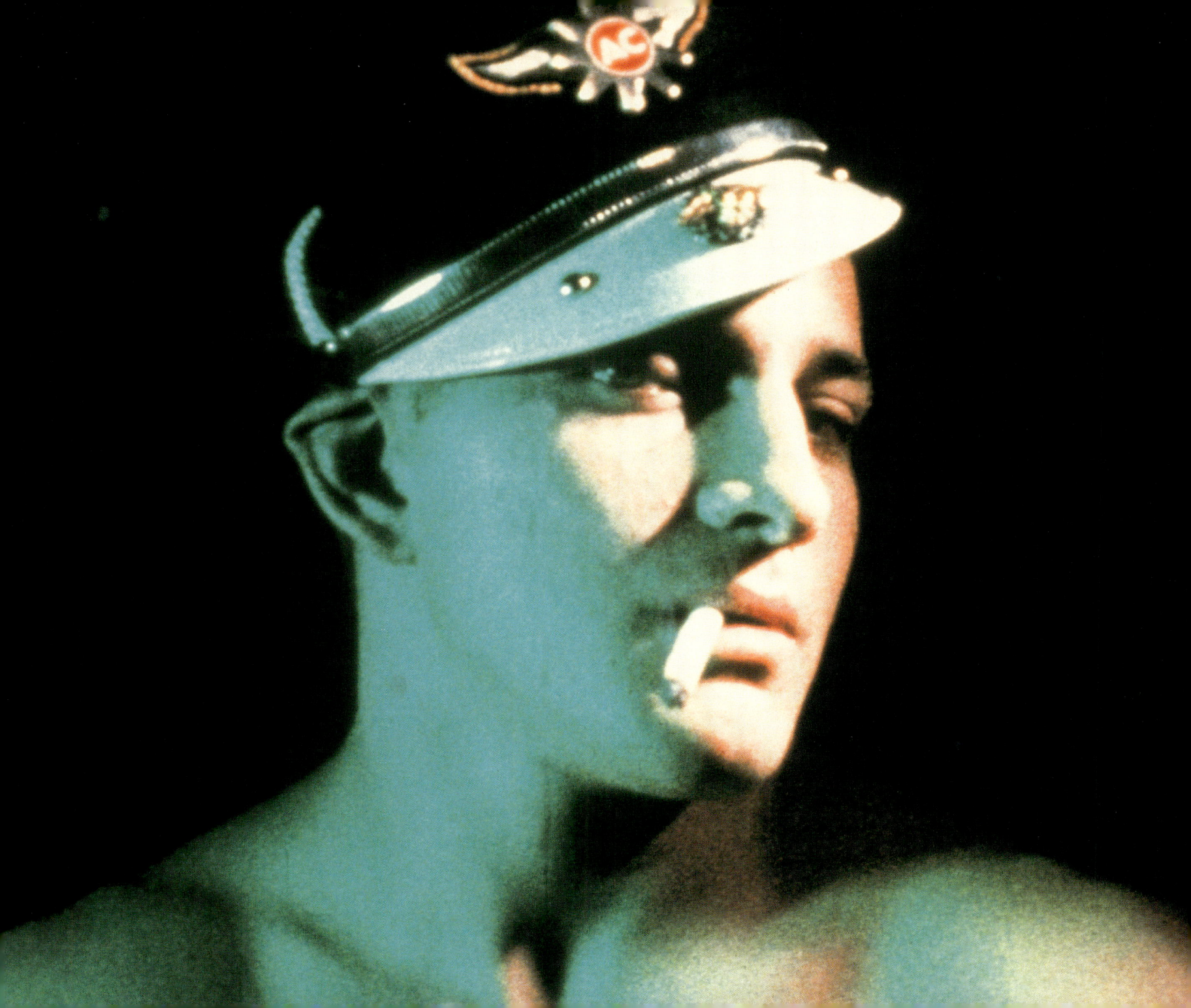

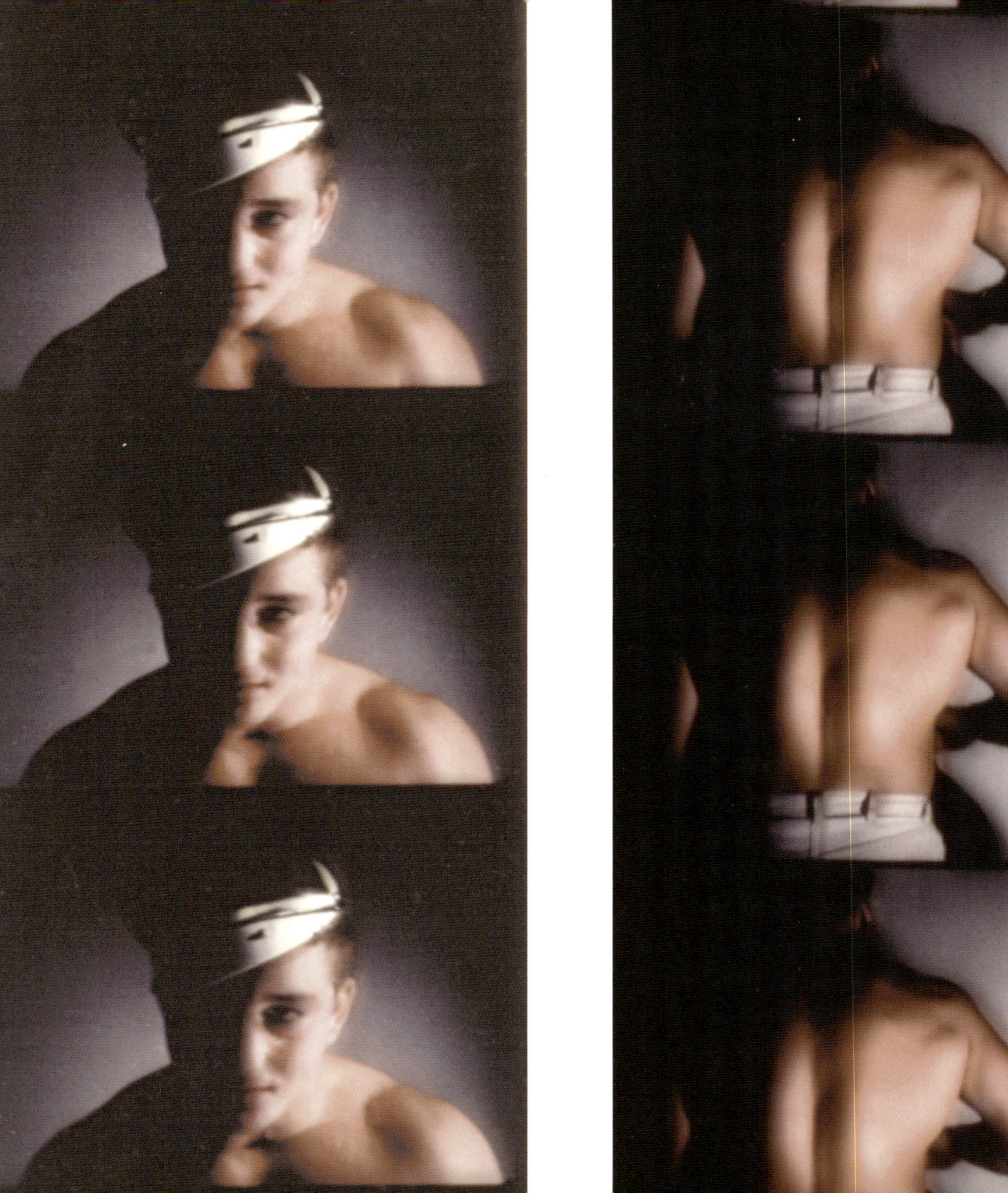

models. Themes of self-immolation, divination, transformation, transubstantiation and alchemy, with the Rosicrucian key primary colors of red, blue and gold, are meshed throughout Anger's iconography. *Scorpio Rising*, in particular, reflects Crowley's *The Book of the Law*, which contained much aggressive neo-Nietzschean sentiment concerning individual strength, while ridiculing the concept of leaders and followers. Following Crowley, Anger's film builds up to an explosive conclusion as *Scorpio* blasphemes against the church (pissing into his gold helmet on the altar). Colliding religious and Hollywood icons, the auto-destructive inter-narrative of the film implies that dying young and staying pretty (for both Dean and Jesus) keeps one's image in perennial circulation. *Scorpio Rising* is structured as a sublimated enticement to a fatalistic climax, and thus the phrase, *le petit mort* ("little death" – French slang for orgasm), provides an apt metaphor for understanding it. The early shots of the film focus upon the ritual of dressing and display. The slow, sensuous, vertical pans down the toned, rippling chests, navels and crotches of the Brooklyn bike-gang boys as they ceremonially deck their bodies with leather and chains, counterpoised with the slow, horizontal pans across the garage floor, motorcycles, tools and spare parts, render these temporarily inanimate objects with the sexualization that has become the modus operandi of the advertising world. America had never produced dandies such as these, too glam to be punk, whose dress signified a codified and elaborate freemasonry, communicated through style and bike culture. And the drama of the light caressing these bodies, making them tantalizingly almost visible, with its echo of Caravaggio's chiaroscuro, inevitably brings into play a metaphor of good and evil. The morality play depicted in the film presents the plunge toward death in the motorcycle crash climax as holding up a mirror to American culture. (As Gregory Markopoulos commented: "*Scorpio Rising* has been made in the image of contemporary America."[13]) The dark erotic imagination becomes an omnipresent underlying theme, particularly palpable in the images of hulking male physiques. These beautiful bodies become sado-masochistic sacrificial lambs in the ritualistic act of self-destruction, as the twinkling lights of a Walpurgis Halloween party morph into the red siren lights of a fatal accident. As Kristeva described, the semiotic "chora" is on the path of destruction, aggressivity, and death.[14]

Anger delved into the suspect ideology embedded in the problematic beginnings of the American (Hollywood) film tradition. While he absorbed the lavish visual qualities of D. W. Griffith's epics, with their sumptuous orgiastic and paganistic microcosms, he also raised questions about the older filmmaker's ideological constructs. Anger's refined editing style reflect both Griffith's and Eisenstein's consummation of narrative exacted by a frame-by-frame montage to create scenes of mythic proportions, a technique few directors at the time were utilizing. The ideal progeny of Eisenstein's intellectual montage, Anger's technique was based on appropriation, re-order, re-selection; cutting and juxtaposing disparate found footage together, creating a brilliant kaleidoscope collage that evokes both pleasure and pain responses from the viewer.

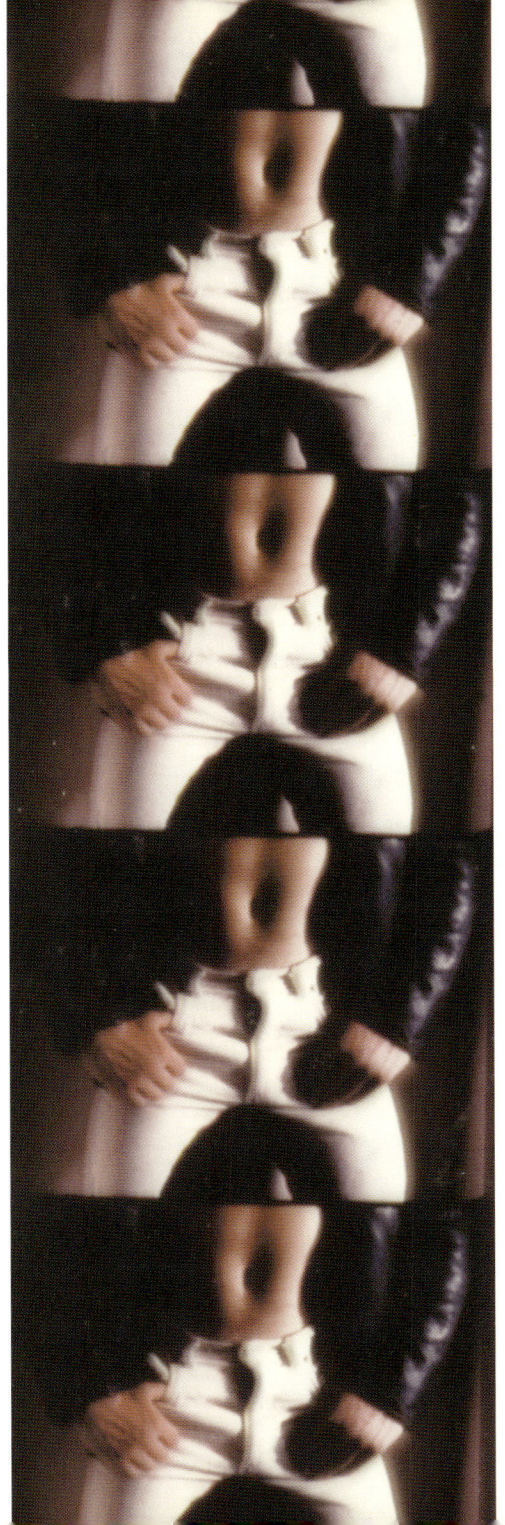

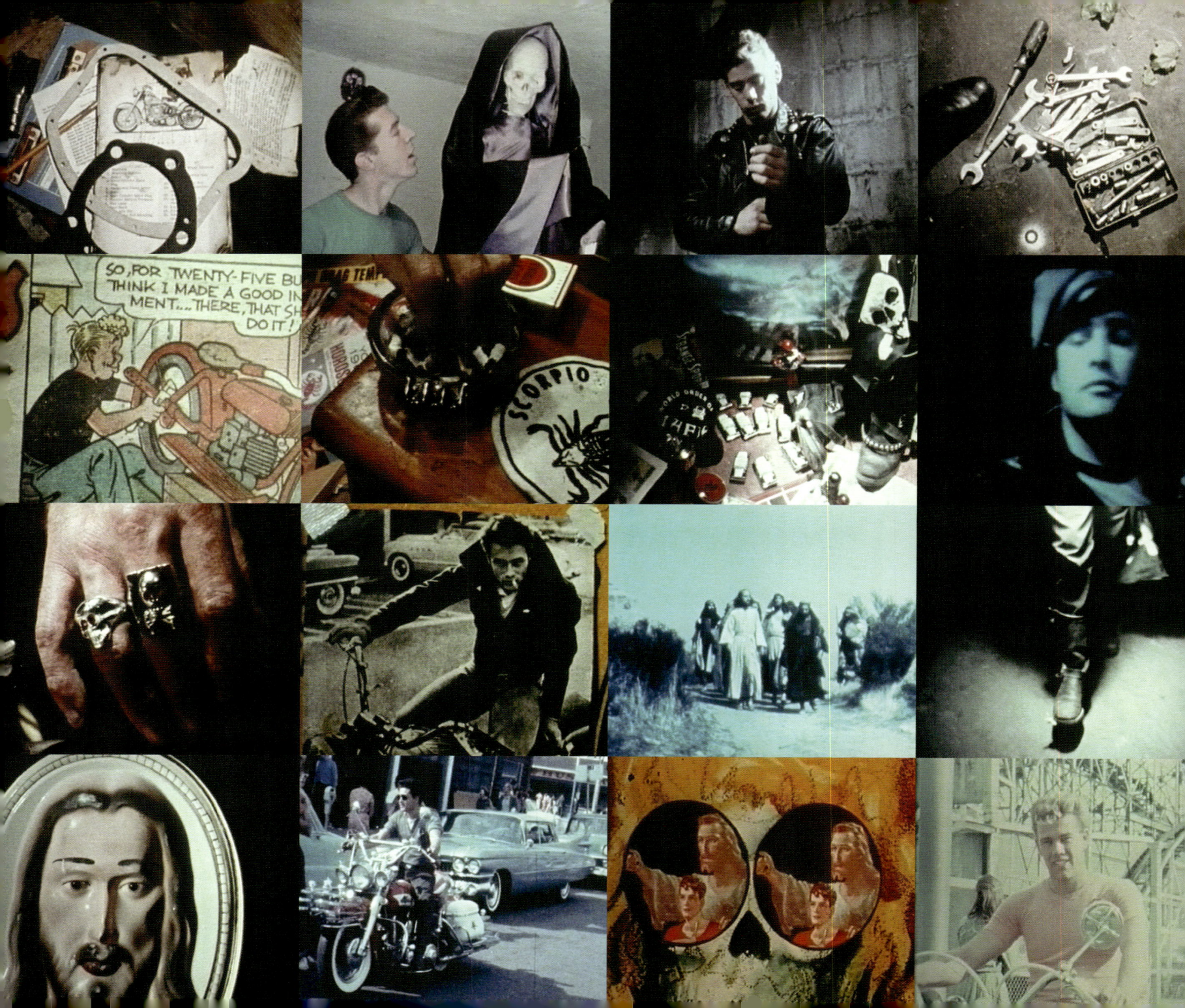

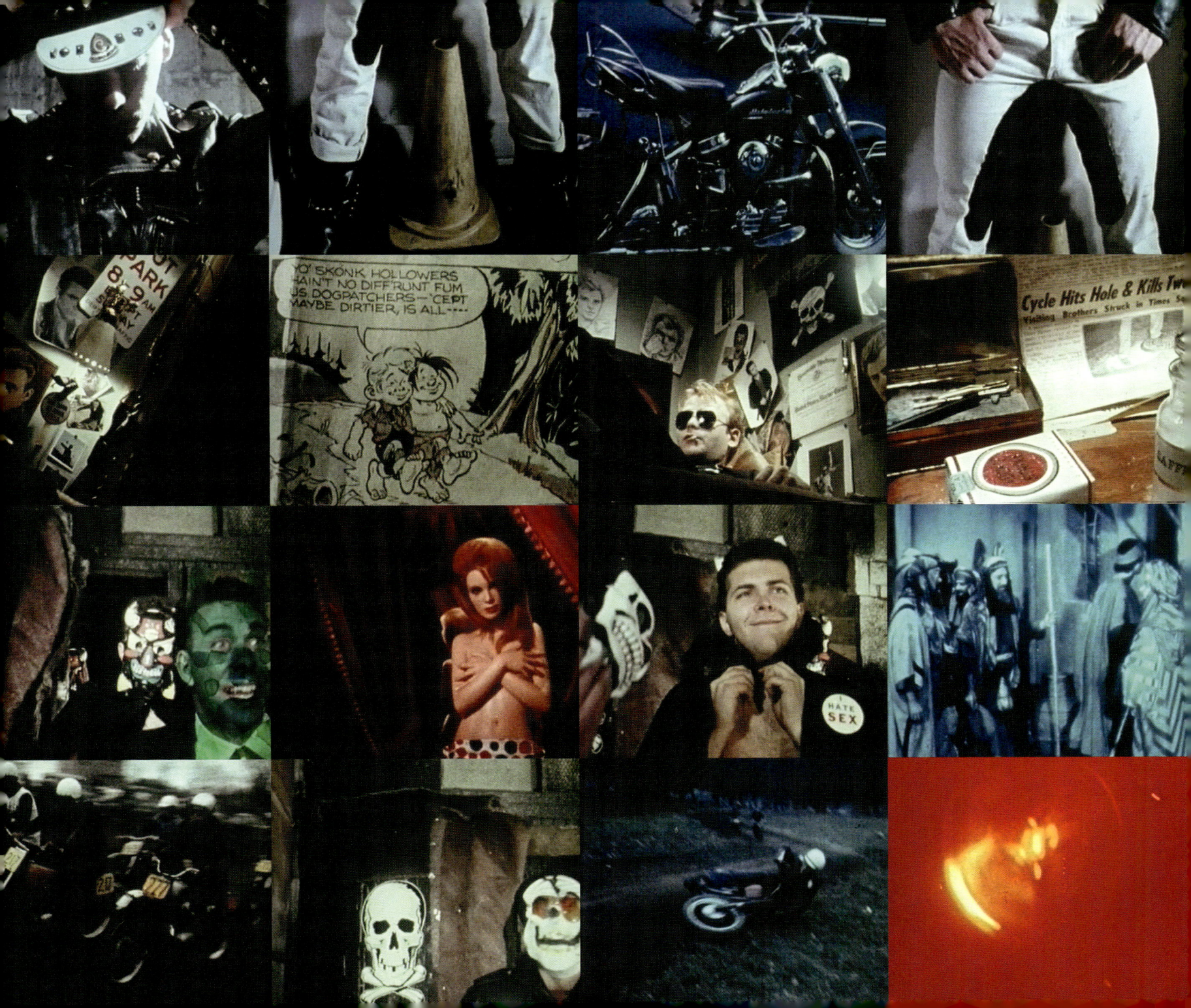

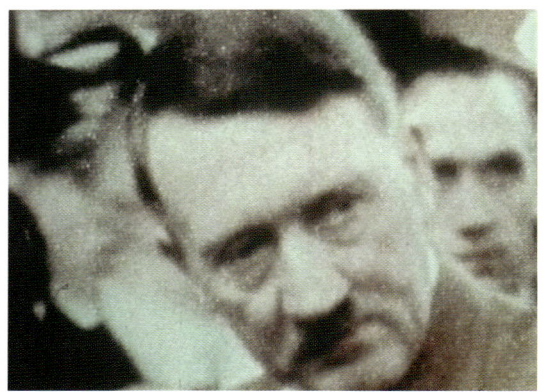

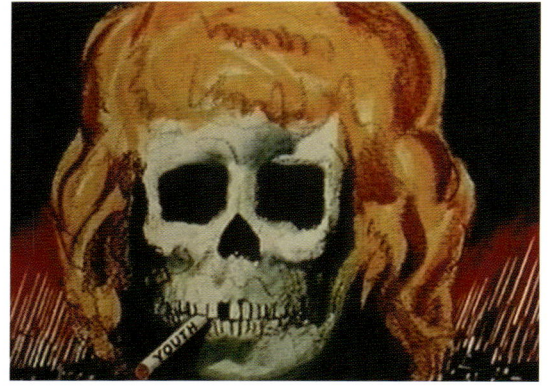

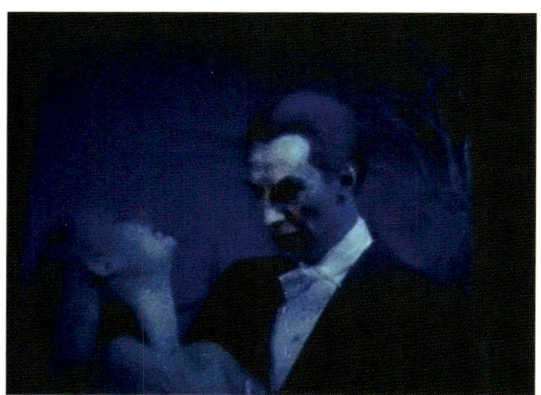

This juxtaposition and increasingly accelerated inter-cutting of opposites – the sacred and profane, master and servant, iconic and iconoclastic – render a proto-pagan world before leaders, before good and evil, transcending politics and religion. Colliding images and icons together, the juxtapositions of ideological opposites create the greatest impact. These images are, in turn, juxtaposed with the lyrics sampled on the soundtrack, further liberating their latent meanings and identities. "If montage is to be compared with something, then a phalanx of montage pieces, of shots, should be compared to the series of explosions of an internal combustion engine, driving forward its automobile or tractor; for, similarly, the dynamics of montage serve as impulses driving forward the total film."[15]

Anger used quasi-subliminal shots, often between one to three frames, to play with a viewer's subconscious level of perception and reception of imagery. *Scorpio Rising* (as is *Invocation of My Demon Brother*) is so full of images, many of which are subliminal, that anybody viewing it for the first time may be unable to recall what has been seen. Stan Brakhage had said that seeing one of Anger's films once is like reading a canto by Ezra Pound on the Times Square sign that flashes news bulletins.

The association of fascism and delinquency obeys the logic of post war paranoia, which translated internal differences – those presented for example, by homosexuality, socialism/communism, and the beats – into threats to national boundaries. *Rebel Without a Cause*, 1954, is symptomatic of the moralizing tendencies of mass media ideology at this time. Youth gangs (with their rigid hierarchies, leader-worship, and lust for violence) were regarded as embryonic fascist units. The references to the Third Reich in *Scorpio Rising* are also to be understood in relation to the brutality of the Los Angeles Police Department at that time, and specifically in relation to the L.A.P.D. Vice Squad. In 1965, *Artforum* magazine reviewed the film, indicating that "The point is not that the cyclists are politically comparable to the Nazi movement but rather that they are emotionally comparable.... The cyclists not only see themselves as Brando and as a holy sect but also as charismatic leaders of supermen. These four sequences present with mordant humor what probably is one of the most grotesque inner landscapes of contemporary life."[16] And yet the review does not indicate Anger's intentional ambiguity.

In this climate of paranoia and repression, *Scorpio Rising* was confiscated by the L.A. Vice Squad. A member of the American Nazi Party, disturbed about Anger's use of Nazi insignia as erotic turn-ons and party games, complained that it was full of obscene images; the print was seized and the art-house cinema manager arrested and thrown into jail for screening it. At that time a First Amendment that tolerated the Ku Klux Klan had little tolerance for art. Indeed artwork came under physical threat during those years, subject to official confiscation and court-ordered destruction. Processing labs were given permission to destroy material they assumed unfit for viewing, such as the collaboration between Kenneth Anger and Stan Brakhage, made in San Francisco, and which was destroyed by Kodak.[17]

This page: "Archetypes of Evil: young Adolf, Death to Cigarettes and Lugosi attacks"
Opposite: "Bruce Byron and the decorated walls of his pad"

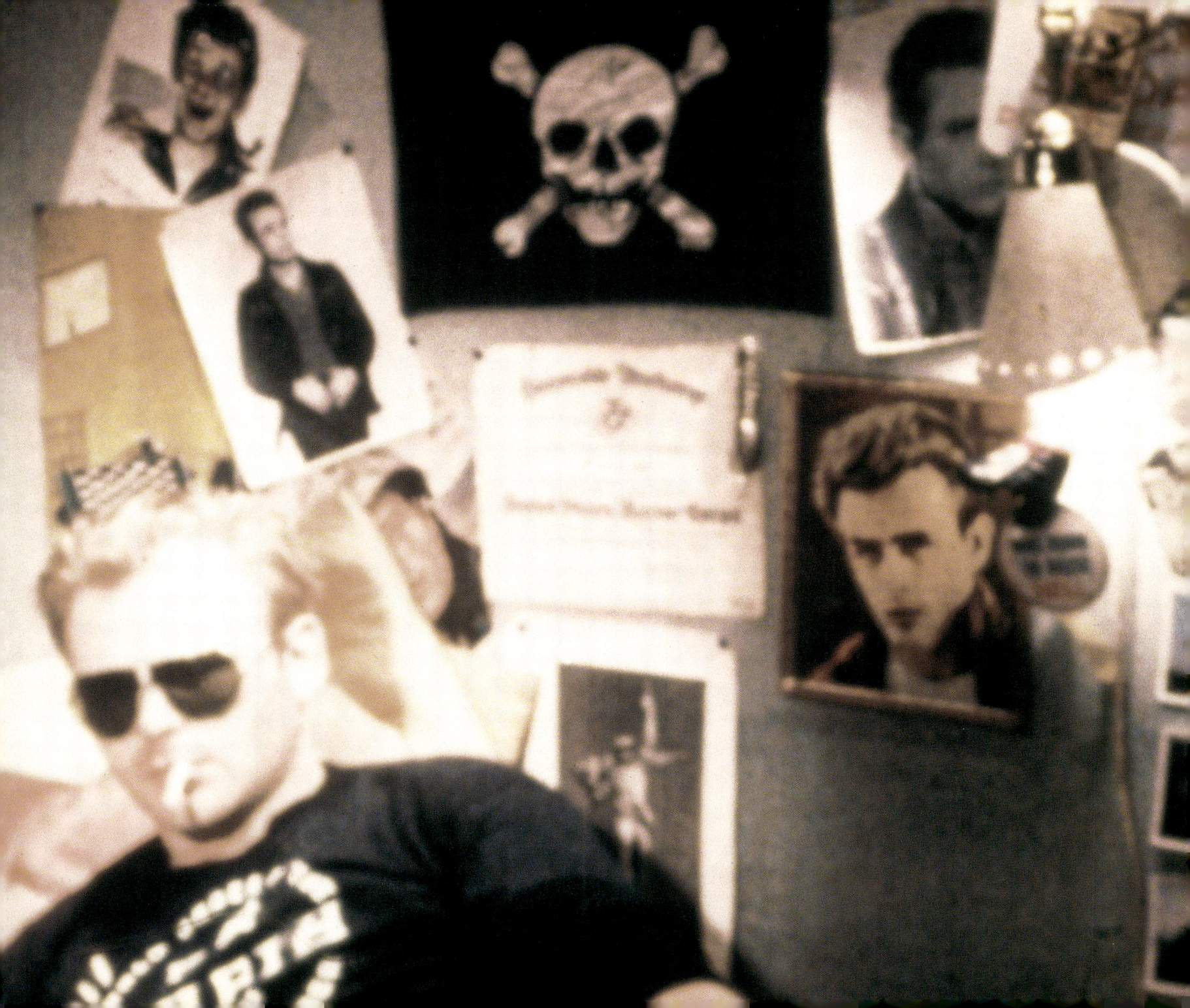

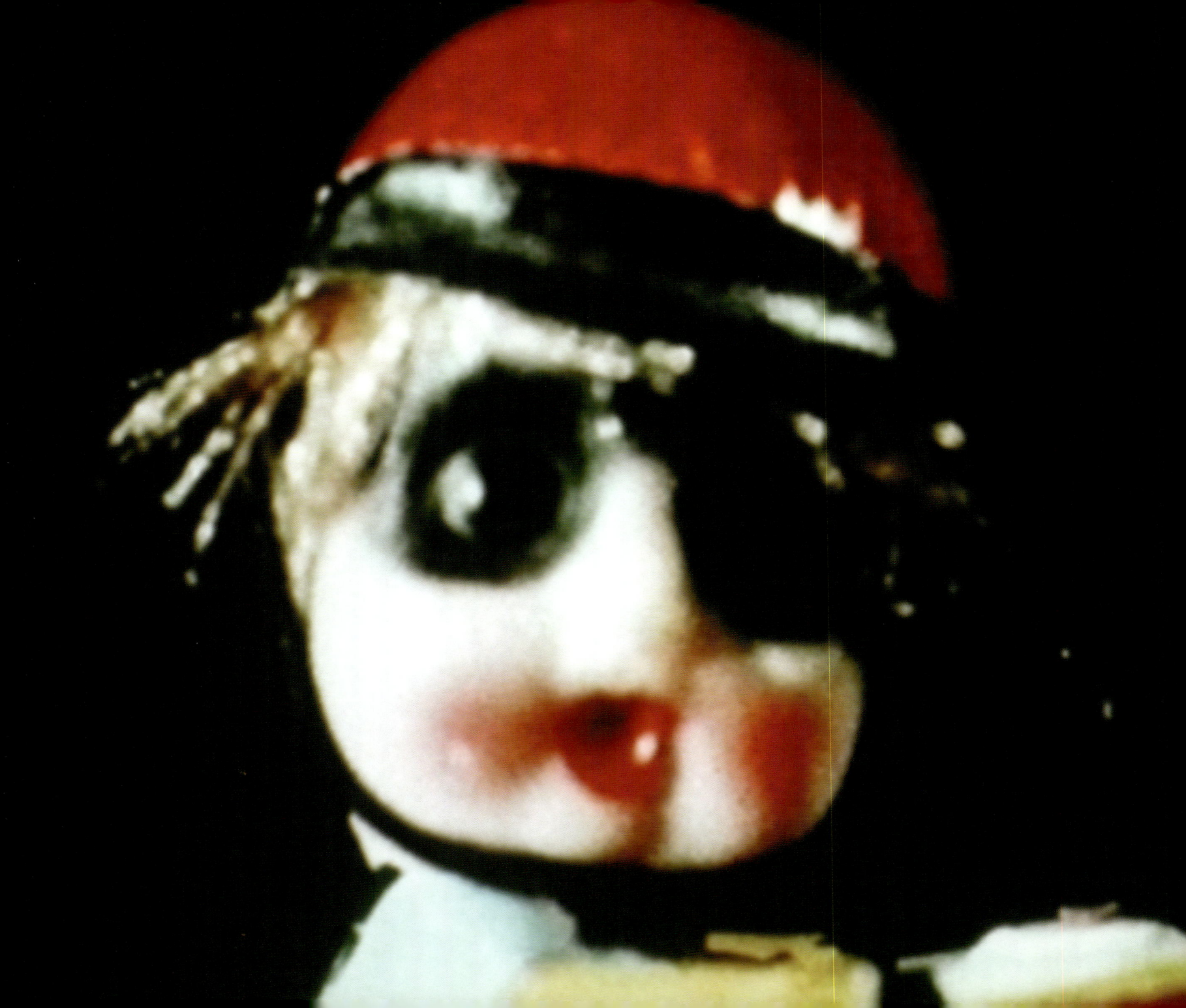

(Brakhage mentioned that at the time, one had a 10% chance of ever getting a film back). Anger, amazingly, won his case with the California Supreme Court in a landmark case stating that the film had "redeeming social merit" and could be publicly screened without any cuts, after having made headlines. (Testifying in court on behalf of the film were Susan Sontag and Allen Ginsberg).

In Robert Smithson's seminal essay "Entropy and the New Monuments," 1966, he makes reference to Anger's *Scorpio Rising*:

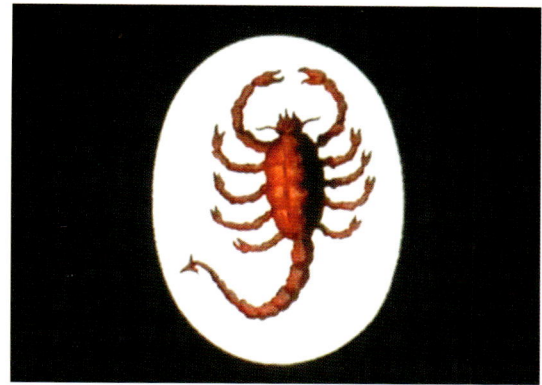

> Stella's immaculate but sparkling symmetries are reflected in John Chamberlain's "Kandy-Kolored" reliefs. "They are extreme, snazzy, elegant in the wrong way, immoderate," says Judd. "It is also interesting that the surfaces of the reliefs are definitely surfaces." Chamberlain's use of chrome and metalflake brings to mind the surfaces in *Scorpio Rising*, Kenneth Anger's many-faceted horoscopic film about constellated motorcyclists. Both Chamberlain and Anger have developed what could be called California surfaces. In a review of the film, Ken Kelman speaks of "the ultimate reduction of ultimate experience to brilliant chromatic surface; Thanatos in Chrome – artificial death" in a way that evokes Chamberlain's giddy reliefs.[18]

Anger's surface fetish was to find its apotheosis in his next project, *Kustom Kar Kommandos*, 1965.

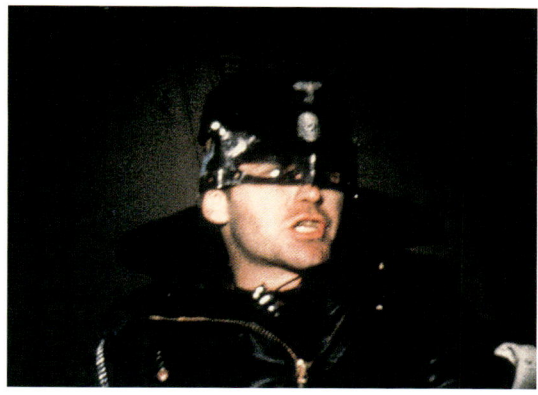

The influence of *Scorpio Rising* has continued up to the present day. In the mid 1970s while Anger was living in London, Malcolm McClaren had called him up to screen *Scorpio Rising* as visual wallpaper for one of the Sex Pistols' first gigs. *Scorpio*'s sado-masochistic leatherboy look was adapted by Westwood/McClaren for their early punk clothing designs. The reception of *Scorpio Rising* was widespread and international: from the art world, to music, to film, to fashion (*The New York Times* reported an overnight motorcycle chic).[19] In 1989 Martin Scorsese noted:

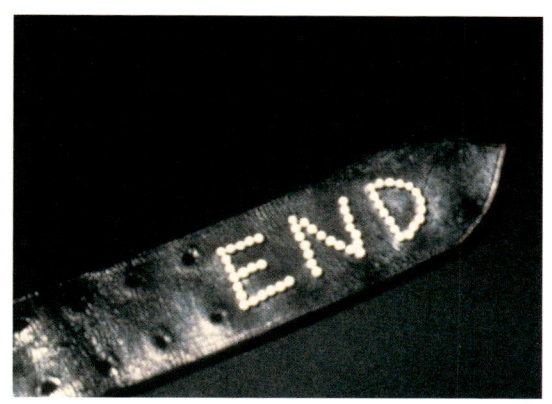

> I well remember the first time I saw a Kenneth Anger film. It was about 1964 at Vernon Simmerman's loft downtown and Jonas Mekas showed us *Scorpio Rising*, after it was banned. Of all his films, it is still the one I like the most. I was impressed by his ironic use of pop music and by his sense of rhythm. I was also fascinated by his ambiguous relationship to Hollywood, his love/hate continuously expressed through the use and abuse of Hollywood imagery, in a romantic, decadent mood. There is a pagan religiosity in his films. His continuous reference to myth and ritual creates a hypnotizing, a dream atmosphere that seems to put the viewer in a state of trance. Kenneth Anger is a unique filmmaker, an artist of exceptional talent.[20]

Kenneth Anger's Scorpio Rising

Carolee Schneemann[21]

Risen. Before our eyes; this journey carries us beyond where we are seated, beyond the screen which we view, and which views us!

Did you see why Love demanded Death? (Priapus shadowing Narcissus in ecstatic addiction, in sadistic fury. It is comprehensible only by the interchange of substances: silver spurs, oily gears, jeweled signals, iron tools, shafts and pipes; their leather torsos, their bodies bound – corseted in silver chains, marked by buttons and buckles; all narrowing parts tied, tightened, tense – as voluptuously indented, shaped, and decorated as their motorcycles are. Follow leather the length of the leg, leather sheathing the foot – the heavy heel reaches the pedal. Image: man and machine as unified, ominous force.)

There is a texture for torture, it builds through whiplash color and speed of lights. Frame by frame each detail grows as intricately as Rodin's "Gates of Hell" remembered in the movement of our own musculature. Watch the steady, incalculable exposure of gesture: the men, their machines, rooms, objects, landscape. (Instance: the flashlight held, poised between his legs, will sweep the dark temple of initiation – flag phallus, twitching legs, helmet... Swastika!) Scorpio: Diurnal, centering the Queen in relation to Mars; under Autumn and Swords, in the realm of the Ox – THE LIGHTNING STRUCK TOWER. (Dark Major Arcana, a psychosexual arcana.) Do not imagine the destruction is not your own. The Scorpion is "falsely reputed to sting itself to death if encircled with fire." Poisoned sting. Eighth sign. (We need at least eight!) "Having an elongated body and a narrow, segmented tail bearing a venomous sting at the tip. Bib. A kind of scourge, prob. One armed with metal points. 1. Kings xii II. Something which incites to action like the sting of a insect."

These images subsume a camera eye; where is Anger? *Scorpio Rising*, so complete to the eye it is impossible to establish the physical actions of "making the film," rather some sense of it sprung complete, in its complex rays and subtle ironies of terror and love, from a lucid dream moving more deeply into consciousness than any intention could provide. Each image and all its details structure a cumulative effect – the total form of the film being implicit in any detail of it. Penetrating visual relationships grow like an organism to an historical/social revelation, inevitable and totally shocking. We recognize that gratuitous curse, the wondrous necessity to juxtapose and combine Christ and Brando – blinding, constructing covenant of division (that split down the center of Western man); they emerge in the film as if they were creations of Anger, insights out of his own body by which we recognize a bridge of psychic torment where energy erupts corrosively and wildly in proportion to its own constraint. The appearance of the "Nazi" regarding the plump sacks of money is not more fantastic than the linkage of love-and-death racing the cyclists, or of the pastry pink and green little boys in the comic strip fragment: "Why haven't our folks gotten together?", or the pin-ups on the wall before which a man's blond head rises.

Motorcyclists. The perfidious shine of their ornaments (depravity – embedded in forms as various and dense as visual worlds of Goya or Bosch). Objects keep striking the eye with a shiny, metallic grace, clear metals and plastic and brilliant glass caught in a mosaic of dis-ease; spun, punned in wheels and spokes of light, ground into chrome and aluminum, leather jackets, fragments of photographs and newspaper clippings. Rock-and-roll sound leads the senses – an even record spin – in three minute belts climaxed with a red light flashing sychronization of all the sound durations. (Our own "dance" music! *Scorpio*'s soundtrack more clear and new than those same scratchy disks we hear spun for love or oblivion.)

The vision is not "symbolic"; it is fleshed, concrete, drawing the metaphoric life-line from every visual unit in tight, dense webs. The beautiful intelligence of Anger's eye causes conjunctions of all-sense response on viewing. The motorcyclists are actual; we are convinced of their every gesture, they pull themselves into the lens, into our eyes harnessing our energies by their own. There is no protection from them.... We are where they are! Demons of potential violence and formalized destruction; we follow as we endure our own nightmares of impotence and rage. The covenant of men. The poisonous mythos. (Christ and his disciples – the mild ones; cyclists/fascists – the wild ones.) That old god submitted to his cross, and these willful ones struggle to intensify their destruction by his own – bearing his cross against their sex.

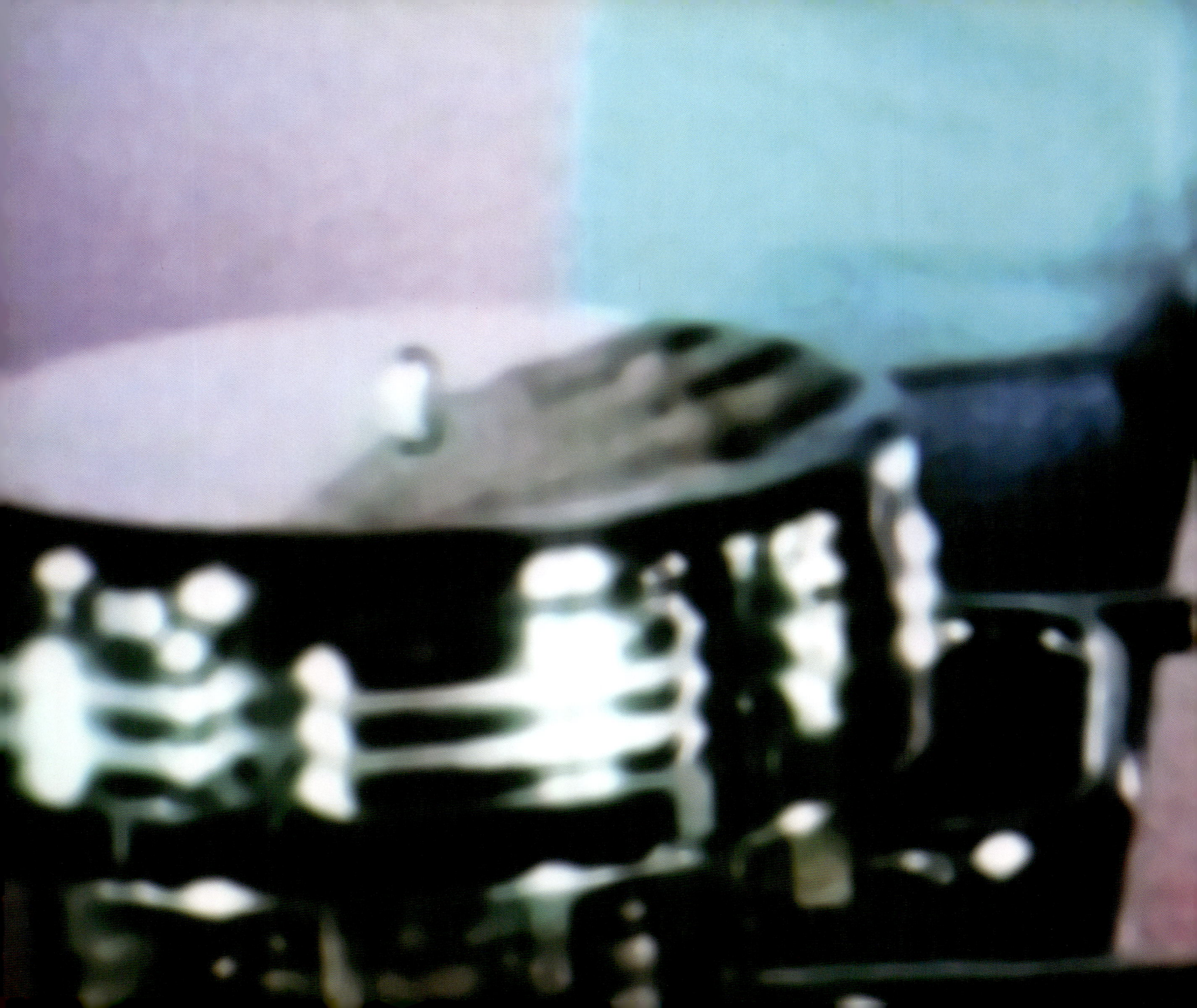

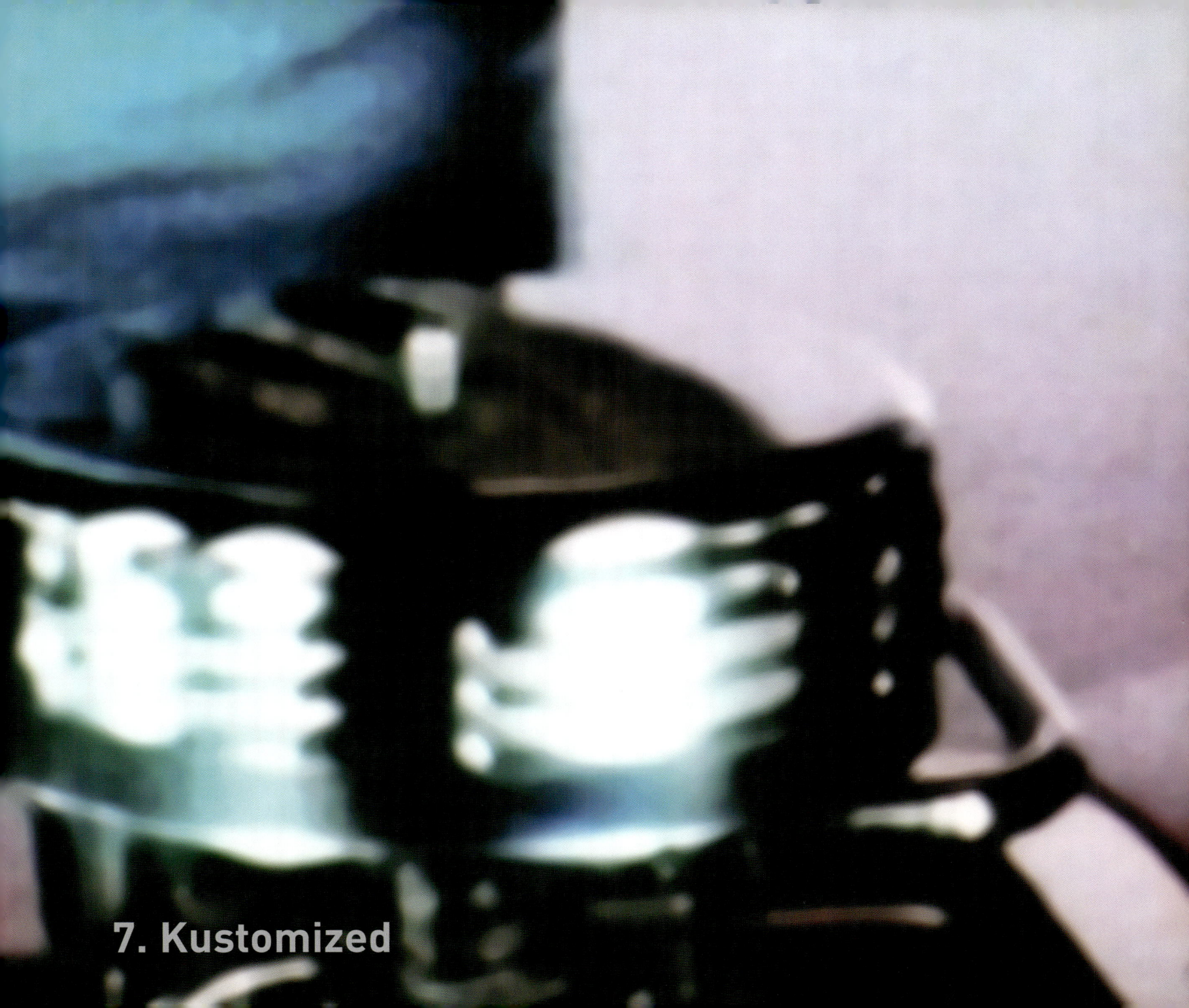

7. Kustomized

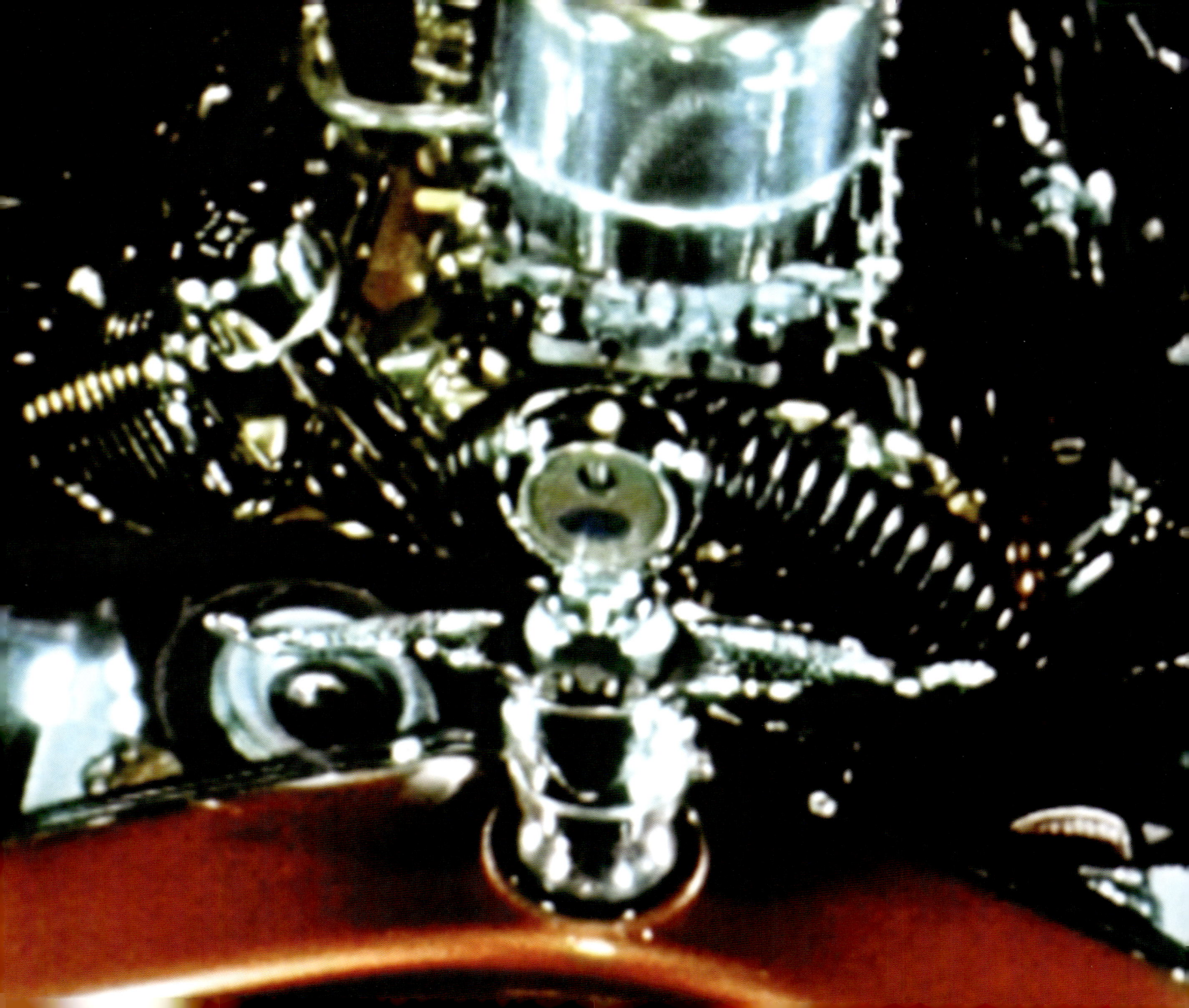

Kustom Kar Kommandos

1965
3 minutes
16mm, color
Music by the Parris Sisters, "Dream Lover"

Following *Scorpio Rising* Anger was the recipient of a Ford Foundation grant to make the film *Kustom Kar Kommandos*, which he originally conceived as feature-length, starring the customized car as fetish object and tribal totem to another American boy cult. But the initial film concept was soon abandoned after attempts to raise funds for its completion were unsuccessful. The footage shot in the actual garages of the kustomizers in California was edited to the single three minute pop song by the Parris Sisters, initiating the music clip as it subsequently evolved: a short film and microcosm compressed into the space of one song. *KKK* is a concept condensed to its essence. The slow and sinuous camera pans mirror the breathless "Dream Lover" lyrics, beginning and ending with the contrapuntal roar of engines. Rather than the frenetic dynamic montage in *Scorpio Rising*, *Kustom Kar Kommandos* features long takes and pans (creating the effect of sensuality and serenity) in a hermetic zone, where the kustom kar and its driver, Sandy Trent, re-enact an initiation rite: as if a sacred experience. In 1958 when a film called *Hot Rod Gang* a.k.a. *Fury Unleashed*, was released apparently it was unthinkable to say "hot-rod" in public for fear of arousing disorder (it couldn't be released under its first title), and it was considered dangerous rabble-rousing stuff at the time.[1] Anger's film explored the forbidden world of these young men and their fetishized machines.

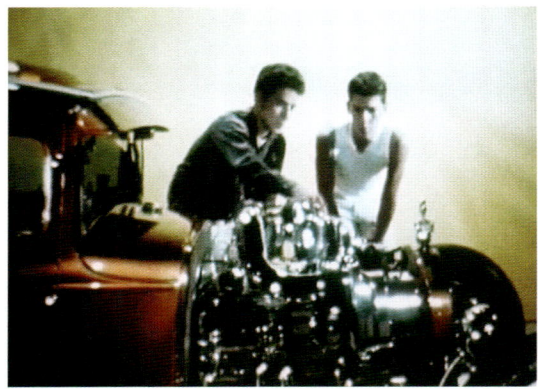

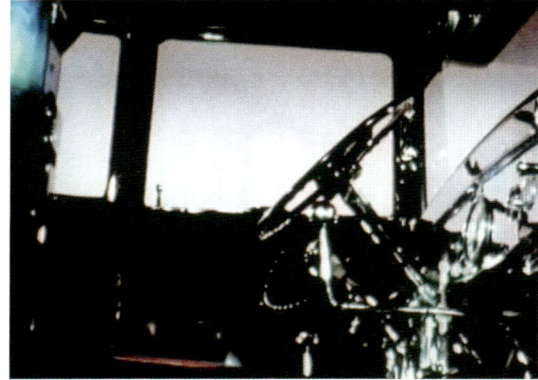

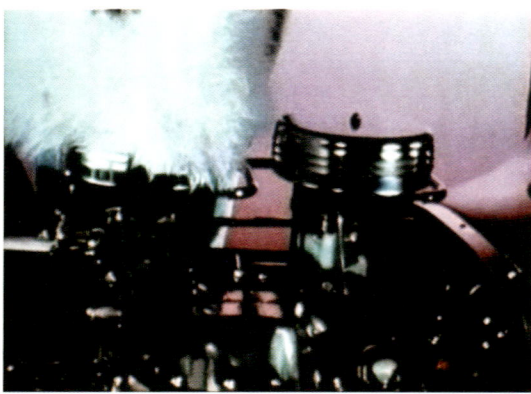

Anger's original proposed scenario was as follows.

"KUSTOM"

Film project by Kenneth Anger utilizing the Eastman rapid color emulsion Ektachrome ER, whose ASA rating of 125 opens up hitherto inaccessible realms of investigation on low-key color location work for the independent creative filmmaker. Running time 30 minutes, track composed of pop music fragments combined with sync location-recorded sound effects and dialog.

KUSTOM is an oneiric vision of a contemporary American (and specifically Californian) teenage phenomenon, the world of the hot-rod and customized car. I emphasize the word *oneiric*, as KUSTOM will *not* be a "documentary" covering the mechanical hopping-up and esthetic customizing of cars, but rather a dream-like probe into the psyche of the teenager for whom the *unique* aspect of the power-potentialized customized car represents a poetic extension of personality, an accessible means of wish-fulfillment. I will treat the custom cars created by the teenager and his adult mentors (such customizers as Ed Roth, Bill Cushenberry and George Barris, whose Kustom City in North Hollywood is a mecca of this world) as the objects of art – folk art if you prefer – that I consider them to be.

The aforementioned adult "mentors," most of whom are located in the periphery of Los Angeles and hence readily accessible for filming, will be shown at work in their body shops on various cars-in-the-process-of-becoming, in the role of "arch-priests" to the teenagers whose commission they are fulfilling. (The locales of body shops and garages will be presented uniquely in gleaming highlighted low-key, in a manner already essayed for the motorcycle garage locations of *SCORPIO RISING*); the idolized customizers (the only adults seen in the film) will be represented as shadowy, mysterious personages (priests or witch-doctors) while the objects of their creation, the cars, will bathe in a pool of multi-sourced (strictly non-realistic) light, an eye-magnet of nacreous color and gleaming curvilinear surfaces.

The treatment of the teenager in relation to his hot-rod or custom car (whether patiently and ingeniously fashioned by himself, as is usually the case, or commissioned according to his fantasy, for the economically favored) will bring out what I see as a definite *eroticization* of the automobile, in its dual aspect of narcissistic identification as virile power symbol and its more elusive role: seductive, attention-grabbing, gaudy or glittering mechanical mistress paraded for the benefit of his peers. (I am irresistibly drawn to the comparison of these machines with an American cult-object of an earlier era, Mae West in her "Diamond Lil" impersonations in the 1930s.)

The formal filmic construct of KUSTOM is planned as follows: (The division into titled "sections" is uniquely for working convenience; these divisions will be "erased" in the finished work. The dominant pop record is indicated in capitals.

1. HAVE MONEY (The Young Conformers)
 An introduction insinuating the spectator into the teen-dream. A fast-shifting visual reverie utilizing the linking device of the lap-dissolve and the wipe to establish patterns of convention followed by the teenage (and sub-teen) group: similarly of hair-styling, style of dress, of language, attitude or manner, taste in dance patterns and pop music; the omniscience of certain popular heroes or ever-shifting masks on Archetypal Images.

2. DAWN (Crystalization)
The concept of individual "style" dawns upon the Teenager. The carefully composed aerodynamics of a crested coiffure is formed. The love-lock. Racked sideburns. The embroidered, self-identifying jacket or painted T-shirt. The "far-out" color combinations in stove-pipe pants, shock-effect shirts and socks. The Grail: the vision of the Teenager as Owner of his own, screamingly individualistic, unique and personalized custom car. (These images of the Grail, "the goal," will be floated across the mirrored image of the Teenager as he arranges his coiffure or clothes.) Subliminal flashes as [he] thumbs through hot-rod magazines or plays juke-box. Closeups of high-school desk tops showing open text books (Science or History) while adolscent hands doodle, first crudely, then with increasing refinement, silhouettes of hot-rod and custom "dream" cars.

3. THE NITTY-GRITTY (Realization)
The Teenager attacks. Dream into action. Abrupt change in formal construct: sharp cuts, swift pans, darting dollies. The night-lit junk-yard, weird derelict cemetery: lifting a "goodie." The first jalopie: a rusty junked car pushed into the dark initiatory cave of the garage. Series of car-frames in the process of being stripped: an almost savage dismantling (analogy to wild animals dismembering a carcass).

4. MY GUY (The Rite)
Under the occult guidance of the shadowy, mysterious adult customizers performing as Arch-Priest, the Teenager's Dream Car is born (allusion to obstetrics). The alchemical elements come into play: phosphorescent blue tongue of the welding flame, cherry glow of joins, spark shower of the buffer. Major operation: dropping the front, raising the back of the car, "channeling" and "chopping." The Priest-Surgeon (customizer) perfects the metal modulations from cardboard mock-ups; plunges in with blowtorch and mallet. The swooping sculpted forms (blackened and rough) materialize in close-ups and their intent is perceived.

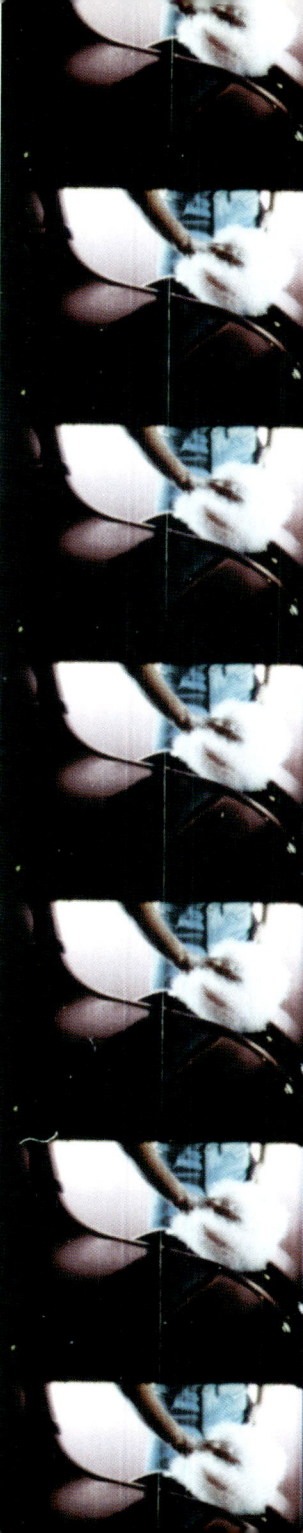

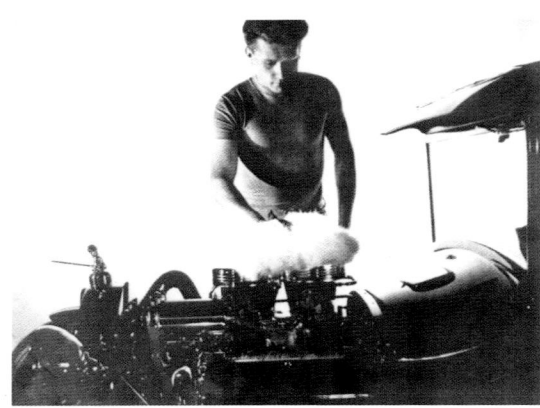

5. IN HIS KISS (The Adorning)

Sudden darting color: the rainbow array as cans are opened, stirred dripping gaudy sticks held up for the Teenager's contemplation and approval. The iridescent "candy-flake" colors and shock-jewel tones in vogue. The Teenager chooses *his* color: tension, decision, joyful release. The cult-object – the shaping-up car body – in the swirl of colored spray-gun mists: rose and turquoise fluorescent fogs as coat upon carefully-stroked, glittering coat, the car-body emerges as a radiant, gem-hued object of adoration. A reflected color-bath splashes over the absorbed faces of the watching teenagers: a whoop of triumph, a jungle-stomp of joy as the custom car is "born."

6. WONDERFUL ONE (Possession)

The Teenager takes possession of his own completed custom or hot-rod car: the painted finish is caressed, the line admired (as would be the line of a girl friend) the chromed shift fondled, firmly grasped. (For this kaleidoscopic montage involving scores of custom and hot-rod cars, it is hoped to include the outstanding examples of customizing currently touring America in the Ford Custom Car Caravan, which could well represent the ideal Dream Cars of America's custom-conscious teenagers. However, for their appearance in KUSTOM, it will be necessary to film them *in movement* against unified black or nocturnal backgrounds – an effect that can be accomplished by camera or optical artifice if it proves impractical to night-drive these valuable machines.)

7. THE FUGITIVE (Flight and Freedom)

The Teenage hot-rodders "rev up" (The Syndrome of the Shift) and take off for a nocturnal drag race (irreal colored light-sources throughout). A lone hot-rodder races down a curving mountain road (Dead Man's Curve). The Custom Boys, *in slow motion*, take command of the controls of their Dream Cars. (This concluding sequence of KUSTOM operates exclusively in the realm of "dream logic": it is intended to create a Science-Fictional atmosphere.) The hot-rodders experience the erotic power-ecstasy of the Shift (the Hurst shift will be employed) to the magnified accompaniment of motor and exhaust. The Custom Boys resemble Astronauts at their controls: their vari-hued craft seem to lift into space. (If possible, a prototype of an actual "air-car" by a noted West Coast designer will be utilized in this section.) The Dragsters streak down the search-light stabbed runway (ideally seen by helicopter) as in cross-cutting the Custom Boys are liberated into weightlessness with their strange craft, and plunge star-ward.

Above and opposite: production stills from
Kustom Kar Kommandos

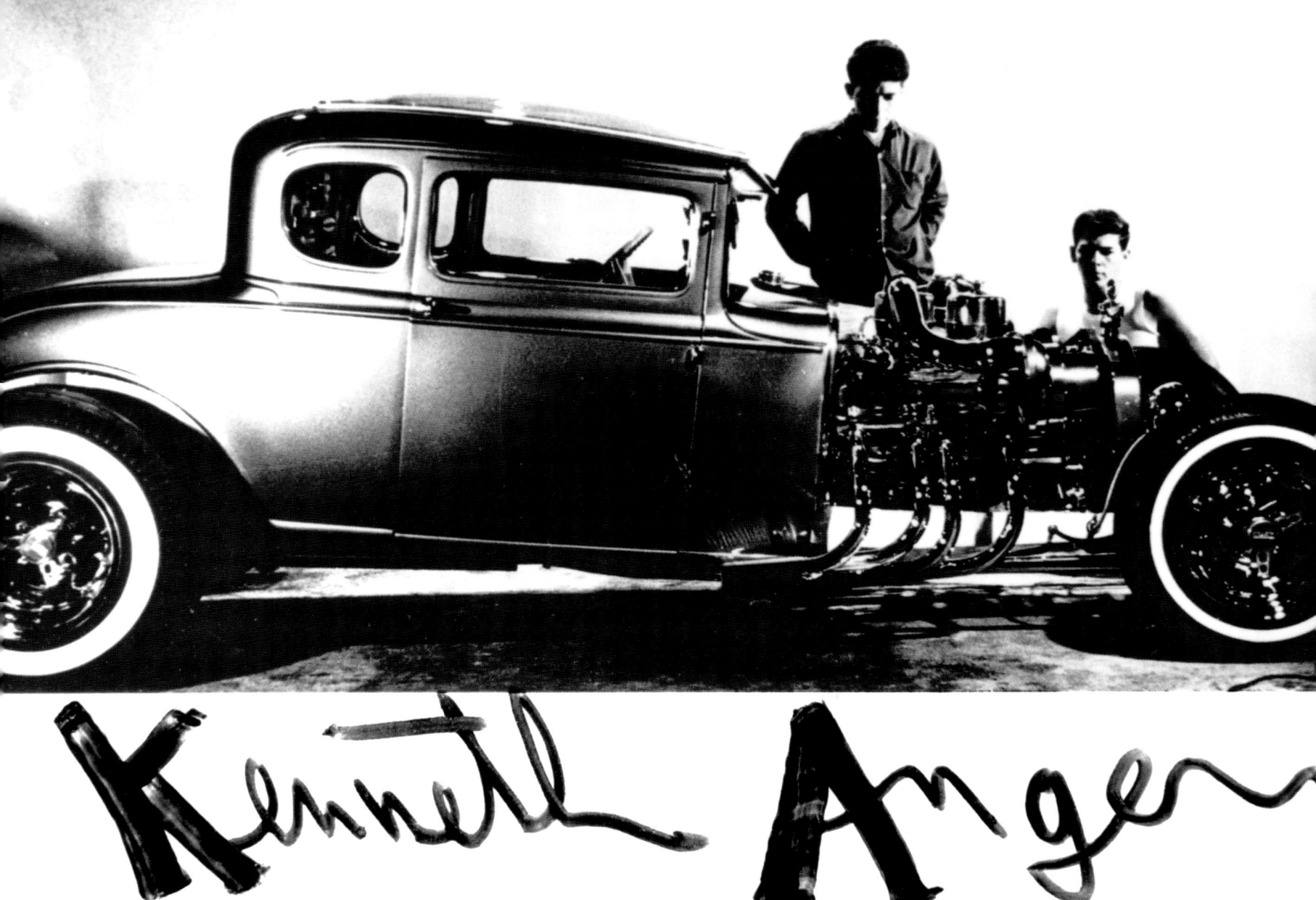

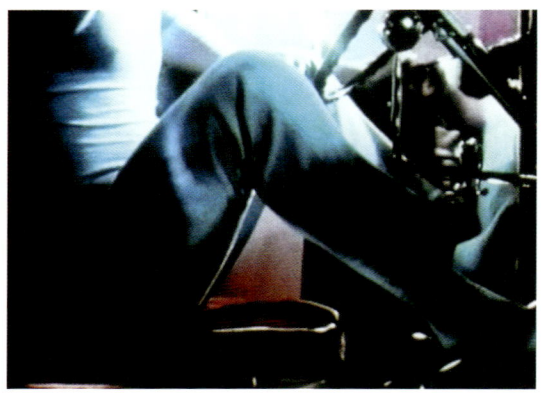

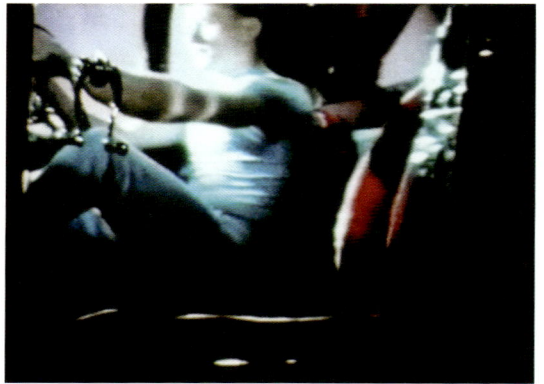

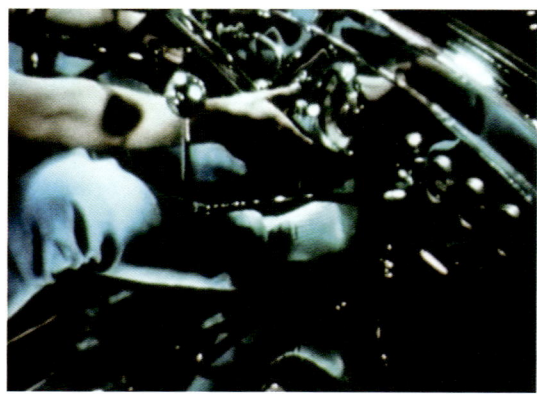

8. SHANGRI-LA (Apotheosis)

The Dragsters streak towards an imposing podium (by montage inference) piled high with towering, animated trophies of glittering gold; the Custom Boys range above the golden mountain of high and free. A nocturnal jostling cheering crowd of teenagers (lit by swinging stabbing searchlights) swing up on their shoulders The Winner – Mr. Hot-Rod, his glowing triumph-filled countenance streaming sweat, his bare arms bearing his Golden Trophy Tower – he exults as The Conqueror, drinks in the adulation of the adolescent sea around him; he is startled by the sky-borne vroom of the upward-sweeping Dream Cars, his beaming face swiftly mirroring, in the moment of his triumph, a greater wonder, a greater goal.

END[2]

In an interview in 1966 Kenneth Anger discussed *Kustom Kar Kommandos*:

When I got the Ford Foundation grant, I was completely breadless, and I conscientiously paid off lab bills and things like that. So by the time I'd taken care of my debts there was a piece missing of the $10,000, and then I got a used station wagon, and some extra equipment I needed. And so a friend and I set off across the country from New York to here to film. The material I'm filming is teenagers in relationship to machines. And one of the machines that across the country they're hung up on in a popular sense, I mean like aside from the transistor, is the car. And so my film is ostensibly about teenagers and drag racing and kustom cars... the complete title is "KKK," which stands for *Kustom Kar Kommandos*. Kustom is spelled with a "k" because that's the way teenagers spell it to show that it's a teenage word and adults keep out. They've invented their own things like that, and they've invented a lot of other things too. The Kommandos being spelled with a "k" turns out to be German, but the kids don't realize it.

In the first place, I subscribe to a thing called "Drag News," which has nothing to do with Finocchio's or drag queens. It's about drag races. It gives scheduled events for the next six months, and it also gives the addresses of various car clubs which meet usually once a week. I've gone to plenty of their meetings and all they talk about are motors and cars. It's just incredible. It becomes very abstract, like some sort of theological discussion.

Spider: Why do you think that teenagers are universally hung up on the automobile? Do you think it's symbolic?

Anger: Well, I suppose my films can be said to have symbolism in them, but I don't see any difference between a symbol and a thing: it's the same. And so, you can say that the cars, particularly the drag racers – what they call the rail jobs – not only are obviously power symbols, terribly phallic and all this, but they're also an involvement in a controlled ordeal, in a controlled death-tempting ritual. The kids I'm interested in are the ones who create the cars themselves, not the ones who have the money to hire one of these super-duper kustomizers to make their dreamboat project.

Spider: What would you say to these kids when you wanted to do some filming?

Anger: Well, I say the same thing that I said with the motorcycle group in *Scorpio Rising*, which is, "I'm making a film," as I said in *Scorpio*, "about bikes," or I say "about kustom cars." And the only similarity of the two groups is that they're terribly touched by anyone that shows any interest in the thing they dig. I've had to do quite a bit of homework, memorizing things that are really quite foreign to me, so that I could talk on their level enough to be accepted.[3]

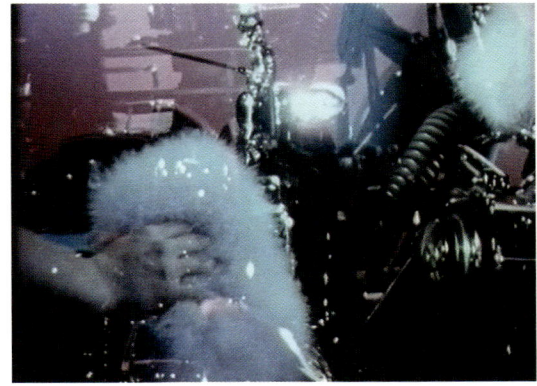

As the three minute "sketch" of *Kustom Kar Kommandos* exists, the "Dream Lover" soundtrack sensuously follows the slow pans across the glistening body of a customized car, and across the taut bodies of the boys tenderly caressing it. Again, fetishizing close-ups are used and attention is given to surface textures: a soft feather-down buffer shivers with a gust across the pristine metal engine and hood, with the car turning slowly in front of the fixated camera. Getting into the car to start up the engine and grip the glistening untouched manual stickshift, it is as if the hot-rod and its rider may never leave their hermetic showroom vacuum.

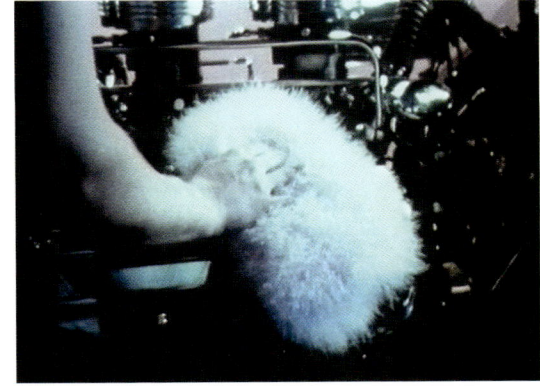

Olivier Assayas gives a detailed appraisal of Anger's influence and relationship to the music clip genre, and the use of music in Anger's work, stating "Anger is the only real precursor of the music clip, providing its essential syntax."[4] As the music video has become one of the dominant aesthetic forms of our time, Assayas addresses the form with cynicism: as a "publicity aesthetic" and "something to sell, and after that a space to fill" (hypnotizing with the speed of montage, by the accumulation not of images, but of visual effects). Assayas likens the singer to one of Anger's "adepts" or Warhol's "superstars," caught in his or her own scenario as a spectacle, presenting themselves for the satisfaction of their own narcissism. Assayas concludes that the music clip inverts what Anger initiated; rather than being inspired by it, simply exploits it.[5]

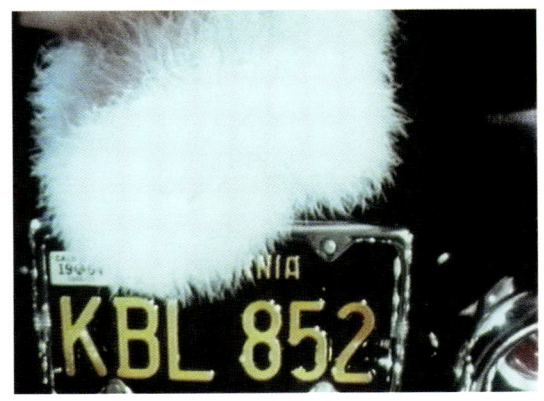

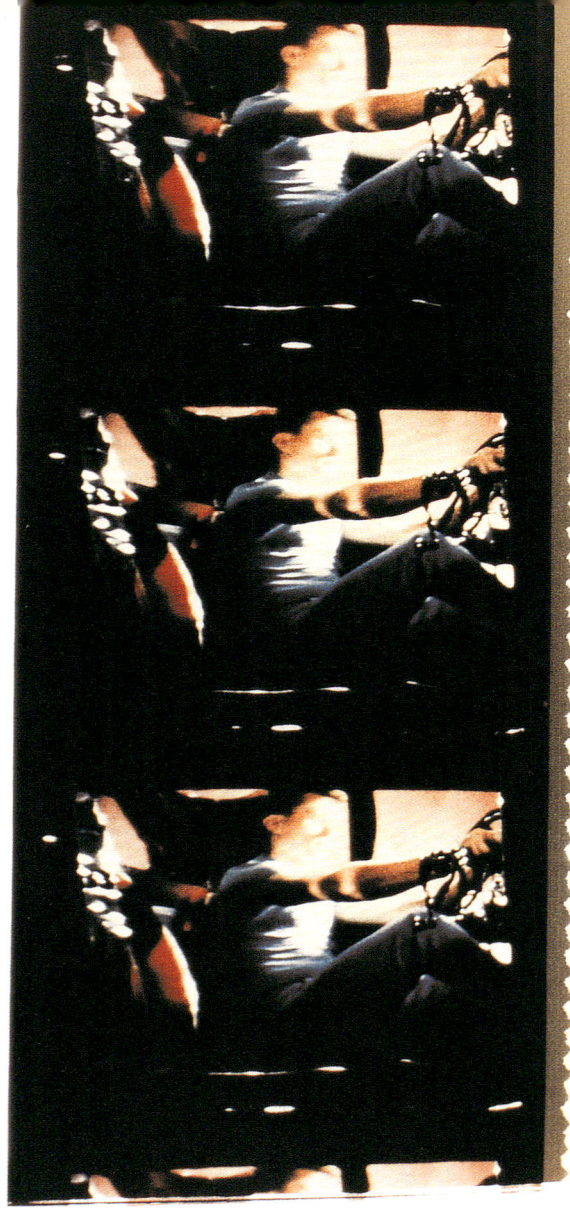

Kustom Kar Kommando's first screening in New York was accompanied by Anger's program notes:

> Excerpt from a work in progress. This sequence invokes the "Dream Lover," a blind for The Charioteer of the Tarot Trumps. Dedicated to Craig Breedlove. Credits: Conceived, Directed, Photographed and Edited by Kenneth Anger. Cast: The All-Chrome Ruby Plush Dream Buggy, and the Maker. Music: The Parris Sisters. Filmed in San Bernadino, California on Ektachrome. Begun with assistance from The Ford Foundation. Note: *KKK* completion costs for 1966, covering optical printing and special effects: $20,000. Interested donors please contact Film-Makers' Co-operative.

As these notes allude, Anger puts into practice Crowley's codified alchemical scale wherein planets are related to colors, sacred alphabets, drugs, perfumes, jewels, plants, magical weapons, the elements of the tarot, etc. In the Royal Color Tables of *777 – The Book of Correspondences*, the "princess scale" denotes the "pure, pastel colors of idealism" which is applied to *Kustom Kar Kommandos*, in an invocation which transposes the Sign of Cancer (sea-shell blue and pink) onto the machine.[6] *Kustom Kar Kommandos* also recalls the "hard sweet pastels" that Donald Judd described in John Chamberlain's crumpled automobile sculptures at this time. Judd reacted with particular enthusiasm to the distinctive surface created by the chromatic luster of the Harley Davidson metallic automotive lacquers that Chamberlain had used. The "California surfaces" that Robert Smithson described when discussing *Scorpio Rising*, were to flourish in the mid to late 1960s and early 70s with the West Coast development of "finish fetish" in painting and sculpture, where the vaunted gestural mark was erased for the machine-like pristine surface of a car or surfboard, using lacquers, metal-flake and airbrushing used for customizing cars.[7] Anger however was soon drawn toward the new psychedelic aesthetic.

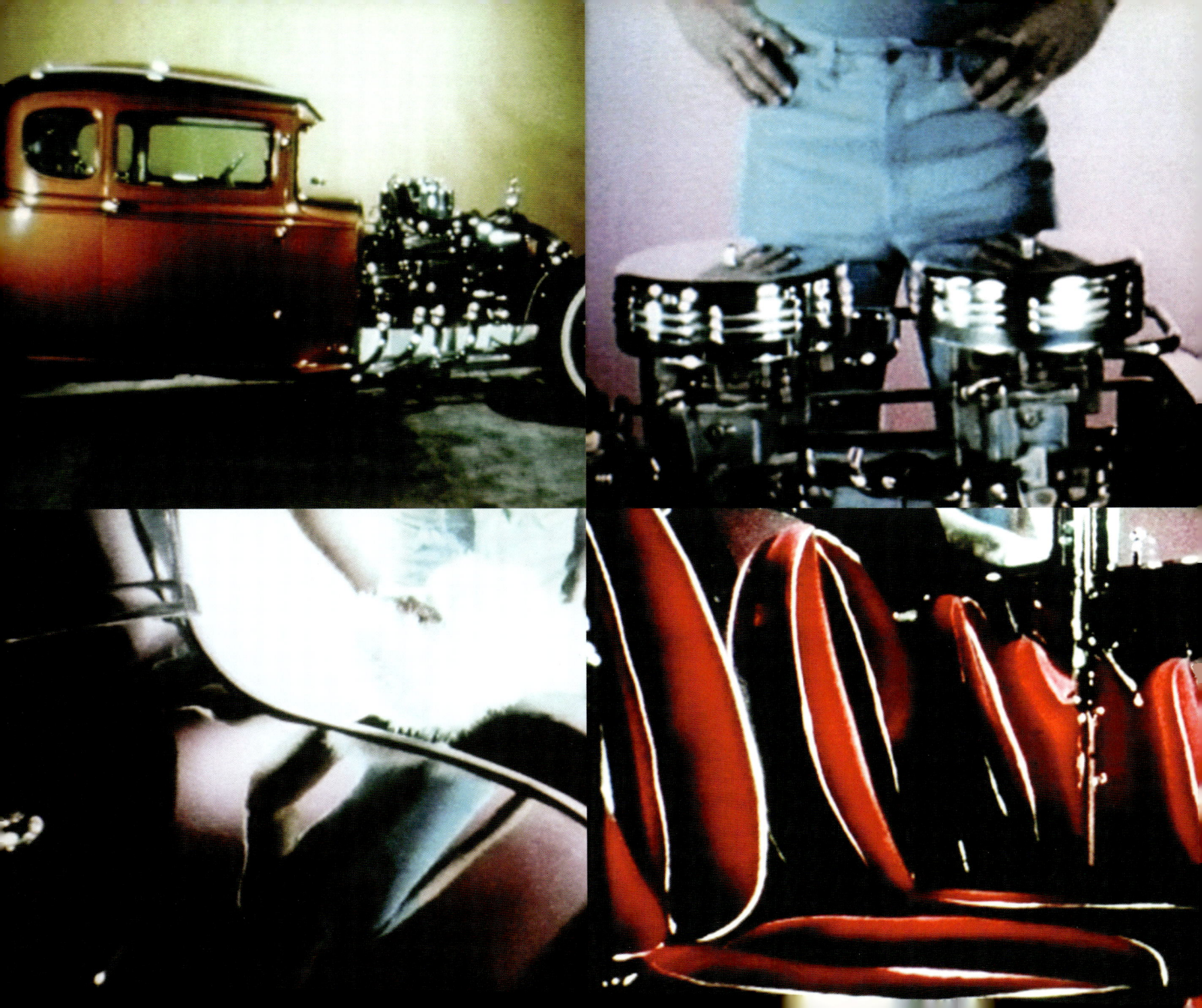

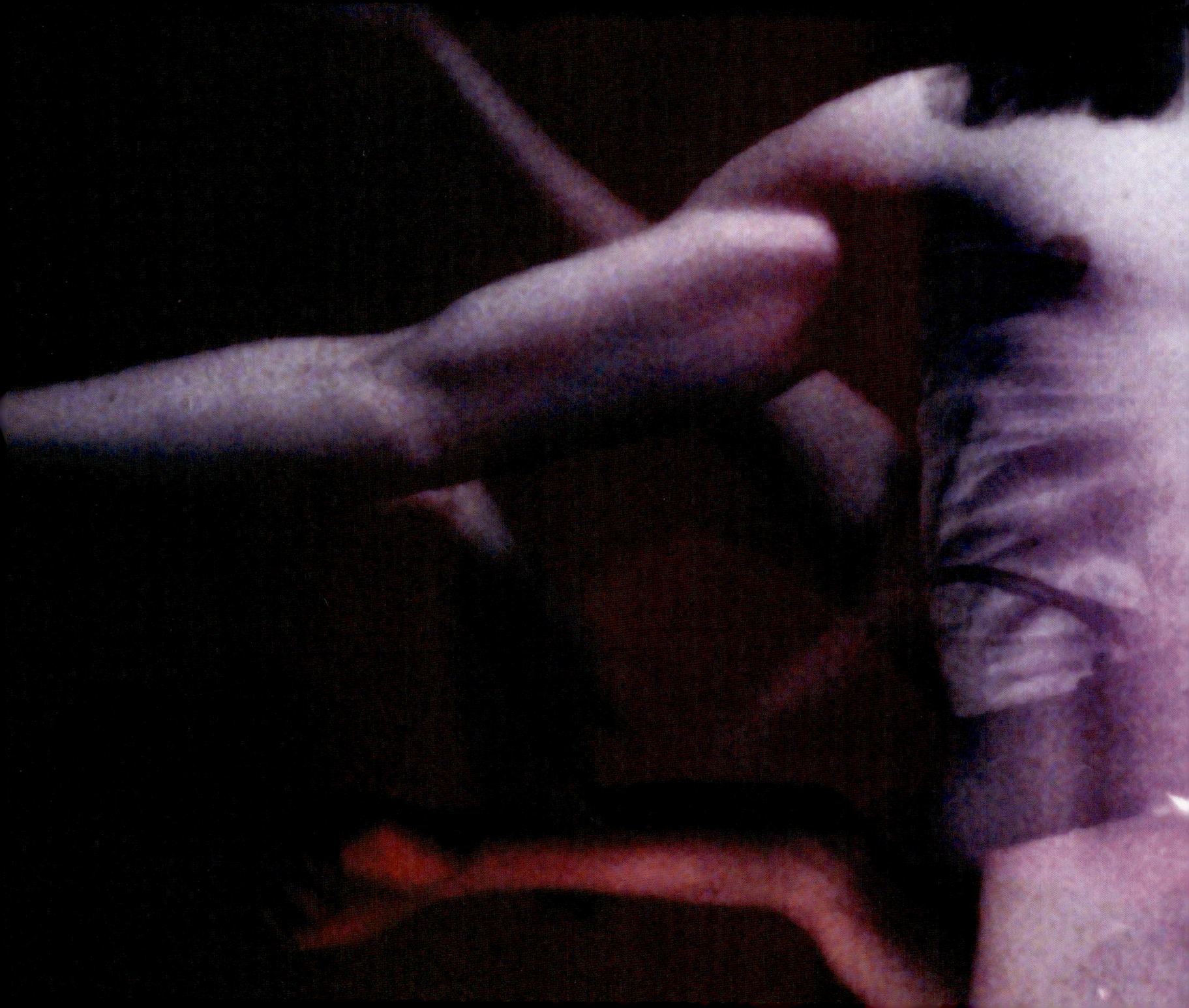

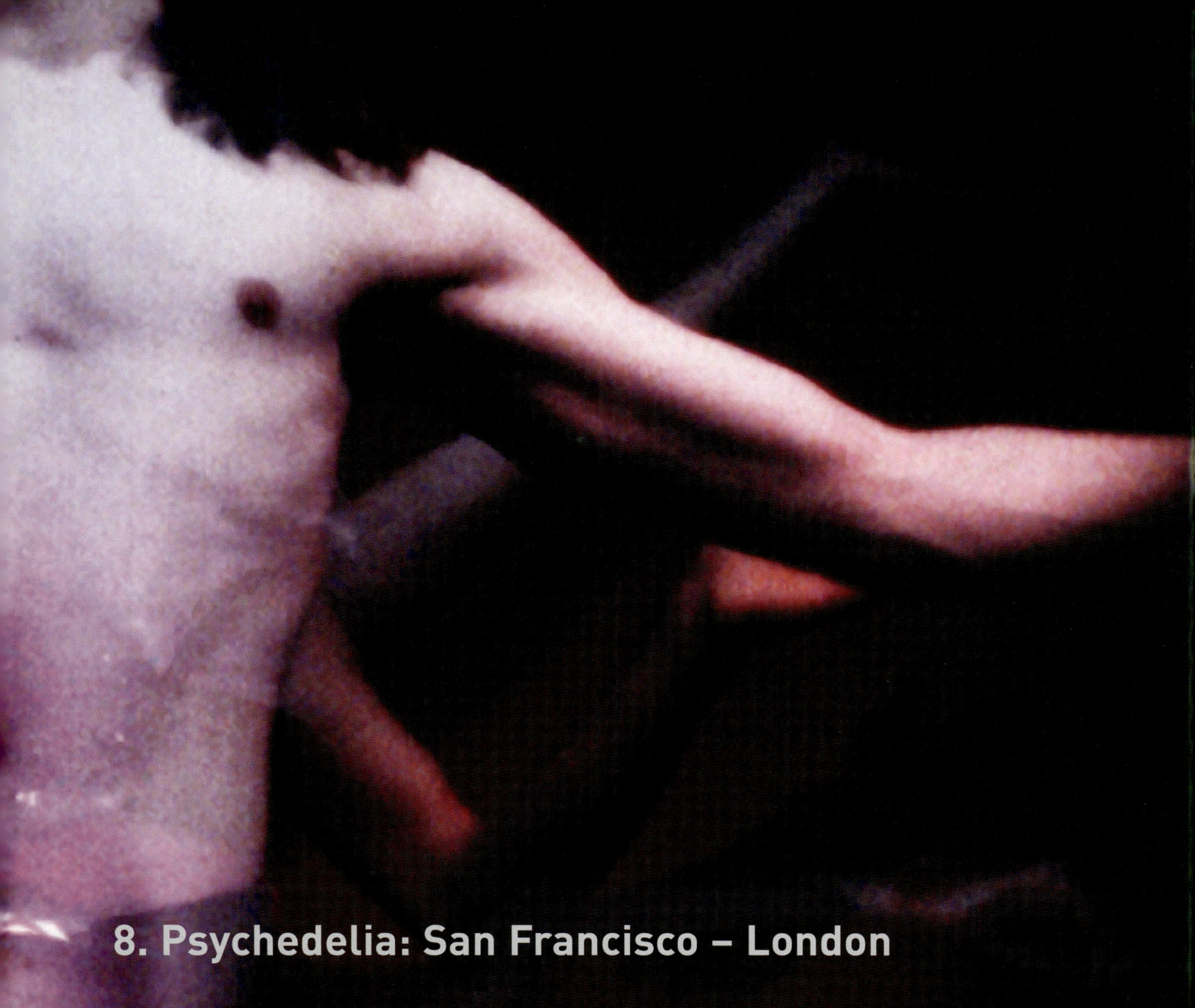

8. Psychedelia: San Francisco – London

Kenneth Anger was integral to the burgeoning psychedelic scene in California, with 1965-1966 marking a dramatic aesthetic change in his work. Nevertheless, his films continued to reflect his interest in ritual and magick, synergizing the pan-cultural symbols and references (departing from Crowley's iconography) with consciousness expanding, abstract psychedelic visuals, and music written specifically to accompany the imagery. This pan-cultural fusion became central to the aesthetics and ethos of psychedelia of the late 1960s as exploration beyond socially prescribed morés became the agenda of the new generation. Anger pioneered visualizing psychedelic states as early as 1954 with *Inauguration of the Pleasure Dome*.[1]

If the doors of perception were cleansed every thing would appear to man as it is, Infinite.... There are things that are known and things that are unknown – in between are the doors.

William Blake

He returned to London in 1965 to prepare the LSD version of *Inauguration of the Pleasure Dome – The Sacred Mushroom Edition (Lord Shiva's Dream)* and to make *Anger Aquarian Arcanum*, 1965, a short sequence of magical symbols for the prelude to his *Magick Lantern Cycle*, a compilation of his best-known work to be screened at the Filmmakers Cinematheque in New York in Spring 1966. The screening featured a prelude of stills of Aleister Crowley as well as images from the *Anger Aquarian Arcanum*, a repertory of symbols and talismans including the Pentagram of the Goat-God Baphomet; The Crowned Dragon of Alchemy; The Sacred Sigil of The Great Beast 666; The Holy Talisman of the Templars, Abraxas. The program, designed by Anger, allowed for a "Brief Intermission": "*Note: Psychedelic researchers desirous to Turn On for Pleasure Dome should absorb their sugar cubes at this point," followed by "*Note: Psychedelic researchers preparing for Pleasure Dome should remain seated during this intermission. The following film should, under ideal circumstances, be experienced in that Holy trance called High."

Anger's increasing interest and experimentation with a psychedelic aesthetic and its concomitant social stance, is a marked and manifold stylistic break from *Kustom Kar Kommados* of the previous year. Whereas most experimented on their own bodies and minds, Anger was to manipulate celluloid to recreate these effects to the highest level of sophistication. Living in the Haight-Ashbury district of San Francisco in a mansion called the Russian Embassy, the next project he conceived was about the "love generation" and his encounter with a certain Joe Lucifer sparked off *Lucifer Rising*, which he began filming in 1966 with a 19 year old guitarist from the band Love, Bobby Beausoleil (who turned out to be less than interested in being directed).

In 1954 Aldous Huxley wrote *The Doors of Perception* and *Heaven and Hell*, exploring the effects of mescaline. The manifestation of the *Mysterium tremendum*, and a quasi-religious ecstasy, is evident in Anger's major work to follow, *Invocation of My Demon Brother* and *Lucifer Rising*.[2] The connection between religion, trance, ritual and hypnosis aided by mind-expanding substances has been widespread from the beginning of time in the rituals and trances of most cultures – shamanistic to Dionysian traditions – from Tibetan Buddhists to Aztecs, ancient Egyptians and practitioners of the occult; a door to paradise or to the infernal regions. Jim Morrison was an avid reader of both Huxley and William Blake, and hence the name The Doors, formed in Los Angeles in 1965, while The Velvet Underground was formed in New York the same year, an integral part of Andy Warhol's *Exploding Plastic Inevitable*. Los Angeles was also home to the burgeoning psychedelic rock scene that gave birth to, amongst others, Steppenwolf, Buffalo Springfield, Love, Kaleidoscope, The Seeds, Frank Zappa, Iron Butterfly and The Byrds.

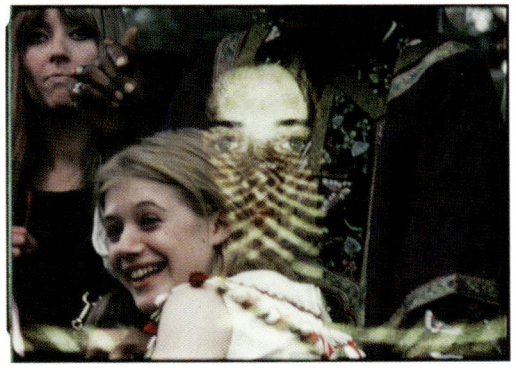

> That humanity at large will ever be able to dispense with Artificial Paradises seems very unlikely.... Art and religion, carnivals and saturnalia, dancing and listening to oratory – all these have served, in H. G. Well's phrase, as Doors in the Wall.[3]

Ritual continued to form a structural framework for Anger's new projects despite the aesthetic change visible in *Lucifer Rising* and *Invocation of My Demon Brother*, in a new context of consciousness expansion of the visionary variety. Symbolism, Decadence and Aestheticism, the automatism of Surrealism, and psychedelia all share what was expressed succinctly by Arthur Rimbaud: "To arrive at the unknown through the disordering of all the senses, that's the point." (It is no coincidence then, that a psychedelic aesthetic adopted styles of Symbolism and Decadence, i.e. Aubrey Beardsley, Art Nouveau, Gustav Klimt and Viennese Jugendstil.)

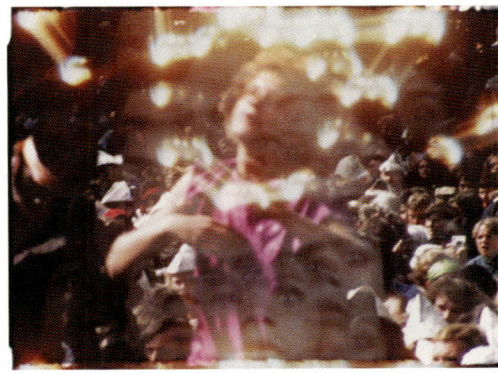

In 1965, Dr. Timothy Leary was a professor at Berkeley experimenting with the new drug lysergic acid diethylamide (LSD). The drug, ingested by pill form or on sheets of brightly painted paper, produced an eight to 12 hour chemical vacation highlighted by profound changes in sensitivity to color, sound, mood; an alternative hallucinatory consciousness. Brilliant illumination seemed to shine from within objects, with preternaturally intense colors on a good trip. LSD was originally intended to be used to help victims of psychological disorders, however, Leary tested it on himself and became enraptured with it. In 1965 LSD was not yet illegal and would only become so in June 1966. So taken with the psychological and sensory effects

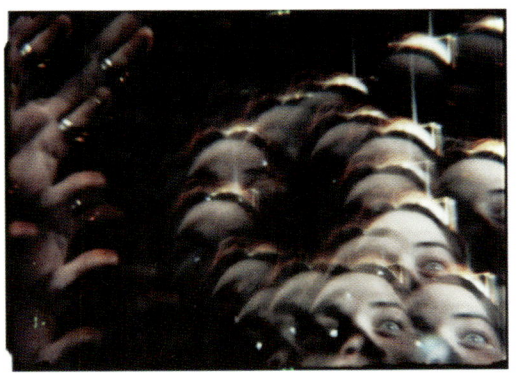

Stills on this page and following are from *Invocation of My Demon Brother*

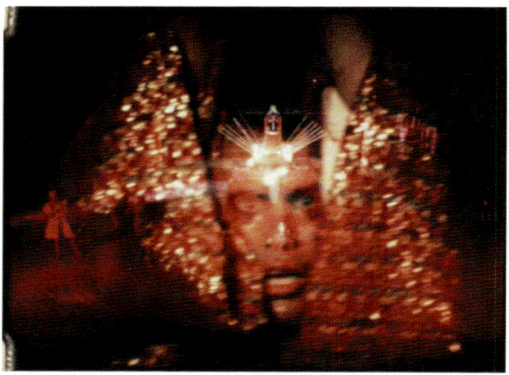

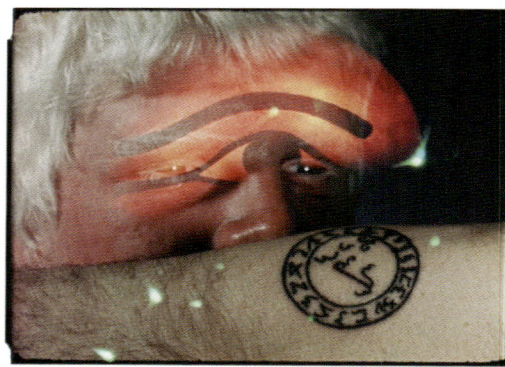

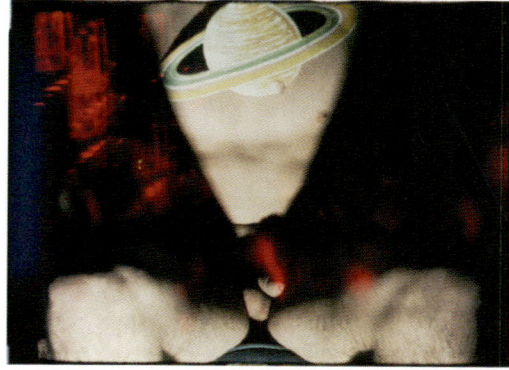

This page middle: "Anger's arm with Lucifer's seal tattoo"
Bottom: "Saturn meets the steelworker"

of acid, Leary organized "be-in's" where attendees dropped acid, danced and grooved to experimental music enhanced by light shows, and generally "freaked out" – it was suggested that attendees would participate in "out-of-body" and mystical experiences.

In San Francisco, Anger was able to borrow electric lamps and projectors used for such light shows for the 1966 *Lucifer Rising* footage with Beausoleil (which was to become *Invocation of My Demon Brother*). It took the world press two years to catch on to this underground movement, which soon took root internationally. Pop music transformed, reflecting psychedelic experience with new electronic sound effects and distortions such as those created with the Moog synthesizer (and the amplifier), creating unearthly experiential sounds as well as reproducing instrumental music once only available in orchestras. This world was light-years away from mainstream film representation, and the visualization of psychedelic states in film was rare (popularized by Dennis Hopper's *The Trip*).[4] While abstract, rhythmic filmmaking had been pioneered by Len Lye and Oskar Fischinger in the 1920s (hand-painted frames, in Fischinger's case, an extension of Kandinsky's search for visual parallels to music, operating directly on the viewers' perceptual faculties), the advent of analogue computer graphics in the 1950s and 60s enabled abstract, psychedelic and personal films: Jordan Belson's *Re-Entry*, 1964, James Whitney's *Lapis*, 1963-1966, the kaleidoscopic *7362* by Pat O'Neill, 1965-1967, among others. Sitney described Sidney Peterson's *The Cage*, 1947: "Even though structurally he related anamorphosis to various forms of madness, his distorting lens offers an alternative to haptic perspectives."[5] The distorted imagery represented the perspective of the "liberated" eye.

> I believe that the use of noise to make music will continue and increase until we reach a music produced through the aid of electrical instruments.... Whereas in the past, the point of disagreement has been between dissonance and consonance, it will be, in the immediate future, between noise and so-called musical sounds.

John Cage, 1956

Opposite: "Anger invokes The Gods at Equinox, Straight Theater, San Francisco, 1967"

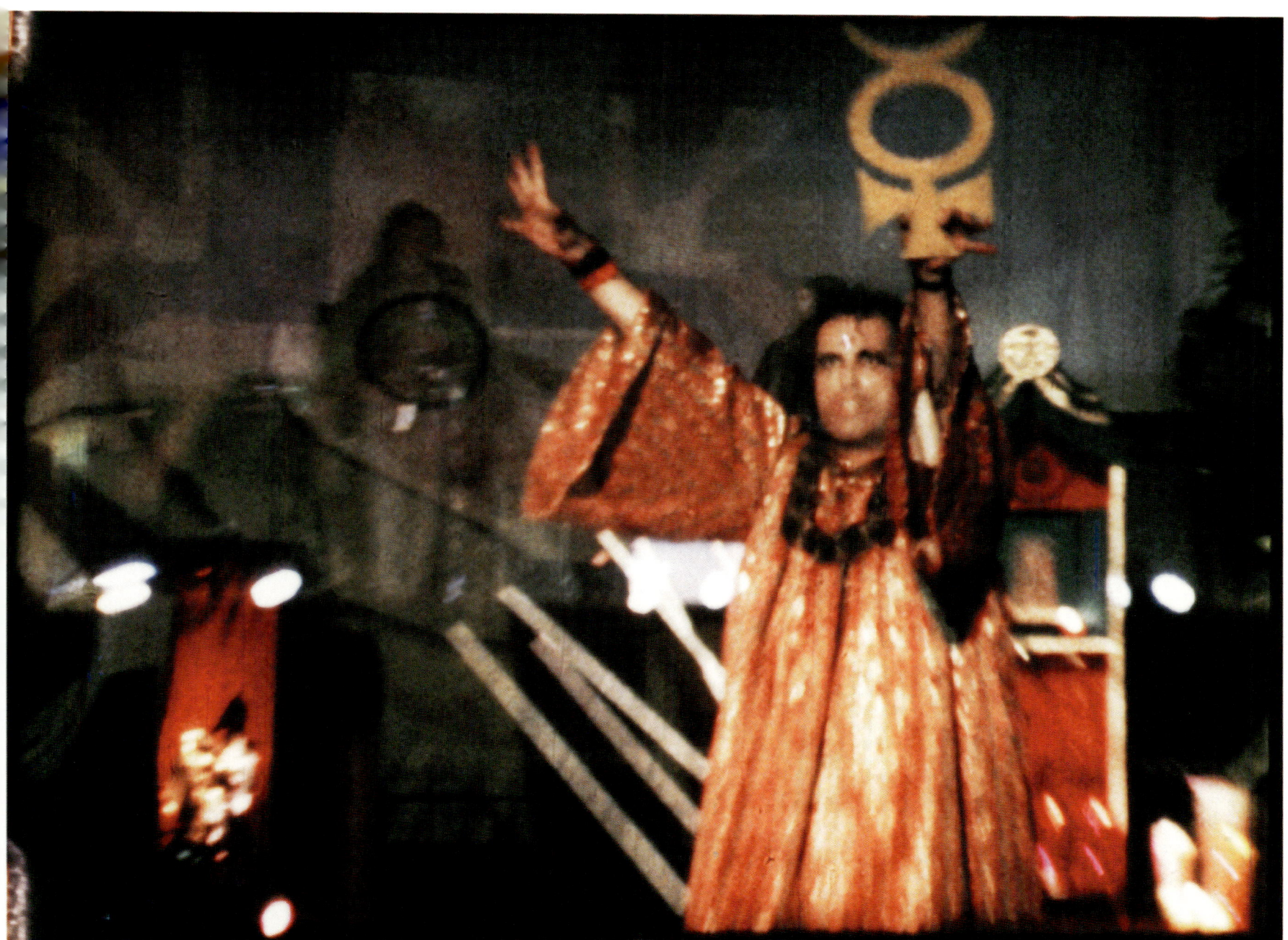

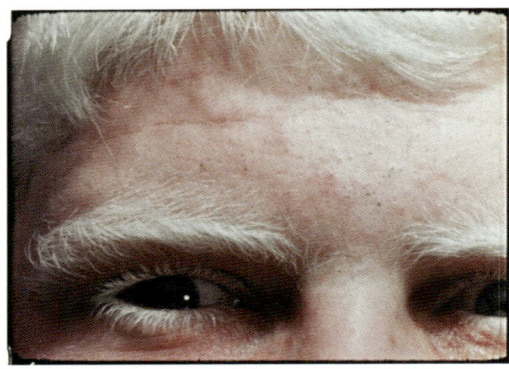

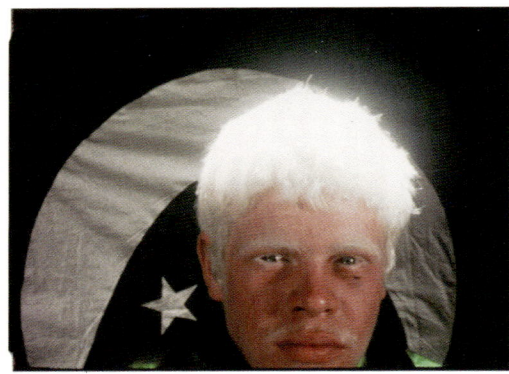

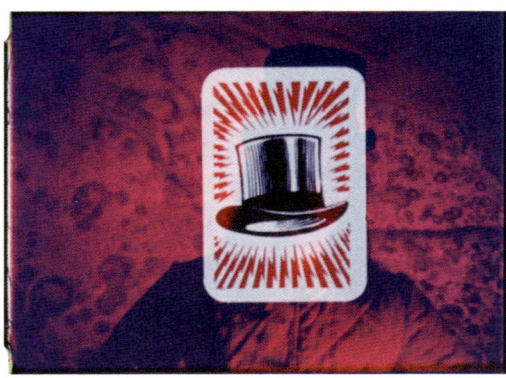

While psychedelic music transcended the rock music boundaries by enhancing, creating or recalling altered states of reality, visual artists explored optical effects and experiments. Op Artists had their leading practitioner in British painter Bridget Riley, and color field painters in the United States explored the optical field and perceptual properties of color. The collaboration of artists and scientists concerned with the physical and experiential properties of light and space evolved, and led to Southern Californian Light and Space artists such as James Turrell and Robert Irwin's explorations of the perceptual and experiential properties of light, space and audio sensory perception. In 1965 the seminal Op Art exhibition *The Responsive Eye* (organized by the Museum of Modern Art, New York) traveled to the Pasadena Art Museum, and Bridget Riley had a solo exhibition in Los Angeles.

September 21, 1967: Kenneth Anger intended to project the footage of his still unfinished *Lucifer Rising* at the Straight Theater on Haight Street, in the Haight-Ashbury "hippie haven" of San Francisco, much of which was of Bobby Beausoleil.[6] The occasion was The Equinox of the Gods, a celebration of the Autumnal Equinox (based on a ritual written by Aleister Crowley), and a benefit with Beausoleil's new band "The Magick Powerhouse of Oz" intended to help the filmmaker finance the film's completion, during which Anger was to conduct an elaborate ritual. Anger asserted in interviews that 1,600 feet of original footage disappeared from the trunk of his car that night. In frustration with the thwarted project, he ran a full-page ad in New York's *The Village Voice* the week of Halloween which read: "In Memoriam Kenneth Anger Filmmaker 1947-1967." It was not an announcement of his death but of the end of his career as a filmmaker. After a "burning ceremony" in New York in front of Jonas Mekas (in which Mekas mistakenly believed Anger was burning his earliest films), he soon departed for London.

Opposite: Advertisement in *The Village Voice* announcing the end of Anger's filmmaking career

In Memoriam

KENNETH ANGER

FILM MAKER

(1947-1967)

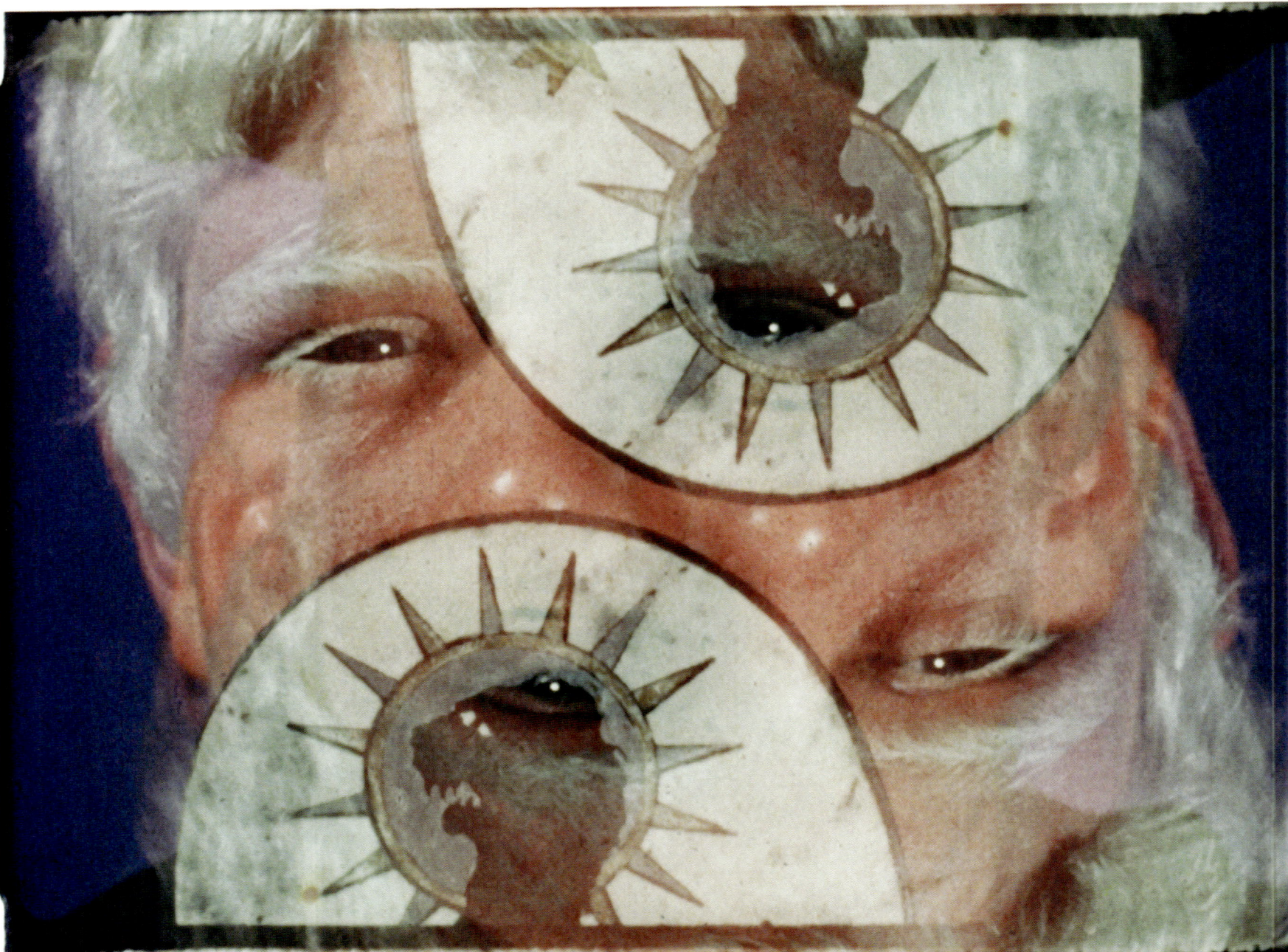

Invocation of My Demon Brother

1969

11 minutes

16mm, color

Music by Mick Jagger on the Moog Synthesizer

Probably more than all of Kenneth Anger's films, *Invocation of My Demon Brother* comes closest to that cinematic state of hypnosis the filmmaker sought. It is a short, intense, ritualistic film with a rough, almost naive synthesizer soundtrack by Mick Jagger. The "shadow prints" and the dialectical relationship between structure and chaos are amplified with the hypnotic waves of mono-tonal synthesized soundtrack. *Invocation's* abstract non-narrative imagery, rough edges and minimal visual flow was technically even more ambitious than previous work such as *Inauguration* with its fast motion, stills and multiple impositions. For the first time, Anger had an original soundtrack to accompany the film, composed by Mick Jagger on his new Moog synthesizer. It is quite possibly the most adventurous and original solo project Jagger ever worked on, and the soundtrack was a gift.

Every film I've ever made has tried to impose upon the mind of the watcher an alternative reality. It's the dedication to create Make Believe.

Kenneth Anger

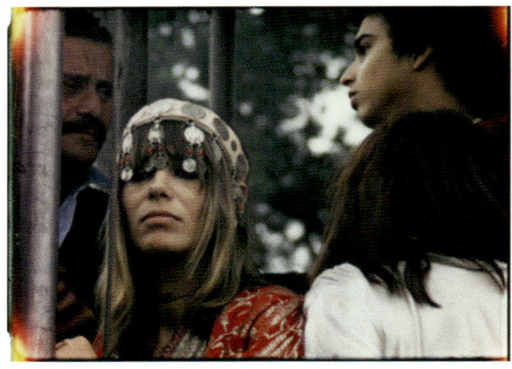

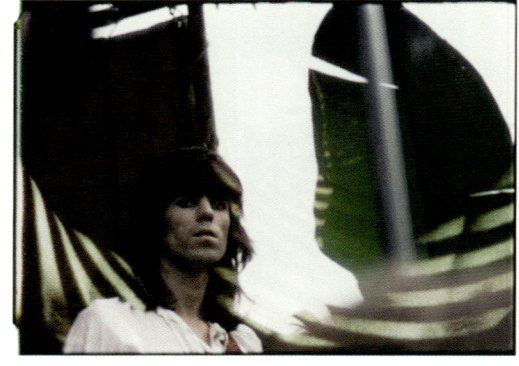

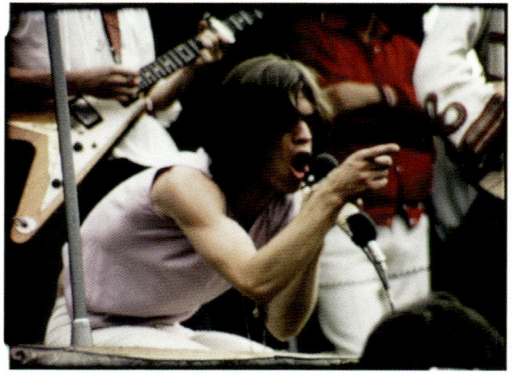

Anger had called it "an attack on the sensorium."[7] Perhaps at his most experimental, Anger moves further away from the stylistic tropes that are synonymous with narrative-driven mainstream cinema, and deeper into the hermetic realm of artifice, symbol, subliminal communication, and spatio-temporal rupture. It attests to the fact that few filmmakers other than Anger have been brave (or imaginative enough) to acknowledge, technically employ and materialize the rapturous, elemental possibilities of film for taking us beyond verisimilitude: exploring to what extent reality and naturalism are just states of perception.

Moving to London in the late 1960s, Anger found himself a pivotal influence in a decadent convergence of rock music, art, and psychedelia, with the Robert Fraser gallery providing a nexus for this convergence.[8] Fraser was also the main conduit for new American art coming into London, particularly American Pop: Robert Rauschenberg, Jim Dine, Bruce Conner, Claes Oldenburg, Andy Warhol and Ed Ruscha, alongside British artists Bridget Riley, Peter Blake, Richard Hamilton and Edward Paolozzi. He was the first to exhibit Gilbert and George, with film screenings by Kenneth Anger, Bruce Conner and Andy Warhol. The legendary openings were peopled by Fraser's friends and clients, including members of the Beatles and the Rolling Stones. Anger and Fraser had become close friends, traveling to India with Fraser in 1968 (with members of the Rolling Stones and others). Versed thoroughly in Crowley's writings and his experiments with altered states through magic and drugs, and already a well-known avant-garde filmmaker and fixture to the Fraser scene, Anger was also taken up by Mick Jagger, Keith Richards, Marianne Faithfull, Anita Pallenberg and subsequently Jimmy Page of Led Zeppelin (an avid collector of Crowley's paintings). The mutual attraction between Anger, Jagger and Page led to original music composed specifically for *Invocation of My Demon Brother* and *Lucifer Rising*. While Fraser was in India, Anger rented his Mount Street apartment in London and used it as the set for *Lucifer Rising*. A decadent rock aesthetic was born, a combination of anger and abjection, Dionysian and shamanistic traditions, Decadence and Dada, which can be placed within a literary context that encompasses de Sade, Lautréamont, Rimbaud, Genet, Bataille, Artaud, Burroughs, and Bukowski.

Originally, Mick Jagger was a contender for the role of Lucifer in *Lucifer Rising*, as it was conceived in 1966. The Rolling Stones' mind-blown 1967 manifesto *Their Satanic Majesties Request* had already illustrated the direction they were taking. Keith Richards' girlfriend, Anita Pallenberg, had first introduced the Rolling Stones' doomed bassist Brian Jones to her her esoteric beliefs. She later appeared as ambi-sexual seductress in *Performance*, 1968, released in 1970, alongside Mick Jagger. The film was co-directed by Donald Cammell, whose father the poet Charles Richard Cammell, was a one-time associate of Crowley in the 1930s. Donald Cammell's reminiscences of the Great Beast as a lad earned him a certain amount of cachet in Luciferian London, as well as the role of Osiris in Anger's *Lucifer Rising*. As Brian Jones drifted into narcotic oblivion, Pallenberg shared her alternative interests with

Jagger and Richards. It was in this climate that Anger integrated his practice, promising to be the Rolling Stones' tutelary Magus, with Pallenberg being particularly captivated by Anger's reputation. Jagger, flirting with film himself, was initially intrigued with what he had heard of Anger's latest opus in progress, *Lucifer Rising*, which had already gained the reputation of being a cursed film (due to its maker's difficulties in casting and financing, and the San Francisco debacle with Beausoleil). It was at this time he made the soundtrack for what was to become Anger's *Invocation*. After the tragic death of Jones, drowning in a swimming pool, the relationship between Anger and Jagger dissipated. The concert thrown for Jones' memory in Hyde Park, fragments of which are captured in *Invocation of My Demon Brother*, turned into a grotesque farce. Hundreds of boxes of white butterflies were meant to have been released into the summer sky, but had shriveled into a dying mess. Jagger became cynical, if not disenchanted with Anger's self-proclaimed role as Magus, while Pallenberg, and Jagger's ex-girlfriend Marianne Faithfull remained on amicable terms, allowing Anger to realize *Lucifer Rising*, with Pallenberg co-producing and Faithfull in lead role as Lilith.

The development and footage of the two films is integrated. *Invocation* as it now stands is based on fragments of a larger-scale unfinished work, a template from which *Lucifer Rising* was produced. Recycling the footage filmed in California from the original *Lucifer Rising* project with the new London material, *Invocation of My Demon Brother* was conceived. It is an extraordinary work in its own right – with all the prismatic refractions onto the magical world in which Anger was involved at the time. It is quite possibly the most "difficult" for viewers in its abstract quality, rapid editing and juxtaposition of alienating yet seductive imagery. "The demands of watching are compounded by the endless repetition of a monotonously abrasive riff on the Moog soundtrack."[9] Anger artfully manipulated dissolves and superimpositions, techniques for undermining conscious control, such as the use of Vietnam footage of a helicopter and troops. Anamorphosis and abstraction increases: this is the first use in Anger's work of a prismatic lens for the kaleidoscopic multiplication of an image, a common technique employed to simulate psychedelic states in the late 1960s. The close-ups on the Wandbearer, the albino Speed Hacker whom Anger had found in San Francisco, recalls Jean Genet's description of his lover's eyes in *The Thief's Journal*: "over which there closed eyelids and lashes so blond, so luminous and thick, that they brought in not the shade of evening but the shade of evil."[10] Anger also recycled the images of Beausoleil (the demon brother of the invocation, who by this time was involved with an L.A. motorcycle gang and soon with the Manson related murder).

In *Invocation of My Demon Brother*, the use of the swastika and Nazi imagery is perhaps even more pronounced than in *Scorpio Rising*, with footage of Anger's ceremonial ritual as Magus. In the invocation "he gyrates widdershins (counter-clockwise) around the "solar swastika" as "Swirling Spiral Force" to enable the Bringer of Light to break through. In the

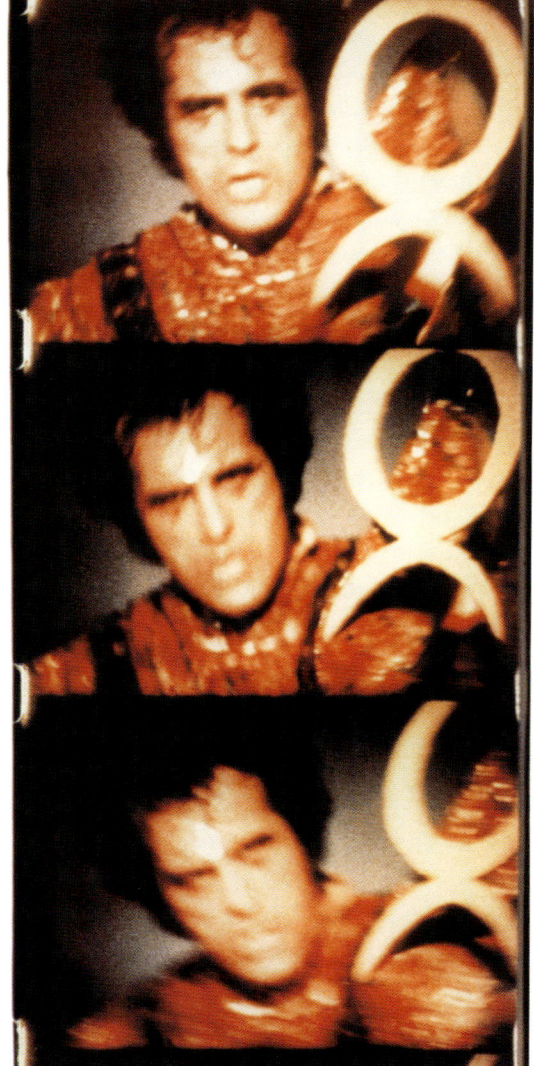

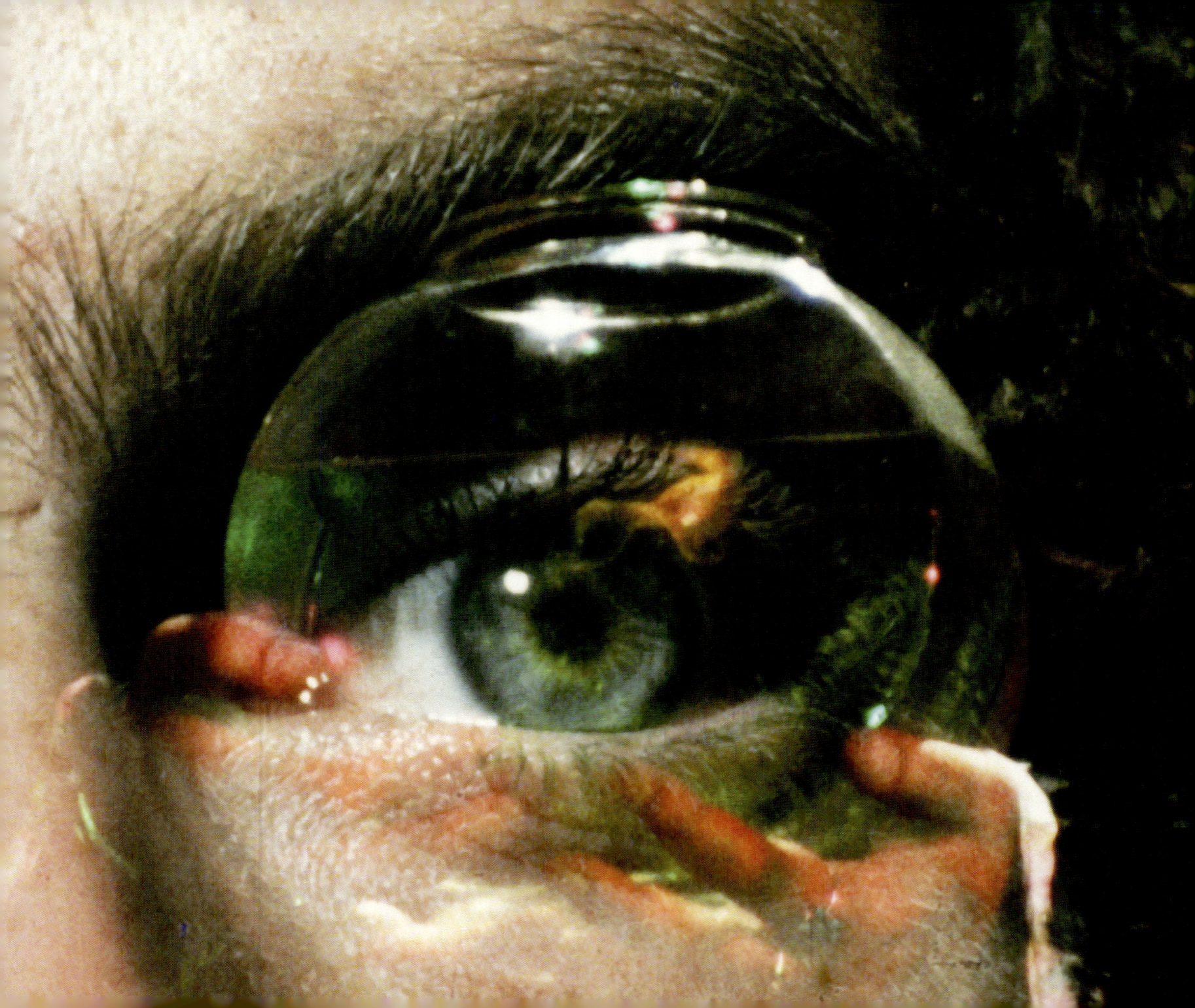

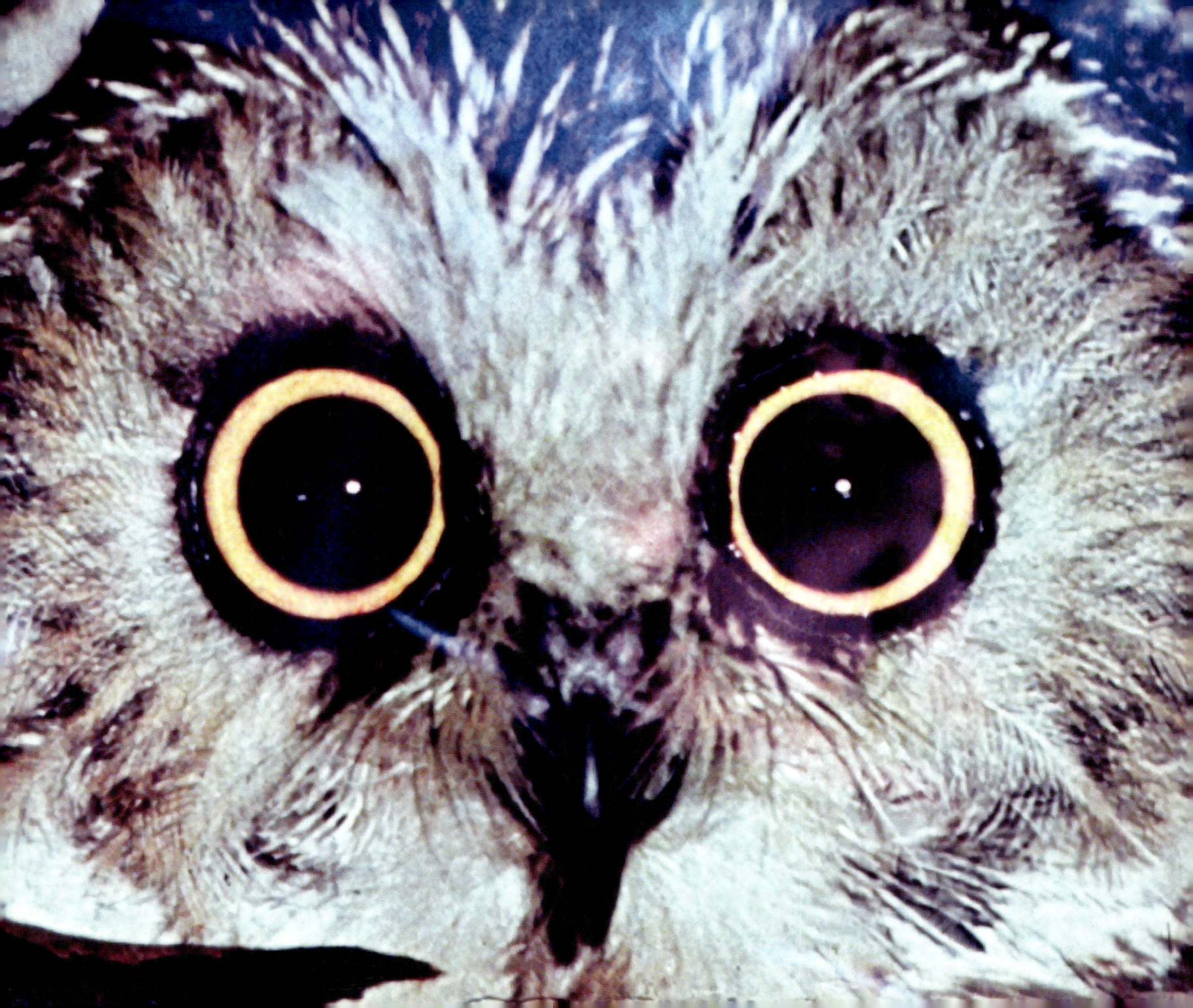

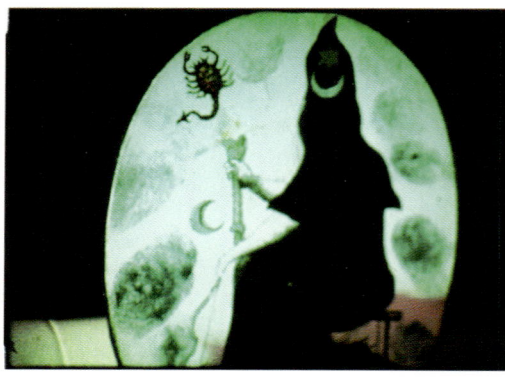

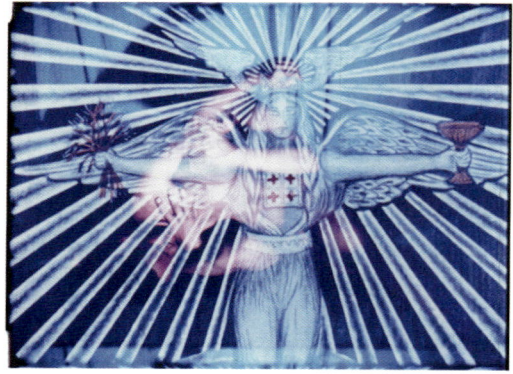

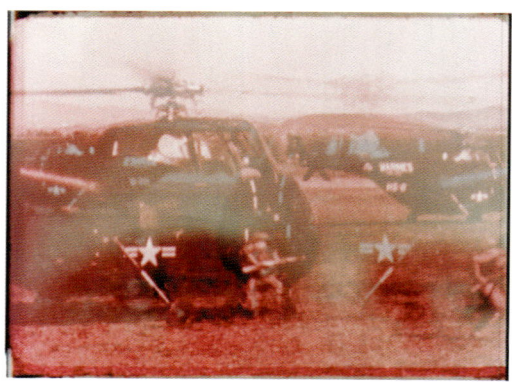

Kabbalah, the swastika is an emblem of continuous spirit."[11] Its symbolic use here as a flag is difficult to dissociate from its historical Third Reich deployment. It has been posited that Hitler was a practicing Satanist and was fully aware of the subconscious power of the symbol with which the Crucifix was replaced. Anger referred to it as "a psychic power pack... Hitler couldn't have done it without the swastika."[12] The swastika has become the most taboo and abject of all symbols, despite its shifting meaning throughout cultures and the ages (it even appears regularly on ancient Greek and Roman ceramic painting). It was appropriated here for its psychic jolt and pan-cultural symbolism. Anger mentioned that the pagan sun-worshipping site of Externsteine, in the Black Forest in Germany, where Marianne Faithfull rises to the altar in *Lucifer Rising*, was used by the Hitler Youth in their initiation ceremonies, carving their names into the tree trunks, which still exist today.[13]

The swastika is used as a repeated motif in the film. It is employed as a hypnosis device, a swirling vortex. The swastika's association with the feminine vortex/passageway into other realms of consciousness was key to this symbol's reappropriation. The Hindu god Ganesha has two primary symbols, the swastika (an emblem of blessing, warding off misfortune) and the mushroom, enhancing psychedelic experience – the keys to the kingdom of knowledge. The drug Soma – which Gordon Wasson has convincingly argued was a hallucinogenic mushroom – was a major formative influence in the early development of Hinduism. Mushroom-like images (known as "chattra" in India) often appear in association with Ganesha, who is appropriately the deity who connects mankind with the divine. Ganesha habitually holds above (or behind) his head what most would take to be an umbrella, but which is also identical to the thin-stemmed psilocybin mushroom. In many depictions of Ganesha he sits below this mushroom which effectively serves to "illuminate" him: the esoteric level of understanding for the initiated (seeing the archetypal form of the sacred mushroom). It is no coincidence then, that in 1966 Anger produced the *Sacred Mushroom* edition of his *Inauguration of the Pleasure Dome*, and the numerous references to Hindu deity in his pantheon.[14] Anger says in retrospect: "I do miss the creative chaos of those years. LSD was great until it became a menace. I wouldn't say LSD influenced my filmmaking, but there was a cosmic quality that came from it. I miss those first trips, when the wallpaper used to dance, when shapes did the hula."[15]

> The image is not an idea. It is a radiant node or cluster: it is what I can, and must perforce, call a VORTEX, from which and through which, and into which ideas are constantly rushing.
>
> Ezra Pound[16]

The cinema in general employs occult (hidden) techniques to simulate physical manifestation. Artaud described an occult model of cinema in which the physical excitement of rotating images communicates directly to the brain. The mind moves beyond the power of representation. For Artaud, "this virtual power of the images probes for hitherto unused possibilities in the depth of the mind. Essentially the cinema reveals a whole occult life with which it puts us directly in contact."[17]

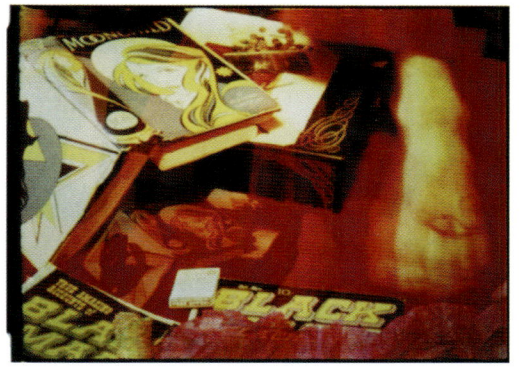

With a number of infamous counterculture figures appearing in *Invocation of My Demon Brother*; The Hell's Angels, Anton La Vey, Anita Pallenberg, Mick Jagger and Keith Richards in the fateful concert in Hyde Park, Marianne Faithfull, and Bobby Beausoleil as he'd been filmed in San Francisco – the intensity of impact is magnified on the spectator's consciousness and recognition. Anton Szandor La Vey was well-known in the 1960s' subculture of social experiment, as the flamboyant High Priest of the Church of Satan and the author of the Satanic Bible. His figure appears in *Invocation* with full horned regalia superimposed with a motorcycle gang wearing Hell's Angels leather jackets.[18]

As if to announce this convocation of potent characters joining forces for the invocation, upon the first screening of *Invocation of My Demon Brother* at the Edinburgh festival of 1969, a nearby church was said to have self-combusted into flames. It is no surprise therefore that with Anger's presence in Britain, the *Invocation* and *Lucifer Rising* projects were subject to high profile media attention which garnered much sensationalized press scandal: "Devil Film To Get State Aid" being one headline due to the fact the film was co-financed by the National Film Board.[19]

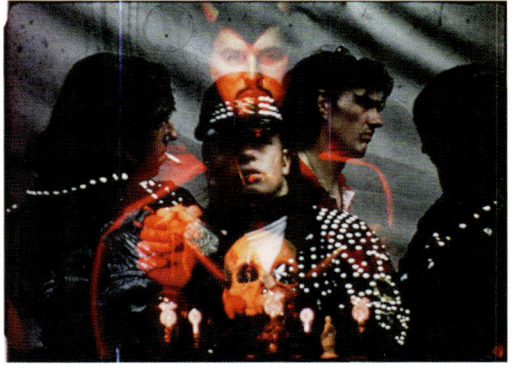

Invocation of My Demon Brother's intense twisted beauty is heightened by proximity to abjection and the powers of horror, ideas central to Kristeva:

"No Beast is there without glimmer of infinity,
No eye so vile nor abject that brushes not
Against lightning from on high, now tender,
Now fierce."

Victor Hugo, *La Légende des siècles*

There looms, within abjection, one of those violent, dark revolts of being, directed against a threat that seems to emanate from an exorbitant outside or inside, ejected beyond the scope of the possible, the tolerable, the thinkable. It lies there, quite close, but it cannot be assimilated. It beseeches, worries, and fascinated desire, which nevertheless, does not let itself be seduced. Apprehensive, desire turns aside; sickened, it rejects.[20]

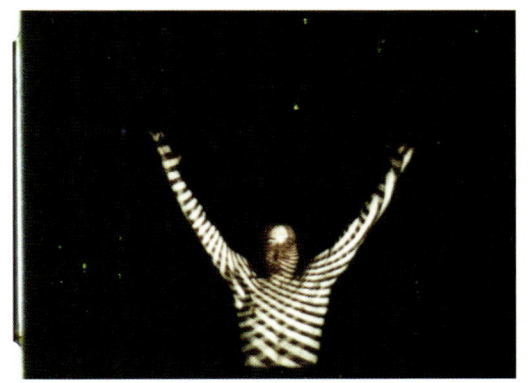

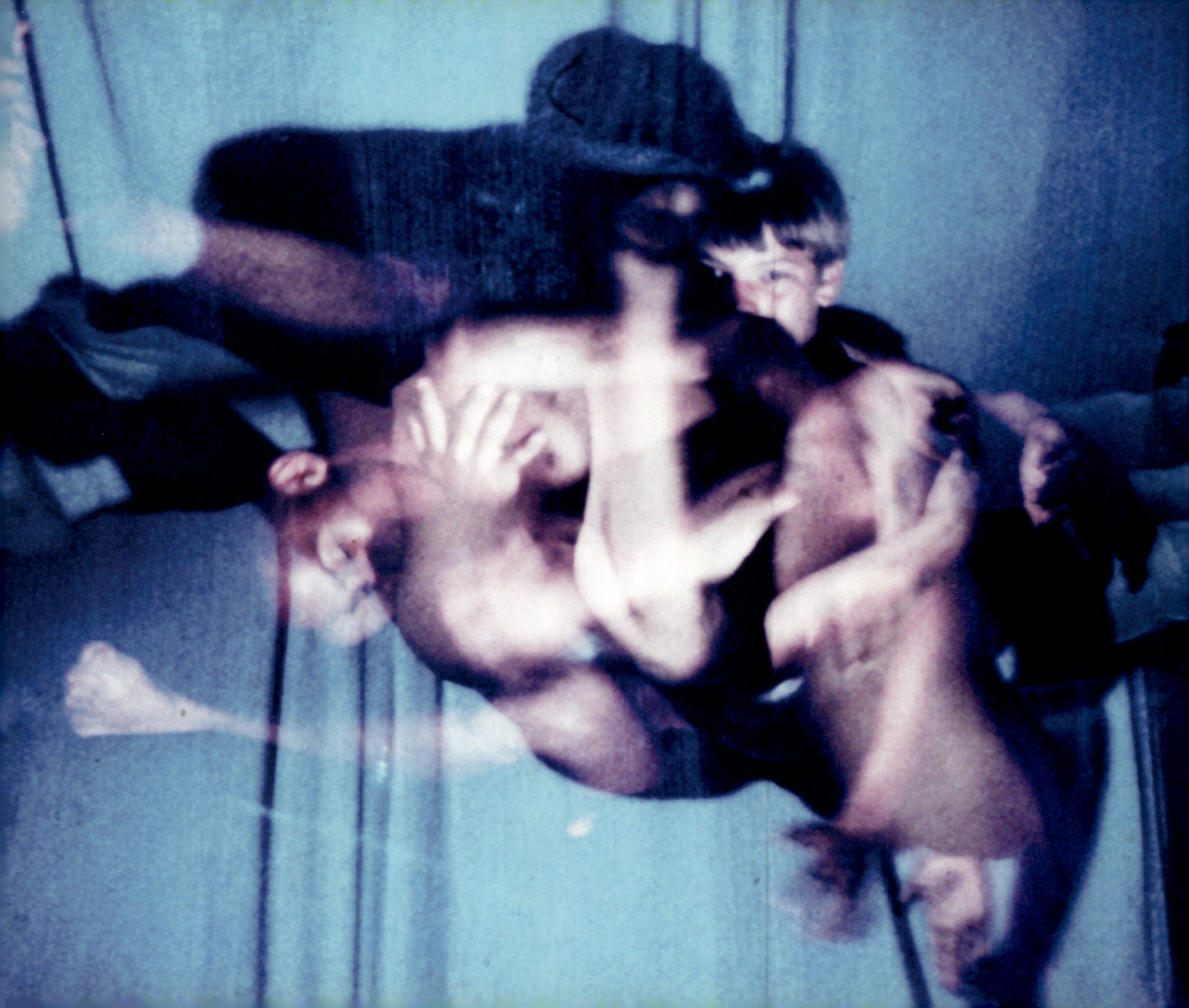

Film Culture's Tenth Independent Film Award was given to Anger for *Invocation of My Demon Brother* in 1969:

> To point out original contributions to the cinema FILM CULTURE is awarding its tenth Independent Film Award (for the year 1969) to Kenneth Anger.
>
> For his film *Invocation of My Demon Brother* specifically, and for his entire creative work in general; for his unique fusion of magick, symbolism, myth, mystery, and vision with the most modern sensibilities, techniques, and rhythms of being; for revealing it all in a refreshed light, persistently, constantly, and with a growing complexity of means and content; at the same time, for doing it with an amazing clarity, directness and sureness; for giving to our eye and our senses some of the most sensuous and mysterious images cinema has created; for being the Keeper of the Art of Cinema as well as the Keeper of the Eternal Magick Directions.[21]

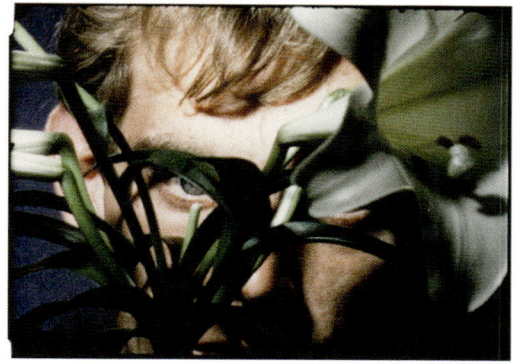

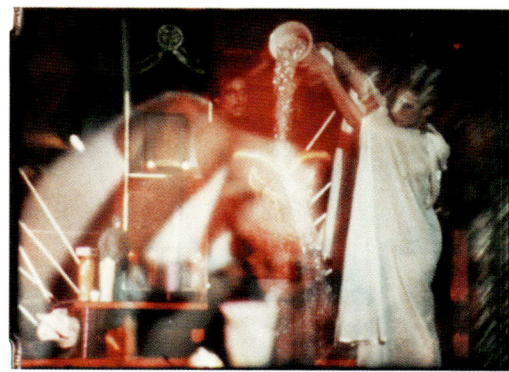

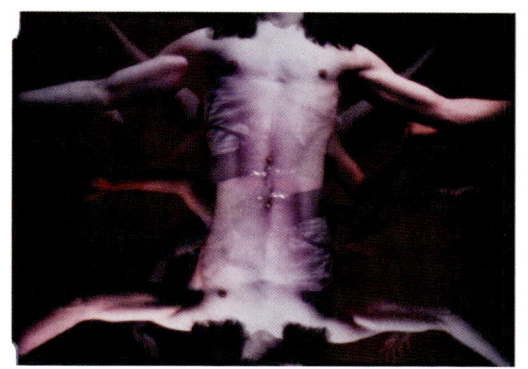

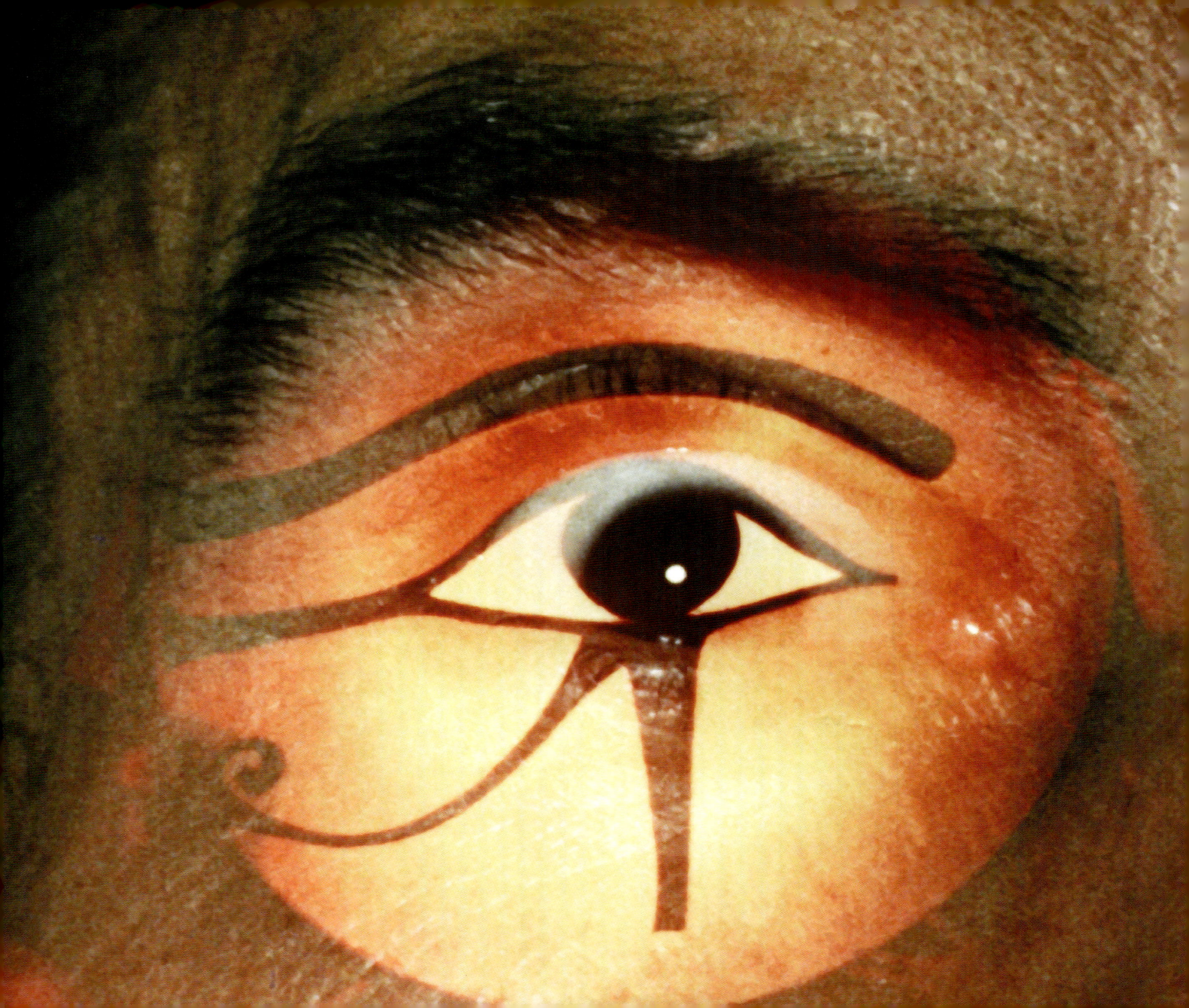

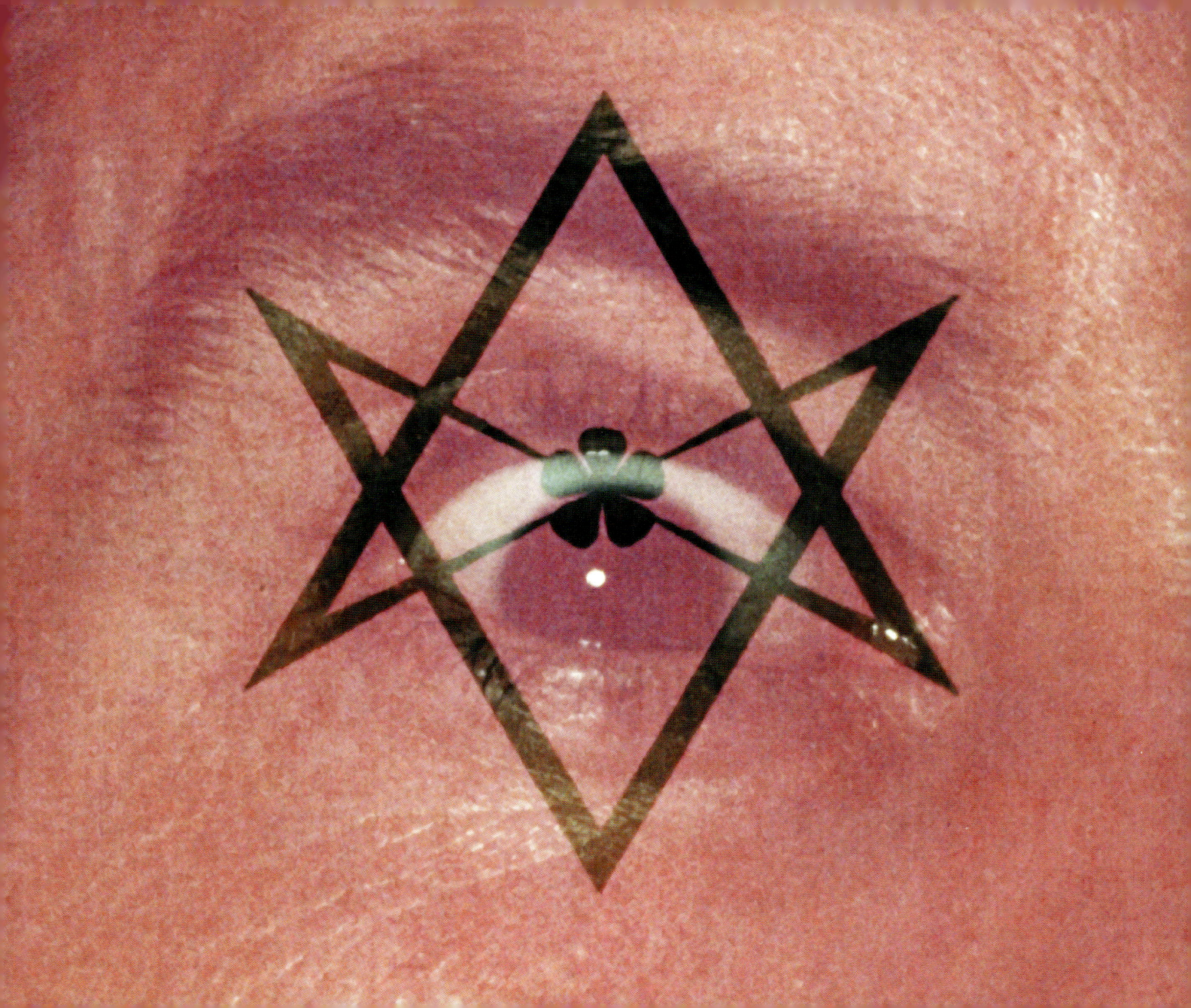

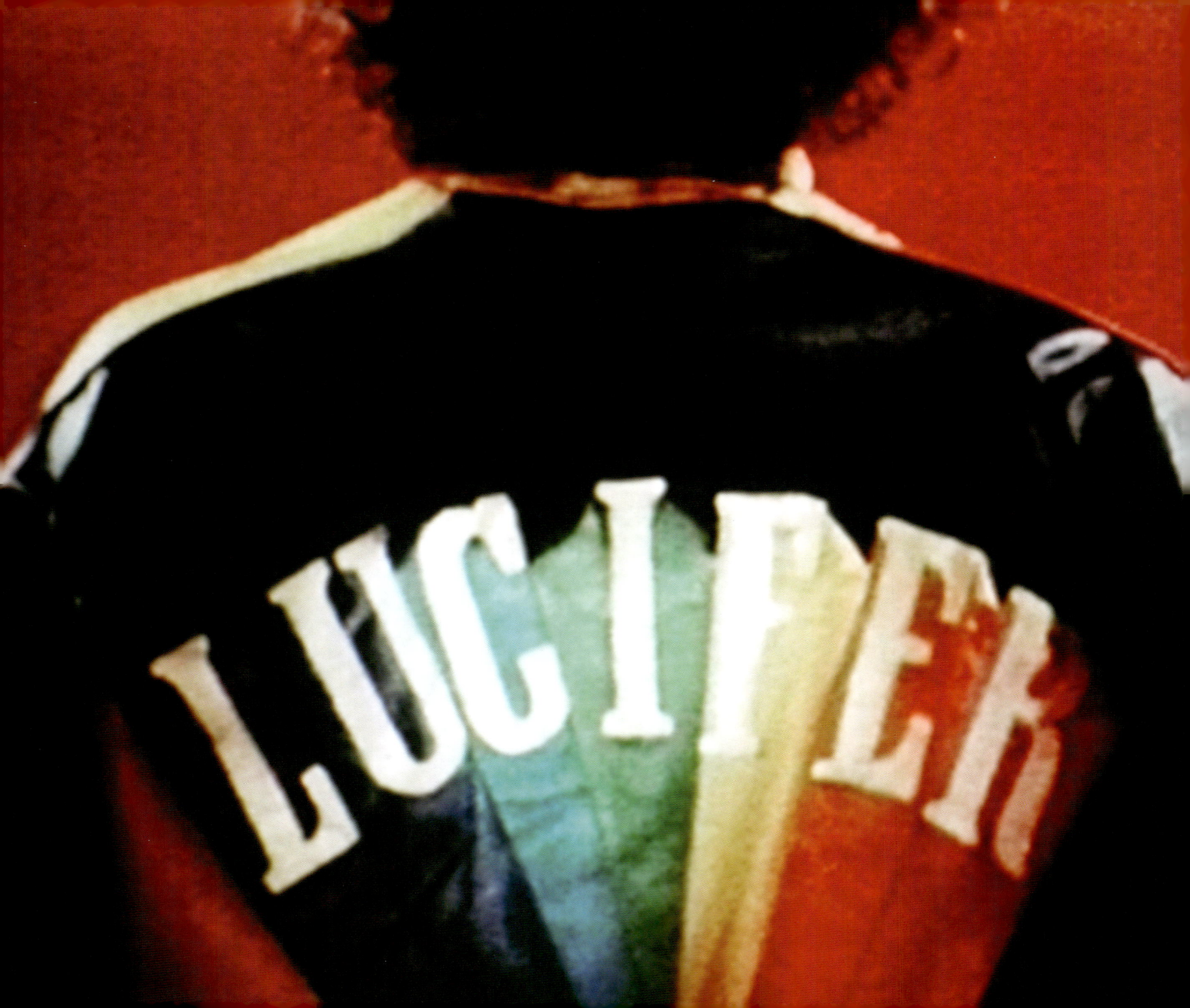

Lucifer Rising

1970-1981
30 minutes
16mm, color
Music by Bobby Beausoleil[22] (originally by Jimmy Page)

We make our destinies by our choice of gods.

Virgil

After these appeared
A crew who under names of old renown,
Osiris, Isis, Orus and their train
With monstrous shapes and sorceries abused
Fanatic Egypt and her priests, to seek
Their wand'ring gods disguised in brutish forms
Rather than human.

John Milton, *Paradise Lost*[23]

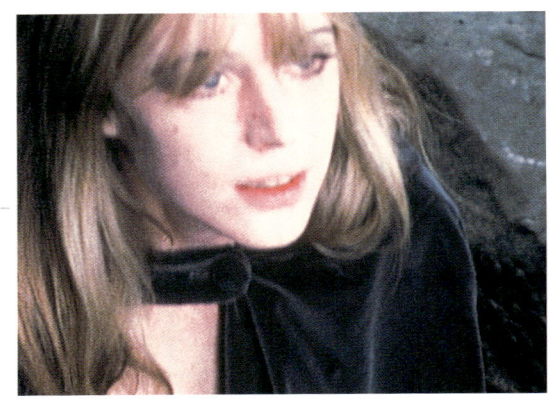

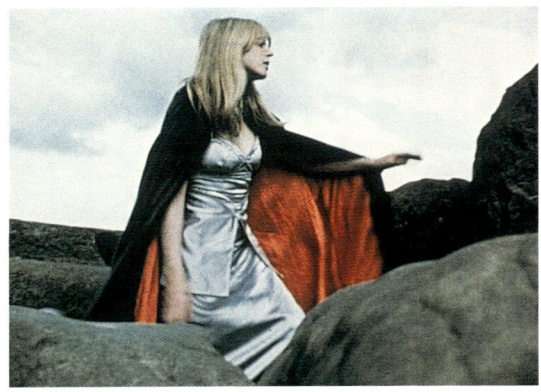

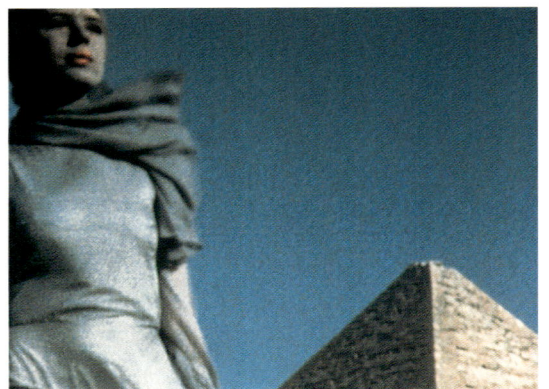

The visual narrative of *Lucifer Rising*, 1970-1981, Anger's most ambitious project to date, was originally inspired by Crowley's poem *Hymn to Lucifer* ("... His body a blood-ruby radiant / With noble passion, sun-souled Lucifer... With Love and Knowlecge drove out innocence / The Key of Joy is disobedience"), which recalls John Milton's epic poem *Paradise Lost*, 1667. It was Milton's version of Lucifer that both Aleister Crowley and Anger took as a departure point in their respective representations of the beautiful and rebellious angel of light: Lucifer not the devil, but Venus, the morning star. The notion of visual narration is expressed in *Paradise Lost* when Milton has the angel Michael guide Adam to the top of a high hill to show him a vision (in narrative form) of things to come. In anticipation of that vision, Adam's eyes had first to be cleansed in an elaborate ritual cleansing: "The Film" was first removed from Adam's "eyes," the "visual Nerve" was then purged by "three drops" from "the Well of Life" and "the inmost seat of mental sight" was finally exposed so Adam could behold that vision of history insofar as Milton could envision it using both scriptural and mythological sources.[24]

Lucifer Rising alludes to the "fallen angel" of orthodox Christian mythology, who in Anger's film is restored to his Gnostic status as "the Bringer of Light"; an implicit part of Crowley's own teachings. Implicit in much of what Anger, and ostensibly Crowley, present is the Gnostic notion that Lucifer was/is a pre-Judeo-Christian deity subsumed into the figure of the Fallen Angel, specifically the ancient Egyptian god Horus. The cosmology of Crowley's Book of the Law introduces a third Aeon, the Age of Horus (Aquarian Age), which follows after Isis' aeon of matriarchy and Osiris' aeon of patriarchy (and Christianity). In Crowley's *777 – Book of Correspondences*, he cross-indexes Greek, Egyptian, and Hindu mythologies. Venus is found in Isis and corresponding goddesses. Lucifer is the Roman name for the planet Venus which was worshipped both as the morning star and Vesper (the evening star). Until these myths were suppressed by the Catholic Church, the Gnostics worshipped Aurora/Lucifer as the Herald of the Dawn, the light preceding the sun. The Crowley/Anger doctrine exchanges Lucifer with Horus as well.[25]

Anger's mythopoesis is a conjunction of personal, social and historic mythologies transcending centuries and cultures, through rich visual metaphor and carnivalesque (also apparent in *Inauguration of the Pleasure Dome*). Mythopoesis is a term of literary criticism with psychological connotations. Sitney adopted it to describe what he saw was a genre of underground film, a sublimated visualization of the links between modern and pagan mythology, and specifically ancient Greek mythology.[26] If myths reflect a culture's efforts to systematize an incoherent world, it can be argued that dreams likewise attempt to bring order to the unruly emotions and desires repressed by the social constraints of everyday life. Mythologies, it has long been argued, authorize the values of the status quo in relation to the dominant culture. By re-imagining myth, Anger reverses this oppressive function, by invoking a poetic re-interpretation, and thereby offering an iconoclastic critique of existing social and

This page: Marianne Faithfull as Lilith
Opposite: "the late Donald Cammell as Osiris, Lord of Death"

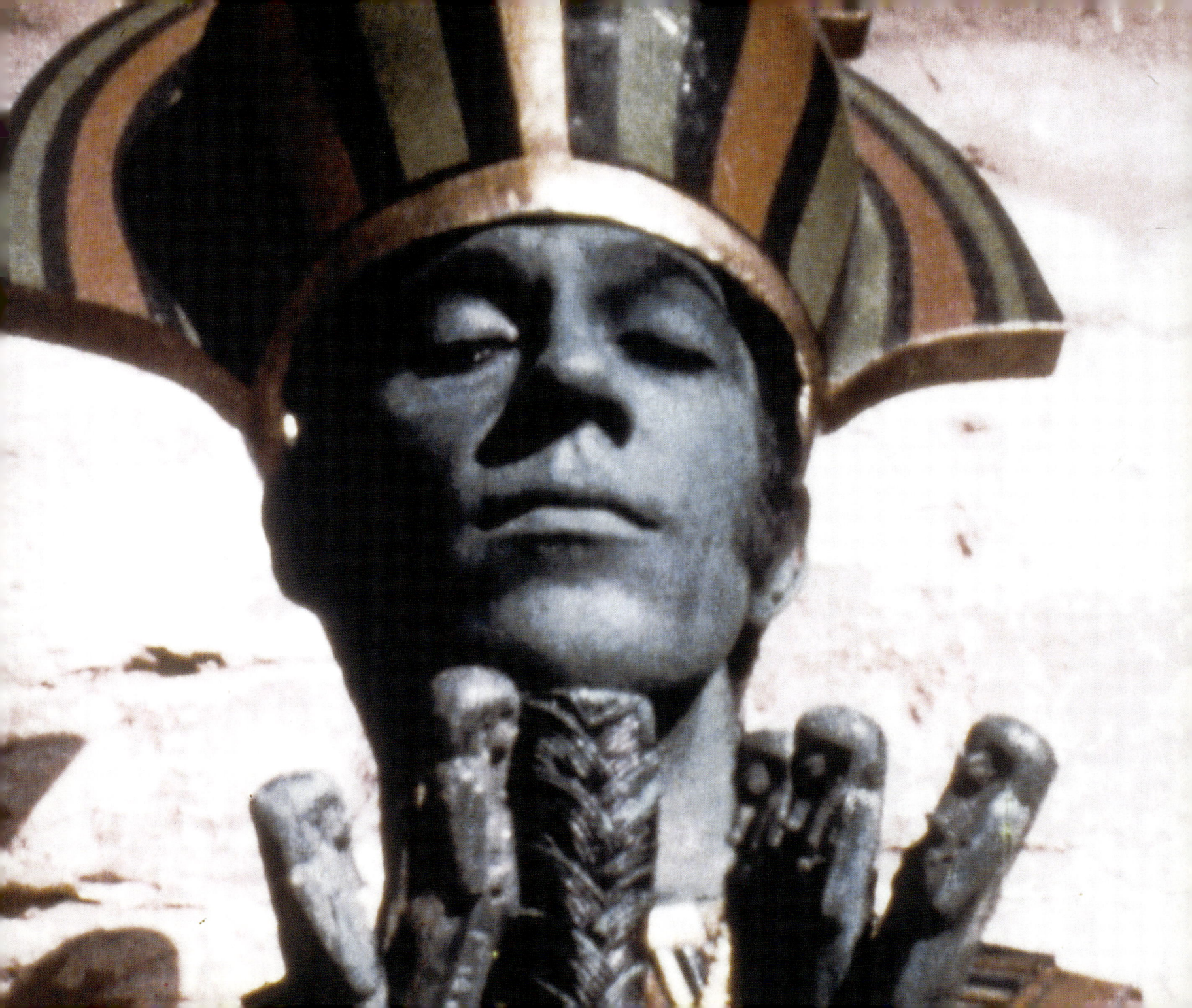

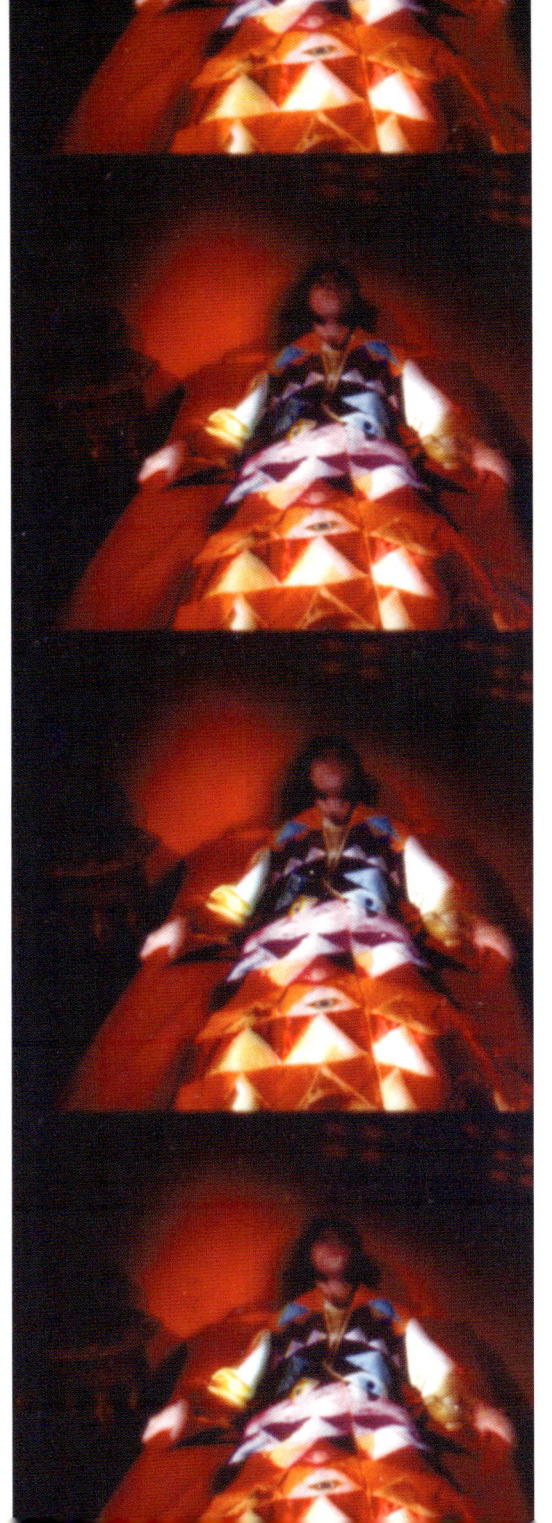

political norms. In the visual narrative of mythopoesis, the inmost seat of mental life suggests a substratum of existence where mental images somehow register both past and future events. This inner existence has been termed "hyponoia," (a Greek term for an underlying sense). It contains the material in which moral and cosmological considerations, even forgotten tales and allegories, form another existence altogether different from rational awareness or conscious self-scrutiny. This web-like "hyponoia" holds all the images and stories, whether remembered or forgotten, that have informed our cultures for literally thousands of years.[27] The pan-cultural stratas of *Lucifer Rising* reflect the "hyponoia" of mythopoesis. Stylistic changes during the making of the film add to this effect. Over 11 years in production and spanning continents, featuring ancient sites for sun worship from an ancient pagan temple in Germany's Black Forest (with Marianne Faithfull rising from a stone sarcophagus to greet the alignment of the sun during summer solstice); to the ancient Egyptian Temples at Karnak and pyramids at Giza; to volcanic islands in Iceland and Stonehenge.

The concept of *Lucifer Rising* began in 1966 while Anger was in San Francisco as a "sequel" or response to *Scorpio Rising*, from the beginning of "the new age." Much of the original footage shot went missing during one of Anger's ritual performances at the Straight Theater (which features in *Invocation of My Demon Brother*), with the rest of the footage shot at this time edited by Anger in London. Led Zeppelin's resident Crowley aficionado, Jimmy Page, composed the original soundtrack for *Lucifer*, which was removed in the 1981 re-edited version and replaced by Bobby Beausoleil's composition.

Lucifer Rising was conceived as a color feature about the "holy" war between the two ages, Piscean and Aquarian, as represented by the rebellious youth of the late 1960s and the repressive and conservative older generation. A planned scene was to have these young hipsters kneeling along the San Andreas Fault in California praying for a liberating earthquake. (Whether or not this was actually performed, it does not remain in any footage, but in 1971 the Sylmar earthquake was devastating). Anger has called it his "religious film."

Robert Haller has commented that Griffith's *Intolerance* and Eisenstein's *Que Viva Mexico!* are the two films which most closely resemble Anger's leap into the unknown in *Lucifer Rising*. Anger discussed the dialectical relationship between the two films in a statement of intention, commenting on the work before filming was completed:[23]

> The film *Lucifer Rising* is my answer to *Scorpio Rising* – which was a death mirror held up to American Culture. And for my own sake I had to make an answer to it even though I still see plenty of thanatic elements at work in America. It's a film about the love generation, but seen in depth – like in the fourth dimension. And I call it a love vision, and it's about love – the violence as well as the tenderness... I began shooting with the spring equinox. I'm type casting in my film, and one thing I've found is that since my film is

about demons – but love demons – I have to work fairly fast because they tend to come and go.... A demon is just a convenient way of labeling a force.... Like *Scorpio Rising*, *Lucifer Rising* is about several things. I'm an artist working in Light, and that's my whole interest, really. Lucifer is the Light God, not the devil, that's a Christian slander. The devil is always other people's gods. Lucifer has appeared in other of my films; I haven't labeled him as such but there's usually a figure or a moment in those films which is my "Lucifer" moment... I'm showing actual ceremonies in the film; what is performed in front of the camera won't be a re-enactment and the purpose will be to make Lucifer rise.... It's the birthday party for the Aquarian Age.... Everything I've been saying so far has been leading up to this. I've been exploring myself and now I've got to communicate it. Lucifer is the Rebel Angel behind what's happening in the world today. His message is that the "Key of Joy is Disobedience."[29]

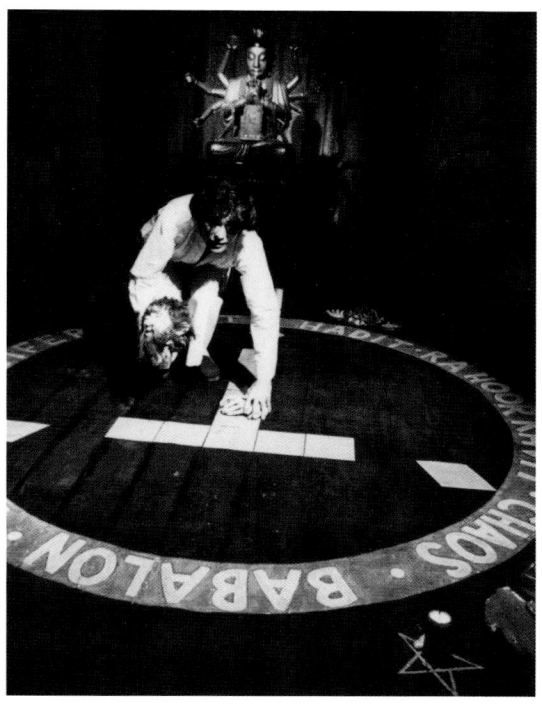

Anger's statement about a film he was yet to make highlight the aspects which have not been retained. Anger's emphasis on light, and Lucifer as the "Light God" reveal aspects of the earlier works – *Fireworks*, *Eaux d'Artifice* and *Rabbit's Moon*. The self-reflexive representation of light – although not apparent in the final version of *Lucifer Rising* – alludes to a continuity of theme throughout the films of the *Magick Lantern Cycle*.

In 1973, Jonas Mekas interviewed Anger, who at that point had modified his conception of *Lucifer Rising* (much of which had been shot, but not edited):

Kenneth Anger: Frankly it's taken me into some very strange corners.... You see, I didn't think it was about demons or hell, really. I was trying to make a film about the Angel of Light. That was his first name. The Son of the Morning, you see. But now I almost believe what the Bible says. Though the Bible says very little about Lucifer. He's censored out, you see. Only a few lines. Satan, you know.... So it's really about the Fallen Angel, the fall from grace, and the hope of redemption, of climbing back up the ladder. It's almost the story in a parable form of the Prodigal Son who goes away and falls from grace and then is accepted back in the family again.

Jonas Mekas: From the footage that I've seen... it looks like you're working much through the forces of nature, with the images of elements of nature.

Kenneth Anger: Yes, absolutely. It's a metaphor. I am trying to get away from identifying with actor or actress as a person. I want to move through nature, and the people are elements of nature also.[30]

Production still from *Lucifer Rising*

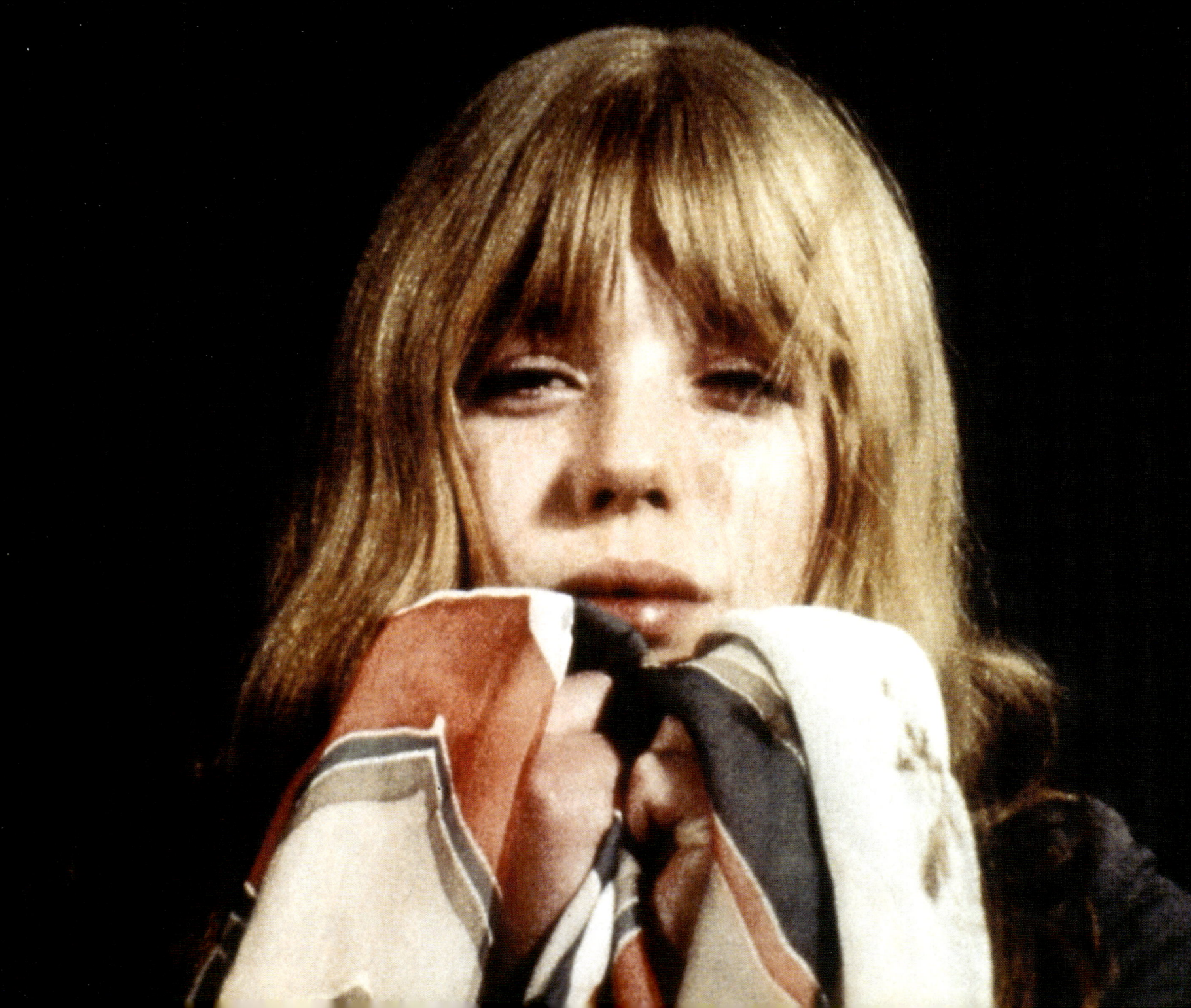

Haller reiterated that it was not clear why some aspects Anger refers to in this interview are not present in the film as of 1980. Perhaps, had Anger been able to complete the 93 minute version, instead of this 45 minute version, the Prodigal Son aspect would have been more visible. Nevertheless, it is present, though not emphatically. Likewise the conception of Lucifer as Fallen Angel (the aspect present in John Milton's *Paradise Lost* and in Crowley's *Hymn to Lucifer*) is not emphasized; his Fall in the film is a consequence of the loss of the knowledge of his lore – he is an invisible, all-but-forgotten force – the Lost God.

The film's location is geographically situated where Crowley purportedly experienced a vision of the Angel Aiwass, source of the revelation of *The Book of The Law* outside Cairo in 1904. The films opening credits (presented by "The War Department") features the flaming letters of "Lucifer Rising" emerging from the ocean. The cinematography from the opening shots introduces billowing Icelandic volcanoes: a mythology about to unfold told through visual juxtapositions and soundtrack. The volcanic eruptions and lava flow manifest the element of fire, which join with sea, land and sky in an elemental conjunction to prepare for Lucifer's rise. We shift between mortal and divine in dizzying vertical edits, which layer different planes or levels of existence. Anger's *Lucifer* features young pagan conjurers, but they are not Satanists in the malignant sense that name usually confers. The mortal adept continues the conjurations of Isis and Osiris to herald the advent of their son Horus. On rising, he sees a golden dawn, a visual metaphor for Crowley's early training.

Lucifer Rising is a celebration, and an invocation, of the power of Magick to summon forth the forces of nature. *Lucifer Rising* begins with images of the subterranean volcanic energy of the Earth, with Isis of Egypt attending to the process of birth under the morning sun, with chains of images that suggest the architecture of Egypt as metaphors for that energy. This opening sequence dissolves to the face of a contemporary Magus, and the spectator must guess as to whether the sequence was dreamed or imagined, experienced or anticipated. For the form of *Lucifer Rising* is not linear but associative: Anger leaps across centuries and millennia, condenses time and space in this film, composing not only a mythological story, but a portrait of a force that has pervaded all of human history. The Magus in the second sequence of the film, the adept or apprentice reappears throughout, but his specific identity is blurred, undercut, by the form of the film, which places attention on transformation. At the close of the second sequence he is impaled on a lance that he commands, sinks into a bath covered in blood, and again Anger dissolves the image – coming "up" with Lilith (Marianne Faithfull) who rises from a stone sarcophagus and makes her way to a Celtic temple in Germany's Black Forest, where she ascends to watch another ceremony, the summer solstice, and alignment of the sun. In all of this Anger wields filmic devices with enormous skill. The darkened adept dissolves to a light blue Lilith, who proceeds to the Pyramids of Giza in the Valley of Kings and Temples of Karnak in Egypt invoking the ancient Egyptian worship of the sun-as-God, Ra. She is then back to the German site where Anger elevates

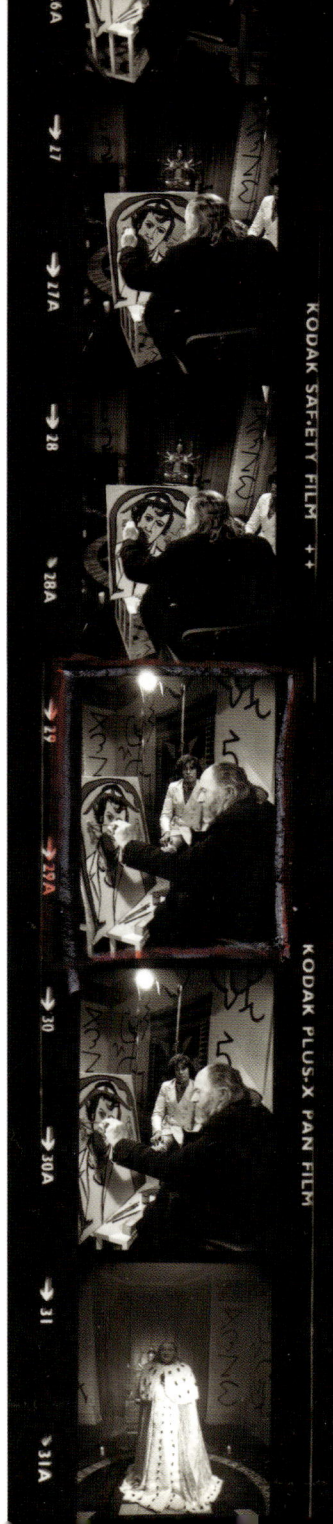

This page: "Sir Francis Rose creates a portrait of the painter," contact sheet from *Lucifer Rising*
Opposite: "Marianne Faithfull: tears that will not come, her own blood on the scarf turned to rust"

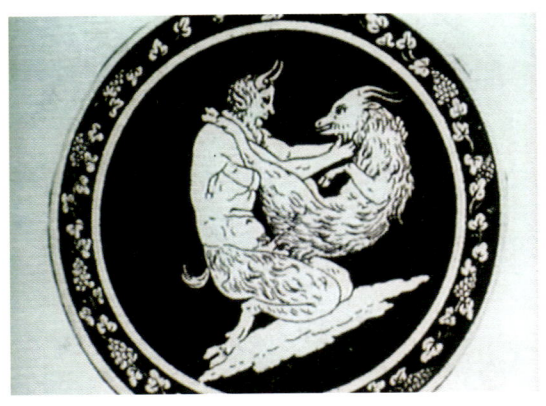

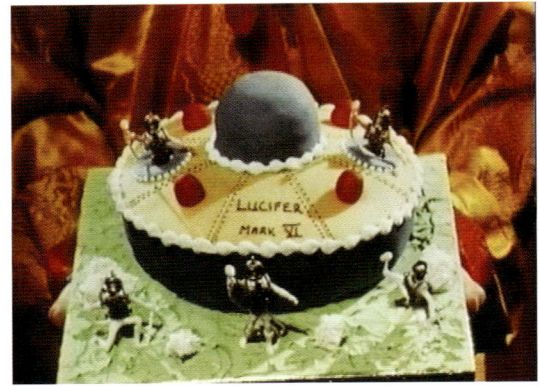

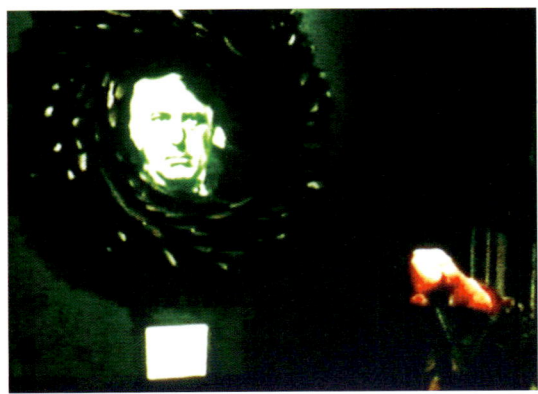

her up the steps with a series of vertical wipes that alternate day and night. To watch the film is to become intensely aware of the kinds and qualities of light, of its presence and absence, of its force (the sun here is somewhat parallel to the moon in *Rabbit's Moon*). Suspended and manipulated temporality intensifies the mythic and oneiric. The goddess Isis, stands upon an immense Egyptian divinity fallen to the ground, wielding an Ankh which is thrice raised to the sky, and a scepter in the other hand. Osiris appears before the temple, then in full sunlight upon a rock responding to his wife Isis, mother of their child Horus, the Hawk-like God of Light, Anger's symbolic deity for the new age, like Lucifer, angel of rebellion against the ancient religions becoming obsolete.

Rather than personifications as in *Inauguration of the Pleasure Dome*, Lucifer's characters represent "actual" divinities wielding their powers in the authentic Egyptian locations. Osiris and Isis have the counterpart of Lilith, female demon, Kabbalistic goddess of destruction, and transcending time and space, the actual adepts of Aleister Crowley practicing rituals of invocation. The serendipitous irony of Bobby Beausoleil's last name (beautiful sun/son) and soundtrack collaboration resonates in the context of the film.

The visual narrative continues as Lilith finds herself in a room, which has been vandalized, destroyed (did she wreak this havoc?); she clutches a bloody scarf, tears roll down her cheeks. Her tears provoke hurricanes and tornadoes. She is again in Egypt before the pyramids (acknowledging the ascendancy of her sister goddess Isis). Thelemite Sir Francis Rose is Chaos, wearing an ermine robe, and prepares to conduct the invocation within a magick circle inscribed with the names of demon-gods: Lucifer, Nuit, Hadit, Chaos, Lilith, Babalon, Ra Hoor Khuit. A statuette of Shiva, the eight-armed Hindu goddess of destruction and regeneration is placed behind the circle. Anger as Magus, wearing a long red tunic leads a procession down a stairwell, and joins Sir Francis. A talisman is thrown into water and cuts to footage in which the splash is suspended by slow motion freezing the droplets into a crown. Anger circumambulates within the circle, progressing to a supernatural speed, (close-ups of his frenzied feet), sparks of red light spray forth as the electric guitar track acts as a sonic mirror escalating in intensity. Smoke and a fiery eruption are cut to lightening bolts, transmuting into rainbow-colored beams embroidered on a satin jacket. Lucifer slowly turns around toward us. The Crowley ritual is looked over by a portrait of the English Magus, which hangs on the wall. An image appears of the Beast 666 in the form of a satyr mating with a goat. Another shot of Crowley is inserted wearing the Masonic triangle (with an eye in its center above his head) as one of the young acolyte pores over the "Stele of Revealing", singled out for its magickal impact by Crowley as exhibit number 666 in the Cairo National Museum.[31] As John Symonds recounted in *The Great Beast*: "Brother Perdurabo advanced to the case. There was an image of Horus in the form of Ra-Hoor-Khuit painted upon a wooden stele of the 26th dynasty. Suddenly Crowley fell back in amazement: The exhibit bore the number 666! His number, the number of the Beast!"[32] A scene from

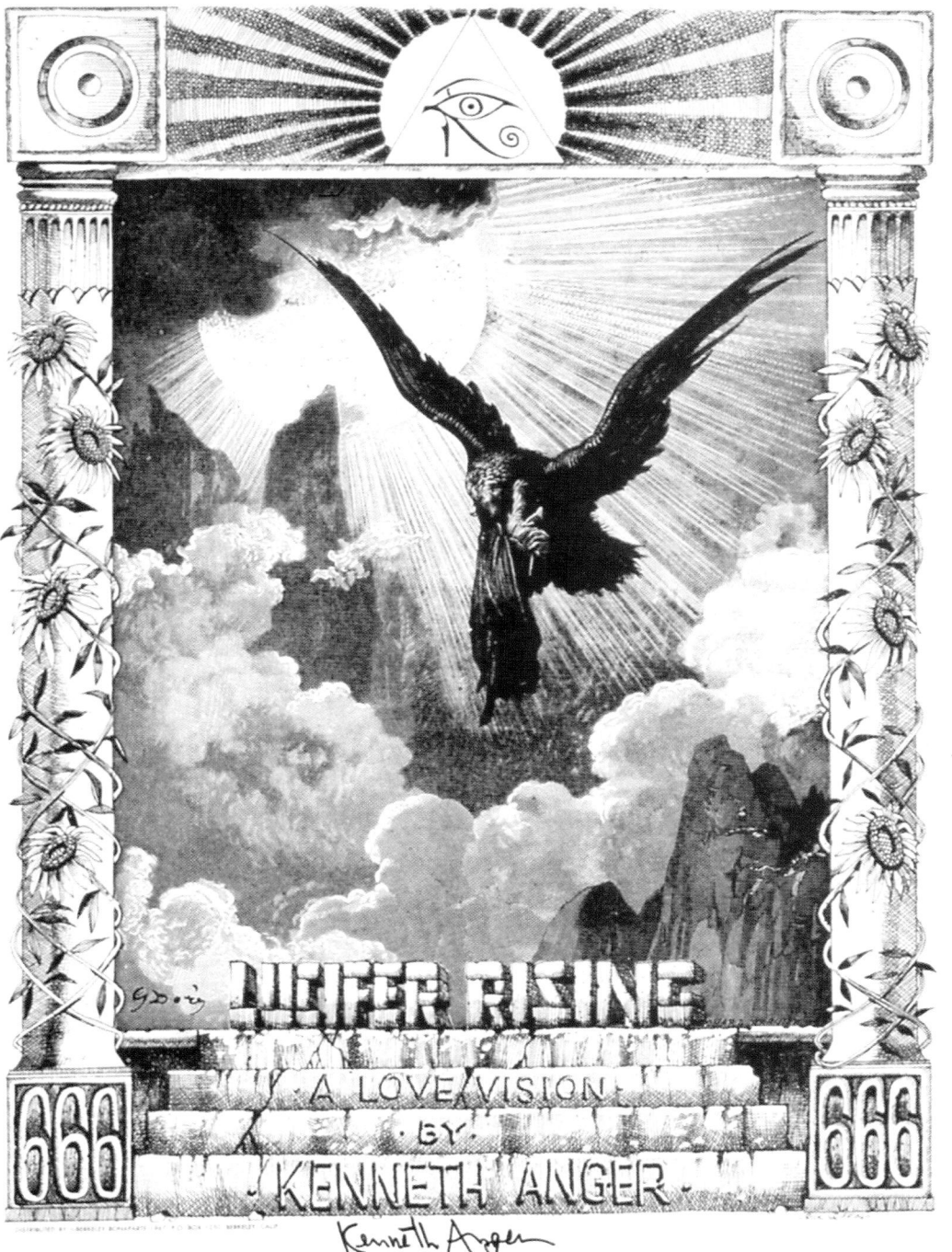

LUCIFER RISING

A LOVE VISION

BY

KENNETH ANGER

666   666

Kenneth Anger

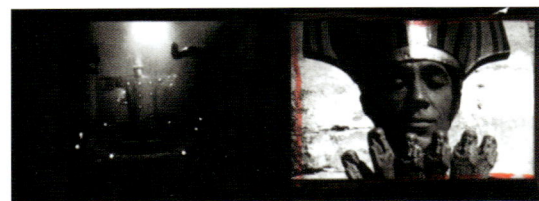

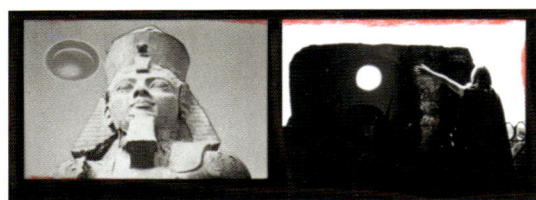

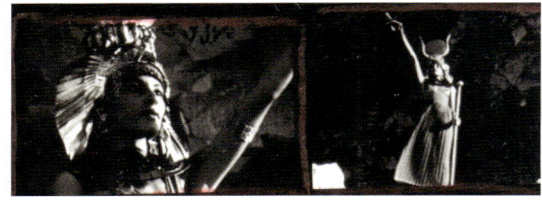

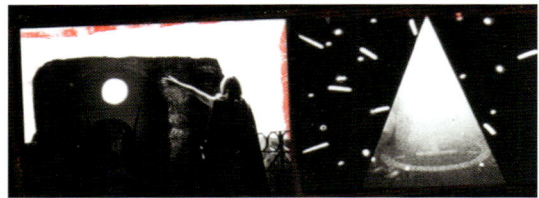

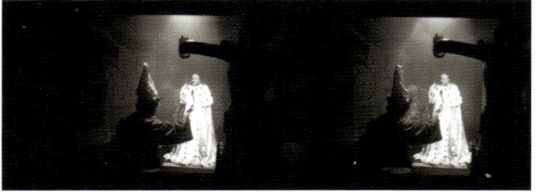

Lachman's *Dante's Inferno* is superimposed, with numerous orgiastic figures dancing. We are then returned to the ancient sites, where storms and eruptions signal the approaching new aeon, as the final sequence in Egypt with Osiris and Isis are greeted with a fleet of flying saucers; the ancient statues of the original deities provide a final shot.

The legend of the birth of Horus is miraculous: Seth, the jealous brother of Osiris, enclosed him into a sarcophagus and threw it into the Nile. Isis succeeded in recovering the body of her husband, but Seth was watching, and cut the body into morsels that he again threw into the river. Isis invoked the forces of light to find all of the pieces of her husband, which were all recovered except for the phallus. By practicing magic rituals she remade him able to impregnate her. She then embalmed Osiris. Thanks to the light of the star Soped, he came back to life and assisted in the birth of their son Horus, child of Light. Isis is frequently referred to as the Great Sorceress, and also overseer of fecundity and protection associated with the "universal mother." She obtained her powers as the daughter of Ra, Sun God of energy and warmth. Conceiving even with the death of her husband, an heir Horus who would re-establish the harmony between the disrupted elements and the terrestrial kingdom. For the Egyptians, Osiris is the image of the cycle of life-death-resurrection. Horus was not born a mortal; and to avenge his father, did not kill Seth. In effect, his mission was not to eliminate evil, the negative, but to master it according to the balance of the two polarities bringing harmony to the universe; reuniting disparate elements. The Ankh is the symbol of human contact with the divine; the rounded head is the vital circuit that animates the divine-human meeting and unceasingly reactivates it. Ankh signifies eternal life, but more precisely, mastery of one's own destiny and future. In *Lucifer Rising*, Osiris and Isis are reunited for the birth of their heir, commanding forces with an ecstatic sense of dominion. The film stands in contrast with *Scorpio Rising* in that it is celebratory; rather than the apocalyptic Final Battle; it offers a declaration of transformation and transcendence.

It is pertinent to mention that in film terms, Eisenstein's montage of opposites mirrors this ancient mythological story: featuring the alchemical "union of irreconcilables," connecting the elemental binaries of sun and moon, water and fire. In ancient Egyptian mythology, the crocodile Sobek, ruling over the lakes and marshes, and all the places where the water is united with the land aided Isis to find the morsels of the dismembered cadaver of her husband. (The opening sequence of *Lucifer Rising* feature shots of crocodiles and the hatching of a newborn out of its egg).

Anger's difficulties in making *Lucifer* were considerable. His first lead actor, a five year old by the name of Godot died in an accident; the second, Bobby Beausoleil, Anger blamed for stealing the footage he had shot in San Francisco in 1966 (which led to the making of *Invocation*). As mentioned previously, as a symbol of protest Anger inserted a full page R.I.P. notice for himself (covering the duration of his film career) in the New York *Village Voice*, vowing to never return to the United States. When filming finally resumed in the 1970s, in Egypt, England, Germany and the United States, Beausoleil, who appeared in *Invocation*, was serving a life sentence in Tracey Prison in California, originally on death row for his involvement in the Charles Manson murders. After their falling out, they reconciled after he contacted Anger in London having learnt of the rift with Jimmy Page, with Beausoleil agreeing to compose and play the film's soundtrack. Forming the Freedom Orchestra in prison, the instruments were delivered by mail order and Anger provided him with the time-sheet for the film to create his shimmering score.

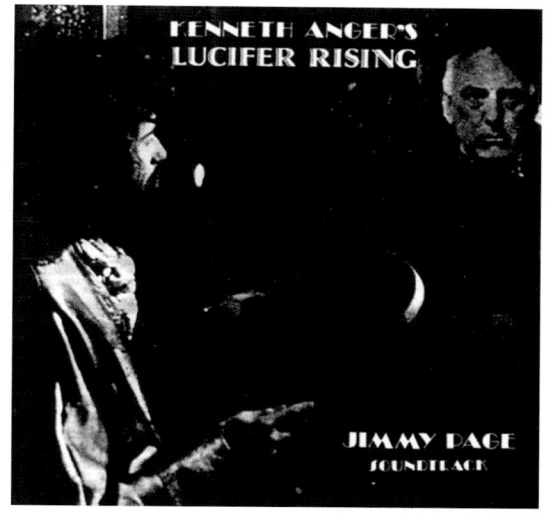

Led Zeppelin guitarist and leader Jimmy Page was fired as composer for the soundtrack of *Lucifer Rising* by Anger due to a succession of problems. Page has been working on the film for three years and had delivered some 28 minutes of completed tape. The story of the collaboration – and the ensuing rift – goes back to 1973 when Page first agreed to compose and perform the film soundtrack. He and Anger first met at Sotheby's, at an auction of Aleister Crowley's books. Page was also a student of Crowley's teachings, owning the second largest collection of his books in the world, as well as Crowley's former residence at Boleskine on the shores of Loch Ness. The collaboration had continued intermittently since their first meeting, with Anger commuting between London and New York to oversee the U.S. publication of his book *Hollywood Babylon*, and Page involved with Led Zeppelin performances and recording. For three months Anger had been using the film-editing facilities in the basement of Page's Victorian mansion in London, to trim the 17 hours of film footage down to one-and-a-half hours. Page had the equipment installed to work on another film project, "Zeppelin Live at Madison Square Garden," provisionally titled, "The Song Remains the Same."[33] Anger's work at Page's house was terminated by an extraordinary sequence of events beginning one night when Anger, apparently the unwitting victim of a domestic fracas, was ordered to leave the house by Page's French girlfriend, who was staying there at the time. No reason was given for his eviction. He returned to the house the next morning to collect his film material and belongings to find the door locked and bolted. By the end of that week, a piqued but by no means disconsolate Anger returned to Page's home, removing the last of his belongings and film artifacts – including the crown of Lucifer, paste studded with rhinestones from a dress once worn by Mae West. It was the media reports of this sequence of events that spurred Beausoleil to re-establish contact with Anger offering to create the films' soundtrack.

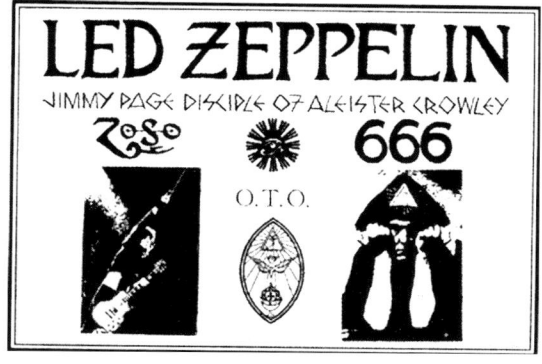

This page: album cover for *Lucifer Rising* soundtrack, Led Zeppelin flyer
Opposite: contact sheets from *Lucifer Rising*

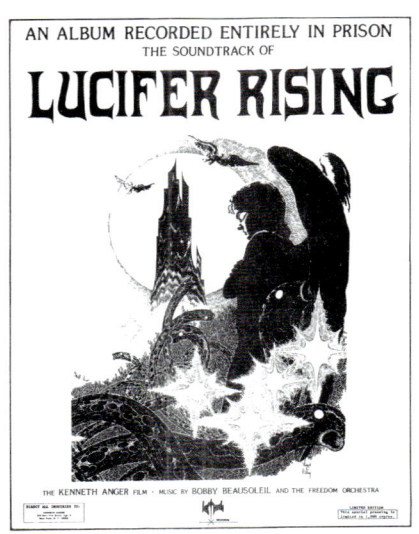

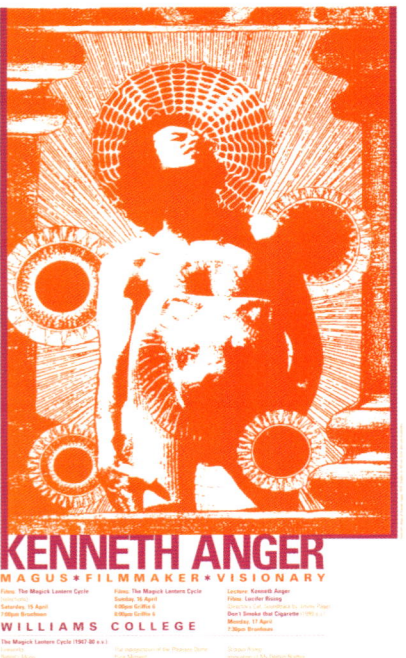

Mick Jagger, who had at one point agreed to take part in *Lucifer*, backed down before shooting began, apparently fearing that the Satanic aura he had once sought to cultivate was becoming too tangible for comfort, particularly as Brian Jones' death occurred at this time. His place was taken by brother Chris, but an on-set row with Anger led to Jagger Jr.'s dismissal. Eventually a Middlesbrough steel worker named Leslie Huggins was recruited for the part, and with Marianne Faithfull and author of *Performance* Donald Cammell, also taking principle roles, filming began.

Nikolas Schreck, in his account of occult/diabolic cinema *The Satanic Screen*, discussed Anger's evocations of Lucifer as forming part of a continuum with earlier evocations in film. George Méliès, who pioneered special effects in cinema, was the original film Magus, often appeared in Luciferian costume; in many of his films he appeared himself as the Devil, Mephisto, Faust, or an alchemist or magician, as Schreck explains:

> It was the proto-surrealist Méliès who used cinema to transcend what the Symbolist painter Gustave Moreau dismissed as "the wretched reporting of positive facts"... Méliès' 1896 *La Manoir Du Diable* is one of the very first presentations of the Devil in the new medium of cinema.... A jumbo-sized bat glides into a *trompe l'oeil* medieval castle hall set.... The bat flaps around menacingly before transforming into a traditionally attired Mephistopheles, none other than Méliès himself. When a cavalier flourished the despised crucifix, the Devil vanishes in a sulphurous puff of smoke. Fin. Essentially, the Devil is portrayed as a stylized grand illusionist, an alter-ego of the filmmaker.[34]

While Anger is not portraying Lucifer as the stock demon of Christian lore in *Lucifer Rising*, but rather as a positive force for a new era, he shares with Méliès a *fin-de-siècle* fascination with artificiality. Anger's works represent a type of film symbolism that is uniquely analogous to the theory of correspondences basic to the Symbolist tradition, as J. E. Cirlot has written:

> ... All cosmic phenomena are limited and serial and... they appear as scales on separate planes... the components of one series are linked with those of another in their essence and in their ultimate significance... there is also a psychological basis for the theory of correspondences related to synaesthesia."[35]

Top: *Lucifer Rising* poster with illustration by Virgil Finley from 1940
Bottom: poster for Kenneth Anger screenings at Williams College

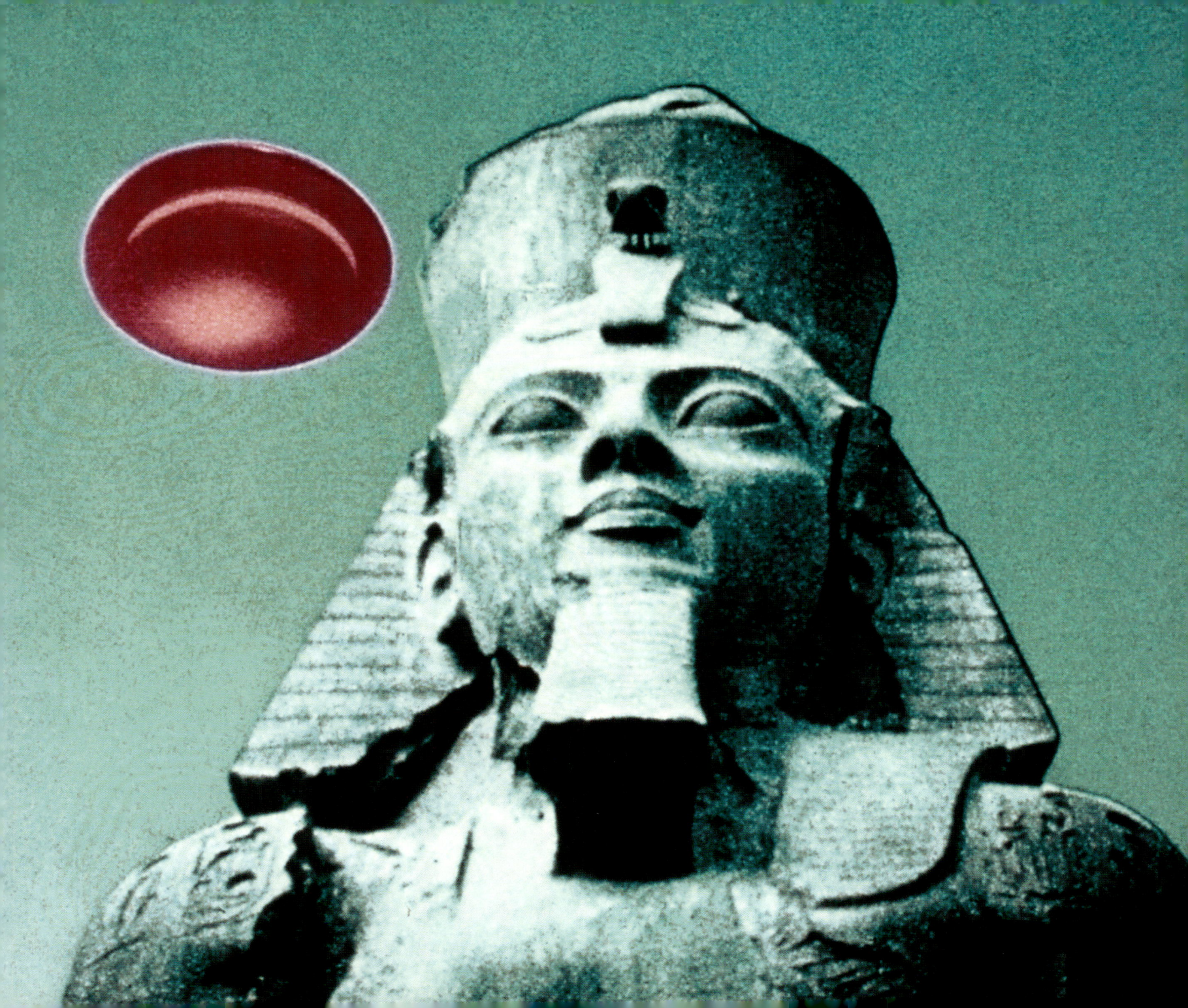

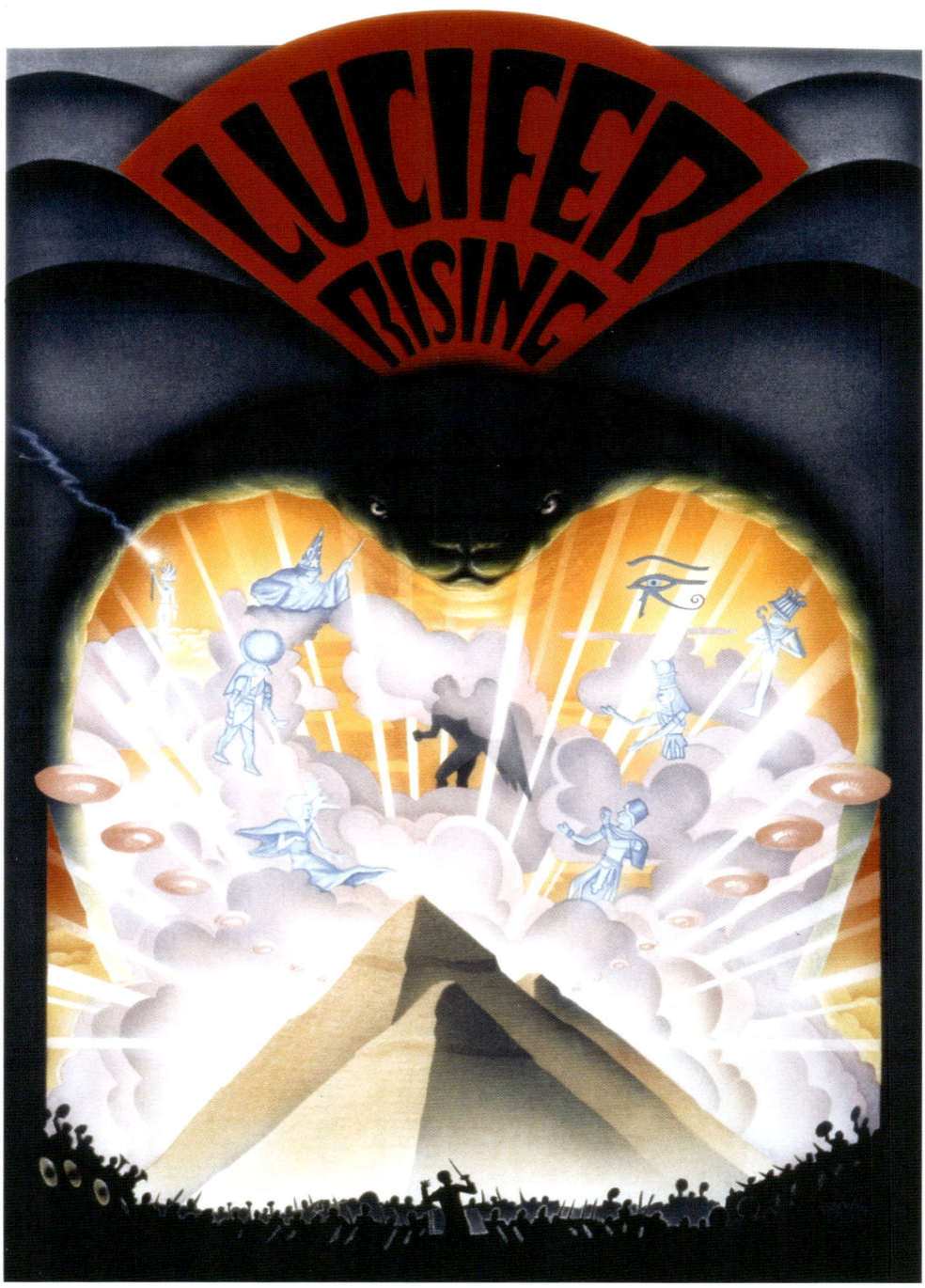

Although the film was premiered at both the Museum of Modern Art and the Whitney Museum in New York in December 1980, and has had numerous screenings internationally since its completion in 1981 (a few changes were made after these initial screenings), this is one of the few discussions of the iconography of the film and quite extraordinary trajectory of its making. What is taken for granted is that such a project could materialize by a solo artist, financing the whole project over 11 years mostly himself, with a vast array of characters playing aspects of themselves in such an extraordinary range of locations. The scale of *Lucifer Rising*, and its place within Anger's *Magick Lantern Cycle* could be seen as anticipating contemporary art film epics such as Matthew Barney's *Cremaster Cycle*, with the internal resonances and symbolism extending beyond a conventional notion of narrative. *Lucifer Rising* was the last major film Anger was to make (although he was to go on to engage in smaller scale film projects). As the final work in the *Magick Lantern Cycle*, it has a dialectical relationship to *Scorpio Rising* (the thanatic death-wish of *Scorpio* is assuaged by the utopian mythopoeia of *Lucifer Rising*), completing the cycle as it forms a conclusive final chapter. Lucifer's theme of an awakening connects it back to *Fireworks*; while reference to light (actual and metaphorical) link it to both *Fireworks* and *Rabbit's Moon*. While the threatening, hypnotic quality of *Invocation of My Demon Brother* perhaps reflects the apocalyptic underside of 1960s counterculture, *Lucifer Rising* as an angel of disobedience and the coming of a new age relates to the utopian countercultural ethos of the 60s and 70s. While each film in itself follows a somewhat cyclical structure, the films relate to one another, with the earliest film *Fireworks* and *Lucifer Rising* as contrapuntal in the whole Cycle, completing through the films a rite of passage, from initiation to realization). Anger considers his films, at least the nine films of the *Magick Lantern Cycle* – as a whole rather than completely separate entities or individual works, with their revisions having also subtly altered their inter-relationships.

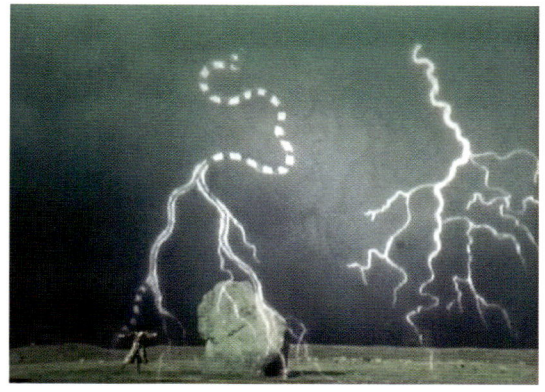

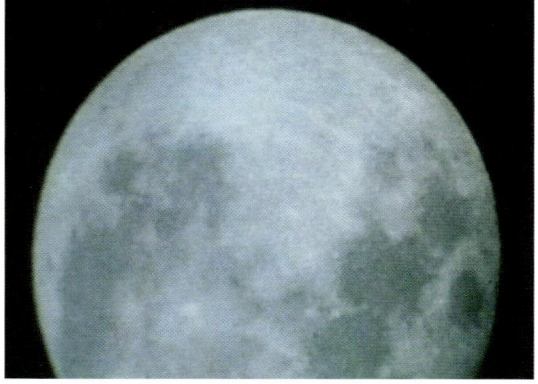

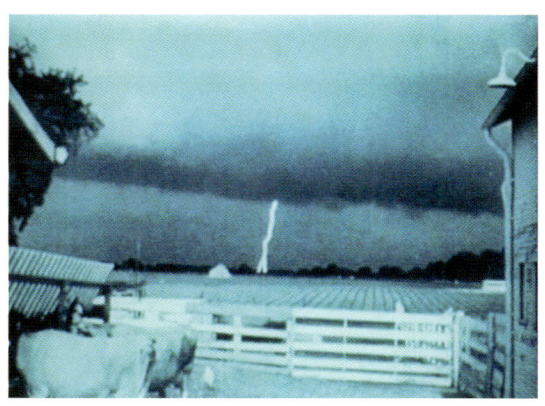

Opposite: poster for *Lucifer Rising*, designed by Page Wood, commissioned for exhibition at the Whitney Museum of American Art, New York, 1980

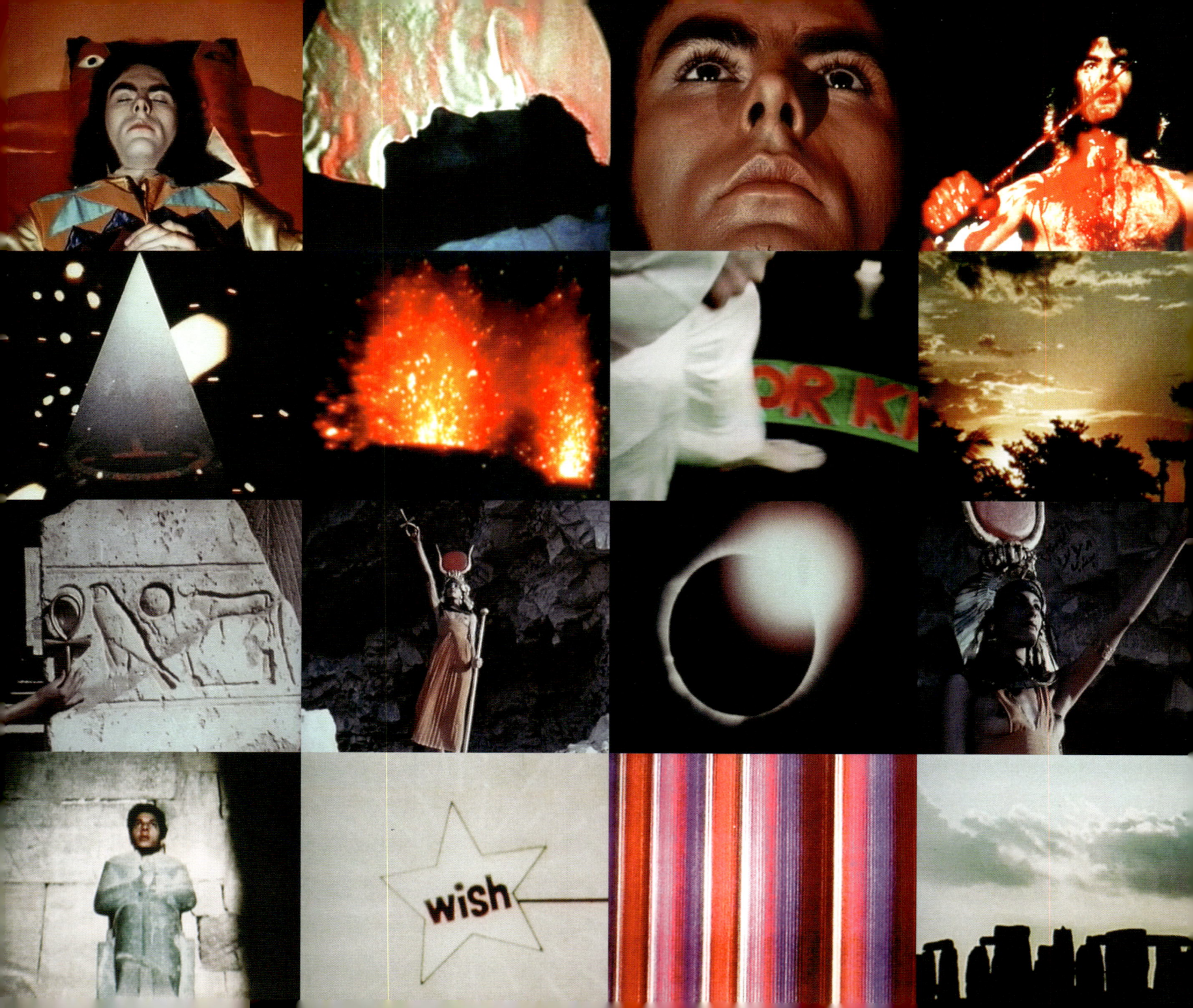

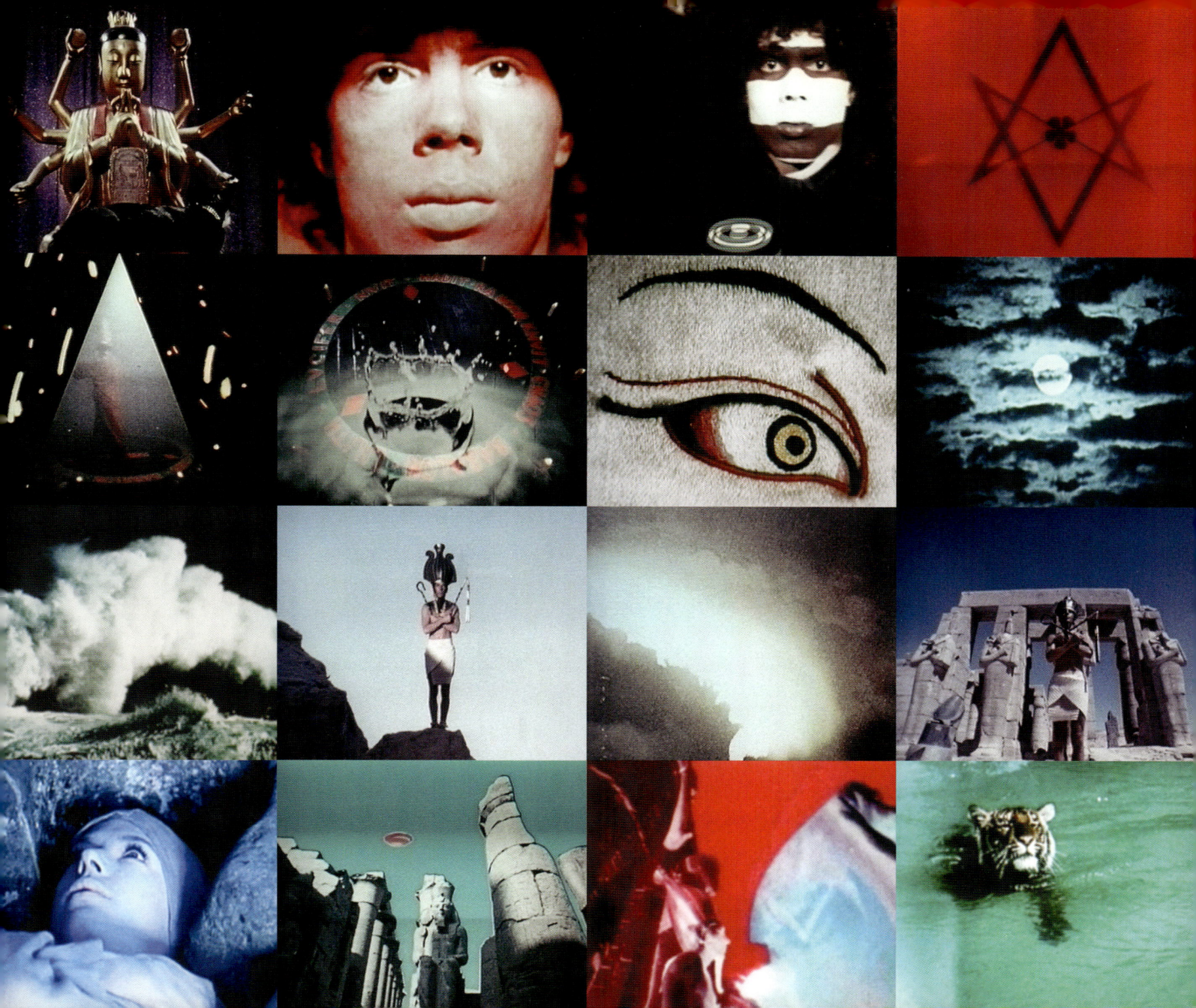

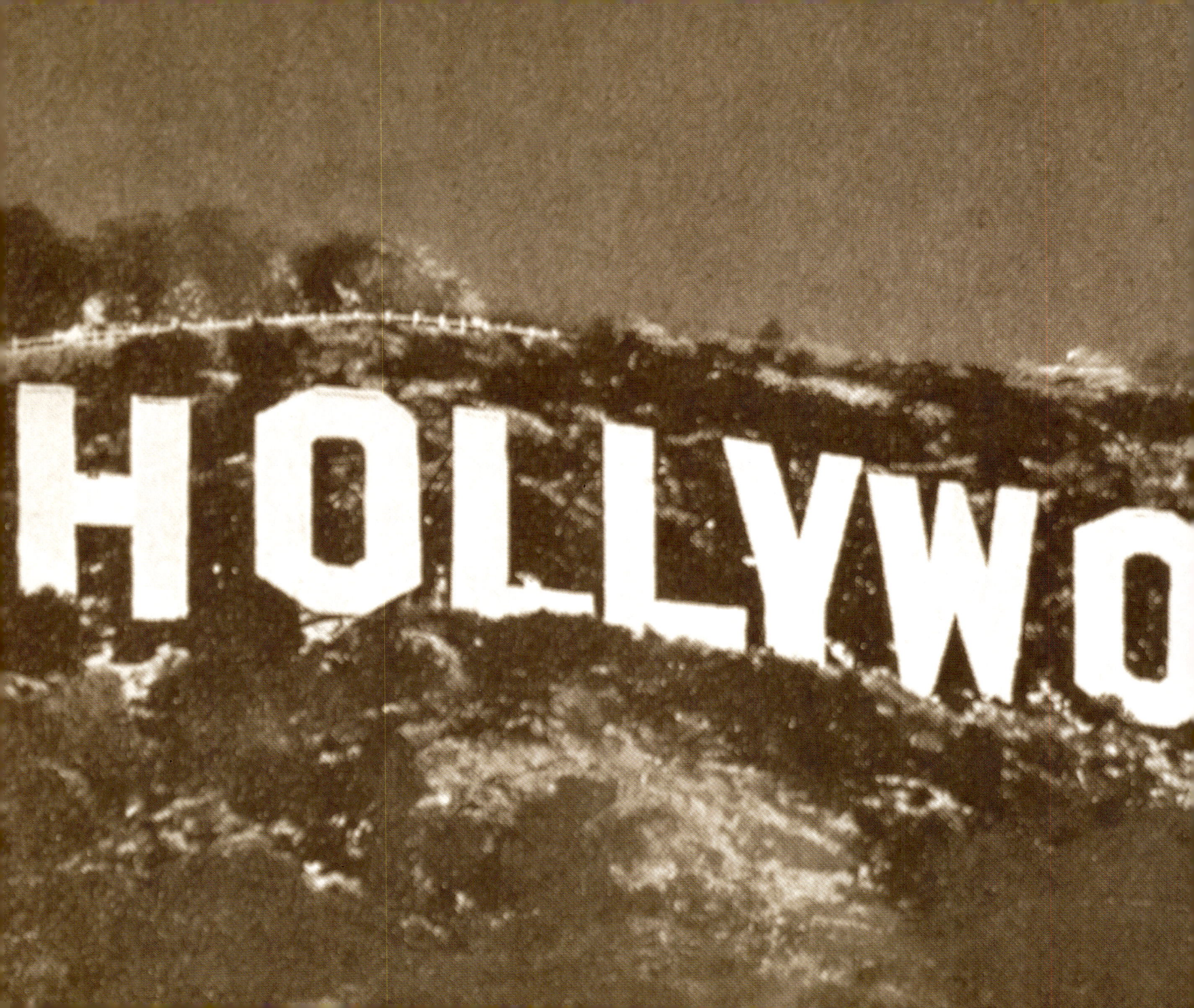

9. Hollywood Babylon

In Paris in the 1950s, Anger had told stories about old Hollywood to the likes of François Truffaut, leading to the suggestion that he do a book. Subscribing to Oscar Wilde's adage that there's nothing else to do with gossip but spread it around, Anger dove into his scrapbook of Hollywood's golden years, using it as a departure point for an investigation into Tinseltown's most infamous scandals.

A book as legendary as its subject

Susan Sontag[1]

There's no doubt in my mind that eventually someone is going to make a so-called underground movie that will revive Hollywood as Kenneth Anger writes of it.

Harry Smith[2]

For him the project was a way to finance his filmmaking, and he found a French publisher, Jean Jacques Pauvert, to sponsor it. The first incarnation – titled *Hollywood Babylone* – was written in French and published in 1959; a picture book chronicling the seedy underbelly of Hollywood, with Jayne Mansfield pouring out of her frock on the cover. It was an instant success in France, and German and Italian editions followed. During the first years of the 1960s, Anger had translated two thirds of the French version to present to an American publisher, but once he submitted the incomplete manuscript, the publisher quickly wrote in the rest, tacked Anger's name on the cover for instant caché and issued the book wrapped in brown paper, to turn a fast profit. This pirated paperback was a crudely written and inaccurate translation, published in 1965. That same year a film based on the book (produced by the same publisher) – again made without Anger's permission – appeared; a third rate soft-porn flick using unknown amateurs to play Hollywood's greats. A federal court injunction finally got both the film and the unauthorized version of the book withdrawn. Although the pirated paperback had sold well over two million copies, Anger didn't see a penny from either unauthorized venture. The first Anger authorized English edition came out under Rolling Stone's book label Straight Arrow Books in 1975.

The international shockwaves that *Hollywood Babylon* created cannot be underestimated in the demythification of America's pantheon. The book has maintained its cult status internationally since its first publication, running into numerous editions. The world is certainly less innocent in its public assumptions, living in a voyeuristic era that hungers for damaging disclosures and exposés. The publication and immediate international consumption of *Hollywood Babylon* certainly contributed to the new voyeuristic age, magnified by the reach of mass media. The commentary upon Hollywood that was first imagined by Anger in *Puce Moment* and popularized by his camped-up, salacious books, amplified the awareness of the mechanization of the star-making factory and the noir side of Hollywood. Precedents for Anger's portrayal of Hollywood include the 1939 novel *The Day of the Locust*, in which author Nathanael West portrayed fandom as an incipient version of fascism, or Hortense Powdermaker's 1950

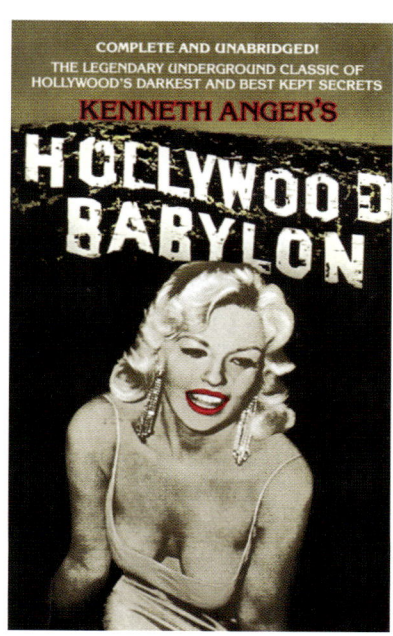

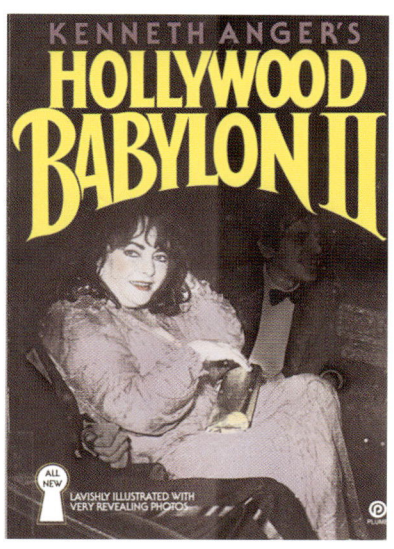

best-seller *Hollywood the Dream Factory*, which was an early exposé of the mechanics of the studio system.[3] Subsequently, these books have given birth to a whole genre of films that explore the seedy underbelly of Hollywood, including Robert Altman's *The Player*, and the recent David Lynch film *Mulholland Drive*.[4] *Hollywood Babylon* has also spawned a whole genre of books utilizing Anger's model.

Thanks to Dr. Alfred Kinsey's vast archives at the Institute for Sex Research, Anger discovered a treasure-trove of early "film work" of certain well-known stars, with Kinsey's research library including pornographic movies confiscated during police raids.[5] With the constant influx of would-be stars and starlets looking for their big break, the porn industry never had a shortage in casting. In preparation for *Hollywood Babylon*, Anger cataloged and had access to every "art" film (many of which were passed down through the authorities), in the Kinsey collection. Just as he had had the unparalleled privilege to explore the vast archives of the Cinémathèque in Paris, his obsession with film and its history was replete with access to the secret archives of the Kinsey Institute, including many cheesy romps with young studs and starlets on the make in Hollywood. Although Anger began writing *Hollywood Babylon* initially as a commercial venture to support his filmmaking, the salacious tales are perhaps the witty flipside of Anger's aesthetic, with his combination of irony, pastiche, and the excavation of history: "The ambivalent mixture of homage and satire [is] characteristic of Anger's fascination: scandal, evil, violence, fascism. His films are the fields in which the dialectic of that fascination is fought."[6] Anger's films and the environment in which they were created are mutually conditioned: sex, violence, scandal, mystery are sublimated in two different directions – one reveling in the quagmire of Hollywood, the other (his films) creating an imaginative sphere that rejects and transcends it. Hollywood is essential to Anger in that it is a key creator of popular culture and propagator of American mythology. The collision between taste and tastelessness generates a camp sensibility, as Anger remarked: "When you deal with a subject like Hollywood, you have to quietly and firmly set taste aside."[7]

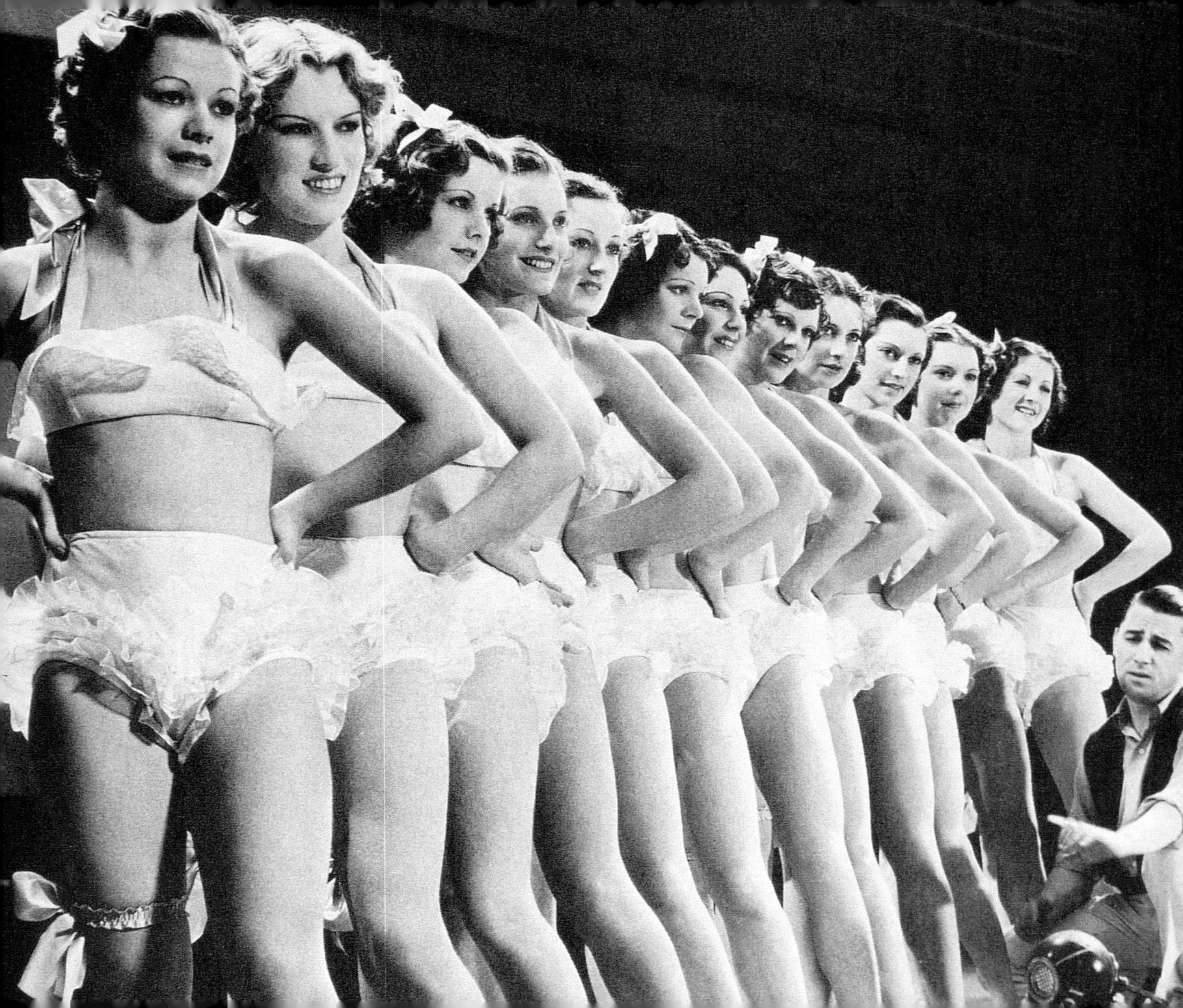

As *Puce Moment* was to be the feature about the glorious goddesses of the 1920s, *Hollywood Babylon* stands in as a substitute for that project, with its inherent nostalgia for a golden age of Hollywood, that of Von Stroheim or Griffith's epic construction of Babylon, albeit littered with unspoken scandal laced with Anger's own *schadenfreude*: "that marvelous German word," says Anger, that describes "that particular Hunnish pleasure in seeing your enemies fall to pieces in front of your eyes. All I've had to do is sit back and wait to see the whole empire of Hollywood Babylon crumble into dust."[8] Original Hollywood maverick David O. Selznick was equally convinced that "Hollywood's just like Egypt. Full of crumbling pyramids. It'll never come back. It'll just keep on crumbling until finally the wind blows the last studio prop across the sands."[9] Although it hasn't crumbled to dust, it is certainly a shadow of its golden age.

If there is continuity to be found between his films and *Hollywood Babylon*, it is the way in which Anger maintained his outsider stance and perspective, as a solo artist apart from the monolithic studio systems, operating as part of a dissenting cinematic and artistic culture. Hollywood was seen as the main cultural adversary to this avant-garde community, representing the arid middle-class values that Anger and others undermined in their films and art work. In this way, *Hollywood Babylon*, could be seen as a continuation of Anger's counterculture critique. However, Anger himself has been discredited by some experimentalists for using many of Hollywood's techniques in his work, such as precision montage editing, dissolves, etc., as for many, an anti-establishment stance was identified with a rejection of cinematic craft. This critique ignores Anger's oppositional stance, which is inflected with a wicked sense of humor and irony, setting him apart not only from the mainstream but from other avant-garde filmmakers.[10] Anger's simultaneous fascination and repulsion with the myth-making of Hollywood made him unusual in experimental circles, as well as making his work more easily accessible for audiences:

Hollywood – A part of its charm was sort of unflinching vulgarity. It always had that brassiness to it. It had the courage of its convictions, crazy as they were. And the studios need to have these incredibly skilled craftsmen, the special effects departments, and the miniaturists; all that sort of hokum movie magic has always interested me very much....[11]

Before *Puce Moment* and certainly *Hollywood Babylon*, the commentary on Hollywood (or nostalgic yearning for its past) did not exist outside the local gossip columns. Rainer Werner Fassbinder was particularly interested in such aspects of Anger's work, and both he and fellow German director Werner Schroeter quoted Anger's imagery and explored representation of same-sex relationships. Fassbinder, for instance in *The Bitter Tears of Petra Von Kant*, 1972, exploits a pastiche of Hollywood glamor, artifice and despair in its dazzling appropriation of studio melodrama with an all-women cast in one of the first internationally visible films depicting lesbian and bisexual relationships. In its gaudy, claustrophobic setting, through an array of decadently gorgeous costumes, emotional wounds are precisely dissected.

Busby Berkeley and his girls: "The sound of taps," *Hollywood Babylon II*

Born and raised in Los Angeles, Anger had as a child heard scandalous, first-hand accounts of Hollywood stars. Anger grew up collecting photographs, clippings and anecdotes of the stars, had danced with Shirley Temple, and participated in Max Reinhardt's magical 1935 *A Midsummer Night's Dream*, portraying the Stolen Prince: The Changeling. Hollywood is an inescapable frame of reference for Anger, as Anaïs Nin recounted in her diary:

> In Hollywood, Kenneth and Curtis [Harrington] took me to the original stars' homes, behind Franklin Boulevard, in the hills. The houses of Valentino, Harold Lloyd, Theda Bara, which may in their time have seemed magnificent but which today looked small, pathetic imitations of Spanish ranches, castles, haciendas. We sat in Harold Lloyd's deserted house by an empty pool, on a broken-down swing covered by a tattered umbrella, and they told me the history of Hollywood, their birthplace.[12]

Researching for *Hollywood Babylon*, Anger pored through newspaper clippings, police files, court reports and mortuary records, he also spoke to butlers, maids, make-up artists, designers, publicists, stand-ins, stars, has-beens, would-have-beens and never-beens: the grapevine. Hollywood did not close ranks to protect the culpable. Old rivalries and jealousies were dragged out of dark corners. One instance of this was when Anger was still at Beverly Hills High School and Lupe Velez, movieland's Mexican Spitfire, committed suicide. Lupe had planned a Snow White suicide, to be found lying on her bed in her finest evening gown, surrounded by bouquets of flowers, OD'ed on sleepers. But at the last moment the tablets reacted with some enchiladas Lupe had eaten that evening. Rather than defile her fantasy-death tableau, she tottered into the lavatory to vomit and it is said, drowned with her head in the toilet bowl. At the time, Anger was living just a block away from Lupe's house on North Alpine Drive. He subsequently went over to get the details from her maid and cook. As Mick Brown describes:

Hollywood Babylon is a perverse prayer to the heyday of Hollywood, a terribly thorough and thoroughly terrible record of the seamy underbelly of Tinseltown's dreamlike façade, with skeletons wrenched out of closets, peccadilloes mercilessly unearthed and corpses scattered liberally throughout. Anger describes it as "an exercise in black humor" and an "allegory of the success myth of America. For all those people who seem to have a firm foothold on the ladder upwards, there's a lot of human wreckage lying at the bottom." – "stories the papers would never have dared to print; the sort of gossip known only to a star's bootlegger, dope dealer, best friend, worst enemy, or mortician...."[13]

The second *Hollywood Babylon*, 1984, was published by Dutton in the U.S. and discussed a few living subjects (most of the subjects in the first book were deceased), featuring a cover with an overweight Elizabeth Taylor. *Hollywood Babylon II* is a bittersweet look at the fabled and foibled stars in their orbit (the privacy of their own homes) including Alfred Hitchcock's predilection for cerebral sado-masochism, how a hundred stars did themselves in, and the real reason Jane Wyman left Ronald Reagan, with before and after shots of James Dean and the Porsche he was killed in. The second volume demonstrated how the real Hollywood could be far more grisly and intriguing than any film noir, with the Black Dahlia murder being a case in point, in which a beautiful 22 year old aspiring actress, Betty (Elizabeth) Short, was brutally murdered in 1947. With dark hair and often dressed in black, Short became known as *The Black Dahlia* in the places she frequented. Her body was found surgically bisected in a vacant lot, occasioning the greatest manhunt in California's history. The murderer has never been identified, with corruption at the highest level of the L.A.P.D. said to have stopped investigations as the leading suspect, a Dr. George Hodel, had files on many high-ranking officers and other public officials as well as many celebrities.[14] His own son Steve Hodel, the author of the chilling *Black Dahlia Avenger*, summarized that while the V.D. files and confidential information Dr. Hodel possessed relating to film industry and police officers personal "indiscretions" was contributory, the real reason for the cover-up related to his detailed knowledge of a

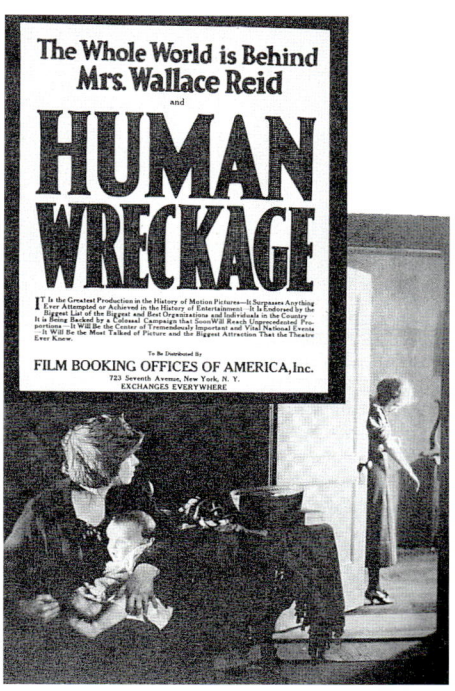

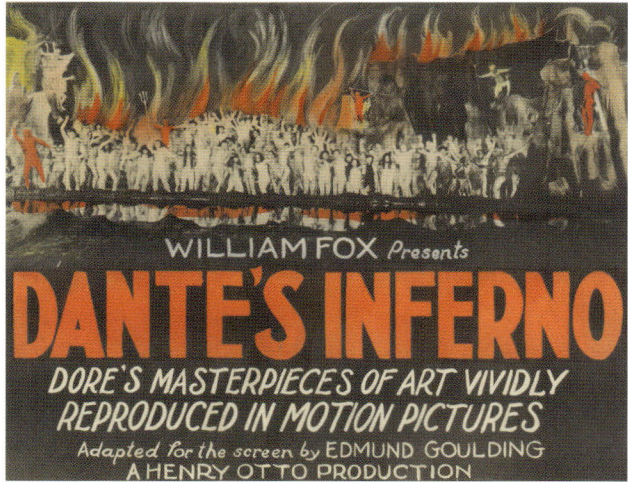

Top: from *Hollywood Babylon*
Bottom: original 1920s silent version of *Dante's Inferno*, hand-painted lobby card, from Kenneth Anger's collection of Hollywood memorabilia

pay-for-protection abortion ring, run by two L.A.P.D. detectives, who were collecting large sums of money from licensed physicians in L.A., in return for allowing them to conduct abortions, without fear of arrest (a felony crime in 1950's L.A.). These same detectives were "friendly" with George Hodel and assisted him in avoiding arrest. When L.A.P.D. high-command learned of the two detectives "cover-up" and the fact that Dr. Hodel had fled the country, they made a "management decision" to remove the damning files rather than expose the Department and the City to public ridicule and financial ruin, in the form of law suits from victims relatives. L.A.P.D. was just recovering from a major corruption scandal in 1939, where 68 high-ranking officers were fired, and a second scandal in less than 10 years was not an option.[15] *Hollywood Babylon II* was the first book in which the photographs of the victim's severed body were presented to an international public – gruesome to the point of transcending reality. Steve Hodel corroborated: "As far as I know, Kenneth Anger's book was the first to use the Elizabeth Short photographs."[16]

Hollywood Babylon II also features a priceless photograph of Nancy Reagan sitting upon the ample knees of the *A-Team*'s Mr. T.

I never had any trouble, except once. The only person I had any trouble with was Gloria Swanson, and her objections were completely off the wall. She didn't have any legal leg to stand on. And she took me to court, saying that I libeled her. There's absolutely no libel in the chapter on her. She was the mistress of Joe Kennedy. I mean, that's a fact. Whether at the time it wasn't known, I mean, it's become known. So her suit was thrown out.[17]

The decline of the classic Hollywood studio system in the 60s ran almost parallel to the peak and groundswell of underground film (and of television); its lumbering enterprise was not lean or nimble enough to keep apace with the volatile social landscape (Hollywood avoided dealing with the great social and political issues of the 1960s, only later grappling with the cultural changes that an independent such as Anger advanced). It too was a symbol and manifestation of a decaying age being replaced by a new invigorated one; and thus its mythical status in Anger's oeuvre. For Anger, the past seems to be an endangered species, hence his affection for the memorabilia of Babylon including old movie theaters and his collection of its trophies. He has campaigned to save old movie palaces all over the U.S. including Radio City Music Hall:

And fortunately for us, Anger, an alert eyewitness to the crumbling of the walls of Hollywood Babylon, was able in his book to raise from the dust of that shambles a bittersweet and often hilarious interplay of text and pictures which does not pander to the current nostalgia craze, but presents a personal collage of Tinseltown in its heyday. The book is written with affection tinged with irony and spiced with Anger's own special blend of black humor.[18]

As television plundered Hollywood archives "making the whole of Hollywood past available to consumers, a fact traditionally regarded as a contributing factor in the decline of the studio system," according to Juan Suarez, "television may have killed Hollywood in the present, but it mythologized its past." Such revivals effectively laid bare the artificiality and conventional formulas of plots, myths and iconographies. It also "led audiences to develop an increasingly ironic attitude toward Hollywood, which appeared as a storehouse of outmoded signs available for recycling through quotation, allusion and appropriation."[19]

Scandals and tragedies are an important part of the historical records of cultures. They reflect at any given time what is considered over-the-edge of behavior, and it's also something that the public can be fascinated with, and afraid of.... They're demonized and glamorized. The books I've written on Hollywood have been about that aspect. The new one will also be Hollywood scandals and tragedies, [referring to *Hollywood Babylon III*] but the trouble is, off the record between you and me, I feel I've used up all the good stories.... And I don't like contemporary Hollywood. The characters aren't larger than life, they're usually smaller than life! (laughs) I can write about someone like Fatty Arbuckle or Jean Harlow or Garbo, but to write about someone like....[20]

According to Anger, prior to its recent gentrification, Hollywood in the 1970s and 80s was sleazy and tacky, with the derelict Hollywood sign a crumbling reminder of its faded glory. Today, despite the newly reinstated annual Oscar ceremonies and premieres at the Chinese Theater, walking down Hollywood Boulevard is a social concoction of Scientology recruiters (having bought up much of the real estate and invariably preying upon the tender insecurities of the down-and-out actor), crack addicts, homeless people, tourists, Goths and mall-shoppers. Perhaps even due to the pervasive influence of *Hollywood Babylon*, a reconstruction of Babylon Court – a large flop of a shopping mall inspired by Griffith's set for *Intolerance* is the main attraction at Hollywood and Highland.[21]

The transformation of Hollywood in the 60s is an essential part of its mythical quality reflected in *Hollywood Babylon*, as Hollywood's crisis served to intensify the myth and nostalgia for it at the height of its glamor. Anger's ambiguous relationship of attraction/repulsion with Hollywood separated him from other avant-garde filmmakers who consciously disavowed any reference to it or the tricks of the trade. But the inveiglings of a camp sensibility were exposed with *Hollywood Babylon* – brutally entertaining, scandalous, and daring, the queering of Hollywood divas sprung from Anger's obsessions. The re-appropriation of the diva became epitomized in the catty dethroning of these goddesses stripped of their props and made all too mortal. This adoration swings to the misogynistic and swings back again to reveal how remarkable it is to have a cavalcade of professionals to create the image of the goddess that we see on screen. The campiness of outrageously flamboyant costume designers, make-up artists and the myriad who were able to sublimate their own personal fantasies into creating the image of the goddess (a drag-queen fantasy no less – where the fantasy of creating the goddess meets that of being made a goddess) has always been the unspoken secret of mythmaking in Hollywood. This camp sensibility can be seen in Jack Smith's description of "moldy glamor" as being "something that is very lush and gaudy and colorful and a bit old, but it could also be very new and have all those qualities or essences, like fans or feathers or costumes...."[22]

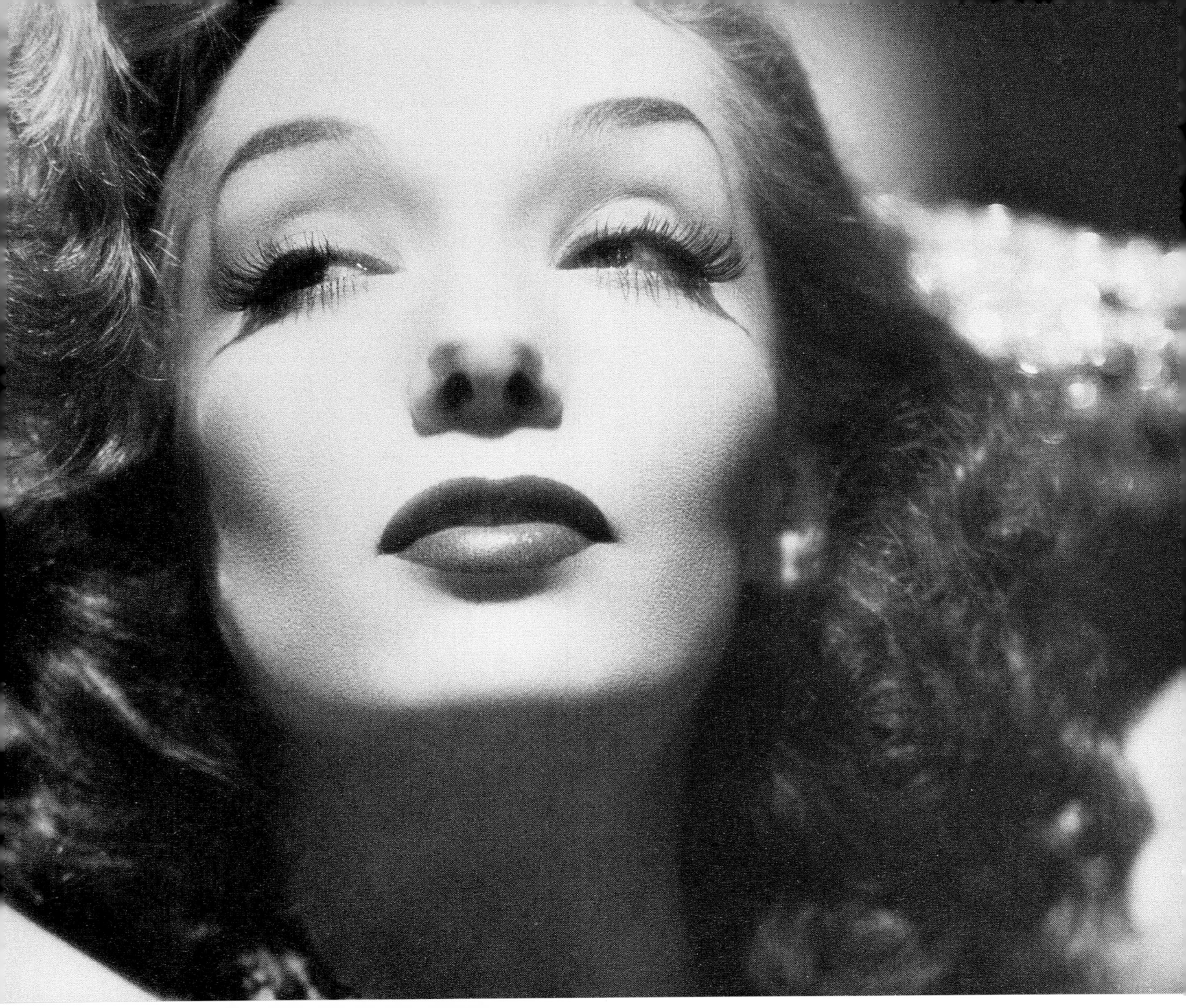

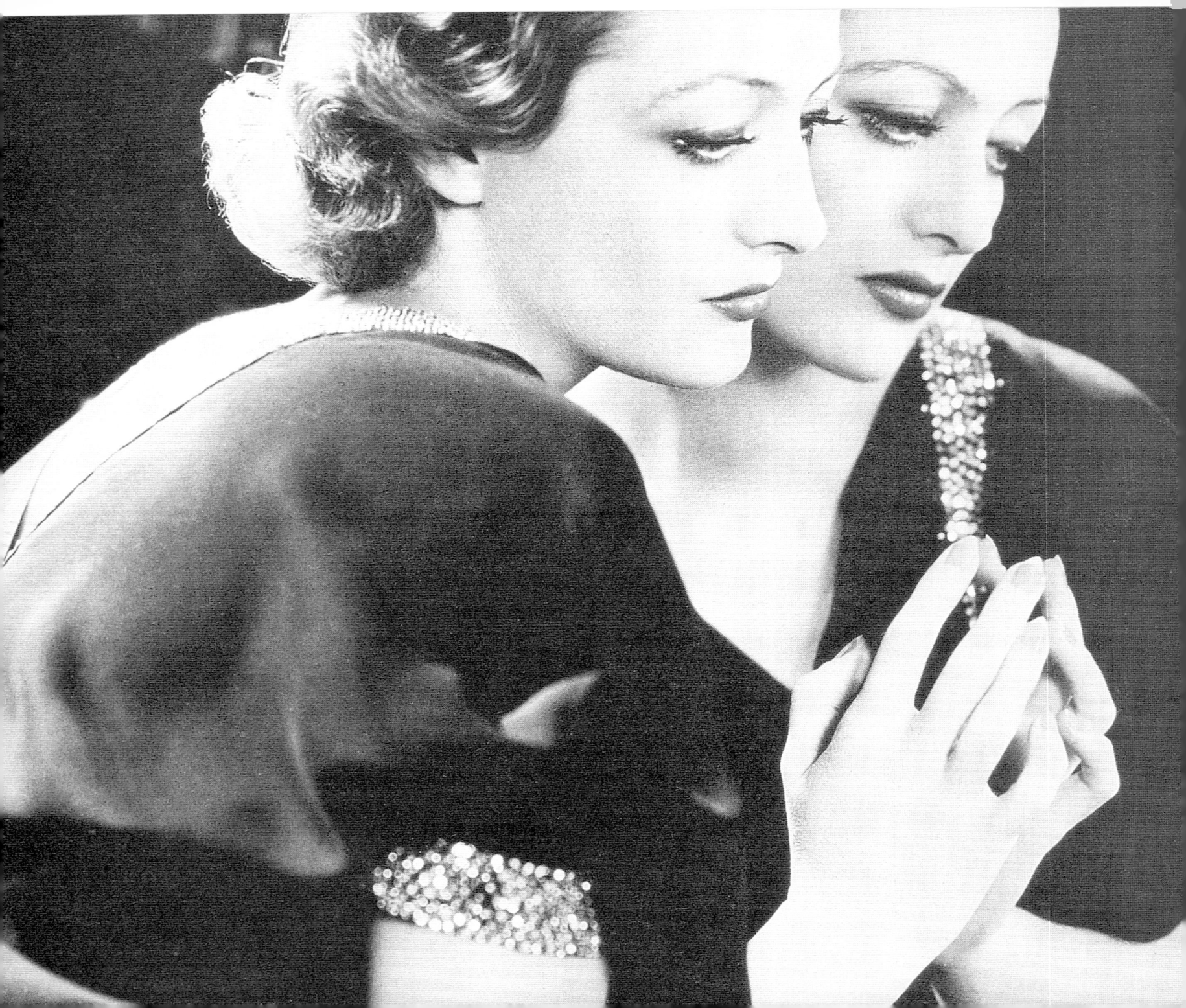

hybrid forms, it also remains true that the two are very uncomfortable bedfellows.

Ed Ruscha's work has pioneered the use of language and imagery drawn from popular media by selecting objects from the sprawling Los Angeles landscape removed from their contexts. Negotiating between abstraction and representation, he lifted portions of L.A. street iconography, and his paintings have often hijacked movie logos (for example, Twentieth Century Fox) and mimicked film. By the same token, the Hollywood sign and revered movie logos were demythified as equally pervasive signs in the landscape as gas stations and parking lots. *The Back of Hollywood*, 1977, in widescreen format, fades into the sunset and traverses a fine line between homage and pastiche – seen from the "other" side and pushed toward hard-edged abstraction. As in the title of one of his works, "Hollywood is a verb."

Like Anger, Andy Warhol was also obsessed with the mechanization of stardom. Emerging from the realm of commercial art (as did James Rosenquist, in effect allowing them both to challenge the elitism of fine art practice), Warhol was to be the artist who decisively re-wrote art's relationship to the star:

The Hollywood we were driving to that fall of 63 was in limbo. The Old Hollywood was finished and the New Hollywood hadn't started yet.... But this made Hollywood more exciting to me, the idea that it was so vacant. Vacant, vacuous Hollywood was everything I ever wanted....[32]

Along with other underground filmmakers, Warhol exposed the manipulation of time and space of commercial Hollywood film production by rejecting editing altogether, as well as creating his own microcosm of "superstars." Warhol relished involvement with mainstream media, making a cameo appearance, lest it be forgotten, on *The Love Boat*. But it has been his degradation and recontextualization of Hollywood icons in his work that have entered the popular imagination.

Anger effectively created an alternate sphere by envisioning a deeply personal universe extending from his Hollywood roots, which encompassed the counterculture and America's youth cults in a radical new filmic vocabulary. *Hollywood Babylon* has unfortunately overshadowed Anger's work as a filmmaker as his films have not been as accessible for viewing.[33] If *Hollywood Babylon* provided a pastiche and scrapbook of Hollywood – Anger's hometown – his films could be seen, to some extent, as an autobiographical pastiche of his life, a scrapbook of characters he has known, places he has been and passages in his own metamorphosis.

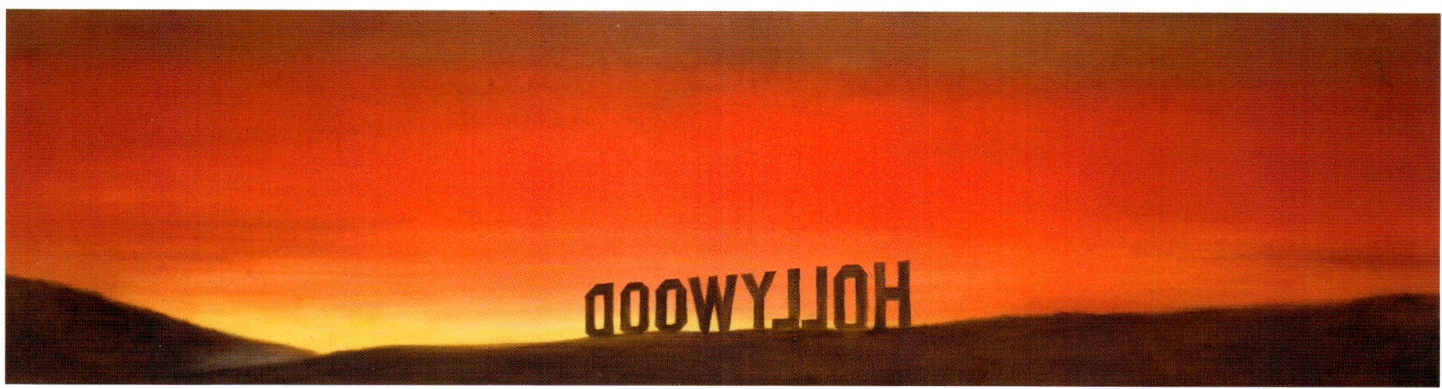

Opposite: Joan Crawford, studio portrait, *Hollywood Babylon*
Above: Ed Ruscha, *The Back of Hollywood*, 1977

Overleaf: Anger's New York apartment

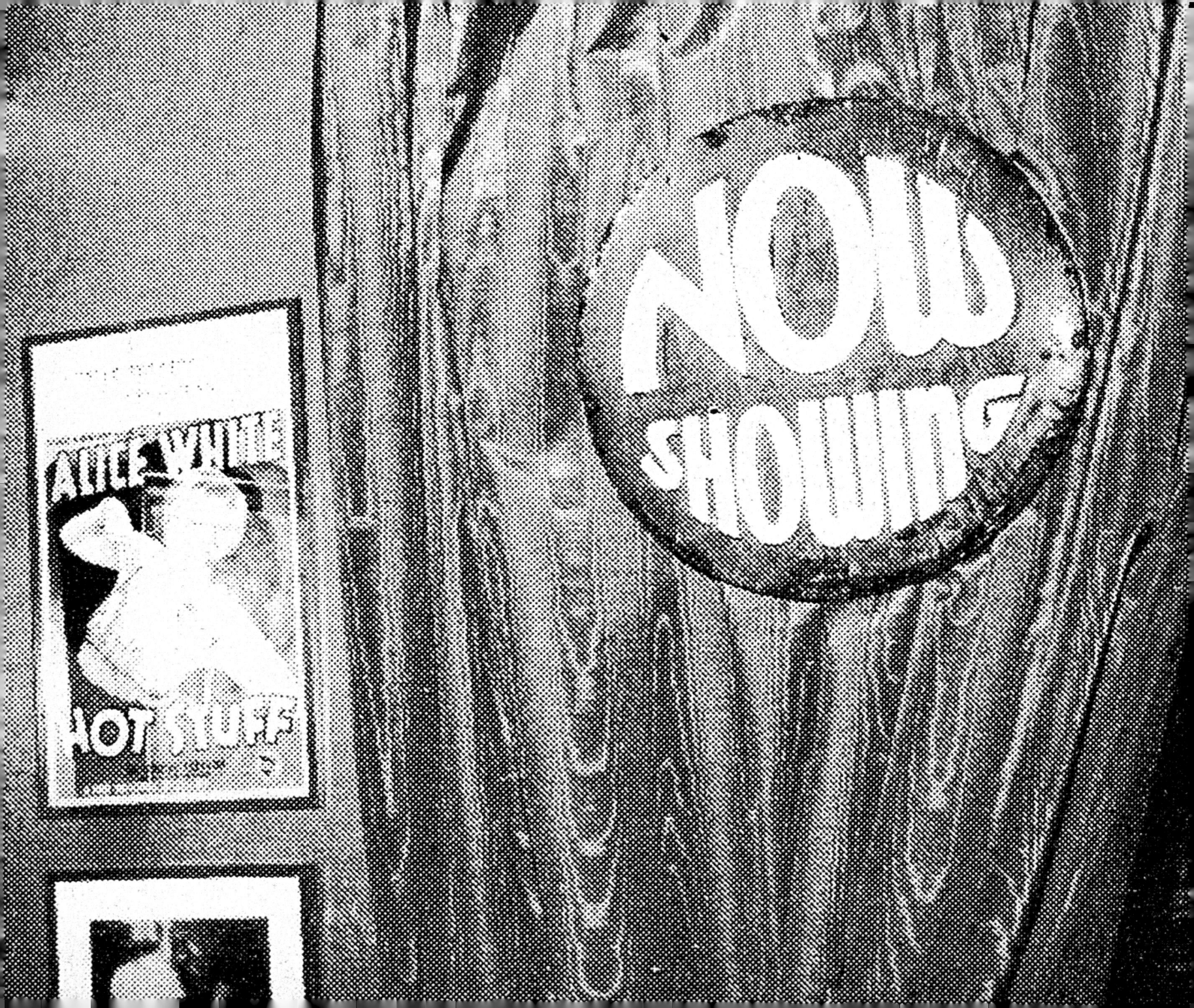

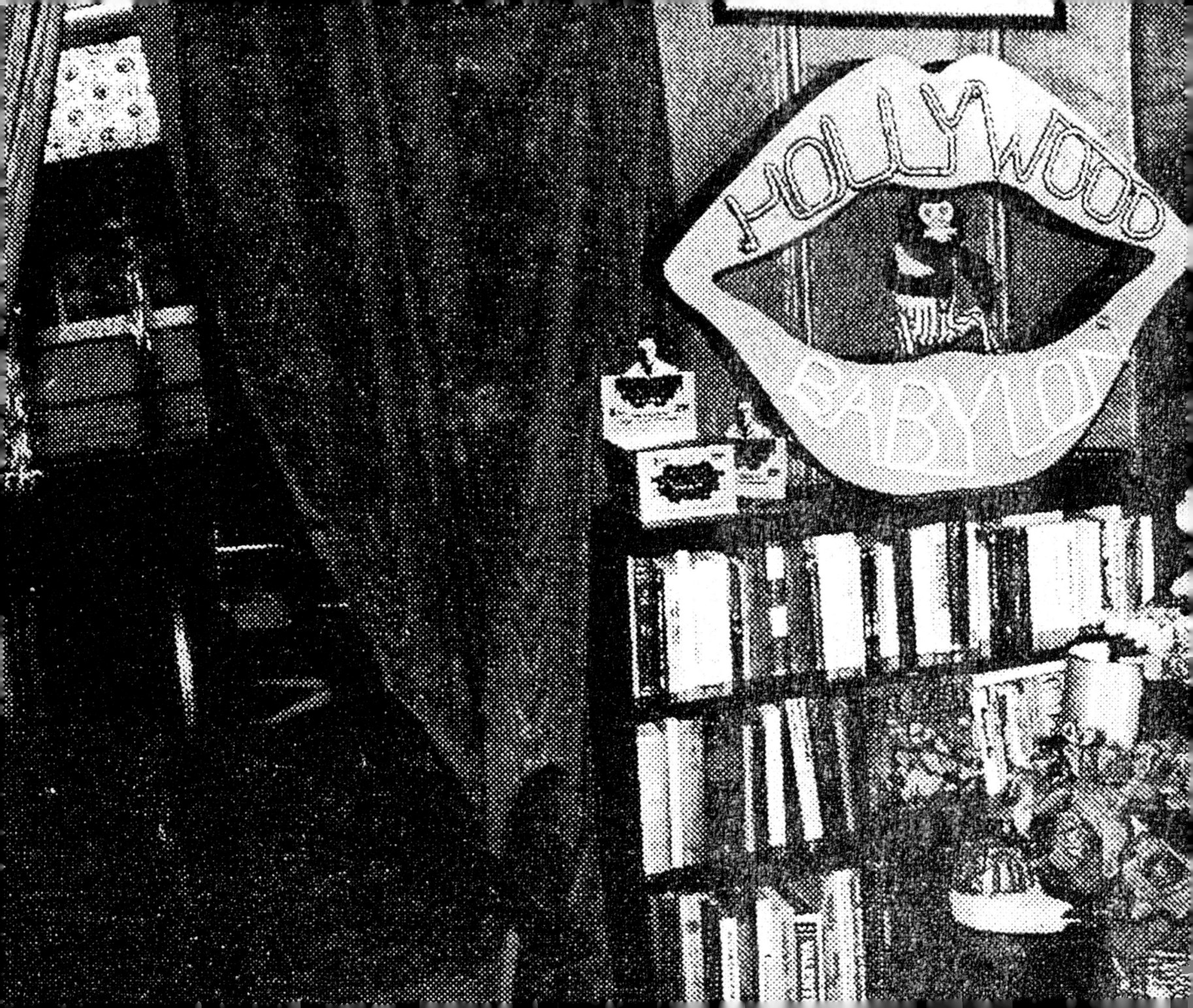

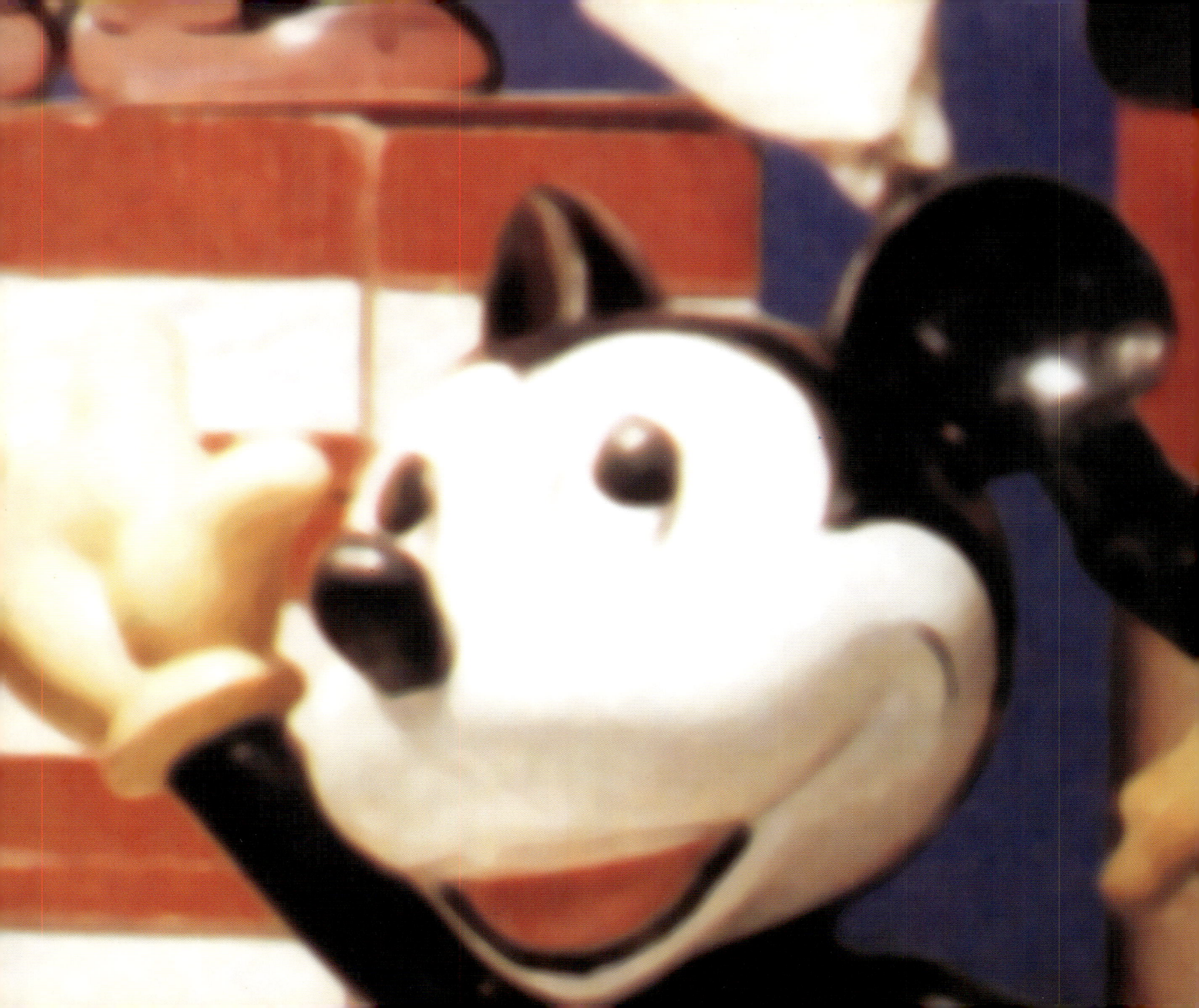

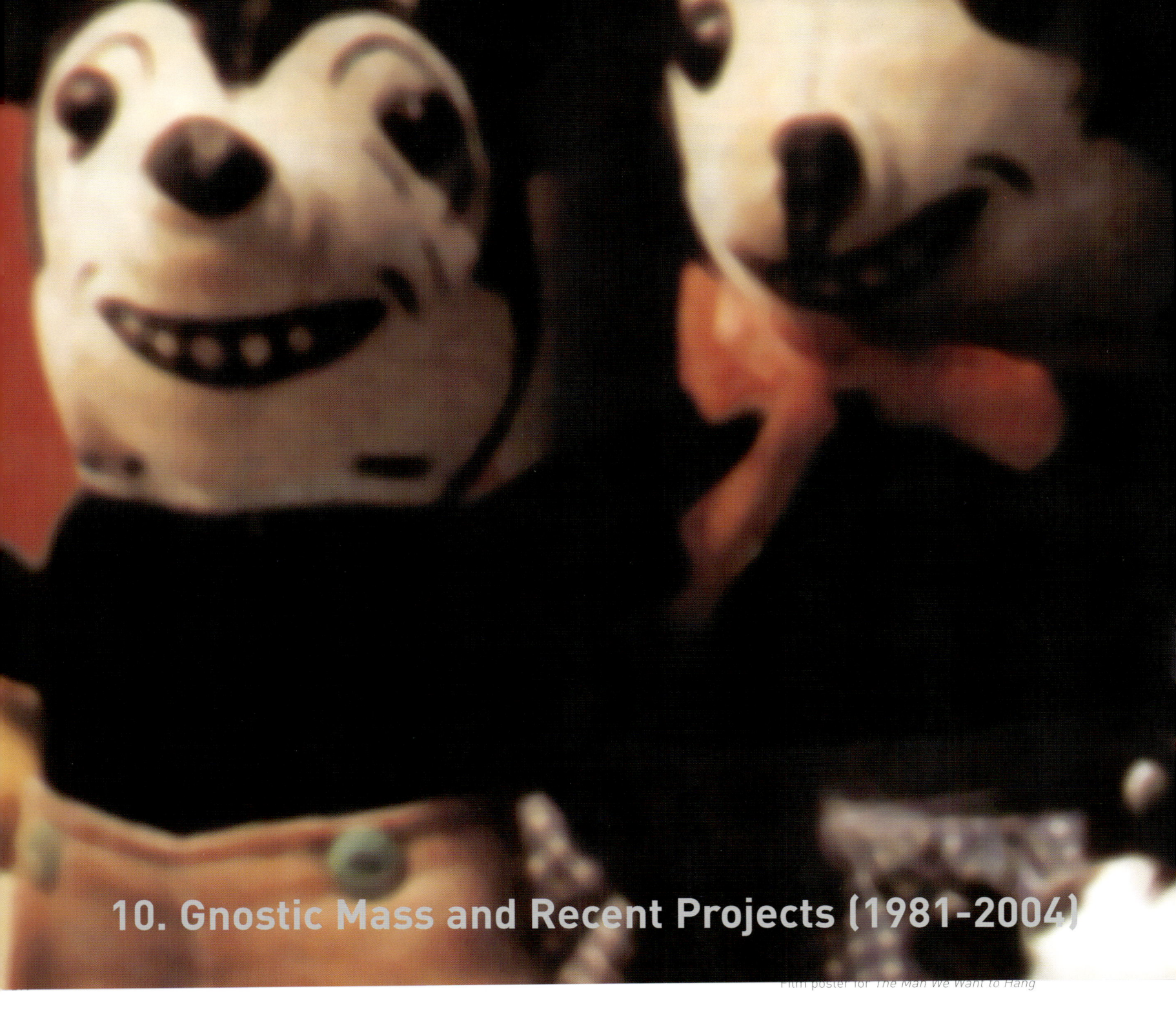

10. Gnostic Mass and Recent Projects (1981–2004)

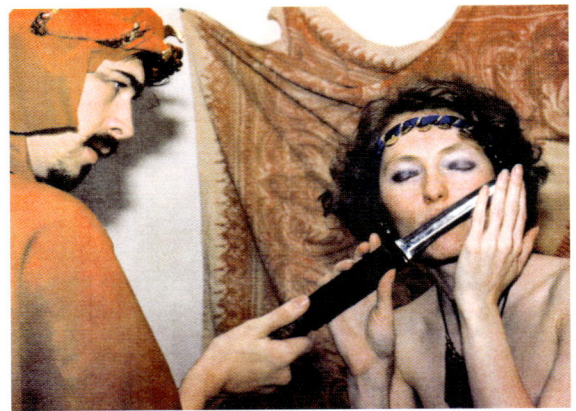

Gnostic Mass ritual will be explicit: "My concept of sensuality and eroticism is through suggestion and inference. To me a shadow is always much more evocative and intriguing than anything explicit. It's a little bit what Marlene Dietrich said: "Desire is everything, having is nothing." It's the longing – the desire – not the nuts and bolts."[5]

During the 1990s, Anger received a number of awards, recognizing his contribution to film. In 1996, the American Film Institute presented him with a Maya Deren Award for Independent filmmaking, in conjunction with an exhibition of his collection of memorabilia and Icons at Anthology Film Archives in New York, and the Los Angeles Film Critics Association endowed an award for lifetime achievement in experimental cinema in January 2003. He also appeared in Bravo's "Art of Influences" television series in 1997 discussing his artistic mentor, Jean Cocteau. (Amongst other interviewees was Helen Frankenthaler who discussed Jackson Pollock). In this interview Anger described Cocteau as a pioneering multi-media artist, and discussed the relationship between film and poetry with reference to Cocteau's *Blood of a Poet* and *Orpheus*. Anger contextualized his film *Fireworks* (recalling Abel Gance) comparing images to hieroglyphs, "letting the power of images as dreams reach the unconscious." Anger's reputation as a seminal figure in both the history of film and contemporary art has been consolidated over the last decade, with exhibitions and screenings such as the 2001 SITE Santa Fe Fourth International Biennial, *Beau Monde: Toward A Redeemed Cosmopolitanism* (curated by Dave Hickey), acknowledging the importance of Anger's work by including a full screening program of the *Magick Lantern Cycle*. He was also endowed with an honorary doctorate from Art Center College of Design, Pasadena in 1999.

An extension from and inspired by Anger's *Hollywood Babylon*, *Suicide in the Entertainment Industry* was compiled by David K. Frasier in 2002.[6] Kenneth Anger wrote the foreword for the "exhaustively researched compendium of cancelled careers," as he put it, and much of the accumulated research material for *Hollywood Babylon II* and *III* was consolidated into this book. An encyclopedia of hundreds of actors, musicians and entertainers

This page: members of the O.T.O. perform *Gnostic Mass*
Opposite: memorial for Elliott Smith, Sunset Boulevard, Silverlake, CA, February 2004

who chose Death, the book charts the demise of characters from Jean Seberg (star of Godard's *Breathless*, the F.B.I. concocted a story about her involvement with one of the Black Panthers to discredit her reputation which drove her to the brink of insanity), to the beautiful French model-actress Capucine (who jumped from the window of her apartment in Switzerland in 1990), to Fantasy Island's Tattoo (Herve Villechaize, who had once attended the École des Beaux Arts in Paris, shot himself in 1993 at the age of 50).[7] What seems to be an all-too frequent trend is the demise of actresses reaching a certain age who are faced with no or little work. These lives and careers are summarized as statistics, with an appendix listing the methods of suicides (under which names are categorized alphabetically and indexed: Airplane, Automobile, Carbon Monoxide, Drowning, Drugs/Pills, Electrocution, Exposure, Fire, Gas, Gasoline ingestion/inhalation, Gun, Hanging, Jumping, Knife/Razor/Scissors, etc.) Yet each portrait provides an insightful and considerate remembrance of those who may have been forever forgotten. In his foreword Anger reiterated Freud: "opposite Eros, the Life Instinct, lies the realm of Thanatos, the Death Instinct. Thanatos, brother of Eros, has his charms, fatal for the merry crew whose calculated conclusions make up the bulk of this book."[8] He pays homage to his own dearly departed suicidal friends; James Whale, the brilliant director of *Frankenstein* and *The Bride of Frankenstein*, Fred Halsted, pioneer in homoerotica; and "Donald Cammell, another Brit who chose to die by the gun in the manner prefigured in his masterpiece *Performance*," and Anger's cameraman Michael Cooper for his film *Lucifer Rising*.[9] Cooper was best known for the album covers for the Beatles' *Sergeant Pepper* and the Rolling Stones' *Their Satanic Majesties Request*.

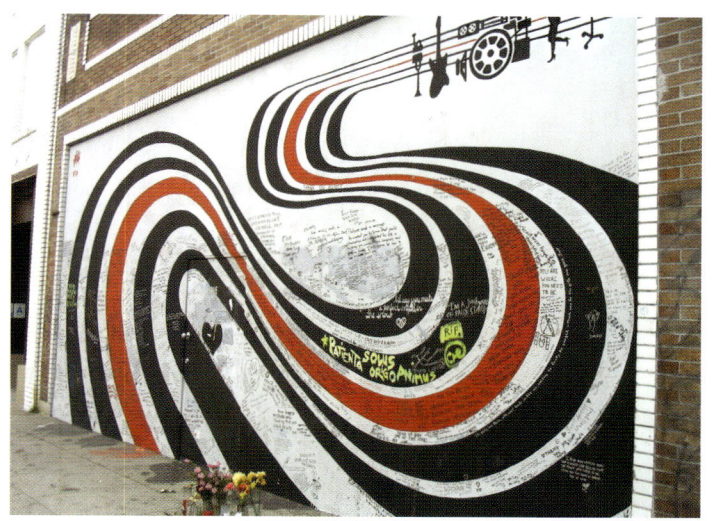

As homage to the memory of his friend and neighbor, Anger has most recently been making a short poetic film *Elliott's Suicide*. In December 2003, the contemporary music world was stunned by the tragedy of the death of talented 34-year-old singer and songwriter Elliott Smith. He had moved to Los Angeles in 1999 and (having previously recorded on independent labels) recorded two albums released by DreamWorks, *XO*, 1998, and *Figure 8*, 2000, and at the time of his death, he had just finished recording a double album (titled *From a Basement on the Hill*), that he had hoped to release on an independent label. Living in Echo Park near Silverlake, he was found dead in his girlfriend's apartment – an apparent suicide – found with a steak knife through his heart. Although a number of sources mention that he was addicted to heroin and was on a steady decline, the melancholia of his lyrics has been overstated while his sardonic humor under-estimated, "the mythology of his depression and drug use grew inflated beyond reality since the singer used them as metaphors for love, relationships and other topics."[10] Anger's film is a personal elegy and eulogy, with some of Smith's music as a soundtrack, and may not be available for public viewing for copyright reasons.

Alongside *Gnostic Mass* and *Arrangement in White on Green* projects, Anger is currently set to film *Mouse Heaven*, following the award of a significant Rockefeller Media grant in 2004. This is a project he has long desired to bring to fruition, at least since 1988; a poetic evocation and fantasy of the various early Mickeys in the private Birnkrant collection of rare vintage Mickey Mouse toys. Anger's preliminary concept for filming the mechanical mice includes setting them against minimal backgrounds (similar in effect to *Kustom Kar Kommandos*). Some will be prancing as mechanical wind-up toys, others stationary. Anger discussed the changing appearance of Mickey Mouse in 1975, with various characteristics either exaggerated or toned down: "Mickey Mouse lost his mouse imp quality. It was Ub Iwerks who drew the best and original Mickey Mouse, the one with the teeth and long tail."[11] He also mentioned that their rivets and metallic masks made them rather alarming characters in close up. Starring Disney's original Mickey Mouse character from 1928-1938, Anger described his proposed film in 1989 as being planned as a fantastical collage. Faced with a gamut of marching Mickey's, the spectator would lose all perspective. Closer in spirit to his earlier films than *Don't Smoke That Cigarette* or *The Man We Want to Hang*, *Mouse Heaven* returns to the hermetic realm of fantasy and perennial childhood, with original music to be composed for the soundtrack by ragtime specialist Ian Whitcomb. The film will be shot on 16mm and then transferred onto 35mm.

Opposite: Kenneth Anger's prints and signature in the "Indie" walk of fame, Vista Theater, Sunset Boulevard, Silverlake, CA

214

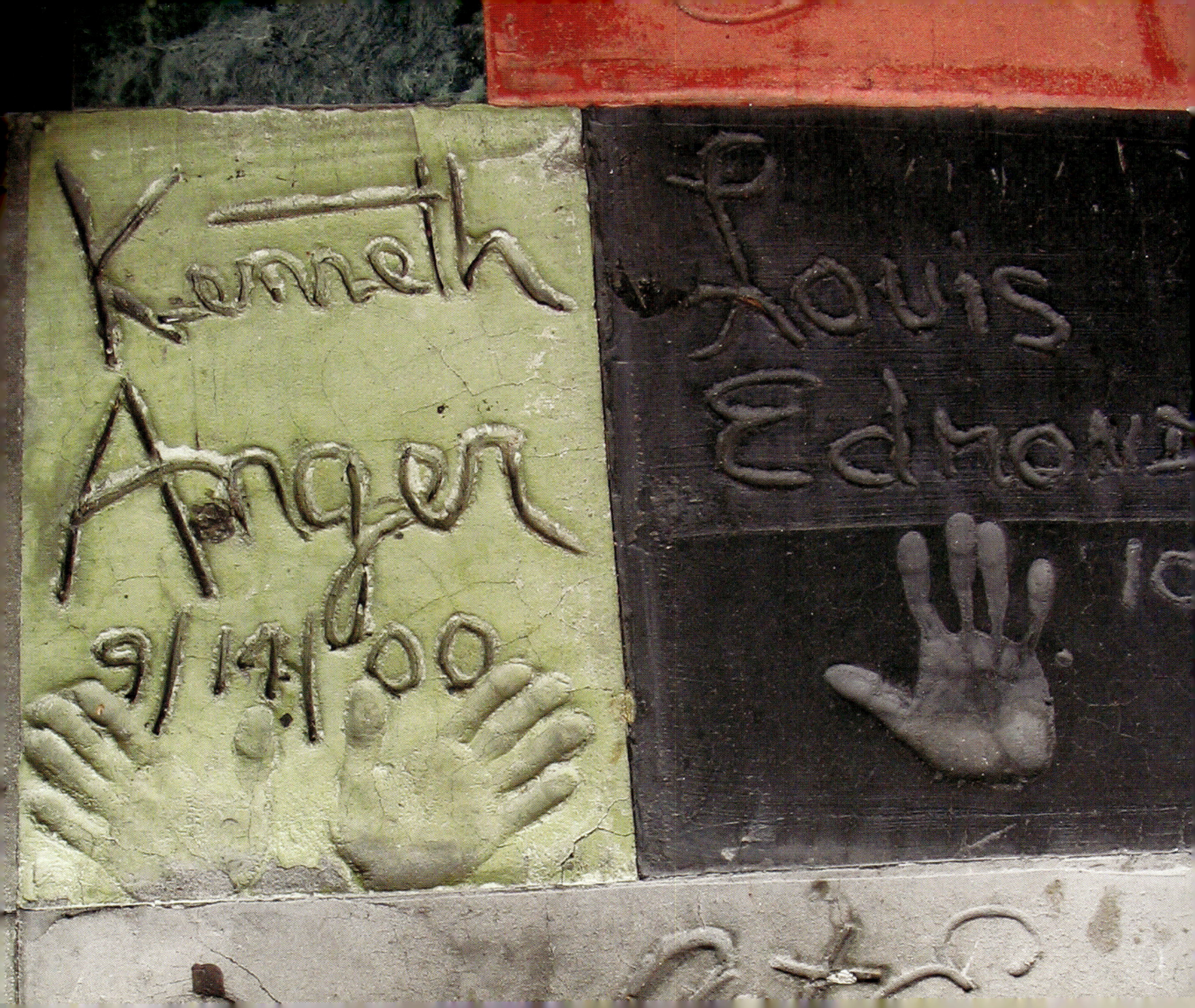

Endnote

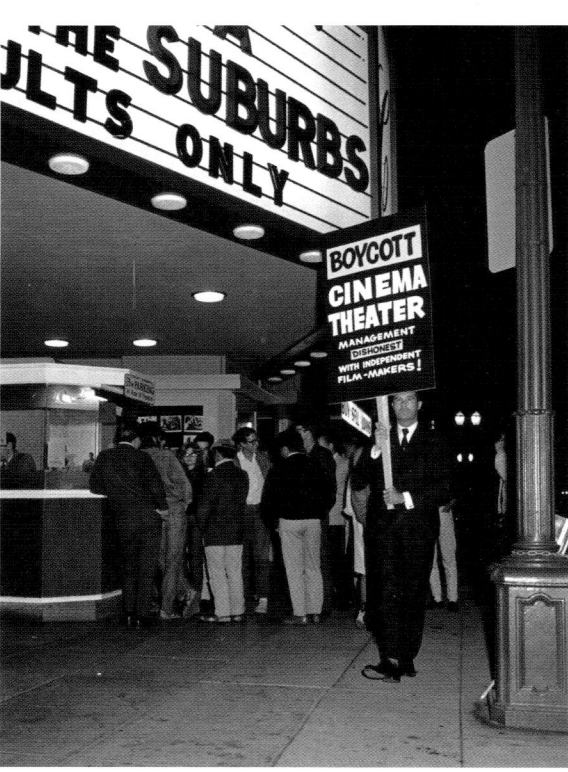

Only one in the picket-line: Anger causes a commotion to protest the illegal copying and screening of his films

Kenneth Anger prompted the blurring of boundaries, blending pop culture and fine art into the moving image. Merging art, film, literature and music, Anger has created an extraordinary contribution to contemporary visual language – a transgressive artist on the threshold between disciplines. Providing a link between the early twentieth century avant-garde filmmakers and today's postmodern media landscape, the visual forms in film, video and contemporary art that we take for granted today can be seen, in part, to stem from Anger's prescient imagination. The reasons for his neglect up to now are complex.

Although alternative production and distribution circuits and midnight screenings in the 1950s, 60s, 70s and 80s created a framework in which Anger's films were often first viewed – signifying a covert niche audience, and a dissent from the mainstream culture market – it has been overlooked that his work was often first presented in an art context (i.e. the San Francisco Museum of Modern Art in the 1940s, the Museum of Modern Art and the Whitney Museum in New York in the 1980s). The impact of these films has been far more universal and ongoing than many in the United States are aware. *Fireworks* has been screened around the world consistently for over six decades and *Scorpio Rising* has had an even wider viewership: with, for example, the film being presented recently by artist Isaac Julien at the Tate Modern in London. The alternative culture of production, distribution, screening and circulation involving personal, independent filmmaking in the United States had begun in the 1940s with Maya Deren and Kenneth Anger, and its groundswell was felt internationally by the 1960s. A culture of dissent has become submerged today within the mainstream, and thus its pioneers such as Anger have been felt but little recognized. With his singular anti-establishment stance, Anger's films have, to a certain degree reflected, processed and contributed to cultural, artistic and socio-political developments. Consistent ambiguity in his films invite multiple interpretations, often contradictory readings, and connections to cultural discourses of the time, blurring the relationship between social currents and works of art.

As Juan Suarez remarked, this new cinema art "signaled the inadequacy of previous critical models for dealing with contemporary cultural developments," explaining that the medley "of "degraded" influences that came together... appeared terribly disconcerting to most critics, who, in coping with it, systematically erased part of its complex cultural identity, assimilating it to modernist high culture or to kitsch."[12] The division between the art market (certainly the art establishment could not readily "claim" it or "sell" it) and the film industry left a gaping void between. Certainly the unmitigated vision and feat of a singular artist as Anger, who usually shot, directed, made costumes, acted in, edited and made props and cast (type-cast) for all his films, is not immediately recognized.

Hopefully the discussion in this book elucidates his contribution to contemporary visual culture, and provides, a little compensation for this neglect, allowing the images from the films to articulate what words cannot. The complexity of his oeuvre, which is often self-contradictory – traversing as it does the stunning, elegantly subversive films of the *Magick Lantern Cycle* to *Hollywood Babylon* – has also made consideration of Kenneth Anger difficult.

This publication has endeavored to consolidate archives and correspondence from Paris, New York, London and Los Angeles; a vast amount of diverse material to provide a larger picture of his oeuvre, and to contain as many voices within the narrative here as time and space would allow. The creation of new stills for this book, facilitated by Anger's distributor Canyon Cinema in San Francisco, and from Anger's own collection of photographs, has allowed for a comprehensive visual illustration of his work. The construction of biographical information was consolidated in Paris with the help of author Pierre Hecker who provided copies of correspondence and archives from the Cinémathèque Française. A chronology was then constructed with material from the Bibliothèque du Film in Paris, the British Film Institute in London, and the film archives of the Museum of Modern Art and Anthology Film Archives in New York, building on conversations with Anger himself.

Kenneth Anger once described his films:

> As enchantment they will last for a while then they will vanish; it's like writing on water.[13]

As rich visual experiences, abounding with explicit and detailed esoteric references and concepts, the energy of his images is such that they can easily be understood on an intuitive level, a direct communication with the senses; their literal references become secondary. On the contrary, then: these unforgettable enchantments have stood the test of time and continue to greet new viewers with a revelation.

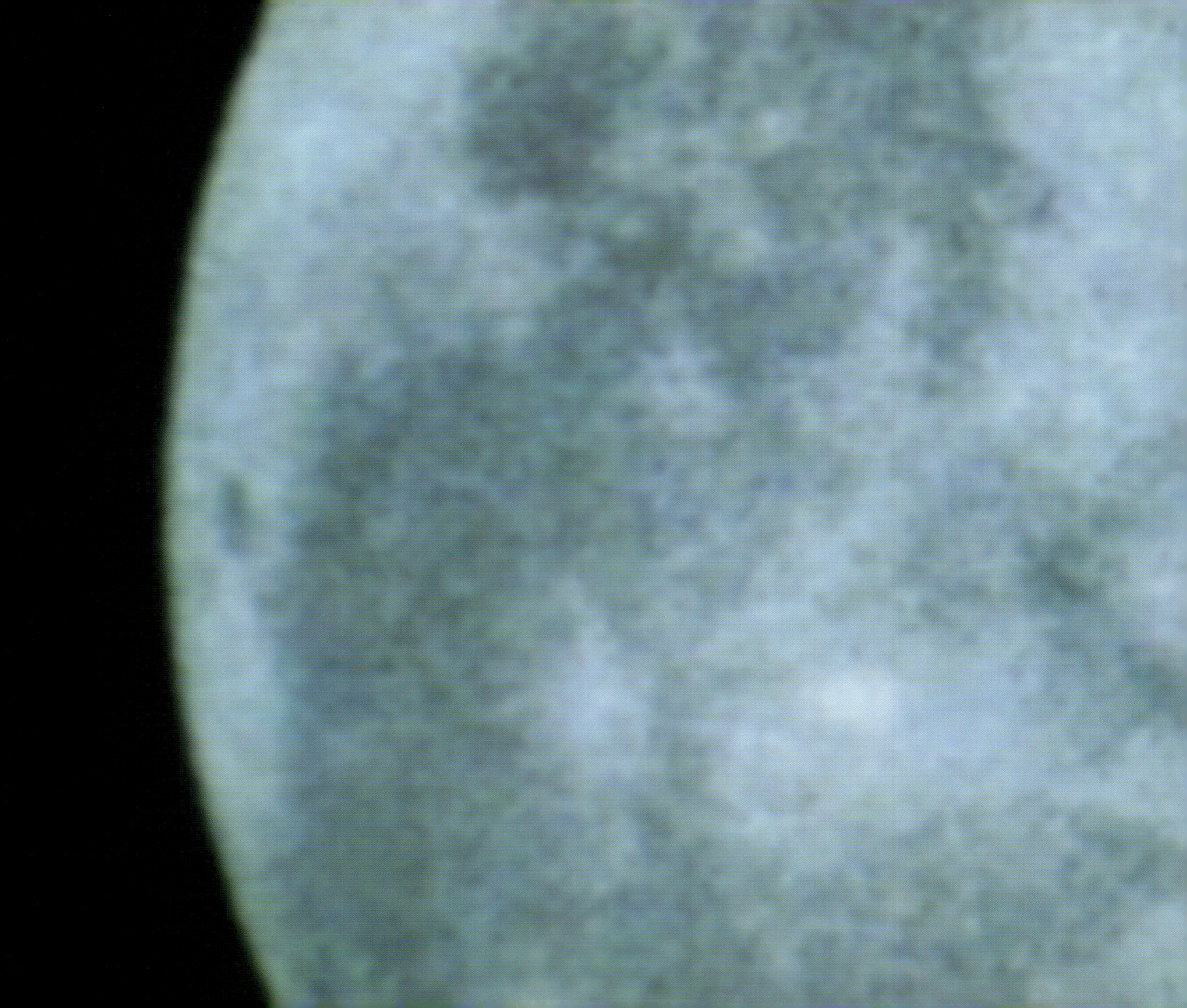

Filmography

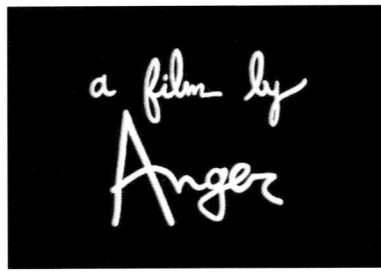

Ferdinand The Bull, 1937

16mm, black and white.

Cast: Boys of Summer Camp at Big Bear Lake.
Based on children's book by Munro.

Anger described these early prototype films up to 1947, as follows in *Film Culture* 31, Winter 1963-1964:

Who Has Been Rocking My Dreamboat?, 1941

7 min., 16mm, black and white, silent, filmed in Santa Monica.

Conceived, directed, photographed and edited by Kenneth Anger.
Cast: A dozen contemporaries recruited from the neighborhood.
Synopsis: Using rapid cross-cutting, the playworld of children shown over-shadowed by war. A montage of American children at play, drifting and dreaming, in the summer before Pearl Harbor. Flash cuts of newsreel mayhem dart across the reverie. Fog invades the playground; the children dropping in mock death to make a misty landscape of dreamers. Smoke billows over the still bodies.

Tinsel Tree, 1941-1942

3 min., 16mm, black and white, hand-tinted, silent, filmed in Santa Monica.

Conceived, directed, photographed and edited by Kenneth Anger.
Cast: A pine silvertip Christmas Tree.
Synopsis: The ritual dressing and destruction of the family Christmas Tree, using hand-colored over-tint. Close-ups as the branches are laden with baubles, draped with garlands, tossed with tinsel. Cut to the stripped discarded tree as it bursts into brief furious flames (hand-tinted gold-scarlet) to leave a charred skeleton.

Prisoner of Mars, 1942

11 min., 16mm, black and white, silent, filmed in Santa Monica.

Conceived, directed, photographed and edited by Kenneth Anger.
Camera Assistant: Charles Vreeland.
Settings, miniatures, and costumes designed and executed by Kenneth Anger.
Cast: Kenneth Anger (The Boy-Elect from Earth).
Synopsis: Science-Fiction rendering of the Minotaur myth. A "chosen" adolescent of the future is rocketed to Mars where he awakens in a labyrinth littered with the bones of his predecessors, previous travelers. First formal use of serial chapter aesthetic: begins and ends in a predicament.

The Nest, 1942-1943

20 min., 16mm, black and white, silent, filmed in Santa Monica, Westwood and Beverly Hills, CA.

Conceived, directed, photographed and edited by Kenneth Anger.
Cast: Bob Jones (Brother); Jo Whittaker (Sister); Dare Harris – later known as John Derek in Hollywood – (Boy Friend).
Synopsis: A precocious study into latent eroticism. A brother and sister relate to mirrors and each other until a third party breaks the balance; seducing both into violence. Ablutions and the acts of dressing and making-up observed as a magic rite. The binding spell of the sister-sorceress is banished by the brother who walks out. Inspired by Cocteau's book *Les Enfants Terribles*, 1929.

Escape Episode, 1944

35 min., 16mm, black and white, silent, filmed in Santa Monica and Hollywood.

Conceived, directed, photographed and edited by Kenneth Anger.
Cast: Marilyn Granas (The Girl); Bob Jones (The Boy); Nora Watson (The Guardian).
Synopsis: Free rendering of the Andromeda myth. A crumbling, stucco-gothic sea-side monstrosity, serving as a Spiritualist Church. Imprisoned within, a girl at the mercy of a religious fanatic "dragon" awaits her deliverance by a beach-boy Perseus. Ultimately it is her own defiance which snaps the chain.

Drastic Demise, 1945

5 min., 16mm, black and white, silent, filmed in Hollywood on V.J. Day.

Conceived, directed, photographed and edited by Kenneth Anger.
Cast: Anonymous street crowds.
Synopsis: A free-wheeling hand-held camera-plunge into the hallucinatory reality of a hysterical Hollywood Boulevard crowd celebrating war's end. A mushrooming cloud makes a final commentary.

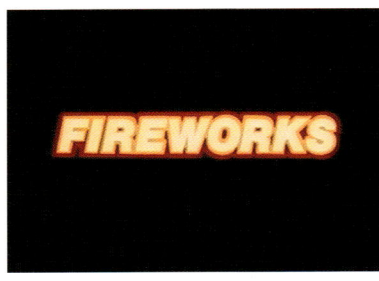

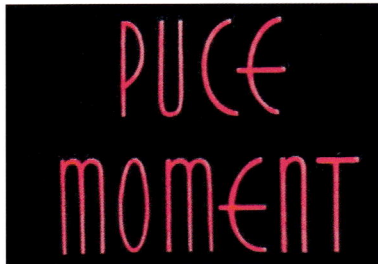

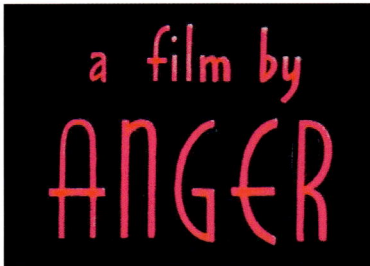

Escape Episode (Sound Version), 1946

27 min., music by Scriabin.

This shorter edition makes non-realistic use of bird, wind and surf sounds, as well as Scriabin's "Poem of Ecstasy" to heighten mood.

In "Experiment in the Film," Lewis Jacobs is the sole source of information about *Escape Episode*:

> Less concerned with cinematic form and more with human conflict are the pictures of Kenneth Anger. *Escape Episode*, 1946, begins with a boy and girl parting at the edge of the sea. As the girl walks away she is watched by a woman from a plaster castle. The castle turns out to be a spiritualists' temple, the woman a medium and the girl's aunt. Both dominate and twist the girl's life until she is in despair. Finally in a gesture of defiance the girl invites the boy to the castle to sleep with her. The aunt informed by spirits becomes enraged and threatens divine retribution. The girl is frustrated, becomes bitter and resolves to escape. The quality of the film is unique and shows an extreme sensitivity to personal relationships. But because the thoughts, feelings and ideas of the filmmaker are superior to his command of the medium, the effect is often fumbling and incomplete, with parts superior to the whole.[1]

Fireworks, 1947

15 min., 16mm, black and white, music by Respighi, filmed in Hollywood.

Conceived, directed, photographed and edited by Kenneth Anger.
Camera Assistant: Chester Kessler.
Cast: Kenneth Anger (The Dreamer); Bill Seltzer (Body Builder Show-Off); Gordon Grey (Body-Baring Sailor); crowd of sailors.
Synopsis: A dissatisfied dreamer awakes, goes out into the night seeking "a light" and is drawn through the needle's eye. A dream of a dream, he returns to a bed less empty than before.

Anger's 1966 Filmmaker's Cinematheque program notes:

> Fireworks Spring Equinox 1947
> "This flick is all I have to say about being 17, The United States' Navy, American Christmas and The Fourth of July,"
> Kenneth Anger's Notebook.... Dedicated to Denham Fouts, who first "turned me on."

Puce Moment, 1949/1970

6 min., 35mm, color, music by Jonathan Halper, filmed in Hollywood.

Conceived, directed, photographed and edited by Kenneth Anger.
Cast: Yvonne Marquis (Star).
Re-edited fragment of never-completed feature-length *Puce Women*.

The Love That Whirls, 1949

16mm, color (Kodachrome).

No credits available. Film confiscated by Eastman-Kodak developing plant in Rochester, who objected to "nudity" in simulated Mexican fertility rites, filmed in Mexico. In 1949, inspired by Frazer's *The Golden Bough*, Anger filmed color footage in Mexico which was subsequently sabotaged by the Kodak laboratories confiscating the film that showed a (faked) nude Aztec human sacrifice, probably also inspired by Sergei Eisenstein's *Que Viva Mexico!* (the Sol Lesser version). Anger described the project:

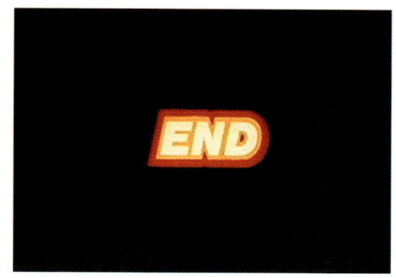

> *The Love That Whirls* was about a human sacrifice – specifically an Aztec ritual in which a youth is chosen to be king. It's about a symbolic Kingship. After one year, the day comes when the King is sacrificed. When his time is up, his flutes are broken and there is a ritual. I found this a compelling situation, but the film had a few glimpses of nudity, which at that time simply wasn't done, even though the context of the nudity made it clear that it was nothing to do with lewdness and obscenity. The film was Kodachrome and had to be developed at the Eastman-Kodak processing plant. Kodak ended up keeping it, saying that they couldn't allow their film to be used for nudity!....[2]

La Lune des Lapins/Rabbit's Moon, 1950/1971/1979

7 min., 16mm, tinted black and white, music by Andy Arthur, filmed in Paris.

Conceived, directed, photographed and edited by Kenneth Anger.
Camera Assistant: Tourjansky.
Cast: André Soubeyran (Pierrot), Claude Revenant (Harlequin), Nadine Valence (Columbine).
Synopsis: "A fable of the Unattainable (the Moon) combining elements of Commedia dell'Arte with Japanese myth. A lunar dream utilizing the classic pantomime figure of Pierrot in an encounter with a prankish, enchanted Magic Lantern." Kenneth Anger

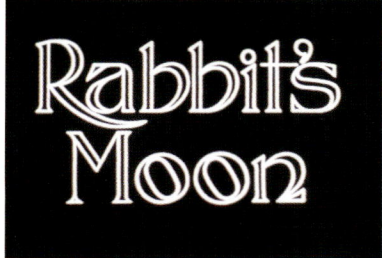

Not released until 1972, then in a 16 minute version with a Temptations soundtrack. In 1979 the seven minute version with music by Andy Arthur was assembled as a "birthday present" for Roark Brakhage.

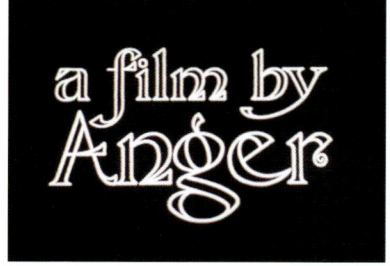

Le Jeune Homme et la Mort, 1951

20 min., 16mm, black and white, silent, filmed in Paris.

Study film from the 1947 ballet by Jean Cocteau.
Cast: Jean Babilée (Young Man); Nathalie Philipart (Death).

Anger filmed this 16mm pilot in the hope of raising funds for a 35mm Technicolor version but, despite Cocteau's full support, the project was not realized due to lack of funding.

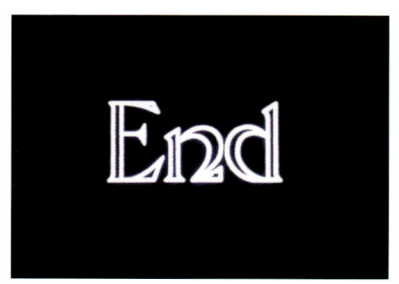

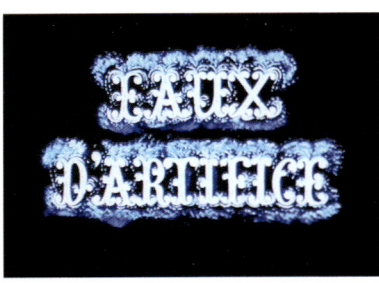

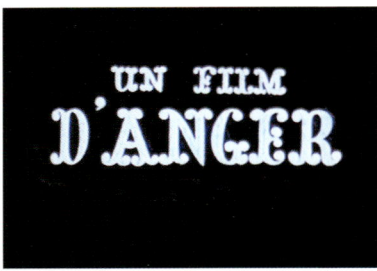

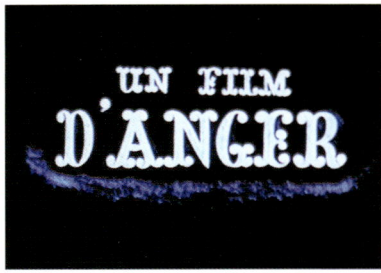

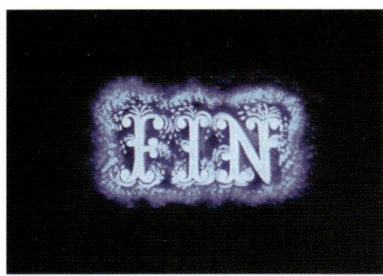

Les Chants de Maldoror, 1951-1952

16mm, black and white, filmed in Paris and Deauville.

Visual adaptation from the book *Les Chants de Maldoror* by Isadore Ducasse – Le Comte de Lautréamont, 1868. Anger states "My scenario follows the "exalted" style of Lautréamont's text finding visual equivalents. "Hymne à l'Océan" segment filmed with members of the Ballets de Marquis de Cuevas on beach at Deauville."[3] A war between flies and pins was also filmed. In addition to lack of funds, Anger reported being threatened by pseudo "Surrealists" who were wary of a "Yank" filming their most revered text.

Eaux d'Artifice, 1953

13 min., 16mm, tinted black and white, music: Vivaldi's "Four Seasons", excerpt from "Winter", filmed in the Gardens of the Villa D'Este, Tivoli, by special permission of the Italian Department of Antiquities, on Ferrania Black and White.

Printed on Ektachrome through a Cyan filter. The fan of Exorcism hand-tinted by Anger with emerald dye.
Conceived, directed, photographed and edited by Kenneth Anger.
Camera Assistants: Thad and Charles Lovatt.
Cast: Carmillo Salvatorelli (The Water Witch).

Anger's 1966 program notes were as follows:

EAUX D'ARTIFICE Summer Solstice 1953

"Pour water on thyself: thus shalt thou be a Fountain of the Universe. Find thou thyself in every Star! Achieve thou every possibility!"
– Khaled Khan, *The Heart of the Master*, Theorem V.
Hide and seek in a night-time labyrinth of levels, cascades, balustrades, grottoes and ever-gushing, leaping fountains, until the Water Witch and the Fountain become One. Dedicated to Pavel Tchelichew.

Inauguration of the Pleasure Dome, 1954/1966

38 min., 16mm, color, music: Janáček's "Glagolithic Mass," filmed at the residence of Samson De Brier, Hollywood.

Printed by Kenneth Anger in Hand Lithography System on A, B, C, D, and E rolls, on Ektachrome 7387.
Conceived, directed, photographed and edited by Kenneth Anger.
Camera Assitant: Robert Straede.
Costumes, lighting and make-up by Kenneth Anger.
Properties and setting courtesy of Samson De Brier.
Cast: Samson De Brier (Lord Shiva, Osiris, Cagliostro, Nero, The Great Beast 666); Cameron (The Scarlet Woman, Lady Kali); Kathryn Kadell (Isis); Renata Loome (Lilith); Anaïs Nin (Astarte); Kenneth Anger (Hecate); Peter Loome (Ganymede); Paul Mathison (Pan); Curtis Harrington (Cesare the Somnambulist); Joan Whitney (Aphrodite).
Synopsis (Sacred Mushroom Edition): "Lord Shiva, The Magician wakes. A convocation of Theurgists in the guise of figures from mythology bearing gifts: The Scarlet Woman, Whore of Heaven, smokes a big fat joint; Astarte of the Moon brings the wings of snow; Pan bestows the grapes of Bacchus; Hecate offers the sacred mushroom, yagé, wormwood brew. The vintage of Hecate is poured. Pan's cup is poisoned by Lord Shiva. The orgy ensues – a magick masquerade at which Pan is the prize. Lady Kali blesses the rites of the children of light as Lord Shiva invokes the godhead with the formula "Force and Fire."
Dedicated to the few; and to Aleister Crowley, and the crowned and conquering child."

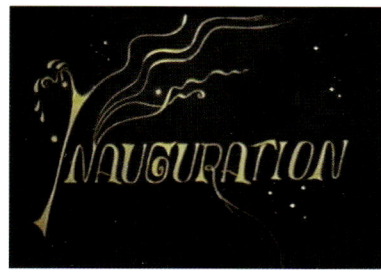

Thelema Abbey, 1955

30 min., black and white, sound, filmed in Thelema Abbey, Cefalù, Sicily.

A documentary by Kenneth Anger on the erotic wall-paintings in Aleister Crowley's ruined temple. With a guest appearance by Dr. Alfred C. Kinsey visiting the Abbey. The film, intended for commercial television in the U.K., was produced for British magazine *Picture Post*, who "lost" the documentary following the sole television broadcast in the U.K.. Anger has made a program in 2004 for Italian television to update the history of the Abbey in continuation from the 1955 project.

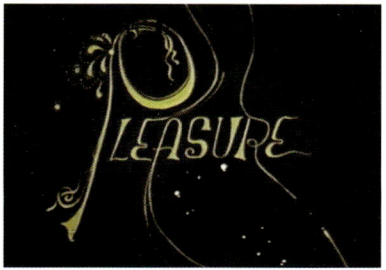

Histoire d'O, 1961

90 min., 16mm, black and white, sound effects and music, filmed in Paris.

From the novel by Pauline Réage, *Histoire d'O*, 1954.

"Follows the narrative of Pauline Réage's book, rendered as a silent film with sound effects and music."[4]

20 minutes of planned 90 minutes filmed. Remnants stored in archives of Cinémathèque Française.

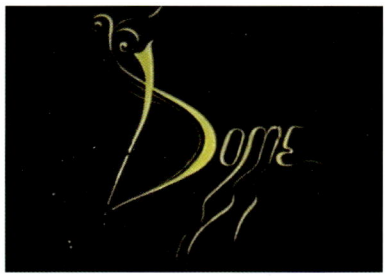

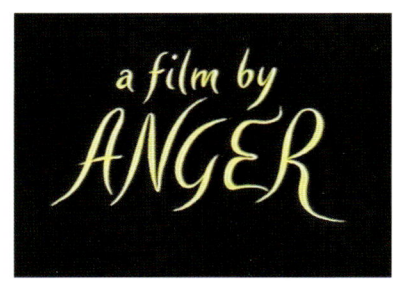

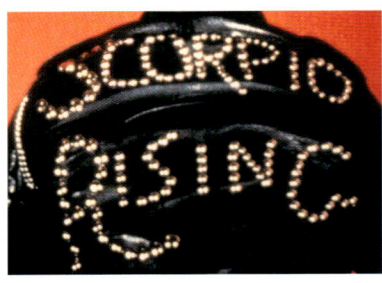

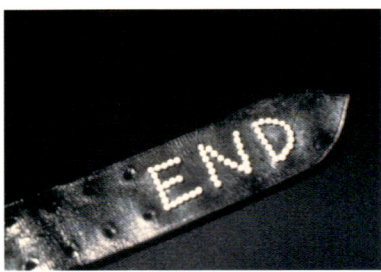

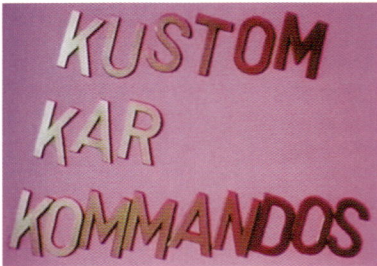

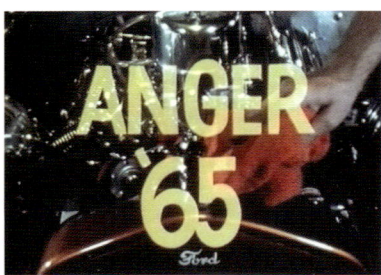

Scorpio Rising, 1963

29 min., 16mm, color, music by Ricky Nelson, Little Peggy March, The Angels, Bobby Vinton, Elvis Presley, Ray Charles, The Crystals, The Ran-Dells, Kris Jensen, Claudine Clark, Gene McDaniels, The Surfaris, filmed in Brooklyn, Manhattan, and Walden's Pond, New York, on Ektachrome ER.

Conceived, directed, photographed and edited by Kenneth Anger.
Filmed by Kenneth Anger in Brooklyn.
Cast: Bruce Byron (Scorpio); Johnny Sapienza (Taurus); Frank Carifi (Leo); John Palone (Pinstripe); Ernie Allo (The Life of the Party); Barry Rubin (Pledge); Steve Crandell (The Sissy Cyclist).

Anger's 1966 Filmmakers Cinematheque program notes:

Scorpio Rising Autumn Equinox 1964

It may be conceded in any case that the long strings of formidable words which roar and moan through so many conjurations have a real effect in exalting the consciousness of the magician to the proper pitch – that they should do so is no more extraordinary than music of any kind should do so. "Magicians have not confined themselves to the use of the human voice. The Pan-pipe with its seven stops, corresponding to the seven planets, the bull-roarer, the tom-tom, and even the violin, have all been used, as well as many others, of which the most important is the bell, though this is used not so much for actual conjuration as to mark stages in the ceremony. Of all these the tom-tom will be found to be the most generally useful."
– The Master Therion, *Magick in Theory and Practice*.

A conjuration of the presiding Princes, Angels and Spirits of the Sphere of MARS, formed as a "high" view of the Myth of the American Motorcyclist. The Power Machine seen as tribal totem, from toy to terror. Thanatos in chrome and black leather and bursting jeans. Part I: Boys and Bolts (masculine fascination with the Thing that Goes). Part II: Image Maker (getting high on heroes: Dean's Rebel and Brando's Johnny; the True View of J. C.) Part III: Walpurgis Party (J. C. wallflower at the cycler's Sabbath). Part VI: Rebel Rouser (the Gathering of the Dark Legions, with a message from Our Sponsor).

Dedicated to Jack Parsons, Victor Childe*, Jim Powers*, James Dean, T.E. Lawrence, Hart Crane*, Kurt Mann*, the Society of Spartans, the Hell's Angels and all overgrown boys who will ever follow the whistle of Love's Brother.
* all suicides

Kustom Kar Kommandos, 1965

3 min., 16mm, color, music by the Parris Sisters, filmed in San Bernadino.

Credits: conceived, directed, photographed and edited by Kenneth Anger.
Cast: Sandy Trent (Car Customizer). Fragment of project originally intended as feature-length. Longer project never completed due to lack of funding and the death of the main actor in a drag race.

Lucifer Rising, 1966

16mm, color, sound, filmed in San Francisco.

Central footage of this version missing.

Invocation of My Demon Brother, 1969

11 min., 16mm, color, music composed by Mick Jagger on the Moog Synthesizer, filmed in San Francisco at the Straight Theater, the "Russian Embassy," and in London.

Conceived, directed, photographed and edited by Kenneth Anger.
Camera Assistant: Michael Cooper
Cast: Speed Hacker (Wand Bearer); Lenore Kandel and William (Deaconess and Deacon); Kenneth Anger (The Magus); Van Leuven (Acolyte); Harvey Bialy and Timotha (Brother and Sister of the Rainbow); Anton Szandor La Vey (His Satanic Majesty); Bobby Beausoleil (Lucifer).
Synopsis:"*Invocation of My Demon Brother (Arrangement in Black and Gold)*. The shadowing forth of Our Lord Lucifer as the Powers of Darkness gather at a midnight mass. The dance of the Magus widdershins around the Swirling Spiral Force, the solar swastika, until the Bringer of Light – Lucifer – breaks through. "The true Magick of Horus requires the passionate union of opposites." Aleister Crowley"

Lucifer Rising, 1970-1981

30 min., 16mm, color, music by Bobby Beausoleil and the Freedom Orchestra, Tracy Prison, filmed in Luxor, Karnak, Gizeh, London, Externsteine and Avebury.

Conceived, directed, photographed and edited by Kenneth Anger.
Assistant Camera: Michael Cooper.
Thelemic consultant: Gerald J. Yorke.
A presentation of Anita Pallenberg.
Cast: Miriam Gibril (Isis); Donald Cammell (Osiris); Haydn Couts (Adept); Kenneth Anger (Magus); Sir Francis Rose (Chaos); Marianne Faithfull (Lilith); Leslie Huggins (Lucifer).

Anger edited a 25 minute version of *Lucifer Rising* in 1973, featuring a soundtrack by Jimmy Page of Led Zeppelin. In 1976 he removed Page from the film and prepared the final edit (with additional footage and optical effects) which Bobby Beausoleil scored from prison. Although originally conceived as the first part of a larger, serial work, this version of Lucifer now stands as a completed film in its own right.
1980: 45 min., 16mm, color, sound. A short, virtually finished version of the longer 1971 film (about 93 min.) that Anger wanted to make, but was unable to complete for economic reasons. This version premiered in New York in 1980 and with slight alterations, is the one included in the current *Magick Lantern Cycle*.

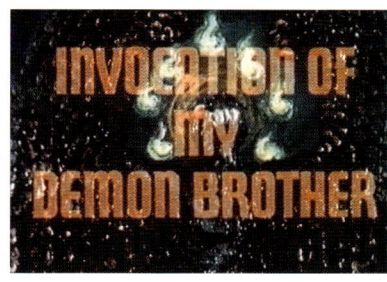
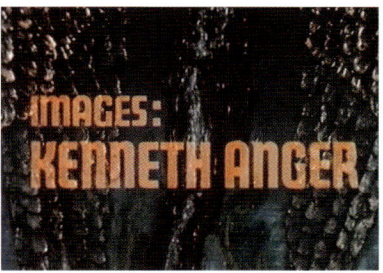
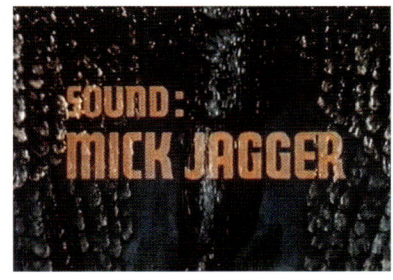
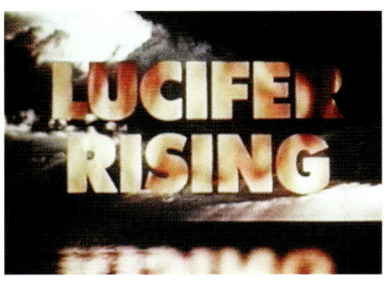

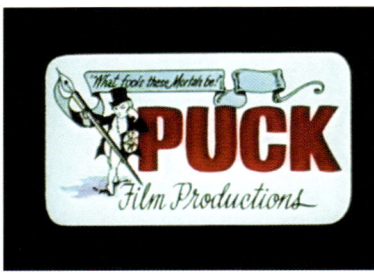

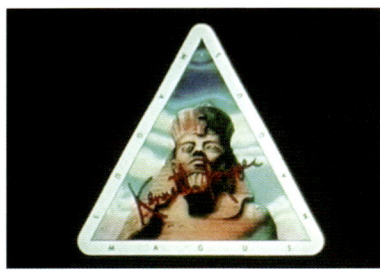

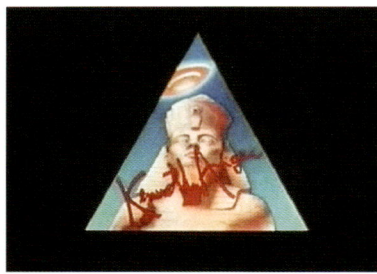

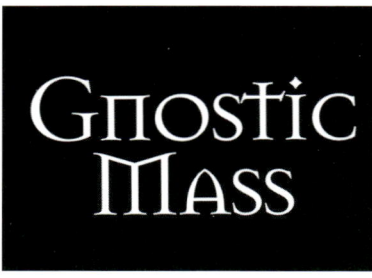

Senators in Bondage, 1976

16mm, color, sound.

"The Eisenstein of Satanism strikes again! Prints of Kenneth Anger's first limited edition *Senators in Bondage*. The master negative will be sealed; no further prints will be struck. Edition strictly limited to 13 copies in honor of the 13 original colonies. Each print individually hand-colored, supplied in a red, white and blue box, bound in chain. *Senators in Bondage* movie metaphor of mighty eminences brought low. A vitriolic bon-bon concocted with malice; a curio for this bicentennial year."[5]

Matelots en Menottes, 1977

16mm, color, sound.

"Matelots en Menottes – a return to the original subject of *Fireworks*. Kenneth Anger's second limited edition. Edition strictly limited to 12 copies."[6]

Denunciation of Stan Brakhage, 1979

7 mins., 12 copies sold.

Confirmed by Jonas Mekas, no other details.

Ich Will!, 2000

27 min.

Ironic re-editing of Nazi propaganda films dealing with the "Boy Scouts" of Nazi Germany, the Hitler Youth or Hitler Jugend.

The Man We Want To Hang, 2002

11 min., 16mm, color, sound, music by Liadov.

Paintings and drawings of and by British occultist Aleister Crowley.

Don't Smoke That Cigarette!, 2000

40 min., video, color, music by Hank Williams, "Smoke, Smoke, Smoke That Cigarette."

"Anger has rifled all the old ad agency back-rooms for banned TV cigarette ads. Combined with jaw dropping cancer images. Come to your own conclusion."[7]

Satirical anti-smoking compilation of early TV cigarette commercials.

Patriotic Penis, 2004

6 min.

Satirical return to the subject matter of *Fireworks*.

Elliott's Suicide – Tribute to Elliott Smith (1969-2003), 2004

16mm, color.

Tribute to the late Elliott Smith, Anger's friend and neighbor who stabbed himself to death in October 2003. Songs written and performed by the late Elliott Smith.

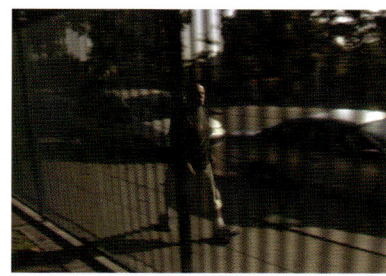

Mouse Heaven, 1987–2004

color, shot on Kodak vision 16mm and transferred onto 35mm, music by ragtime specialist Ian Whitcomb.

Cameraman: Doug Henry.

This film project was "postponed" after 1987. Now with a Rockefeller Foundation Media Arts grant to finish it, the film is scheduled for completion late 2004. "*Mouse Heaven* has an "all toy" cast based on Walt Disney's original character (1928-1938). Planned as a fantastical collage. Faced with a gamut of marching Mickeys, the spectator would lose all perspective."[8] "A fantasy featuring the Birnkrant collection of extremely rare vintage Mickey Mouse toys; many of which when filmed in ultra close up with moving riveted jaws, seem charmingly menacing."[9]

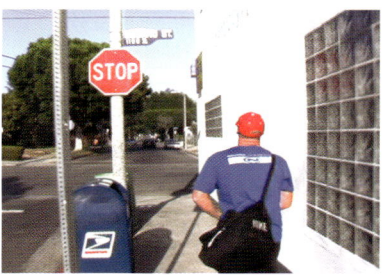

Gnostic Mass, 2004

40 min.

First text version completed (with two cameras) at Lake Elsinore.

Anger sees RED, 2004

7 min., hi-definition video, soundtrack: pop music.

Camera: Michael Chadwick
Featuring: Red (as Himself)
Location: De Longpre Park, Hollywood, Valentino Memorial, streets of Hollywood.

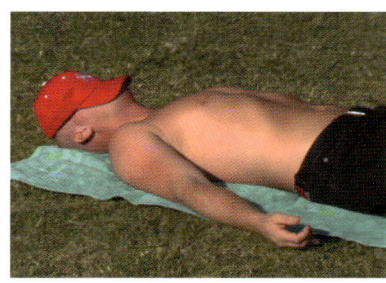

The Anger Magick Lantern Cycle

3 hours, 16mm

Vol. 1: *Fireworks*, *Rabbits Moon*, *Eaux d'Artifice*
Vol. 2: *The Inauguration of The Pleasure Dome*
Vol. 3: *Kustom Kar Kommandos*, *Puce Moment*, *Scorpio Rising*
Vol. 4: *Invocation of My Demon Brother*, *Lucifer Rising*

The *Magick Lantern Cycle* will be available in 2005 on DVD from Fantoma Films, San Francisco. Film rentals may be organized through Anger's primary distributor, Canyon Cinema in San Francisco. Volumes 1-4 on video are available in the U.S. through many independent video rental outlets, and the British Film Institute has released the series on video in the UK.

Canyon Cinema: www.canyoncinema.com, BFI: www.bfi.org.uk

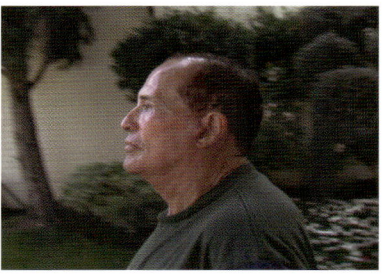

This page: *Anger sees RED*, 2004

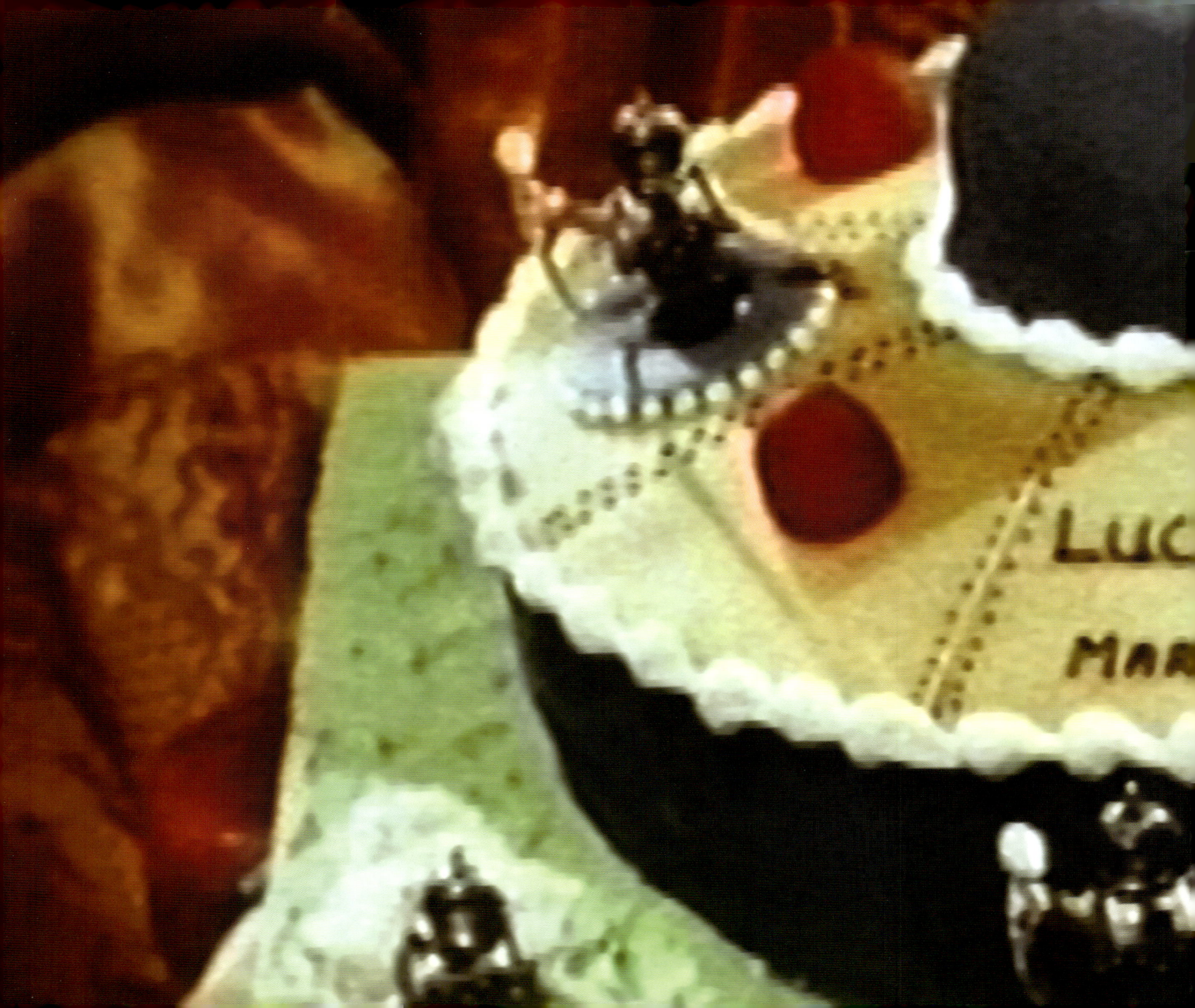

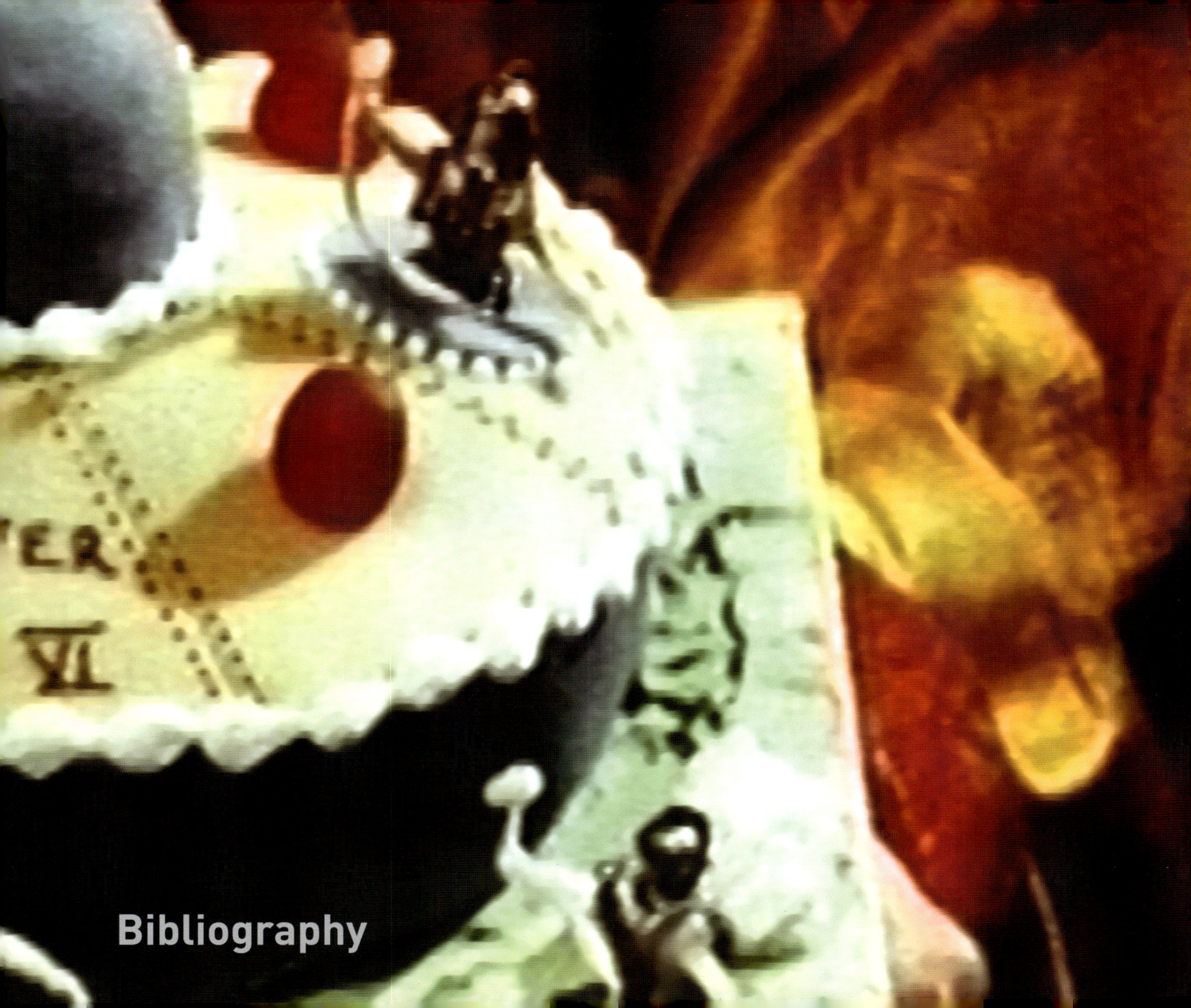
Bibliography

Articles and Books by Kenneth Anger

All texts are in reverse date order.

"Diva de la decadence: Salomé," in *En Marge de Hollywood: la première avant-garde cinématographique américaine 1893 –1941*, Jean-Michel Bouhours, Bruce Posner and Isabelle Ribadeau Dumas eds., Paris: Musée d'Art Américain Giverny/ Éditions du Centre Pompidou, 2003, pp. 92-101.

Frasier, David K, *Suicide in the Entertainment Industry*, foreword by Kenneth Anger, London: McFarland & Company, Inc., 2002.

"Letter to the Editor: Concerning the Maya Deren Awards," *The Village Voice*; reprinted in *Motion Picture*, no. 3, 1987.

Hollywood Babylon II, New York: E.P. Dutton, 1984.

"A Short Review of *Close Encounters of the Third Kind*," *Film Comment*, vol. 14, no. 1, January 1978.

"In Memoriam; Henry Langlois," *Film Comment*, vol. 13, no. 2, March 1977.

Hollywood Babylon, San Francisco: Straight Arrow Books, 1975.

Atlantis: The Lost Continent, New York: Dover Press, 1970.

"The Erotic Art of Bobby Beausoleil," *Puritan*, (no other reference).

"*Invocation of My Demon Brother*," in *Film Culture*, no. 48-49, 1971.

Anger Magick Lantern Cycle, A Special Presentation in celebration of The Equinox, Spring 1966, (limited edition catalog designed and written by Anger), New York: Film-Makers' Cinematheque, 1966.

A History of Eroticism, adapted from the French edition, *Bibliothèque Internationale d'Erotologie*; Paris: J. J. Pauvert, 1961.

Hollywood Babylone, (French), Paris: J. J. Pauvert, 1959.

"Aux Enfers," *Cahiers du Cinéma*, (French), vol. 14, no. 79, January 1958.

"Hollywood ou le comportement des mortels," *Cahiers du Cinéma*, (French), vol. 13, no. 77, December 1957.

"L'Olympe, ou le comportement des dieux," *Cahiers du Cinéma*, (French), vol. 13, no. 76, November 1957.

"Modesty And the Art Of Film," *Cahiers du Cinéma*, (French), no. 5, September 1951.

"Application d'Artifice," *St. Cinéma des Près*, (French), no. 2, 1950.

Books and Catalogs

Rowe, Carel, and Anna Powell, *Moonchild: The Films of Kenneth Anger*, Persistence of Vision, vol. 1, Jack Hunter ed., New York: Creation Books, 2002.

Hickey, Dave, *Beau monde: toward a redeemed cosmopolitanism: SITE Santa Fe's Fourth International Biennial, July 14, 2001-January 6, 2002*, Santa Fe: SITE, 2001.

Hecker, Pierre, *Jeune, dure et pure! Une histoire du Cinéma d'avant-garde et Expérimental en France*, Nicole Brenez and Christian Lebrat eds., (French), Paris: Cinémathèque Française and Editions Mazzota, 2001.

Sitney, P. Adams ed., *A Film Culture Reader*, New York: Cooper Square Press, 2000.

Assayas, Olivier, *Kenneth Anger – Vraie et Fausse Magie au Cinéma*, (French), Paris: Collection Auteurs, Éditions de l'Étoile/Cahiers du Cinéma, 1999.

Hecker, Pierre, *Les Films "Magicks" de Kenneth Anger*, preface by Nicole Brenez, (French), Paris: Classiques de l'Avant-Garde, Éditions Paris Expérimental, 1999.

Vyner, Harriet, *Groovy Bob – The Life and Times of Robert Fraser*, London: Faber and Faber, 1999.

Camper, Fred, "Material and Immaterial Light: Brakhage and Anger," *First Light*, New York: Anthology Film Archives, 1998.

Suarez, Juan A., *Bike Boys, Drag Queens, and Superstars*, Bloomington: Indiana University Press, 1996.

Brougher, Kerry, and Russell Ferguson, *Hall of Mirrors: Art and Film Since 1947*, Los Angeles: The Museum of Contemporary Art and The Monacelli Press, 1996.

Wees, William C., *Light Moving in Time: Studies in the Visual Aesthetics of Avant-Garde Films*, Berkeley: University of California Press, 1992.

Mellenkamp, Patricia: *Indiscretions: Avant-Garde Film*, Bloomington: Indiana University Press, 1990.

Pilling, Jayne and Mike O'Pray eds., *Into The Pleasure Dome – The Films of Kenneth Anger*, London: British Film Institute, 1989.

James, David E., *Allegories of Cinema: American Film in the 1960s*, New Jersey: Princeton University Press, 1989.

Fonoroff, Nina and Melanie Curry, *Canyon Cinema – Catalog 6*, Ann Arbor: McNaughton and Gunn, 1988.

Rowe, Carel, *The Baudelairean Cinema: A Trend within the American Avant-Garde*, Ann Arbor: University of Michigan Press, 1983.

Haller, Robert, *Kenneth Anger: A Monograph*, Minneapolis: The Walker Center for Art/Film in the Cities, 1980.

Mekas, Jonas and P. Adams Sitney, *The Pleasure Dome – Amerikansk Experimentfilm 1939-79/American Experimental Film 1939-79*, Stockholm: Moderna Museet, 1980.

Dwoskin, Steve, *Film Is...*, New York: Overlook Press, 1975.

Sitney, P. Adams, *The Essential Cinema: Essays on the Films in the Collection of Anthology Film Archives*, New York: New York University Press, 1975.

Sitney, P. Adams, *Visionary Film: The American Avant-Garde 1943-1978*, Oxford: Oxford University Press, 1974, 1979, 2002.

Durgnat, Raymond, *Sexual Alienation in the Cinema*, London: Studio Vista, 1974.

Mekas, Jonas, *Movie Journal: The Rise of the New American Cinema 1959-1971*, New York: Collier Books, 1972.

Sitney, P. Adams, *The American Independent Film*, Boston: Museum of Fine Arts, 1971.

Tyler, Parker, *Underground Film: A Critical History*, New York: Grove Press, 1969.

Renan, Sheldon, *The Underground Film*, New York: Studio Vista, 1968.

Renan, Sheldon, *Introduction to the American Underground Film*, New York: E.P. Dutton and Co, 1967.

Battcock, Gregory ed., *The New American Cinema*, New York: E. P. Dutton, 1967.

Journals and Articles

Pallenberg, Anita, *Vogue* (British), September 2004.

Hutchison, Alice L., "Kenneth Anger," *Contemporary*, November 2003.

Horton, Roger (text), and Alain Le Garsmeur, unpublished photographs taken on the set of *Lucifer Rising*, *Another magazine*, issue 4, Spring-Summer, 2003.

Calendar, "Barbican Center: *California Image / California Sound*," *Time Out*, London, June 11-18, 2003 (featuring Anger's *Fireworks*).

Hutchison, Alice L., "Courting Anger," *Afterall*, Summer 2003, pp. 56-71.

Moore, Rachel, "Cultural Bolshevism at Capital's Late-Night Show: *Scorpio Rising*," *Afterall*, Summer 2003, pp. 72-77.

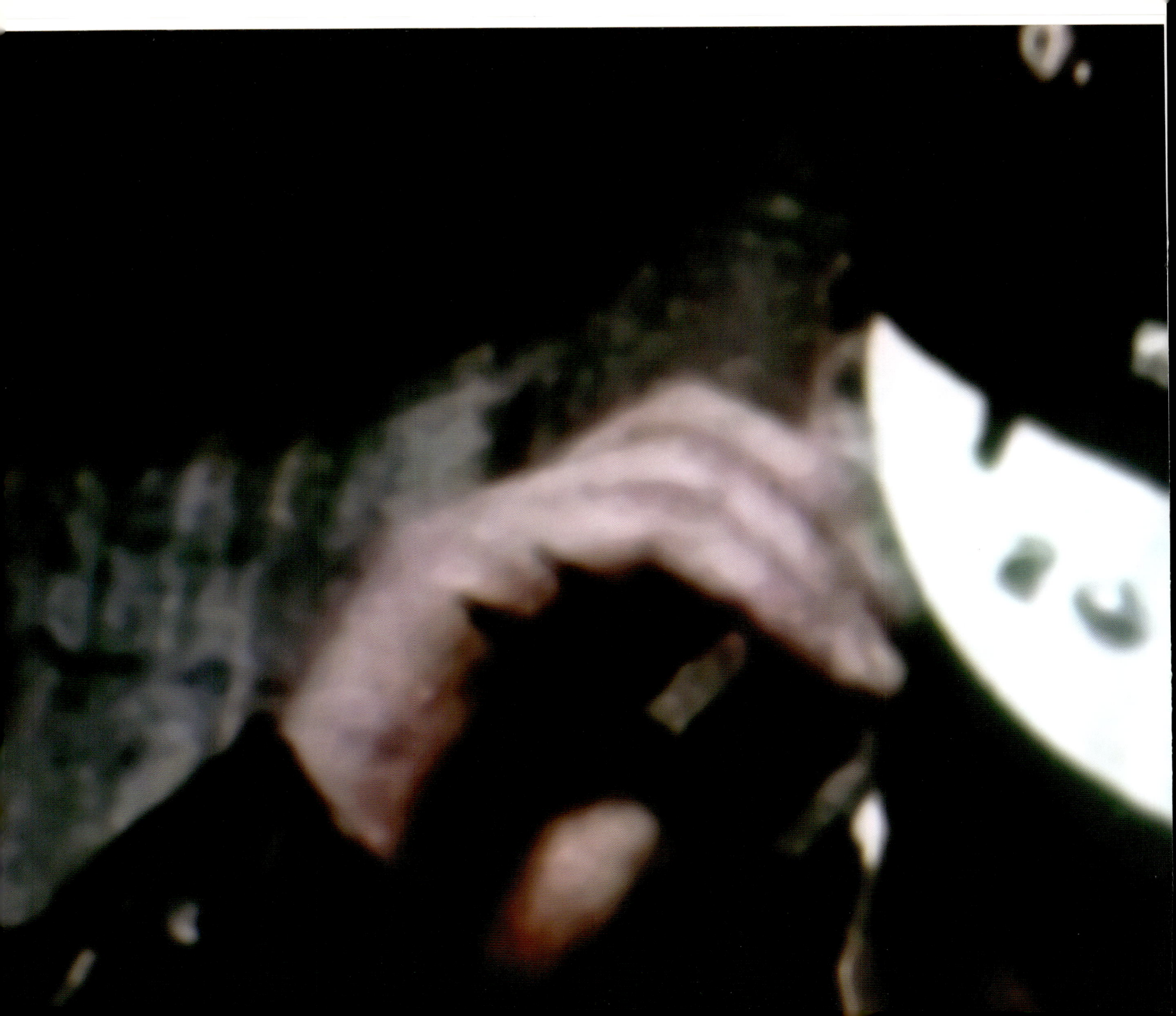

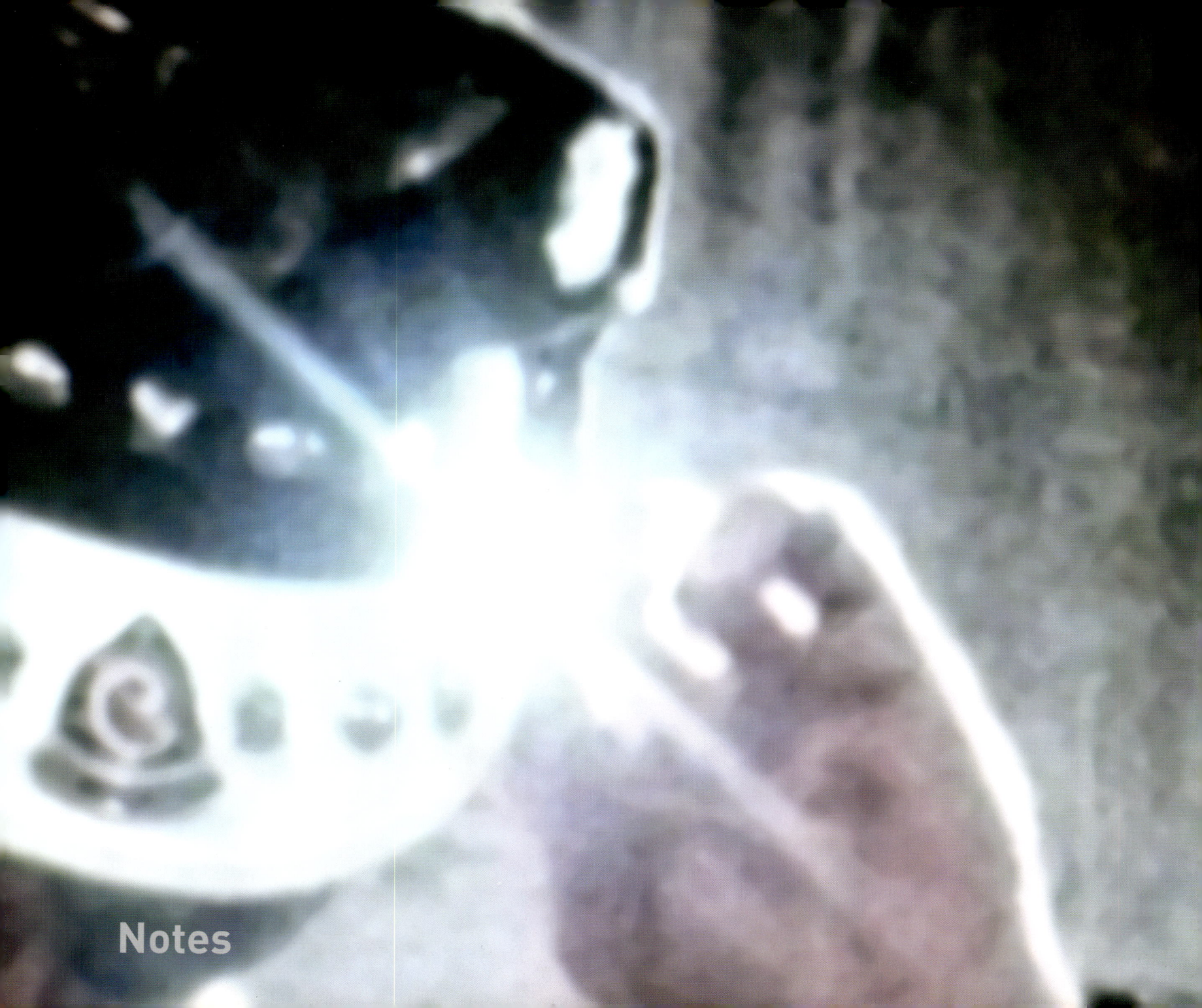

Notes

Introduction

1 "Underground" is a term Anger disdains, along with "avant-garde," "experimental," etc.. "I reject them all. Avant-garde is too pretentious. Experimental makes it sound like tinkering in the garage. And underground, that I never accepted. It's just another way of staying outside the mainstream. I'm an independent filmmaker. It may sound colorless, but that's what I am." Quoted in Eleanor Ringel, "The Visions of Anger," *The Atlanta Constitution*, February 11, 1980.

There have been a three small monographs published on Anger recently (two in French), but none cover his career as comprehensively as this publication. See, for example, Jack Hunter ed., *Moonchild*, London: Creation Books, 2002, and, in French, Olivier Assayas, *Kenneth Anger: Vraie et Fausse Magie au Cinéma*, Paris: Collection Auteurs, Cahiers du Cinéma, 1999.

2 Hanhardt, John C., Curator, Film and Video, Whitney Museum of American Art, New York. Quoted in *Film Folio*, February 1981, Courtesy of MOMA Film Archives, New York.

3 Warhol produced over 4000 reels, many of which have never been screened, in contrast to the nine primary films of Kenneth Anger's *Magick Lantern Cycle*. Olivier Assayas makes an extensive and fruitful comparison between Anger and Warhol, and Anger's relationship to Pop Art in his book *Kenneth Anger: Vraie et Fausse Magie au Cinéma*.

4 Sontag, Susan, quoted in "Night of the Locust," *Newsweek*, June 16, 1975, p. 73.

5 Anger's time in France instilled in his work an aesthetic which embodied multiple histories, mythologies and pan-cultural references. However, this fertile decade in France has not been discussed in any detail in English up until this point.

6 Anger's own assiduously applied system of "Magick" is a form of Symbolism in which his development of a cinema of correspondences is based on the associative tables of Aleister Crowley (1875-1947). Anger experiments with the technique of parallel montage, which forms a complementary system of correspondences, asserting his understanding and application of Sergei Eisenstein's structural principles. The Symbolist system at work in Anger's montage is a realization of what Eisenstein had defined as a form of synaesthesia in the chapters "Synchronization of the Senses," and "Color and Meaning" in his book *The Film Sense*. Eisenstein's interest in Symbolism was of great influence in his later work. Peter Wollen has remarked that: "the dominant strand throughout the rest of his [Eisenstein's] life was to be the investigation of the 'synchronization of the senses' a return to the symbolist infatuation with Baudelaire's correspondences." Quoted in Carel Rowe, *The Baudelairean Cinema: A Trend within the American Avant-Garde*, Ann Arbor: University of Michigan Press, 1983, p. 72.

7 Bobby Beausoleil, one-time guitarist for the band Love, is serving a life-sentence for his involvement with the Charles Manson murders, further discussed in Chapter Eight.

8 For example, the film was barely addressed in P. Adams Sitney's indispensable guide to avant-garde American cinema art, *Visionary Film: The American Avant-Garde*, New York: Oxford University Press, 1974, 1990, 2002.

9 Murry, John Middleton, quoted by Rowe, *The Baudelairean Cinema*, p. 13.

10 Benjamin, Walter, *Charles Baudelaire: A Lyric Poet in the Era of High Capitalism*, Henry Zohn trans., London: NLB, 1973, p. 59.

11 Benjamin, *Charles Baudelaire*, p. 117.

12 The term "Baudelairean cinema" was first coined by Jonas Mekas, (possibly also in reference to Ken Jacobs' film *Baudelairean Capers*), "Movie Journal," *The Village Voice*, New York, May 2, 1963, pp. 84-86.

13 Rowe, *The Baudelairean Cinema*. Comparing 1960s avant-garde American film with the French Decadent Symbolists, Rowe discusses the variations of myths of death and rebirth, and myths of the Apocalypse (and the fall of Babylon). Decadence has been defined as more than a perverse expression of pre-apocalyptic dissatisfaction; it includes the Apocalypse proper – the celebration which signals a new age; consistently finding classical Greek and biblical myths which reflect cyclic themes of death and rebirth. The phoenix born from the ashes can be seen as a metaphor in Anger's *Fireworks*.

14 Baudelaire, Charles, *Selected Writings*, quoted in Rowe, *The Baudelairean Cinema*, p. 16.

15 Baudelaire, *Intimate Journals*, pp. 11-12, quoted in Rowe, p. 16.

16 Baudelaire, *Intimate Journals*, pp. 11-12. Baudelaire's motif and cult of artificiality was to continue to evolve as an important motif in Decadent aesthetics taken up by Anger, and inherent in what would evolve as Camp (as defined by Sontag in 1964).

17 As Rowe has stated, "Jack Smith visualized Decadence and Warhol allowed it to expose itself." *The Baudelairean Cinema*, p. 65. Warhol often used identical material to Anger, i.e. Hollywood stars such as Marlon Brando's publicity shot from *The Wild One*, and his 1967 film *Bike Boy*. There are instances of Warhol mimicking Anger's iconography, subject matter and even shots: for instance in *Sleep*, Warhol recreated the sleeping dreamer reclining on a bed from Anger's *Fireworks*. *Bike Boy* was also an obvious derivation of *Scorpio Rising*. Warhol openly praised Anger's work, as in Peter Sempel's film *Jonas in the Desert* in which he is interviewed. The admiration was not reciprocated.

18 Benjamin, Walter, "The Work of Art in the Age of Mechanical Reproduction," (1936), *Illuminations – essays and reflections*, Hannah Arendt ed. and intro., Harry Zohn trans., New York: Harcourt, Brace and World, Inc., 1968, p. 244.

1. Los Angeles in the 1940s

1 *Baby Burlesques*, 1934, director unknown, Educational Pictures, Hollywood. "Baby exploitation at its tackiest. Featuring caricatures of contemporary politicians and figures from Hollywood." Kenneth Anger Filmography, *Into The Pleasure Dome – the films of Kenneth Anger*, Jayne Pilling and Mike O'Pray eds., London: British Film Institute, 1989, p. 53.

2 Anger provided a filmography of his work prior to *Fireworks* in *Film Culture*, no. 31, Winter 1963-1964, p. 8. Reproduced in P. Adams Sitney's *Visionary Film*, 1974 and in this filmography, courtesy of *Film Culture* and Anthology Film Archives, New York. "Six Films Before *Fireworks*" was compiled by Rebekah Wood in conversation with Kenneth Anger, "Notes on the Hidden Camera of Kenneth Anger," *Into The Pleasure Dome – the films of Kenneth Anger*, p. 58-59.

3 Wood, "Notes on the Hidden Cinema of Kenneth Anger," p. 60.

4 "Original spoken prologue in a husky adolescent tenor by the 17 year old Anger, as the film begins in darkness, the black lack of image replacing the title "Fireworks"," Kenneth Anger for Canyon Cinema catalog, San Francisco, and in conversation with the author, 2004.

5 "Anger is a fanatical non-smoker – this cigarette is the only "fag" Anger has ever smoked – to point out he is playing a "non-Anger" part." Comment from conversation between the author and Anger, 2004.

6 Baker, Robb, "The Trials of Lucifer: An interview with Kenneth Anger," *Soho Weekly News*, October 28, 1976, p. 16 (reproduced in Robert A. Haller, *Kenneth Anger: A Monograph*, Minneapolis, MN: Film in the Cities, 1980, p. 5).

7 *Lot in Sodom*, 1933, dir. James Watson, a quasi-erotic retelling of the Biblical parable, could be considered a precursor. The first films with homosexual content were made in Germany: *Anders als die Andern* (*Different from the Others*) premiered in 1919, the tragedy of a violinist pushed into suicide by a blackmailer (Nazi's destroyed every reel of the film). An explosion in gay subculture in the late 1920s in Berlin saw the release of a number of films: *Gesetze der Leibe* (*The Laws of Love*) by Magnus Hirschfeld and Richard Oswald, 1927, also destroyed; *Geschlecht in Fesseln* (*Sex in Chains*) by William Dieterle, 1928; *Lulu* by G.W. Pabst, 1929, and *Mädchen in Uniform* by Leontine Sagan, 1931.

8 Sitney, P. Adams, "The Achievement of the American Avant-Garde Cinema 1960-70," *Into the Pleasure Dome, American Experimental Film, 1939-79*, Stockholm: Moderna Museet, 1980, p. 21.

9 As discussed by Lucy Fischer, *A History of the American Avant-Garde Cinema*, catalog for a film exhibition organized by the American Federation of Arts, 1976, New York, p. 77.

10 The catalog for which first featured Antonin Artaud's "Witchcraft and the Cinema", 1949, in which he stated "raw cinema, taken as it is, in the abstract, exudes a little of this trance-like atmosphere, eminently favorable for certain revelations" ... "cinema is made primarily to express matters of the mind, the inner consciousness...."

11 Cocteau never officially claimed authorship of the homoerotic book which is rarely referred to in English ("The White Book").

12 *The Diary of Anais Nin, vols. 1-5*, New York: Harcourt. Reproduced in Chapter Four as "Come As Your Own Madness."

13 Renan, Sheldon, *Introduction to the American Underground Film*, New York: E.P. Dutton and Co., Inc, 1967, p. 42.

14 Anger on Cocteau, Bravo "Art of Influences" television series made in 1997.

15 Anger on Cocteau, Bravo "Art of Influences". Serge Diaghilev was the legendary impresario behind the Ballets Russes in Paris, with Nijinsky and Stravinsky, with whom Cocteau ingratiated himself upon during his youth.

16 Sitney, *Visionary Film*, p. 33.

17 Sitney, *Visionary Film*, p. 33.

18 A classic of avant-garde cinema, *Meshes of the Afternoon* has been discussed extensively in a number of publications including Sitney's *Visionary Film*. Deren's formal concern with cinema had been from dream (*Meshes of the Afternoon*, 1943) to ritual (*Ritual in Transfigured Time*, 1946) and myth (*The Very Eye of Night*, 1958). While based in New York, *Meshes* was filmed in Los Angeles.

19 Keller, Marjorie, "*Rabbit's Moon* by Kenneth Anger," *Film Culture*, nos. 67-69, 1979, pp. 200-210.

20 Markopoulos, Gregory, *Psyche*, 1947-1948, 25 min, 16mm, color.

21 Harrington, Curtis, *Fragment of Seeking*, 1946, 14 min, 16mm, black and white. "A classic West Coast experimental psychodrama second only in importance to Kenneth Anger's *Fireworks* as the leading example of Freudian surrealism produced during the experimental film movement of the 1940s. It deals with teenage narcissism and latent homosexuality, with the film artist portraying the protagonist." Los Angeles: Creative Film Society catalog, 1975.

22 Harrington didn't know about *Fireworks* until he had seen it screened for the first time. Similarities were coincidental despite their converging mutual interests. Conversation with Curtis Harrington, April 2004.

23 Sitney, *Visionary Film*, p. 58, 2002 edition, in reference to James Broughton.

24 "*Fireworks* is a pure example of the psycho-dramatic trance film... pictures of the sailor and the dreamer scattered beside the bed, as if they were the objects of a masturbation fantasy before sleeping." *Visionary Film*, p. 100, 1974 edition. Within each work, Anger's films created their own aesthetic. Sitney's discussion neglects the initial impact these films had, their startling and daring originality, and the pioneering context in which they were made, as well as skirting around the issue of homoeroticism.

25 Nin, *The Diaries of Anaïs Nin, vols. 1-5*, Spring 1948, p. 352.

26 Quoted in John Caliendo, "Kenneth Anger Rising," *Oui*, 1976, p. 113.

27 The attribution of Deren's title was noted by Curtis Harrington, conversation with the author, April 2004.

28 Deren, Maya, *Poetry and the Film: A Symposium* (with Arthur Miller, Dylan Thomas, Parker Tyler. Chairman, Willard Maas), organized by Amos Vogel, October 28, 1953 at Cinema 16, quoted in *Film Culture*, no. 29, summer 1963, pp. 174-175.

29 Miller, Arthur, *Poetry and the Film: A Symposium*, p. 181.

30 Anger, October 30, 2003 presentation at the Getty Museum, Los Angeles, with Curtis Harrington and Larry Jordan. The "zoot-suiters" were flamboyantly dressed dandies (a style typified by exaggeratedly long, brightly colored jackets with huge shoulder pads and tapered waists, baggy pants and brogues). Initially an African American youth fashion, closely connected to jazz culture, the zoot suit was co-opted by a generation of Mexican American kids, who made it their own largely in reaction to their social marginalization. The oversized suit was both an outrageous style and a statement of defiance. Zoot suiters asserted themselves, at a time when fabric was being rationed for the war effort, and in the face of widespread discrimination. In the summer of 1943, Los Angeles erupted in violence. For ten straight nights, American sailors armed with make-shift weapons cruised Mexican American neighborhoods, dragging boys – some as young as 12 years old – out of movie theaters and diners, bars and cafes, tearing the clothes off the young men's bodies and viciously beating them. Police stood by as servicemen stripped, beat and battered the "zoot suiters," invariably innocent teenagers,

then dragnet-style, threw hundreds of the victims in jail making indiscriminate arrests. Media reports portrayed them as juvenile delinquents who were asking for trouble.

31 W. H. Auden also attempted to account for the fascination: "It is not an accident that many homosexuals should show a special preference for sailors, for the sailor on shore is symbolically the innocent god from the sea who is not bound by the law of the land and can therefore do anything without guilt."

32 Fischer, *A History of the American Avant-Garde Cinema*, p. 77.

33 Conversation with Curtis Harrington, April 2004.

34 Anger, Kenneth, "Application d'Artifice," *St. Cinema des Près*, no. 2, Paris,1950, author's translation, 2004. (n. p.) MOMA film archives, New York.

35 Boullet, Jean, *St. Cinema des Près*, no. 2, Paris, 1950, author's translation, 2004.

36 Boullet, *St. Cinema des Près*, no. 2.

37 Anger, 1971 interview with Tony Rayns, "Dedication to Create Make Believe," reproduced *Into The Pleasure Dome – the films of Kenneth Anger*, 1939, p. 23.

38 Sitney, "The Magus," *Visionary Film*, 2002 edition, p. 83.

39 Anger, *Icons*, Vienna: Institut Française de Vienne, 1995, p. 17.

40 Anger, in Wood, "Notes on the Hidden Camera of Kenneth Anger," p. 45.

41 Rowe, Carel, "Illuminating Lucifer," *Film Quarterly*, vol. 27, no. 4, summer 1974, p. 30.

42 Anger, in Wood, "Notes on the Hidden Camera of Kenneth Anger," p. 45.

43 Olivier Assayas described this poetic evocation as "richer, more profound and enigmatic than the laborious reconstructions that Hollywood works away at and wants to resemble.... In 1948 in Hollywood, the commentary on Hollywood did not exist and the charm or poetry of certain of its isolated motifs had not yet been described.... It wasn't until later that it was formulated and much later still that it appeared in cinema under the form posed by Anger, perhaps by the intermediary of the generation of German filmmakers such as Schroeter and Fassbinder at the beginning of the 1970s...." p. 30. Assayas drew the connection between *Puce Moment* and R. W. Fassbinder's *Petra*

Von Kant, 1972, p. 28. Olivier Assayas, *Kenneth Anger: Vraie et Fausse Magie au Cinéma*, Paris: Cahiers du Cinéma: Collection Auteurs / Editions de l'Étoile, 1999, (author's translation).

44 Edwards, Roy, *Cinema 16 Film Notes*, 1955/1956, April 4, 1956, MOMA film archives.

45 In "Diva de la decadence: Salomé" authored in French by Kenneth Anger, he describes Nazimova as the female Orson Welles of her time; starring, producing and creating her costumes (with Rambova) and mise-en-scènes, as Mae West was to similarly take the reins. Jean-Michel Bouhours, Bruce Posner, Isabelle Ribadeau Dumas eds., *En Marge de Hollywood: la première avant-garde cinématographique américaine 1893-1941*, Paris: Musée d'Art Américain Giverny / Éditions du Centre Pompidou, 2003, pp. 92-101.

46 Ridge, Ross, *The Hero in French Decadent Literature*, Athens, Georgia: University of Georgia Press, 1961, p. 57.

47 Anger, 1971 interview with Tony Rayns, "Dedication to Create Make Believe," p. 24.

2. Paris 1950-1960

1 Echoing Bataille's obsession with sexuality and death, Cocteau returned to themes in *Orpheus*. A desperate young painter meets a beautiful artist's model with whom he falls passionately in love. But she is the archetypal figure of Death, conveying through masks and gestures his fate (placing the mask of Death over his face), and he ultimately hangs himself.

2 The resulting film, *Le Jeune Homme et la Mort*, 1951, was described by Anger: "The first few months after I arrived in Paris, I was fortunate enough to see, at the Theater Champs Elysées, a wonderful performance of Jean Cocteau's *Le Jeune Homme et la Mort* danced by the original cast of Nathalie Philipart and Jean Babilée. The ballet was set to Bach's *Passacaglia*. The set was a beautiful backdrop of the Paris skyline in the 1920s. I discussed the ballet with Cocteau and told him I'd like to film it. He gave me permission and wrote me a letter to find a producer – saying that he had full confidence and wanted me to direct it. I went round, approaching some of the big names like Pauvert. Despite the fact that I had Cocteau's name, my budget was too high. I never found a producer. I wanted to film in 35mm,

Technicolor with a sound stage. I managed to shoot a 16mm, black and white study-film. Just to have light, I filmed in Jean Babilée's garden. The young man hangs himself from a tree. It was winter – cold, every movement was accompanied by visible breath from the chill air. When death comes to take the young man, she is wearing a mask and stilts – like the image of death in *Orphée*." Quoted in *Into The Pleasure Dome – the films of Kenneth Anger*, London: British Film Institute, 1989, p. 64.

3 "American Du Wop of the 50s," annotation by Anger, 2004. This version was interspersed with a Balinese "Ramayana monkey chant" throughout.

4 Anger, letter to Stan Brakhage, unpublished letters of Brakhage, Anthology Film Archives, New York, cited in Keller, Marjorie, "*Rabbit's Moon* by Kenneth Anger," *Film Culture*, no. 67-69, 1979, pp. 211-215.

5 Aldous Huxley discussed the *Lanterna Magica*, the ancestor of cinema and Anger's metaphor for the projector, and his art of wielding preternatural light. In 1802 the inventors of this new kind of peepshow coined the word "phantasmagoria." Huxley, *Heaven and Hell*, New York: Harper and Rowe, 1990 edition, p. 166.

6 Anger, Kenneth, unpublished letter to Stan Brakhage, Anthology Film Archives, New York, cited in Keller, "*Rabbit's Moon*," pp. 211-215.

7 Keller, "*Rabbit's Moon*," pp. 200-210.

8 Keller, "*Rabbit's Moon*," Anger letter to Brakhage, p. 204. Anger's sentiments recall Milton's description of Adam in *Paradise Lost* shedding "the film" from his eyes in order to really see.

9 Kenneth Anger letter to Stan Brakhage, read at School of Art Institute of Chicago, Spring 1973, quoted in Keller, "*Rabbit's Moon*," p. 203.

10 Keller, "*Rabbit's Moon*," p. 210.

11 Keller, "*Rabbit's Moon*," p. 204.

12 Interview with Kenneth Anger, *Film Culture*, no. 40, 1966.

13 Haller, Robert A., *Kenneth Anger: A Monograph*, Minneapolis, MN: Film in the Cities/The Walker Art Center, 1980, p. 5.

14 Anger's version of *Que Viva Mexico* was a silent 16mm study for a festival sponsored by Henry Langlois and was only shown twice,

once at the festival, c. 1950-1951, and again at the Cinématèque Français.

After half a century of negotiations the original film reels were given back to the Russian State Film Archives. The film had been developed and printed in Hollywood, and was later passed to the Museum of Modern Art in New York. Although Eisenstein and cameraman Eduard Tisse had passed away; assistant director G. V. Alexandrov was finally able to re-edit the film as close to Eisenstein's original conception, from memory and the director's sketches and original scenario, in 1979. The release of a digitally enhanced 35mm restoration of the film is currently underway.

15 Alexandrov, G. V., *Que Viva Mexico!* Video-recording, 1979, AFI Louis B. Mayer Library archives, Los Angeles.

16 Eisenstein, Sergei M., *Que Viva Mexico!*, introduction by Ernest Lindgren, Arno Press Cinema Program, New York: Arno Press and The New York Times, 1972, p. 27.

17 Anger interview with Robert Haller and John Burchfield at Pittsburgh Filmmakers Inc. November 1979, in Haller, *Kenneth Anger*, p 17.

18 First published in *Cahiers du Cinéma*, no. 5, Paris, September 1951, reprinted courtesy of Kenneth Anger and *Cahiers du Cinéma*. Translated by David Wilson.

19 Literally, "a peppercorn," i.e. a futile exercise.

20 Lautréamont, *Maldoror and the Complete Works of the Comte de Lautréamont*, Alexis Lykiard trans., Cambridge: Exact Change, 1994, pp. 68-69.

21 God is alternately referred to as "the Great Exterior Object," "the Celestial Bandit," and "The Supreme Drunkard." "So one day, then, tired of trudging along the steep track of earthly voyage and of staggering like a drunkard through life's dark catacombs, I slowly raised my morose eyes (ringed with huge bluish circles) toward the concave firmament, and, though so young, dared penetrate the mysteries of heaven! Not finding what I sought I raised my dismayed gaze higher, still higher, until I caught sight of a throne fashioned of human excrement and gold upon which, with idiotic pride, body swathed in a shroud made of unwashed hospital sheets, sat he who calls himself the Creator! He held in his hand a corpse's decaying torso and bore it in turn from eyes to nose, from nose to mouth: once in his mouth one can guess what he did with it. His feet were emersed in a vast pool of boiling blood, to whose surface two or three cautious heads would suddenly rise like tapeworms from a full chamberpot, and immediately slip back again quick as arrows...." Lautréamont, *Maldoror*, pp. 76-77.

22 Lykiard, Alexis, introduction, *Maldoror*, p. 4.

23 Aranda, Francisco, *Buñuel: A Critical Biography*, London: Secker and Warburg, 1976, p. 62.

24 Wood, Rebekah, in conversation with Kenneth Anger, "Notes on the Hidden Camera of Kenneth Anger," *Into The Pleasure Dome – the films of Kenneth Anger*, Jayne Pilling and Mike O'Pray eds., London: British Film Institute, 1989, p. 64.

25 Lykiard, *Maldoror*, p. 21.

26 Paris-based film critic Ado Kyro (Adonis Kyrou) authored two books on Buñuel (including *Buñuel: An Introduction*: translated by Adrienne Foulke, NY: Simon and Schuster, 1963).

27 Letter to author, October 2003.

28 Kenneth Anger discussed the project in 1989: "I discovered the book when I was quite young. I loved it, put a lot of passion into it. I found people to play the parts, I found settings, gaslit corners, places still had the romantic look of a Second Empire. It was a terrific ambition to make this epic film-poem. I found ways to translate the text's extraordinary images. I planned to film a mid-nineteenth century story taking place in twentieth century Paris. I filmed "the hymn to the ocean," on the beach at Deauville, with Hightower and members of the Marquis de Cuevas Ballet. They danced in the sea; tables were placed beneath the water line so the dancers could stand on their points. It looked as though they were standing on waves. The people who called themselves "surrealists" were furious – this group of punks threatened me – they didn't want a Yank messing round with their sacred text. I just told them to go to hell! I also managed to film the war of the flies and pins. I put bags of pins and dozens of flies into a glass container; revolved the container and filmed in close-up. As the pins dropped, the flies zigzagged to escape. In slow motion, an impressive image." Quoted in *Into the Pleasure Dome-The Films of Kenneth Anger*, p. 64.

29 Kristeva, Julia, *La Révolution du langage poétique*, presented as her State Doctorate in July 1973, at the Sorbonne, Paris, was originally published in 1974 by Editions du Seuil. Margaret Waller translated one third of original text in 1984.

30 Kristeva, *Revolution in Poetic Language*, Margaret Waller trans., New York: Columbia University Press, 1984, p. 35.

31 Kristeva, "The Subject in Signifying Practice: Revolution of Poetic Language," Kelly Oliver ed., *The Portable Kristeva*, New York: Columbia University Press, 1997, p. 82.

32 "For the capitalist mode of production produces and marginalizes, but simultaneously exploits for its own regeneration." Kristeva, "The Subject in Signifying Practice: Revolution of Poetic Language," pp. 29-30.

33 Kristeva, "The Subject in Signifying Practice: Revolution of Poetic Language," pp. 29-30.

34 Rimbaud, Arthur, *A Season in Hell*, Bertrand Mathieu trans., preface by Anaïs Nin, etchings by Jim Dine, Cambridge, MA: The Pomegranate Press, 1976, p. 21.

35 Artaud, Antonin, "Nerves Scales," *Collected Works*, vol. 1, London: Calder and Boyars, 1968, pp. 76-77.

36 Anger, Bravo "Art of Influences" interview, New York, 1997.

37 The author's identity was much debated until Dominique Aury claimed authorship in *The New Yorker* in 1995. Albert Camus exclaimed that it could not have been written by a woman as he couldn't conceive of a woman delving into such depths of sado-masochism.

38 Anger, letter to author, October 2003.

39 The girl's father thought "his daughter was slipping out of the house to take harpsicord lessons, not skirting the fine line between the artistic and the pornographic." *After Dark*, December 1977. Anger described the boyfriend as a "flaming swindler" who took it upon himself to be the film's producer. Anger also promised the girl that he would not screen it for her sake; for her "it was a bit of a youthful folly, now she has children." Interview with Vincent Ostria, 1997, quoted in Olivier Assayas, *Kenneth Anger: Vraie et Fausse Magie au Cinéma*, Paris: Cahiers du Cinéma: Collection Auteurs / Editions de l'Étoile, 1999, p. 63 (author's translation).

40 Anger, interview with Linda Dubler, *Atlanta Art Papers*, vol. 4, no. 2, March/April 1980, p. 2.

41 Assayas, *Kenneth Anger: Vraie et Fausse Magie au Cinéma*, p. 61.

42 "O" could also be viewed as The Scarlet Woman. The book had certain affinities with the rigorous ceremonial precision of Crowley's ritualistic sex-magick.

43 Anger, interview with V. Ostria, quoted in Assayas, *Kenneth Anger: Vraie et Fausse Magie au Cinéma*, p. 63.

44 Both share a portrayal of sexual liberation through humiliation.

3. Eaux d'Artifice

1 Anger's comment: "The fact is Mary Meerson never answered any letters A multi-linguist of amazing versatility, Mary was strictly a telephone person." His mention of a "crise d'angoisse irrationelle" further on in the letter refers to Anger's bi-polar disorder, which he lives through without medication such as lithium. His roller-coaster condition has meant deserts of depression which sometimes go on for months.

2 Literally "Baroque waters" and "mystery of the waters" respectively: timesheets and budget, archive collection of Cinémathèque Française, Paris.

3 Anger, *Magick Lantern Cycle*, Filmmakers Cinematheque program, 1966, New York, p. 2.

4 Anger, unpublished letter to Mary Meerson, January 19, 1953.

5 Anger, Cinema 16 program notes, cited Sitney, *Visionary Film*, New York: Oxford University Press, 1974 edition, p. 102.

6 Haller, Robert, *Kenneth Anger: A Monograph*, Minneapolis: Film in the Cities/The Walker Art Center, 1980, p. 6.

7 Haller, *Kenneth Anger*, p. 6.

8 Ralph Steiner's *H2O*, 1929, pre-empted *Eaux d'Artifice* as purely formal invention, with its shots of light on water.

9 Anger has cited Whistler as an influence, and full titles such as *Invocation of My Demon Brother (Arrangement in Black and Gold)* pay homage to the artist.

10 Sergei Eisenstein introduced "Synchronization of the Senses" in *The Film Sense* by quoting E. M. Forster: "...indeed the more the arts develop the more they depend on each other for definition. We will borrow from painting first and call it pattern. Later we will borrow from music and call it rhythm." *The Film Sense*, New York: Harvest/Harcourt Brace Jovanovich, 1947, p. 68.

11 Eisenstein, *The Film Sense*, p. 71.

12 Sitney, *Visionary Film*, 2002 edition, p. 71.

4. Inauguration of the Pleasure Dome

1 "Dedication to Create Make Believe," Anger interviewed by Tony Rayns (*Time Out*, 1971), *Into The Pleasure Dome – the films of Kenneth Anger*, London: British Film Institute, 1989, p. 26.

2 Anger, Kenneth, interview with Bruce Martin and Joe Medjuck, *Take One*, 1, no. 6, 1967, p. 13.

3 Cinema 16, program notes, April 4, 1956, courtesy of Museum of Modern Art film archives, New York.

4 The most thorough diegetic analysis of shot-by-shot sequences of Anger's pre-*Lucifer Rising* films has been made by P. Adams Sitney, *Visionary Film*, specifically for *Inauguration of The Pleasure Dome*.

5 Religious art has frequently made use of these vision-inducing materials; from the shrines and statues of India, Nepal and Tibet, to ancient Egypt, China, the Greeks, the Incas, the Aztecs. Aldous Huxley discussed the experiences of visionaries and the vision-inducing arts in *Heaven and Hell*, gems and temple stone transported thousands of miles, which remind one "obscurely or explicitly, of the preternatural lights and colors of the Other World". *Heaven and Hell*, New York: HarperCollins, 1955, p. 112. Huxley goes on to discuss the visionary power of great works of art, the struggle between Darkness and Light, which often draw upon the realm of archetypal symbols (pp. 117-119). The Sufi poetry and music in Persia, devoted to praises of intoxication; sexual union and intoxication partake of that essential otherness characteristic of all vision, echoing the rites of Dionysus.

6 Overtonal montage is roughly defined as arising from the conflict between the tone and the overtone (which Eisenstein briefly discussed in operation).

7 Barna, Yon, *Eisenstein*, New York: Secker and Warburg, 1973, p. 81.

8 De Brier, Samson, December 9, 1977, *Film Culture*, nos. 67, 68, 69, 1979, pp. 211-215. In De Brier's text he asserts that the scene where the young boy Peter appears to be drinking from Cameron's breast was not shot, whereas in the following text by Anaïs Nin she states that the scene did take place. The scene was shot, but the drinking from the breast was simulated.

9 Nin, Anaïs, *The Diary of Anaïs Nin: 1947-1955, vol. 5*, New York: Harcourt Publishing, 1974, taken from December 1953, pp.138-140. Nin was understandably annoyed that her screen debut was overshadowed by Cameron, The Scarlet Woman. Anger seemingly played a Machiavellian role improvising with his cast whose interaction became a volatile social experiment. "Kenneth lived entirely in a world of his own. Who entered into it, who inhabited it, who did he love or trust or confide in?" Nin wondered. Anaïs Nin, Spring 1960, *The Diary of Anaïs Nin: 1955-66*, vol. 6, New York: Harcourt Publishing, p. 231.

5. Thelema Abbey

1 Anger, Kenneth, in conversation with Rebekah Wood, "Notes on the Hidden Camera of Kenneth Anger," *Into The Pleasure Dome – the films of Kenneth Anger*, Jayne Pilling and Mike O'Pray eds., London: British Film Institute, 1989, p. 61.

2 The German Ordo Templi Orientis joined forces with Crowley to form a British division of the O.T.O., for which he rewrote O.T.O. rituals around 1918. The German O.T.O drew upon Freemasonry, Rosicrucianism, and the Illuminist movements of the eighteenth and nineteenth centuries, the rituals of the Knights Templars, early Gnostic teaching and paganism. Differing from the Freemasons, with a leaning toward oriental religion and philosophy, the O.T.O. regarded sexuality as an intrinsic part of magic. Its members believed that sexual ecstasy could lift one to a different plane of consciousness and spirituality. The concept was common in India and China but was generally dismissed by European cultures as eccentric obscenity. Crowley adopted the sex-magick rites and rituals that have been used in Indian Tantric and Shivaite practices comparable with those of certain Gnostic sects. While retaining the use of certain convenient customs and terminology used in early Freemasonry, Crowley revised the O.T.O. rituals, insignia

and modes of recognition to avoid infringing upon the legitimate privileges of the established and recognized authorities of modern Freemasonry, and also to specifically reflect the teachings of Thelema.

3 Crowley was also the role-model for the Magus Oliver Haddo in Sommerset Maugham's first novel *The Magician*, 1926.

4 Westcott, William Wynn, "The Rosicrucians, Past and Present, At Home and Abroad, Address to the Soc. Rosic. in Anglia", unpublished speech, 2001, courtesy of the O.T.O. / Kenneth Anger.

5 Crowley, Aleister, quoted in Lawrence Sutin, *Do What Thou Wilt – A Life of Aleister Crowley*, New York: St. Martin's Press, 2000, p. 7.

6 Klingsor (the Landulf of Capua) was a magician who lived in Sicily one thousand years earlier, around whom Wagner based Parsifal.

7 Lawrence Sutin creates a multifaceted portrayal of Crowley in *Do What Thou Wilt*. Another detailed portrait of life at Thelema Abbey can be found in Martin Booth, *A Magickal Life: A Biography of Aleister Crowley*, London: Hodder & Stoughton, 2000.

8 Letter to Crowley dated February 23, 1946. The Babalon Working (the invocation of the "elemental") was conducted in early January 1946 with Hubbard as Parson's Scribe. Quoted in John Carter, *Sex and Rockets – the Occult World of Jack Parsons*, Feral House: Venice, CA, 1999, p. 130.

9 *Wormwood Star*, 1955, color. Cameron, a painter and poet based in Los Angeles, burnt each of her works having completed them as a part of a cycle of creation. The film, in which she reads the lines of one of her dark sonnets, has images of her attired in brightly colored silks, in an ornate set by Paul Mathison, with images of her graphic, demonic paintings: rare existing images of her work.

10 Anger, "Kenneth Anger on *Lucifer Rising*," American Independent Film AFA Newsletter, 1981, courtesy Museum of Modern Art film department archives, New York.

11 Anger, Kenneth, letter to author, October 2003.

6. Scorpio Rising

1 Interview with Stan Brakhage, P. Adams Sitney, *Film Culture*, no. 30, Fall 1963, *Film Culture Reader*, 2000, pp. 201-229 (pp. 220-221).

2 Carlos Clarens, Cuban film historian.

3 "An Interview with Kenneth Anger," *Spider* magazine, reproduced in *Film Culture*, no. 40, 1966, p. 68.

4 Brando, Marlon, quoted MB filmography, www.brando.crosscity.com.

5 "An Interview with Kenneth Anger," *Spider* magazine, pp. 69-70.

6 Among Menken's films was *Arabesque for Kenneth Anger*, 1961, 4 min. (Although Anger does not appear in the film physically, he is present as an idea, as well as the subject of the film's dedication.)

7 In one recent reappraisal of the film, Jaime N. Christley states: "To the untrained moviegoer, *Scorpio Rising*... will seem like a senseless barrage of homosexual biker imagery, leather and chains and engines, juxtaposed with religious imagery... Nazi references, and set to about a dozen... pop tunes ("Leader of the Pack" and "My Boyfriend's Back" to name just two). To the seasoned cineaste, the film pretty much remains that way – but a consideration of the period (the early 60s) and technique (the kind of hyperactive editing not seen outside the films of Eisenstein, Gance, Vertov, and a few others) raises the movie to the level of lost classic, a true cult artifact that had an incalculable impact on a whole generation of contemporary filmmakers. It can be held responsible for the term "MTV editing" that uncomplimentary trope that's in every working or amateur critic's phrasebook – and it may be that *Scorpio Rising* qualifies as the granddaddy of the music video, which gives it a Star Wars-like stature in film history. Anger's techniques of montage have also had a positive influence, direct or indirect, for better or worse, on the movies of Scorsese, Cassavetes, Aronofsky, Korine, Luhrmann, Bruckheimer, Spike Lee, Roeg, and countless others. Self-indulgent, incoherent, heavy-handed, and a landmark of undergound cinema." *Filmwritten* magazine, quoted in online film critics society, ofcs.rottentomatoes.com, 2003.

8 Renan, Sheldon, *Introduction to the American Underground Film*, New York: E.P. Dutton and Co, 1967, p.111.

9 Anger, quoted in *Film Culture*, no. 40, 1966, p. 71.

10 Anger, quoted in *Film Culture*, no. 40, 1966, p. 71.

11 Bruce Conner did not use music to nearly the same ironic degree as Anger, and in Jack Smith's *Flaming Creatures*, 1962-1963, it is the nostalgic resonances of pop music that are used to create an out-of-date and camped up aesthetic. The music is "used," lifted from soundtracks of old films.

12 Rowe, *The Baudelairean Cinema*, Ann Arbor: University of Michigan Press, 1983, p. 8.

13 Markopoulos, Gregory, *Film Culture*, no. 31, Winter 1963-1964, pp. 5-6.

14 Kristeva, Julia, *Portable Kristeva*, Kelly Oliver ed., New York: Columbia University Press, 1997, p. 37. Freud notes that the most instinctual drive is the death drive. Though disputed and inconsistent, in Freudian theory the "death drive is transversal to identity and tends to disperse "narcissisms" whose constitution ensures the link between structures and, by extension, life. But at the same time and conversely, narcissism and pleasure are only temporary positions from which the death drive blazes new paths. Narcissism and pleasure are therefore inveiglings and realizations of the death drive." p. 64.

15 Eisenstein, Sergei, *The Film Sense*, New York: Harvest/Harcourt Brace Jovanovich, 1947.

16 Dienstfrey, Harris, "Film: Two Films and an Interlude by Kenneth Anger," *Artforum*, June 1965, pp. 48-50.

17 In 1954 Anger collaborated on a project with Stan Brakhage and artist Jess Collins in San Francisco. Collins had made collages from bodybuilding magazines, and used them to make a giant puzzle. Anger was going to utilize a similar process cinematographically and Brakhage was the cameraman. With optical effects and montage, the puzzle was thus put into movement, but the fruits of this unique collaboration was confiscated by the processing laboratory for what they assumed to be obscene material.

17 Smithson, Robert, "Entropy and The New Monuments" (1966), *Robert Smithson: The Collected Writings*, Jack Flam ed., Berkeley/ Los Angeles: University of California Press, 1996, p. 20.

18 Lester, Elenore, "From Underground: Kenneth Anger Rising," *The New York Times*, Feb. 19, 1967, "Almost overnight, display windows of elegant uptown boutiques had wicked motorcycle chains thrown over plush velvet couches, and models in couture dresses, poised between the handlebars of motorcycles, casting enigmatic glances at dangerous-looking drivers. The fad for the motorcycle look got a shot in the arm. Leather and goggles became standard gear for both sexes for doing the galleries on the upper East Side, as well as the bars on the lower West...."

19 Scorsese, Martin, quoted in *Into The Pleasure Dome – the films of Kenneth Anger*, Jayne Pilling and Mike O'Pray eds., London: British Film Insititute, 1989, p. 55.

20 This text was first published in *Film Culture*, no. 32, Spring 1964.

7. Kustomized

1 American International Pictures, black and white, starring Gene Vincent.

2 Anger, Kenneth, original *KKK* scenario, 1964, Museum of Modern Art film archives, New York.

3 Conducted by *Spider* magazine, reproduced in *Film Culture*, no. 40, Spring 1966, pp. 68-71. Courtesy of *Film Culture*, Jonas Mekas and Anthology Film Archives, New York.

4 Assayas, Olivier, *Kenneth Anger, Vraie et Fausse Magie au Cinéma*, Paris: Collection Auteurs, Cahiers du Cinéma, 1999, p. 103.

5 Assayas' negative appraisal doesn't take into consideration contemporary artists such as Chris Cunningham who have made inventive videos for the likes of Aphex Twin, or artist Doug Aitken who has also made music videos.

6 Rowe, Carel, "Illuminating Lucifer," *Film Quarterly*, vol. 27, no. 4, summer 1974, p. 28.

7 The artists John McCracken, Craig Kauffman and Judy Chicago could be mentioned here.

8. Psychedelia: San Francisco – London

1 A possible precursor alluding to psychedelic consciousness was Harry Smith's 1947 feature-length animated film *Death and Trancefiguration*, whose prime dynamic was "constant transformation, division, reassembly, or multiplication of objects and creatures, either inspired or in reference to one aspect of Hindu cosmology." Ken Kelman, *Film Culture*, no. 34, Fall 1964, p. 51. Oskar Fischinger, one of the first pioneers of abstract filmmaking and Len Lye's abstract, rhythmic films of the 1920s should also be mentioned here as influential precursors.

2 "The literature of religious experience abounds in references to the pains and terrors overwhelming those who have come, too suddenly, face to face with some manifestation of the "Mysterium tremendum." In theological language, this fear is due to the incompatibility between man's egotism and the divine purity, between man's self-aggravated separateness and the infinity of God... by unregenerate souls, the divine Light at its full blaze can be apprehended only as a burning, purgatorial fire. An almost identical doctrine is to be found in *The Tibetan Book of the Dead*, where the departed soul is described as shrinking in agony from The Pure Light of the Void, and even from the lesser, tempered Lights, in order to rush headlong into the comforting darkness of selfhood as a reborn human being, or even as a beast, an unhappy ghost, a denizen of hell. Anything rather than the burning brightness of unmitigated Reality – anything!" Aldous Huxley, *The Doors of Perception*, London: Harper and Row, 1954, 1990 edition, pp. 55-56.

3 Huxley, *The Doors of Perception*, p. 62.

4 Saul Bass' title sequence for Hitchcock's *Vertigo*, 1958, created an early abstract animation alluding to altered reality: the eye merges into a circular vortex, a metaphor for visual hypnosis. The British feature film *Wonderwall*, 1968, featuring George Harrison's original soundtrack, The Beatles' *Magical Mystery Tour*, 1967 and Frank Zappa's 1969 *Captain Beefheart And The Grunt People* also attempted to visualize psychedelic states utilizing contemporary music to amplify the visual effects; Walt Disney's animated *Fantasia* (with animation by Oskar Fischinger) and *Alice in Wonderland* also gained a new audience. Stanley Kubrick's *2001: A Space Odyssey*, 1968, provided a wide-screen panorama for abstract perceptual phenomena. John Cage and Ronald Nameth collaborated in the ambitious *HPSCHD*, 1969, that used 52 loud-speakers, seven amplified harpsichords, 8,000 slides, and 100 films, while The Yardbirds' performance in Antonioni's *Blow Up*, 1966, was a quintessential reflection on the London art and rock scene.

5 Sitney, *Visionary Film*, 1974 edition, p. 54.

6 Ex-guitarist of the band Love, Beausoleil fell under the influence of cult leader Charles Manson soon thereafter. He was convicted of killing music teacher Gary Hinman, July 1969, two weeks earlier than the murders at the home of Sharon Tate. Beausoleil was not involved in the Tate killing as he was already in police custody. Having become involved with a motorcycle gang upon his return to L.A., he had been sent out on an initiatory mission to buy the gang drugs, which Hinman had sold him. When the gang claimed the drugs were ineffective, they wanted their money back and Hinman became the unwitting victim for payback. The sequence of events was complicated by the fact that Beausoleil, who had settled the dispute with Hinman, was accompanied by two of Manson's girlfriends, who had telephoned Manson to tell him there was an argument. Manson showed up at the door of Hinman's house and viciously slashed the man's face, leaving by stating that Beausoleil needed to finish the job (in another interview Beausoleil stated that this incident did not take place and Manson was never present). Beausoleil claims that his attempts to bandage his face and resist taking him to hospital led up to the fatal stabbing. Beausoleil's arrest was instrumental in leading the police to Manson. Beausoleil also states that Truman Capote spun a completely fictitious tale about him in his book *Music For Chameleons*.

7 Anger quoted in Tony Rayns, "Lucifer: a Kenneth Anger Kompendium," *Into The Pleasure Dome – the films of Kenneth Anger*, p. 16. Originally published in 1969, in *Cinema*.

8 See Simon Frith and Howard Horne, *Art into Pop*, London: Methuen, 1987, a survey of the relationships between pop music and art. Anger was present for Yoko Ono's *White* exhibition, where everyone came dressed in white, the whole exhibition was of white objects and guests were encouraged to take

part in the white hallucinogenic elixir beverage, the occasion which introduced Ono to Lennon. (from a conversation between the author and Anger, 2003). When Antonioni arrived in London to shoot *Blow Up*, he announced that the film was to be "everything Robert Fraser, and more." It was Fraser who arranged for Robert Blake and Jann Haworth to design the cover for the Beatles' *Sgt. Pepper's Lonely Hearts' Club Band*, 1967, featuring Aleister Crowley amongst the pantheon, and for Hamilton to design their *White Album*, 1968. Fraser was adamant about breaking barriers between the hermetic realm of "high art" and pop culture, which continued through punk. See *Art and Artists*, vol. 2 no. 5, August 1967, pp. 12-13.

9 Powell, Anna, *Moonchild: The Films of Kenneth Anger*, Jack Hunter ed., London: Creation Books, 2002, p. 84.

10 Genet, Jean, *The Thief's Journal*, New York: Grove Press, 1964, p. 17.

11 Powell, *Moonchild*, p. 87.

12 Anger, quoted in Rayns, "Lucifer: a Kenneth Anger Kompendium," p. 16.

13 Conversation between author and Anger, December 2002. Punk's adoption of the swastika is also discussed by Dick Hebdige in *Subculture: the Meaning of Style*, London: Routledge, 1979. Hebdige discusses bricolage, appropriating another range of commodities by placing them in a symbolic ensemble, which served to erase or subvert their original meaning. Although Hebdige makes no reference to Anger, his discussion is pertinent to Anger's work: from Kristeva's *Revolution of Poetic Language*, examining the subversive possibilities within language through a study of French symbolist poetry, pointing to poetic language as the place where the social code is destroyed and renewed, as discussed earlier, to his discussion of Jean Genet's romantic emphasis on deformity, transformation and refusal, p. 138.

14 And likewise, Indian instruments such as the sitar were adopted, George Harrison having come under the influence of Ravi Shankar (The Beatles' "Norwegian Wood, This Bird Has Flown," featured the first use of a sitar in a pop song, *Rubber Soul* album, 1965).

15 Vyner, Harriet, *Groovy Bob: The Life and Times of Robert Fraser*, London: Faber and Faber, 1999, p. 121.

16 Pound, Ezra, *Gaudier-Brzeska: A Memoir*, New York: New Directions, 1960, p. 92.

17 Artaud, Antonin, "Sorcery and the Cinema," *Collected Works*, vol. 3, London: Calder and Boyars, 1972, pp. 65-66.

18 La Vey (1930-1997) served as an ideal bogeyman for the sensation-seeking American media of that tumultuous period. His curious celebrity was based largely on a self-created legend (not unlike that of Aleister Crowley). La Vey disseminated his legend through interviews with journalists, personal discussion with his disciples, and two La Vey-approved [auto]biographies (apparently ghostwritten by La Vey himself). The first of these, 1974's *The Devil's Avenger*, embellished on the fabrications already sketched in the introduction to the Satanic Bible. The second, 1990's *Secret Life of a Satanist*, contradicted many of La Vey's own claims in the earlier volume, while putting forth new legends for public consumption.

19 London *Sunday Telegraph*, 28 March 1971, n. p.

20 Kristeva, Julia, "Powers of Horror: Approaching Abjection," *The Portable Kristeva*, New York: Columbia University Press, 1997, p. 229.

21 Independent Film Award, reproduced in *Film Culture Reader*, P. Adams Sitney ed., New York: First Cooper Square Press, 2000, p. 429. (c) 1970 *Film Culture* Non-Profit Corporation.

22 Bobby Beausoleil recorded the soundtrack in prison with the Freedom Orchestra, Tracy Prison, California.

23 Milton, John, "Paradise Lost" (476- 482), *Complete Poems*, John Leonard ed., London and New York: Penguin, 1998, p. 133.

24 Parker, Lois J., *Mythopoesis and the Crisis of Post-Modernism: Toward Integrating Image and Story*, New York: Brandon House, 1998, p. 145. "Implied also is the notion that this inmost seat of mental sight is characterized in such a way that one can mythologically envision all that is to follow... and suggest that there is indeed a "magical" "substratum of ... existence" (Ahsen, 1968/73) where mental images somehow register both past and future events... a mythmaking consciousness affecting our perceptions." p. 146.

25 For a recent discussion of Lucifer, see Jan Verwoert's "Bring on the devil: On the romantic cult of radical individualism," *Afterall*, issue 7, 2003, pp. 8-17.

26 Sitney first applied the term to avant-garde film in regard to Brakhage's *Dog Star Man* in *Film Culture* in 1964. Gene Youngblood then discussed mythopoeia in the context of "expanded" cinema in his book, *Expanded Cinema*, New York: E.P. Dutton, 1970.

27 Parker, *Mythopoesis and the Crisis of Post-Modernism*, p. 146.

28 Haller, Robert, *Kenneth Anger: A Monograph*, Minneapolis: Film in the Cities/Walker Art Center, 1980, p. 8.

29 1970 interview with Kenneth Anger, "Aleister Crowley and Merlin Magick," *Friends* 14, September 18, 1970, p. 16, reproduced in Haller, *Kenneth Anger*, p. 9.

30 Mekas, Jonas, "Movie Journal," *Village Voice*, May 17, 1973, quoted in Haller, *Kenneth Anger*, p. 9.

31 Which in 1904 was known as the Boulak Museum in Cairo. The museum having moved, the ancient painted wooden funerary stele has been renumbered. It depicts Horus receiving a sacrifice from a deceased priest.

32 Symonds, John, *The Great Beast*, London: Rider and Company, 1951, p. 58.

33 The Zeppelin film, based around a 1974 Madison Square Garden concert, is lifted out of the arena by fantasy and documentary sequences. Although it may be considered a documentary it is more of a musical. Page complained: "It's so time consuming. It's a horrible medium to work in. It's so boring! So slow! Just shooting the fantasy sequence. Can we do it again so we can get a different angle? Can you do it again so we can get a different angle? Can you do it again? I'm not used to that. It's a silly attitude, okay, but nevertheless... the Anger things are completely different. Working with him is a unique experience." In Page's words, "I felt it quite an honor that he asked me. The version I was involved with was the third version. After being shown the initial rushes I've messed around with the instruments and the only recognizable instrument is the 12 string guitar, though even that doesn't sound like a 12 string. Plus the synthesizers sound like a horn instrument. The danger with synthesizers is that if it just sounds like a synthesizer, you've had it really and then

there's drum combined with a pulse sound which sounds like a heartbeat as if there's a presence, plus a sound like ethereal breathing, out of that comes the horn sound. It is a very small part I play and in no way sensational." "Anger Rising," *Sounds*, October 2, 1976, p. 8.

34 Schreck, Nikolas, *The Satanic Screen: An Illustrated History of the Devil in Cinema*, London: Creation Books, 2000, p. 15. Schreck also aligns the role of the changeling prince in *A Midsummer Night's Dream* 1935 (in which Anger appeared), with whom he identified, with the mischievous Puck, connected with the darker side of the faery domain. Watching with amusement the perils of mere mortals, in the case of *Scorpio Rising*, Puck, as played by Mickey Rooney, watches the motorcyclists head to their doom. Puck Productions, a logo designed by Beausoleil identifies the films in the *Magick Lantern Cycle*.

35 *A Dictionary of Symbols*, New York: Philosophical Library, Inc., 1962, quoted in Carel Rowe, *The Baudelairean Cinema*, p. 65.

9. Hollywood Babylon

1 Sontag, Susan, quoted in "Night of the Locust," *Newsweek*, June 16, 1975, p. 73.

2 Smith, Harry, interview with P. Adams Sitney, *Film Culture*, no. 37, Summer 1965, reprinted in *Film Culture Reader*, New York: Cooper Square Press, 2000, p. 276.

3 West, Nathanael, *The Day of the Locust*, New York: Random House, 1939; Hortense Powdermaker, *Hollywood the Dream Factory*, Boston: Little, Brown, 1950.

4 Earlier films, *Sunset Boulevard*, 1950, *The Bad and the Beautiful*, 1952, Godard's *Le Mépris* (*Contempt*, 1963), Fellini's *8 1/2*, 1963, contributed to the deconstruction and de-mythologizing of Hollywood; often as self-reflexive representations reflecting the construct of filmmaking and actors. Weegee published *Naked Hollywood*, 1953 – a new approach to documenting the film industry, a comical exposé of the dream factory, while Diane Arbus conflated Disneyland with Hollywood in such work as *Rocks on Wheels, Disneyland, Cal.*, 1962 – an outcrop of prop rocks on dollies simulating a mountainscape sunset.

5 Anger had been in contact with Kinsey since the late 1940s when Kinsey had requested a copy of *Fireworks* for his collection, and the two subsequently worked together on a documentary on Aleister Crowley's Thelema Abbey, as discussed in Chapter Five.

6 Sitney, P. Adams, *Visionary Film: The American Avant-Garde*, New York: Oxford University Press, 1974 edition, p. 95.

7 Anger, quoted in Eleanor Ringel, "The Visions of Anger," *The Atlanta Constitution*, Monday, February 11, 1980, p. 4b.

8 Anger, interview with Tony Rayns, *Into The Pleasure Dome – the films of Kenneth Anger*, London: British Film Institute, 1989, p. 23.

9 Quoted in Ben Hecht, *A Child of the Century*, New York: Ballantine, 1970, p. 467.

10 Parker Tyler summarized that the technical crudity of many underground films was an almost paranoid rejection of commercial Hollywood filmmaking, which had perfected the technical form of film to the point of invisibility for the spectator. For Tyler, underground film's expression of dissent often led to inhibiting the resourceful language of film, resulting in the production of work of little aesthetic value. As Tyler mentioned, both Anger and Brakhage, more than other avant-garde filmmaker's, create "films that have both filmic craft and poetic style." Parker Tyler, *Underground Film: A Critical History*, Harmondsworth, Middlesex: Penguin, 1974, p. 39.

11 Anger, quoted in Ken Turan, "The Underground Man," n.p, n.d, Anthology Film Archives, New York.

12 Nin, Anaïs, *The Diary of Anaïs Nin, 1955-66*, vol. 6, New York: Harcourt, p. 352.

13 Brown, Mick, "Hollywood Anger," *Crawdaddy*, September 1976.

14 See *L.A. Confidential* author, James Ellroy's 1987 novel *The Black Dahlia* written from the perspective of a police officer who becomes obsessed with the case. Steve Hodel, a retired L.A.P.D. cop, re-released *Black Dahlia Avenger*, in 2004, with foreword by Ellroy. The book claims to have finally solved the murder case with ample grim evidence; the suspect being the estranged and deceased father of the author himself, who was taped as saying "Supposin' I did kill the Black Dahlia. They couldn't prove it now. They can't talk to my secretary anymore because she's dead..." The blurring of fact and fiction, art and reality is amplified by the fact that Ellroy's own mother was the victim of an unsolved murder.

15 Steve Hodel, letter to author, June 9, 2004.

16 Steve Hodel, letter to author, June 9, 2004.

17 Anger, Reel.com interview.

18 Abby Hirsch press release for *Hollywood Babylon*, c. 1976 (ghost-written by Anger?). MOMA film archives, New York.

19 Suarez, Juan, *Bike Boys, Drag Queens and Super Stars: Avant-Garde, Mass Culture, and Gay Identities in the 1960s Underground Cinema*, Bloomington: Indiana University Press, 1996, p.124.

20 Anger, Reel.com interview.

21 Accessed from Hollywood Boulevard via the Grand Staircase, this gathering place features two massive, 33 foot tall elephants weighing 13,500 pounds each perched on columns 73 feet above the plaza, and made of thick fiberglass-reinforced concrete. To the left of the elephants, Babylon Court's arch, engraved with larger-than-life Egyptian motifs, frames the "Hollywood" sign.

22 Interview with Jack Smith, Gerald Malanga, *Film Culture*, no. 45, 1967, p. 14.

23 ... "an archetype of the human face. Garbo offered to one's gaze a sort of Platonic Idea of the human creature, which explains why her face is almost sexually undefined, without however leaving one in doubt... but Garbo does not perform in it any feat of transvestism; she is always herself..." Barthes also quips "A few years earlier the face of Valentino was causing suicides." Roland Barthes, "The Face of Garbo," *Mythologies*, London: Random House, 2000 edition, p. 56.

24 Sontag, Susan, "Notes on Camp," (1964), *Against Interpretation and Other Essays*, New York: Anchor Books/Doubleday, 1990 edition, p. 283.

25 Sontag could well be discussing Anger or Warhol: "The connoisseur of Camp has found more ingenious pleasures... in the coarsest, commonest pleasures, in the arts of the masses. Mere use does not defile the objects of his pleasure, since he learns to possess them in a rare way. Camp – Dandyism in the age of mass culture – makes no distinction between the unique object and the mass-produced object. Camp taste transcends the nausea of the replica." "Notes on Camp," p. 289.

26 Sontag, "Notes on Camp," p. 291.

27 Sontag, "Notes on Camp," pp. 279-280.

28 Anger, quoted in Ed Sikov, "Hollywood Babylon," *Christopher Street Reader*, issue 88, May 1984, pp. 55-56.

29 "Down by the Murky Rivers of Babylon," *The Sunday Times Magazine*, December 22, 1985, pp 26-28. (Thanks to Gillian Cuthill, Foundation Manager, Robert Mapplethorpe Foundation, New York).

30 This exhibition was accompanied by a catalog of the same name, edited by Michael Webb. The neon violin is now in the collection of the Museum of the Moving Image, London.

31 Brougher, Kerry, "Introduction," *Hall of Mirrors – Art and Film Since 1945*, Los Angeles: Museum of Contemporary Art, 1996.

32 Warhol, Andy, in Andy Warhol and Pat Hackett, *POPism: the Warhol Sixties*, 1980, New York: Harper and Row, p. 40.

33 There are plans to release his films on DVD in 2005 by Fantoma Films of San Francisco.

10. Gnostic Mass and Recent Projects (1981-2004)

1 Anger, Kenneth, "Flames In The Night," interview by Rebekah Wood, *Into The Pleasure Dome – the films of Kenneth Anger*, London: British Film Institute, 1989, p. 50.

2 At the Institut Français de Vienne, Vienna, Austria, June 1995.

3 I am grateful to Walter Cassidy and to Stuart Shave of Modern Art, Inc., London for reproduction of these images in this book. Anger agreed to the reproduction of all of his Icons, including the most recent, for this book. As the rare prints of his films have often been returned from various screenings in very bad shape – often with frames or sections taken out as "souvenirs", or even worse, whole reels having been copied, and screened without his knowledge or that of his distributor, it is no wonder then that he is cautious about their screenings. It is remarkable therefore that, for the first time, he has permitted the creation of new frame enlargements from the original films for the images to be used in this book (a selection first appearing in *Afterall* including the cover, Summer 2003), most of which are being reproduced here for the first time and in color.

4 "A three-night retrospective of films by renowned independent filmmaker Kenneth Anger, screened in the outdoor spaces of the Schindler House and at the University of Southern California School of Film and Television.... His transgressive and provocative films influenced a post-War generation of avant-garde filmmakers." Schindler House/MAK Center program, October 10-12, 2002.

5 Anger, interview with Wood, *Into The Pleasure Dome – the films of Kenneth Anger*, p. 46.

6 Frasier is a long-time assistant of Kinsey's and associate at the Institute for Sex Research in Bloomington, Indiana.

7 Seberg's vocal and financial support of counterculture political groups like the Black Panthers prompted the F.B.I. (under the direction of bureau Chief J. Edgar Hoover) to wage a smear campaign against her. See David K. Frasier, *Suicide in the Entertainment Industry*, Jefferson, North Carolina: McFarland & Co., Inc, 2002, p. 286.

8 Anger, Kenneth, Foreword, Frasier, *Suicide in the Entertainment Industry*, p. 1.

9 Anger, Foreword, Frasier, *Suicide in the Entertainment Industry*, p. 2.

10 Wood, Luke, Smith's DreamWorks A & R rep, quoted in "Long Road Down," Calendar, *Los Angeles Times*, February 15, 2004, pp. E37-39. Smith had not overdosed; no drugs were found in his system besides prescription medication, and friends say that in his last few months he seemed newly optimistic and free from drug addiction. The Frasier book was published just before Smith's death.

11 Anger, Kenneth, quoted in Robert Heide, *The Soho Weekly News*, New York, September 25, 1975, p. 11.

12 Suarez, *Bike Boys, Drag Queens and Super Stars*, p. 100.

13 Anger, Kenneth, interview with Tony Rayns, *Friends* 14, London, September 18, 1970, p. 17.

Filmography

1 Jacobs, Lewis, "Experiment in the Film," *Avant Garde Production in America*, Roger Manville ed., London: Grey Walls, 1948, p. 136, reproduced in *Film Culture*, no. 31, winter 1963-1964, p. 8.

2 Anger, Kenneth, quoted in Rebekah Wood, "Notes on the Hidden Cinema of Kenneth Anger," *Into The Pleasure Dome – the films of Kenneth Anger*, London: British Film Institute, 1989, p. 61.

3 Anger, Kenneth, letter to author, October 2003.

4 Anger, letter to author, October 2003

5 Abby Hirsch publications, New York, June 1976, quoted in *Into the Pleasure Dome – the films of Kenneth Anger*, p. 68.

6 Abby Hirsch publications, New York, June 1977, quoted in *Into the Pleasure Dome – the films of Kenneth Anger*, p. 68.

7 Canyon Cinema catalog, San Francisco, www.canyoncinema.com.

8 Anger, *Into the Pleasure Dome – the films of Kenneth Anger*, p. 68.

9 Anger, Kenneth, conversation with author, 2004.

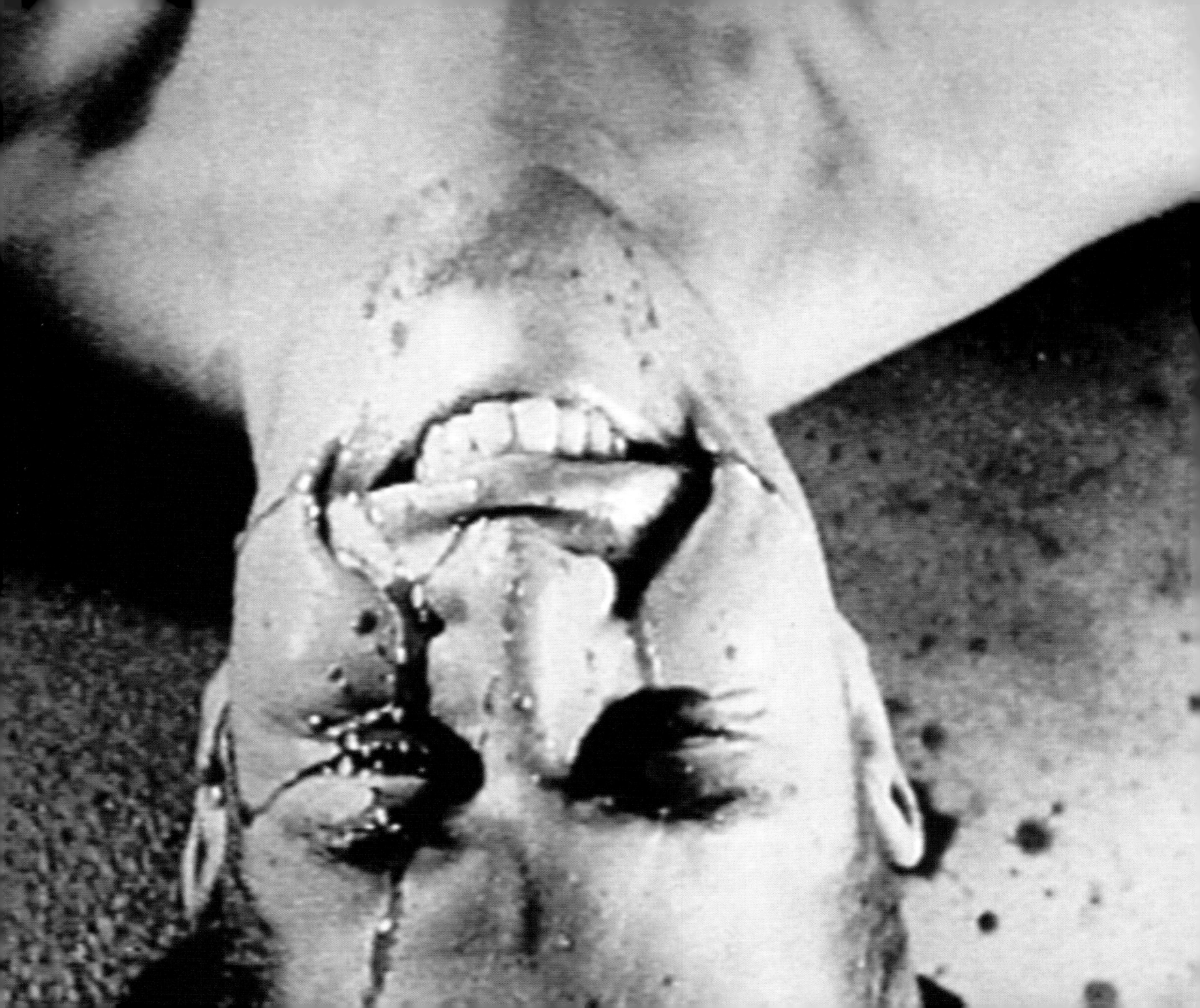

Text credits

Credits for small sections of text are acknowledged in the relevant footnote. Quotations in the text from *Film Culture* are reproduced by permission of *Film Culture* Inc., Jonas Mekas and Anthology Film Archives, New York.

p. 8, Kenneth Anger, "Time Must Have A Stop." Text was written in Palm Springs, 24 April 1995, for *Kenneth Anger Icons*, Institut Français de Vienne, Vienna, June 1995, reprinted courtesy of Kenneth Anger.

p. 38, Kenneth Anger, "Application d'Artifice" (Application of Artifice). First published in *St. Cinema des Près*, no. 2, Paris, 1950. Author's translation, 2004. Reprinted courtesy of MOMA film archives, New York and Kenneth Anger.

p. 60, Kenneth Anger, "Modesty and the Art of Film." First published in *Cahiers du Cinéma*, no. 5, Paris, September 1951. Translated by David Wilson. Reprinted courtesy of *Cahiers du Cinéma* and Kenneth Anger.

p. 76, *Hymn to the Sun*, manuscript, Bibliotèque du Film, Paris with thanks to Pierre Hecker, courtesy of Kenneth Anger.

p. 77, Kenneth Anger, letter to Mary Meerson, December 19, 1951. All letters reprinted courtesy of Kenneth Anger

p. 78, Kenneth Anger, letter to Mary Meerson, February 26, 1952.

p. 79, Kenneth Anger, letter to Mary Meerson, November 17, 1952.

p. 98, Samson De Brier, "On The Filming of Inauguration of the Pleasure Dome", *Film Culture* 67, 68, 69, 1979, pp. 211-215. Reprinted courtesy of *Film Culture* and Anthology Film Archives with thanks to Jonas Mekas and Robert Haller. © *Film Culture* Inc.

p. 101, Anaïs Nin, "Come As Your Own Madness," from *The Diary of Anaïs Nin: 1947-1955*, vol. 5, p. 133-134, 138-140. © 1974 by Anaïs Nin, reprinted by permission of Harcourt, Inc.

pp. 108-109, Kenneth Anger, letter to Henri Langlois, October 15, 1955. Translated by the author from the original French letter.

p. 119, Kenneth Anger, letter to Henry Langlois, April 5, 1962. Translated by the author from the original French letter.

p. 120, Kenneth Anger, letter to Mary Meerson, April 26, 1962.

p. 121, Kenneth Anger, letter to Henry Langlois, c. 1962. Translated by the author from the original French letter.

p. 122, Stan Brakhage, "The Dead", from an interview with Stan Brakhage, P. Adams Sitney, *Film Culture*, no. 30, Fall 1963, reproduced in *Film Culture Reader*, 2000, pp. 220-221. Reprinted courtesy of the Estate of Stan Brakhage, *Film Culture* and Anthology Film Archives with thanks to Jonas Mekas and Robert Haller. © *Film Culture* Inc.

p. 140, Carolee Schneemann, "Kenneth Anger's *Scorpio Rising*", *Film Culture*, no. 32, Spring 1964. Reprinted courtesy of Carolee Schneemann.

Acknowledgments

New York: Charles Silver, Curator of Film, Museum of Modern Art; Jonas Mekas and Robert Haller, Anthology Film Archives; P. Adams Sitney; Gillian Cuthill, Robert Mapplethorpe Foundation; The Smithsonian Institute.

Paris: Pierre Hecker, Tav Falco, Cinémathèque Française.

Los Angeles: Thomas Lawson, CalArts, Curtis Harrington; Ed Ruscha and Gagosian Gallery; The Louis B. Meyer Research Library, American Film Institute.

London: Catherine Grant and Duncan McCorquodale, BDP; Paul Nunneley, Hoop Associates; Walter Cassidy and Stuart Shave, Modern Art, Philip Huntley.

Berlin: Miriam Dagan.

Auckland: Roger Horrocks.

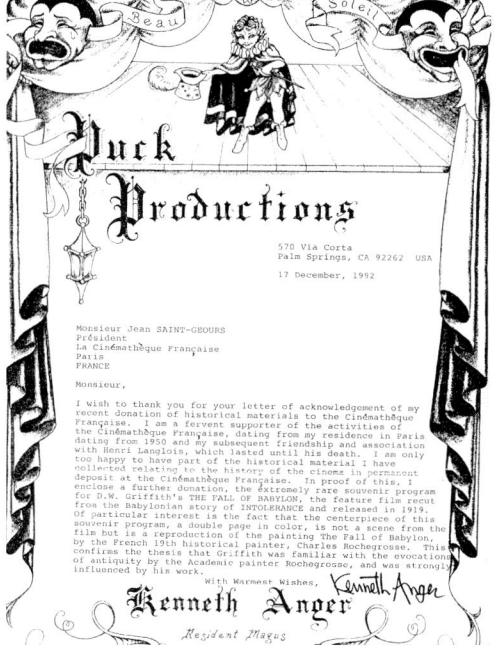

Picture credits

Unless otherwise stated, all images are courtesy Alice L. Hutchison and Kenneth Anger. Captions in quote marks are by Kenneth Anger.

Front cover: *Scorpio Rising*, 1963, film still.

Endpapers: Astrum Argentinum symbols courtesy of the O.T.O. and Kenneth Anger. "The famous – or infamous – Unicursal Hexagram of the Ordo Templi Orientis. Dr. Anger has meditated long and hard on its possible meaning – where all Roads lead back to the Beginning. The Original Black Hole? Blatant Invitation to Anal Sex? Anger's meditation produced the whispering voice of Marjorie Cameron, deep and throaty, who appealed " Follow me into the flower called NOWHERE." And then after a period of silence the whispered invitation (or Command): "COME TO BED." Following the vehicular suicide at the conclusion of his film *Scorpio Rising* of the conflicted by Christian Guilt handsome Catholic abuse victim Jim Powers, the meditation voiced "BLESSED, BLESSED, OBLIVION."

Frontispiece: *Puce Moment*, 1949/1970, Icon, courtesy of Kenneth Anger.

Preface

pp.6-7, *A Midsummer Night's Dream*, featuring Kenneth Anger as The Stolen Prince: The Changeling, William Dieterle and Max Reinhardt dirs., 1935, production still, collection of Kenneth Anger.

Introduction

pp.10-12, 18-19, *A Midsummer Night's Dream*, 1935, production stills, collection of Kenneth Anger.

p. 15, Edmund Teske, portrait of Kenneth Anger, 1954, Topanga Canyon, superimposed with etching by Gustav Doré, gelatin silver (composite) print, 34 x 24cm. Courtesy The J. Paul Getty Museum, Los Angeles, © Edmund Teske Archives/Lawrence Bump and Nil Vidstrand, 2001.

p. 17, Robert Haller, portraits of Kenneth Anger, 1950, courtesy of Anthology Film Archives, New York.

1. Los Angeles in the 1940s

pp.20-21, 23, 24, 26, 27, 28, 31, 33-37, *Fireworks*, 1947, film stills and strips.

p. 27, Jean Cocteau, *Film Maudit* poster, private collection, courtesy of Kenneth Anger.

p. 29, Jean Cocteau, *Blood of a Poet*, 1930, film stills, courtesy Photofest, New York.

p. 30, top: Curtis Harrington, *Fragment of Seeking*, 1946-1947, courtesy Curtis Harrington; middle: Gregory Markopoulos, *Psyche*, 1947-1948, courtesy Anthology Film Archive, New York (with thanks to Robert Haller); bottom: Jean Cocteau, *Orpheus*, 1949, courtesy Photofest, New York.

p. 32, *Fireworks*, film still. "The diagonal scar across Anger's right eyebrow, which he bears to this day, resulted from backyard bare-knuckle fisticuffs with fellow 15 year old school chums in Santa Monica High prior to Anger's transfer to Beverly Hills High School. Bloody noses and scars caused by school rings: the "Ultimate Fighting" of Anger's adolescence.

p. 34,"Got Milk? Anger's female cleansing following bloody beating."

p. 40, Yvonne Marquis in *Puce Moment*, 1949/1970, Icon, courtesy of Kenneth Anger.

pp.42-45, *Puce Moment*, film stills. "The late Yvonne Marquis, one of the few females Anger adored. (He also adored the Borzoi dogs)."

2. Paris 1950-1960

pp.46-47, black and white portrait of Kenneth Anger taken in Paris, 1951, courtesy of Cinémathèque Française, thanks to Pierre Hecker.

p. 49, black and white portraits of Kenneth Anger in Paris, 1950 (photographer unknown).

p. 50, 54-55, 57, *Rabbit's Moon*, 1950/1971/1979, film stills.

p. 59, Sergei Eisenstein, *Que Viva Mexico!*, 1931, film stills, courtesy of Arcadia Films, London and Russian State Film Archives, Moscow .

p. 66, portrait of Kenneth Anger as a young Magus, c. 1950 (photographer unknown), collection of Kenneth Anger.

p. 71, *Histoire d'O*, 1961, production still, courtesy of Kenneth Anger. This film is stored at the Cinémathèque Française, but efforts to retrieve it have been unsuccessful.

3. Eaux d'Artifice

pp.72-73, Kenneth Anger, *Eaux d'Artifice*, 1953, Icon, courtesy of Kenneth Anger.

pp.75-85, *Eaux d'Artifice*, 1953, film stills.

4. Inauguration of the Pleasure Dome

pp.86-87, *Inauguration of the Pleasure Dome*, 1954/1966, Icon, courtesy of Kenneth Anger.

pp.88, 92, 94, 96-97, *Inauguration of the Pleasure Dome*, film stills.

p. 90, *Inauguration of the Pleasure Dome*, top: Cameron as the Scarlet Woman, film still; middle: Anaïs Nin as Astarte, Icon, courtesy of Kenneth Anger; bottom: Renate Druks, film still.

p. 91, top and middle: Lachman's *Dante's Inferno*, hand-painted lobby cards, 1935; bottom: Samson De Brier as Cagliostro, black and white photograph from set of *Inauguration of the Pleasure Dome*, collection of Kenneth Anger.

pp.93, 104-105, Kenneth Anger, black and white photographs from set of *Inauguration of the Pleasure Dome*, courtesy of Anthology Film Archives, New York.

p. 95, Samson De Brier in *Inauguration of the Pleasure Dome*, Icon, courtesy of Kenneth Anger.

5. Thelema Abbey

pp.106-107, Dr. Alfred C. Kinsey with Kenneth Anger at Thelema Abbey, 1955, black and white photograph, collection of Kenneth Anger

p. 110, details of frescos by Alistair Crowley, Thelema Abbey, photographed by Marco Pasi, courtesy of O.T.O. and Kenneth Anger.

p. 111, Frater Kybernetes, photographs of exterior and interior of Thelema Abbey, courtesy of Frater Kybernetes, www.inventati.org/amprodias/.

p. 112, top: Aleister Crowley, conducting *Rite of Saturn*, 1910, courtesy of Kenneth Anger; bottom: Kenneth Anger with lantern, collection of Kenneth Anger.

p. 113, top: Kenneth Anger with lantern; bottom: cover of Aleister Crowley's book *Moonchild*, courtesy of O.T.O., originally designed by Beresford Egan for 1929 edition published by Mandrake Press.

pp.114-115, Astrum Argentinum symbols courtesy of the O.T.O. and Kenneth Anger.

Black Dog Publishing

Architecture Art Design Fashion
History Photography Theory and Things

© 2004 Black Dog Publishing Limited, the artists and authors

All rights reserved

Conception and text by Alice L. Hutchison

Edited by Catherine Grant

Designed by Hoop Associates

Printed in the European Union

Back Dog Publishing Limited
Unit 4.4 Tea Building
56 Shoreditch High Street
London E1 6JJ

Tel: +44 (0)20 7613 1922
Fax: +44 (0)20 7613 1944

Email: info@bdp.demon.co.uk
www.bdpworld.com

All opinions expressed within this publication are those
of the authors and not necessarily of the publisher.

British Library Cataloguing-in-Publication Data.

A catalogue record for this book is available from the
British Library.

ISBN 1 904772 03 X

I have found a definition of the Beautiful, of my own conception of the Beautiful. It is something intense and sad... I can scarcely conceive... a type of Beauty, which has nothing to do with Sorrow.

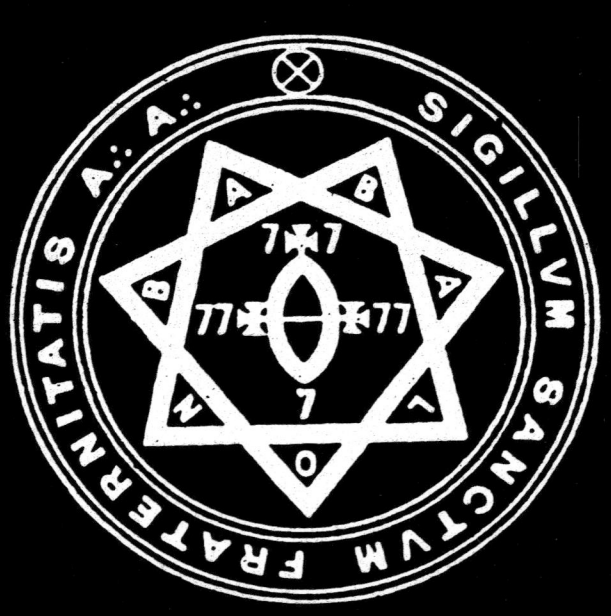